DIN SAUR SANCTUARY
1

STORY AND ART BY
ITARU KINOSHITA

RESEARCH CONSULTANT: SHIN-ICHI FUJIWARA

CONTENTS

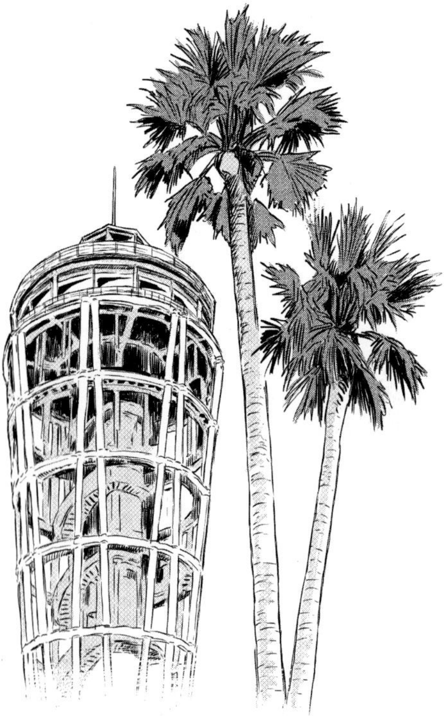

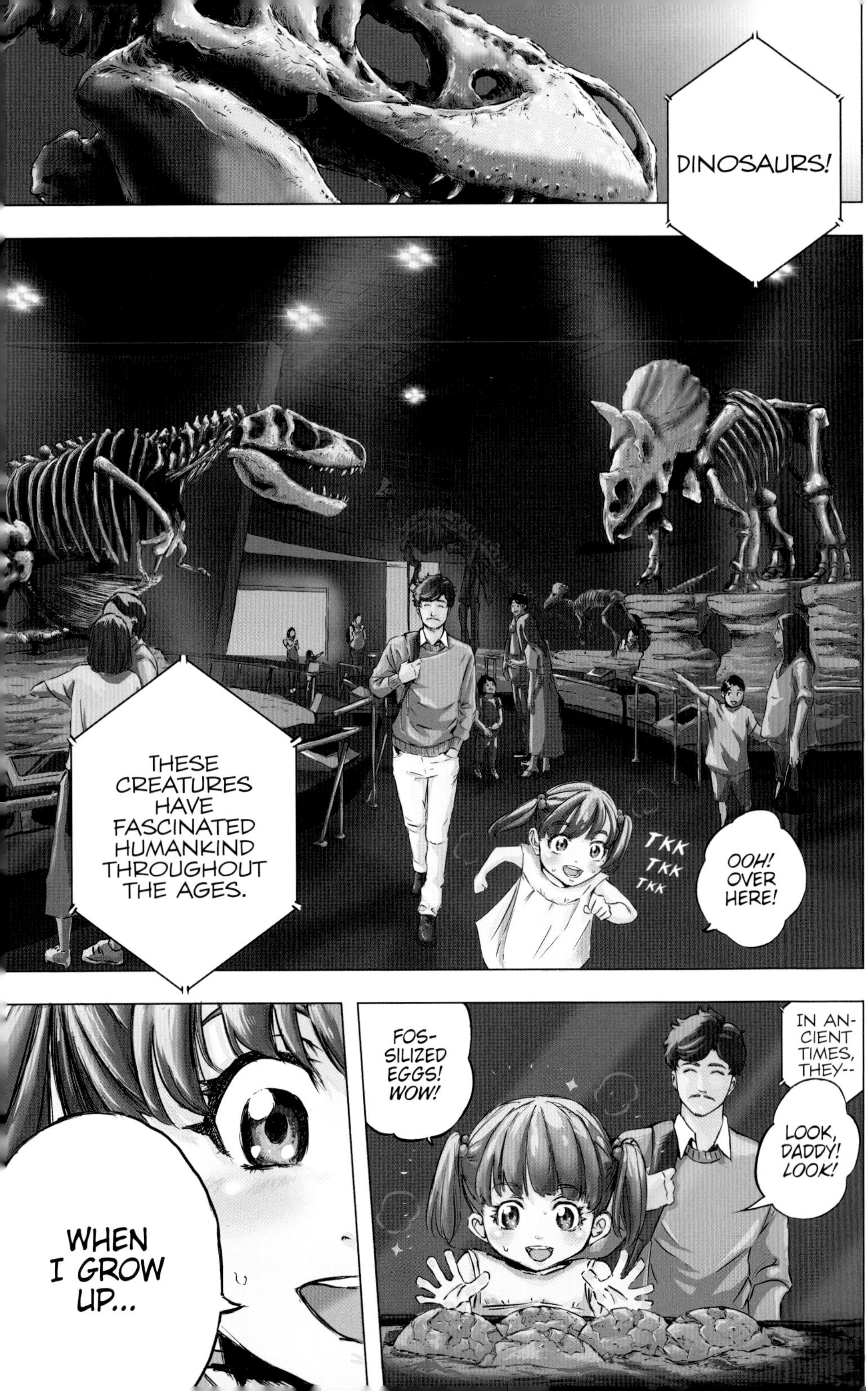
DINOSAURS!
THESE CREATURES HAVE FASCINATED HUMANKIND THROUGHOUT THE AGES.
TKK TKK TKK
OOH! OVER HERE!
IN AN-CIENT TIMES, THEY--
FOS-SILIZED EGGS! WOW!
LOOK, DADDY! LOOK!
WHEN I GROW UP...

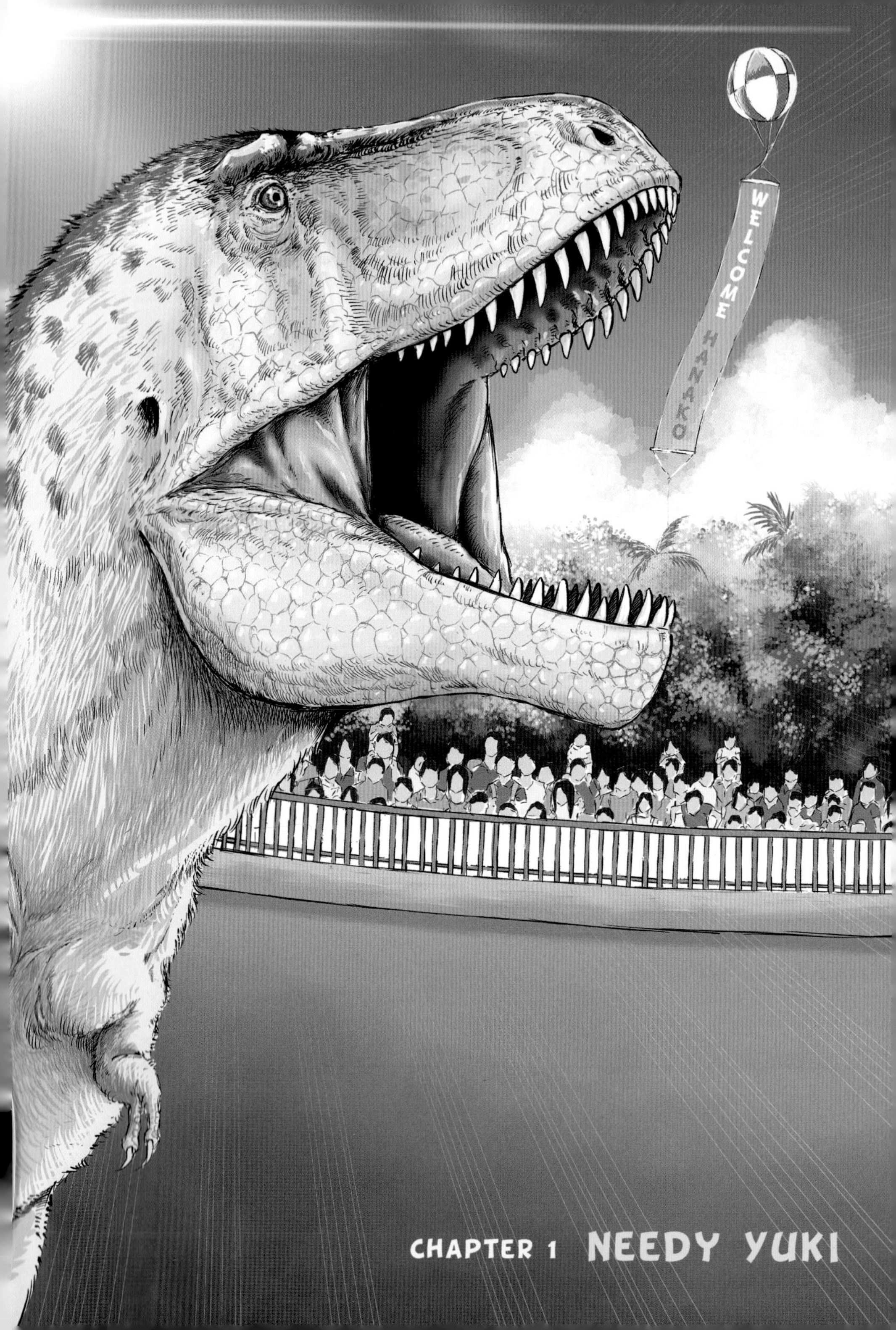
WELCOME HANAKO

CHAPTER 1 NEEDY YUKI

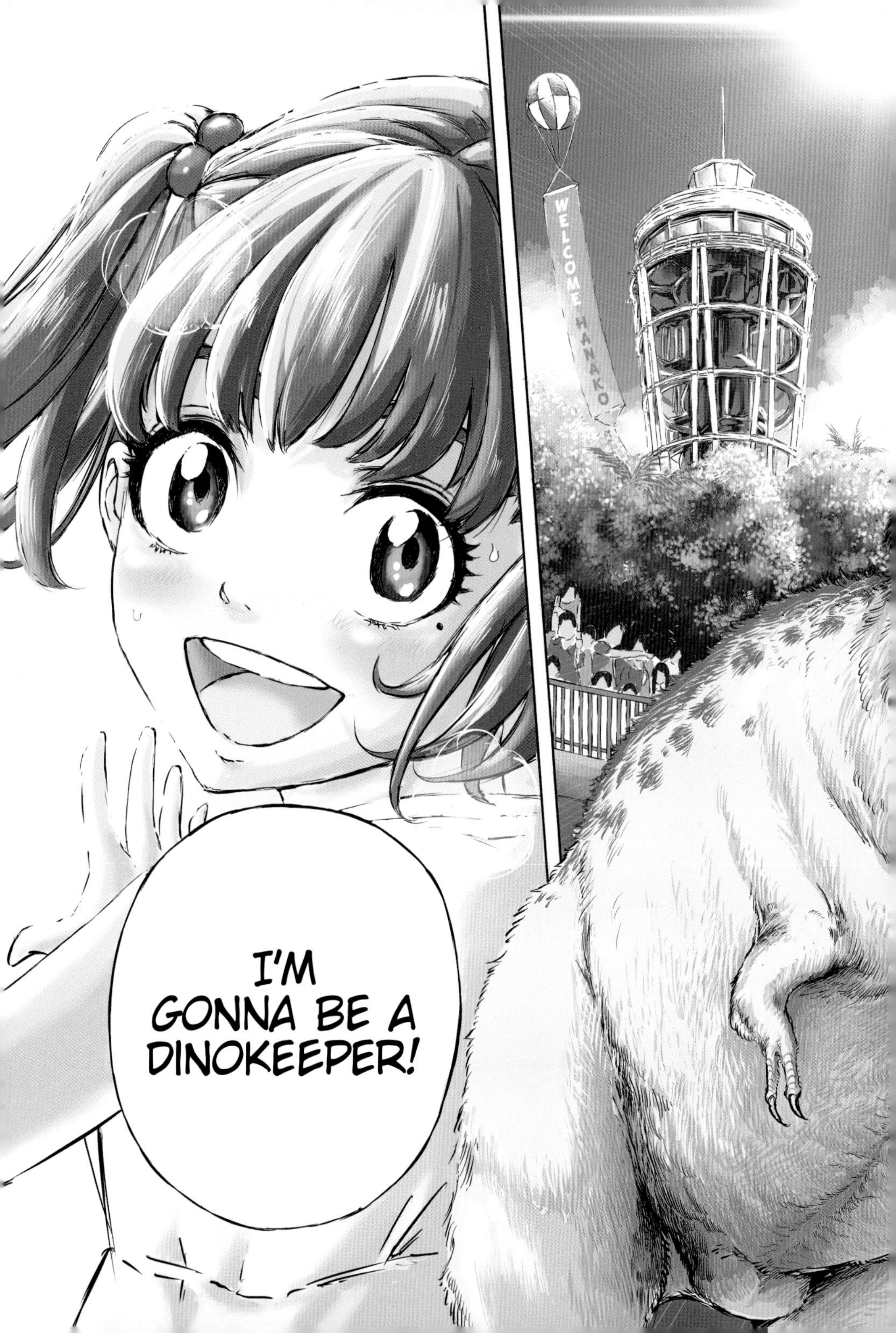

WELCOME HANAKO
I'M GONNA BE A DINOKEEPER!

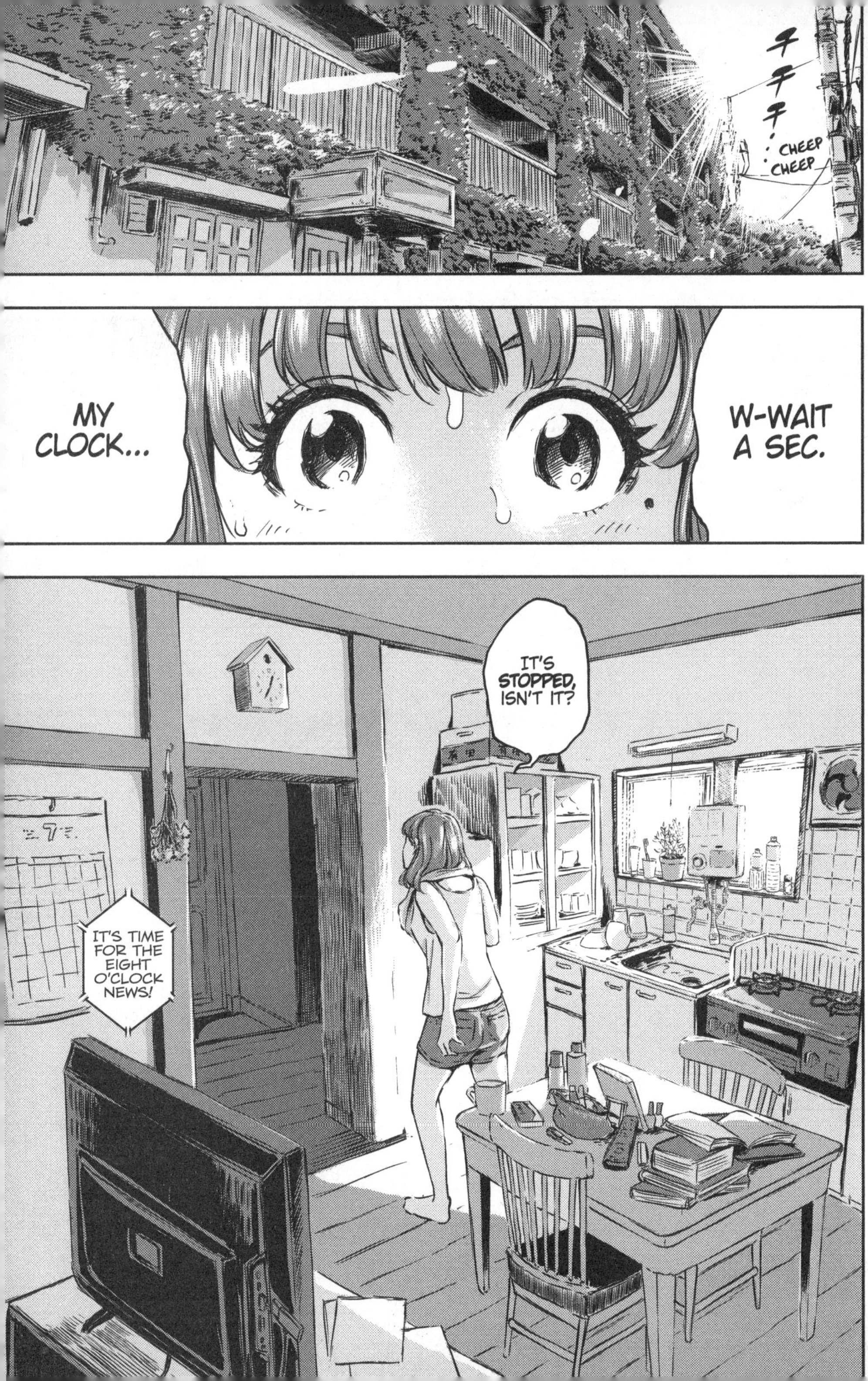
チチチ・・
CHEEP CHEEP
W-WAIT A SEC.
MY CLOCK...
IT'S STOPPED, ISN'T IT?
IT'S TIME FOR THE EIGHT O'CLOCK NEWS!

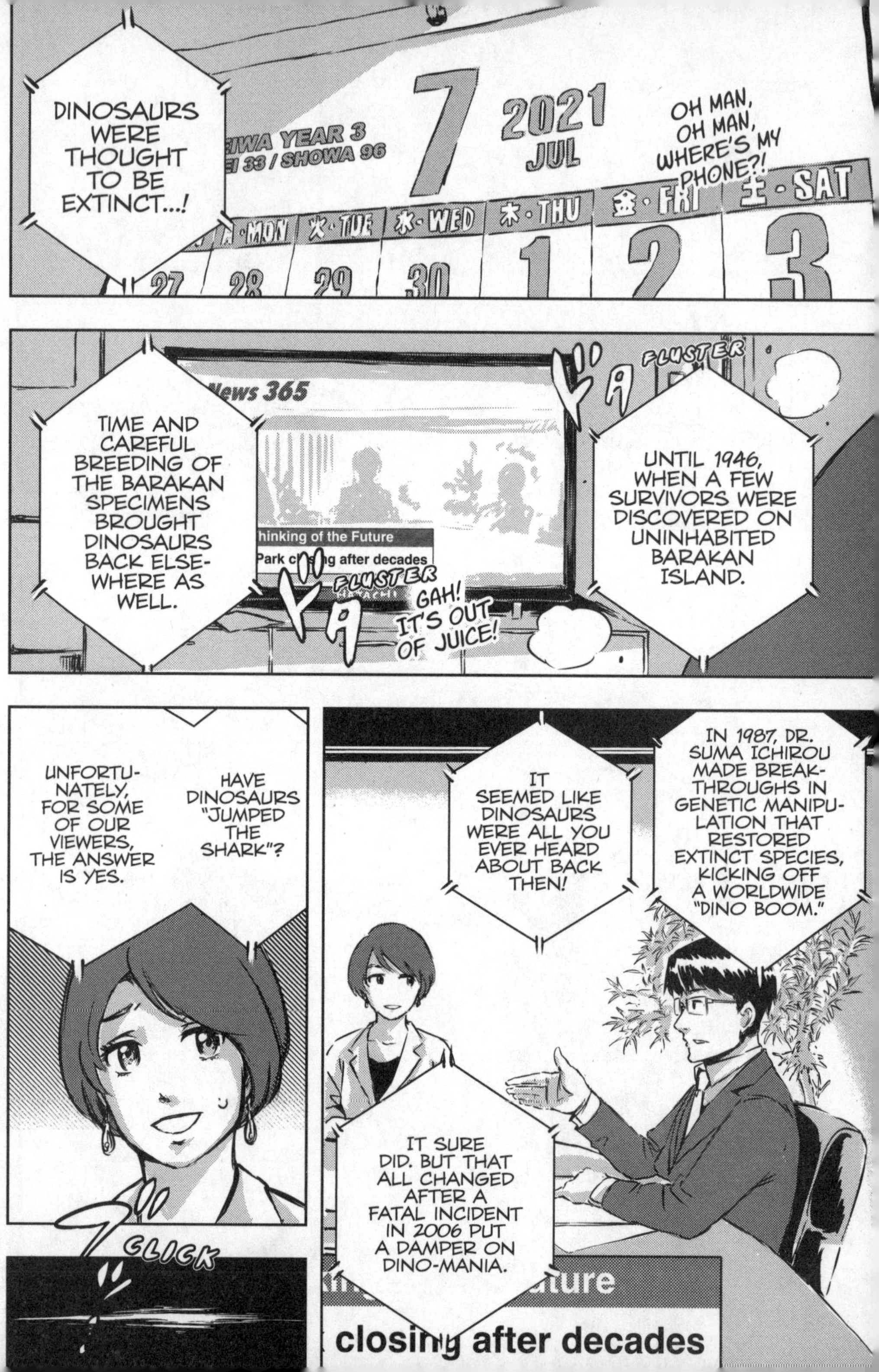

OH MAN, OH MAN, WHERE'S MY PHONE?!
2021
JUL
7
EIWA YEAR 3
EI 33 / SHOWA 96
土・SAT
金・FRI
木・THU
水・WED
火・TUE
月・MON
3
2
1
30
29
28
27
DINOSAURS WERE THOUGHT TO BE EXTINCT...!
UNTIL 1946, WHEN A FEW SURVIVORS WERE DISCOVERED ON UNINHABITED BARAKAN ISLAND.
FLUSTER
News 365
Thinking of the Future
Park closing after decades
TIME AND CAREFUL BREEDING OF THE BARAKAN SPECIMENS BROUGHT DINOSAURS BACK ELSE-WHERE AS WELL.
FLUSTER
GAH! IT'S OUT OF JUICE!
IN 1987, DR. SUMA ICHIROU MADE BREAK-THROUGHS IN GENETIC MANIPU-LATION THAT RESTORED EXTINCT SPECIES, KICKING OFF A WORLDWIDE "DINO BOOM."
IT SEEMED LIKE DINOSAURS WERE ALL YOU EVER HEARD ABOUT BACK THEN!
IT SURE DID. BUT THAT ALL CHANGED AFTER A FATAL INCIDENT IN 2006 PUT A DAMPER ON DINO-MANIA.
uture
closing after decades
HAVE DINOSAURS "JUMPED THE SHARK"?
UNFORTU-NATELY, FOR SOME OF OUR VIEWERS, THE ANSWER IS YES.
CLICK

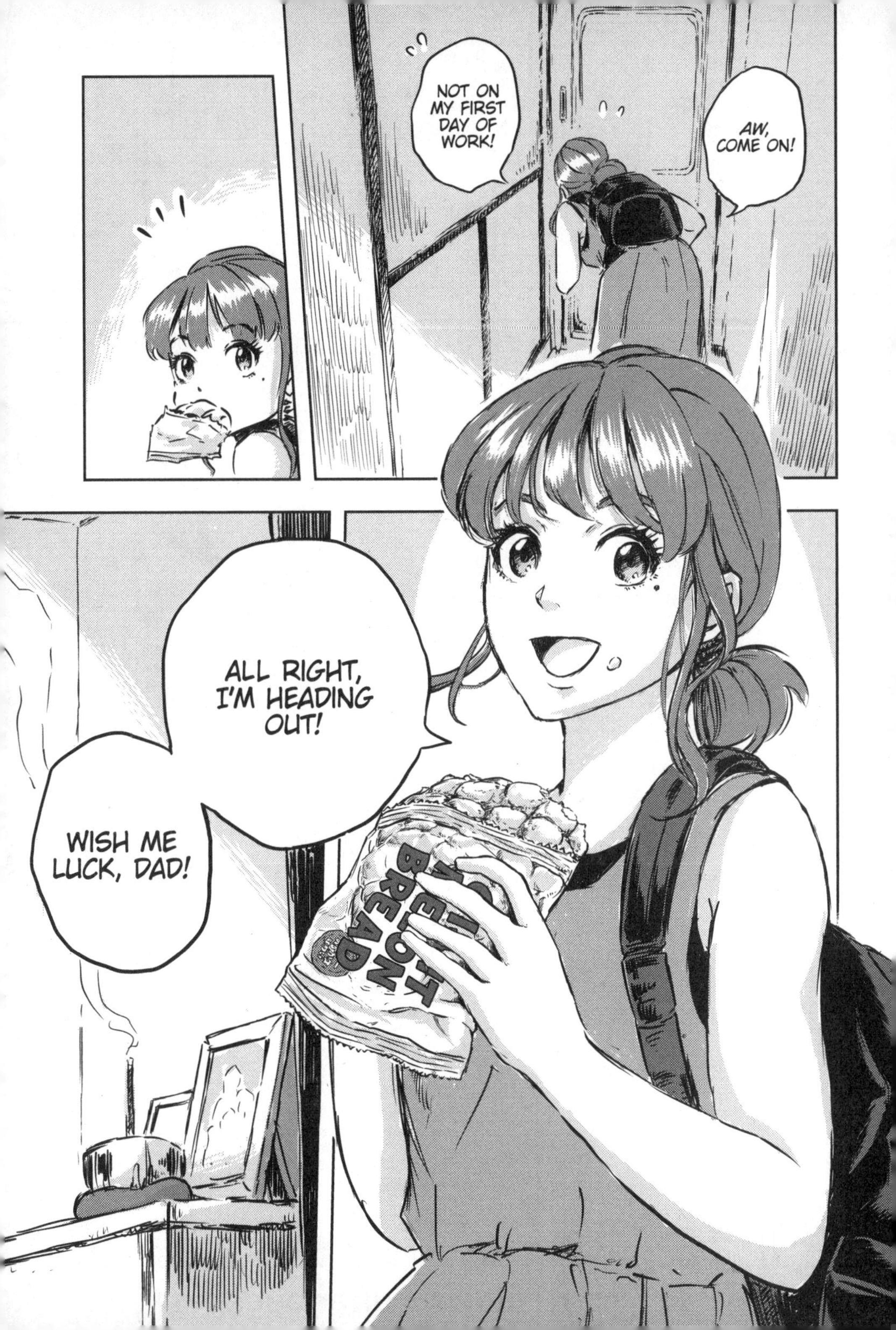
AW, COME ON!
NOT ON MY FIRST DAY OF WORK!
ALL RIGHT, I'M HEADING OUT!
WISH ME LUCK, DAD!

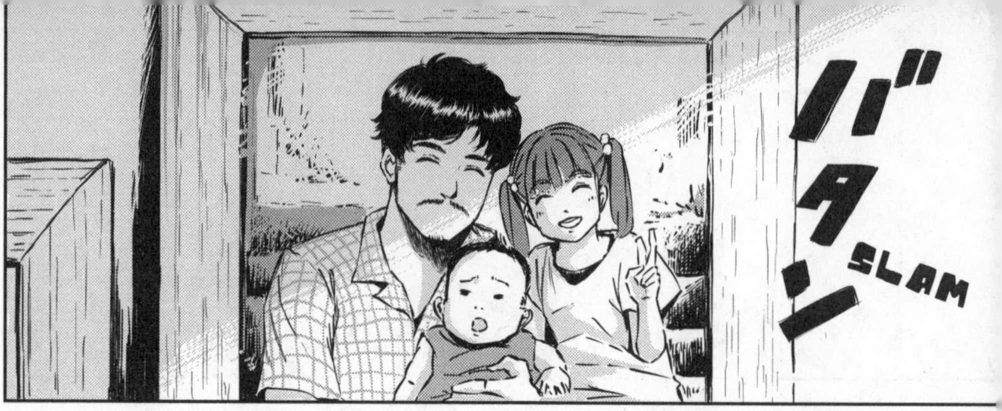
バタン
SLAM

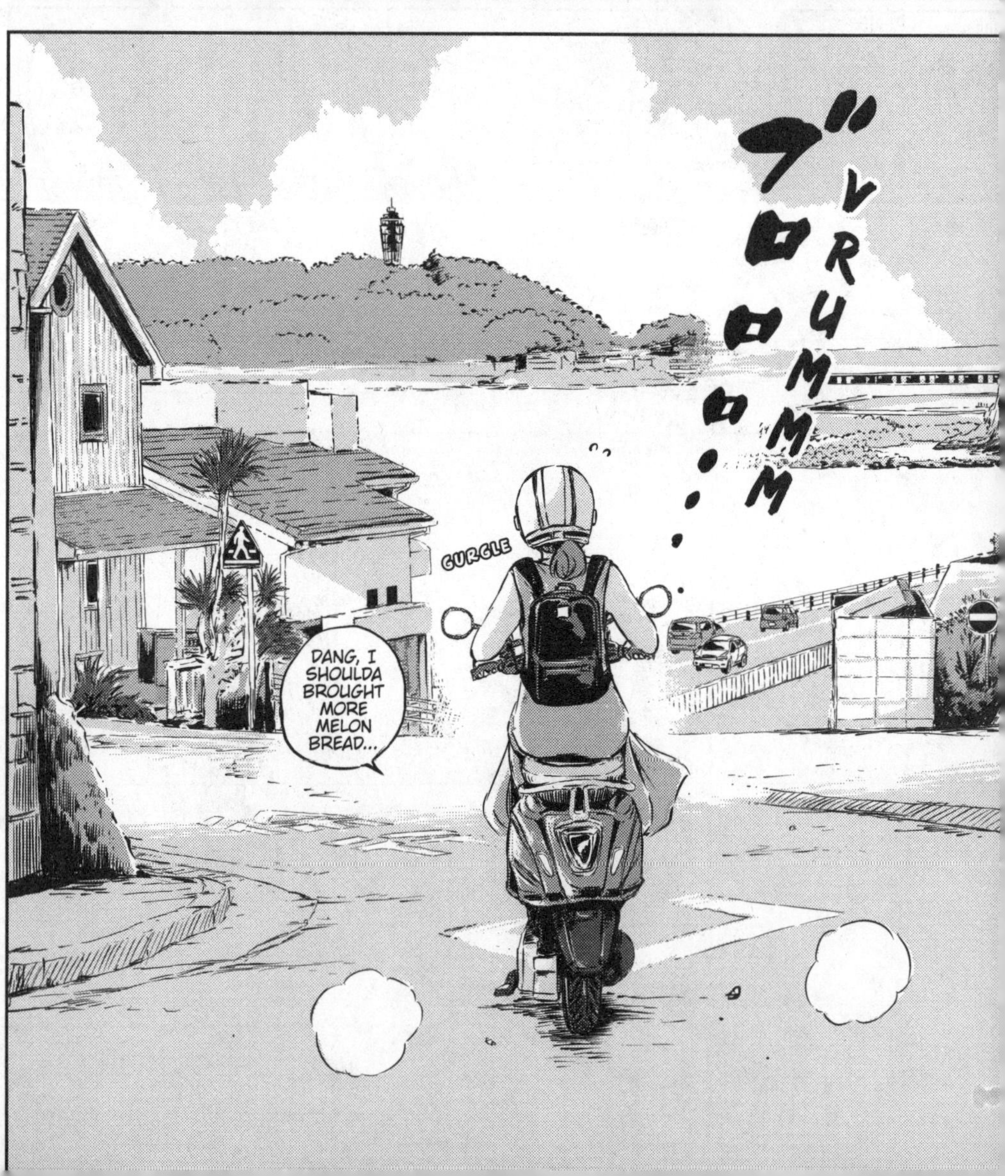
ブロロロ…
VRUMMMM
GURGLE
DANG, I SHOULDA BROUGHT MORE MELON BREAD...

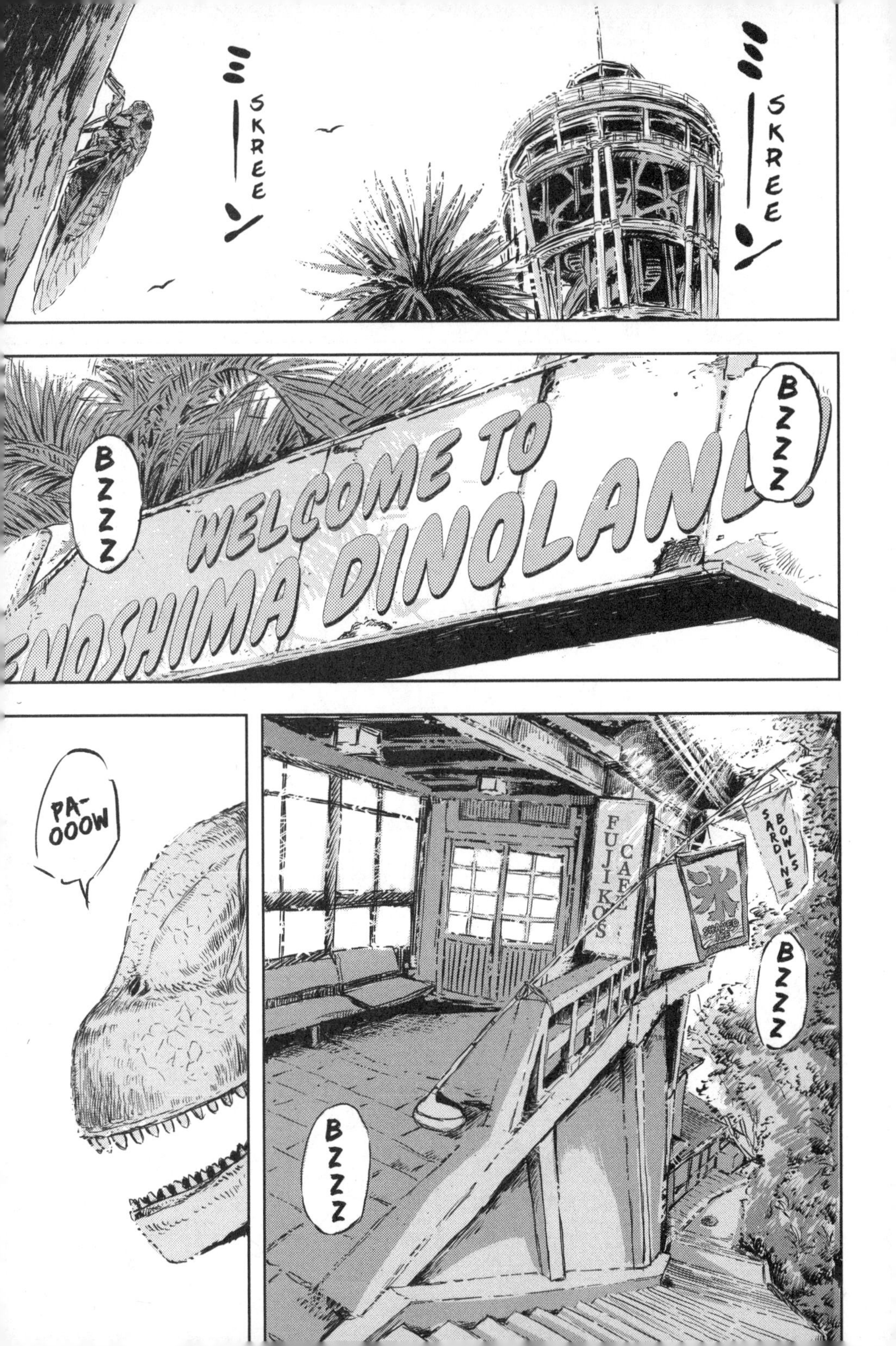
SKREE
SKREE
BZZZ
WELCOME TO
NOSHIMA DINOLAN
BZZZ
SARDINE BOWLS
FUJIKO'S CAFE
SHAVED ICE
BZZZ
BZZZ
PA-OOOW

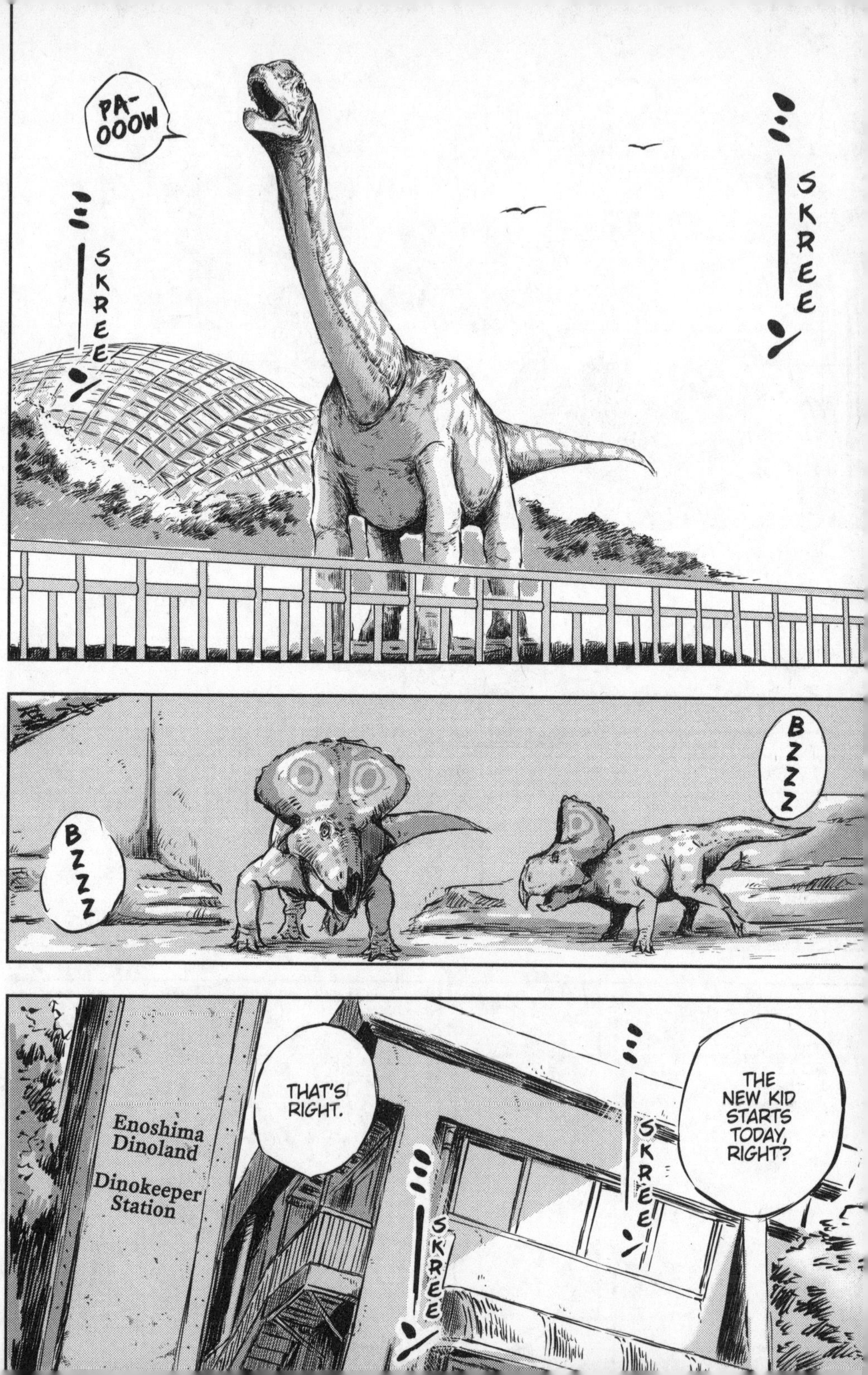

SKREE
PA-OOOW
SKREE
BZZZ
BZZZ
THE NEW KID STARTS TODAY, RIGHT?
SKREE
THAT'S RIGHT.
SKREE
Enoshima Dinoland
Dinokeeper Station

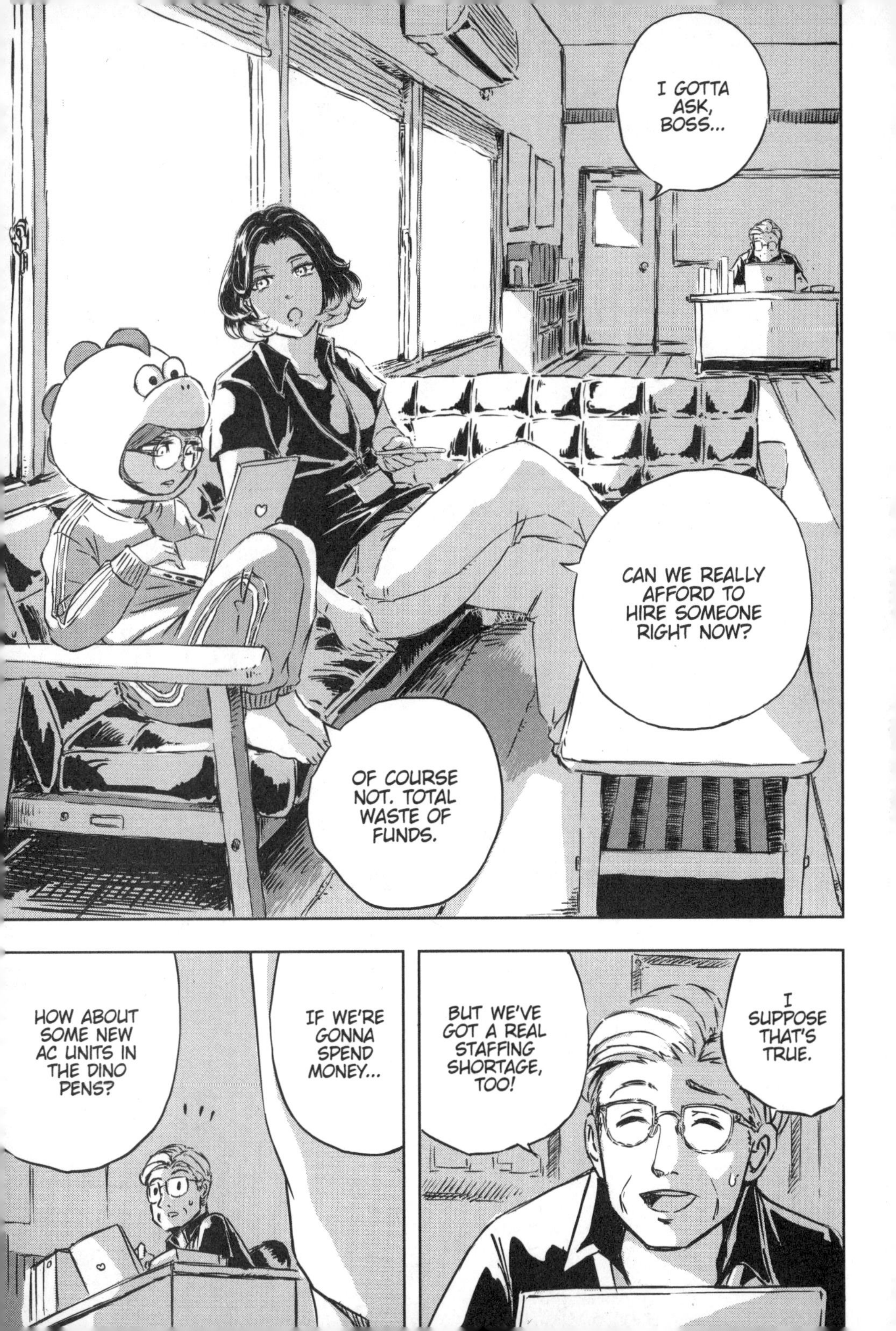
I GOTTA ASK, BOSS...
CAN WE REALLY AFFORD TO HIRE SOMEONE RIGHT NOW?
OF COURSE NOT. TOTAL WASTE OF FUNDS.
I SUPPOSE THAT'S TRUE.
BUT WE'VE GOT A REAL STAFFING SHORTAGE, TOO!
IF WE'RE GONNA SPEND MONEY...
HOW ABOUT SOME NEW AC UNITS IN THE DINO PENS?

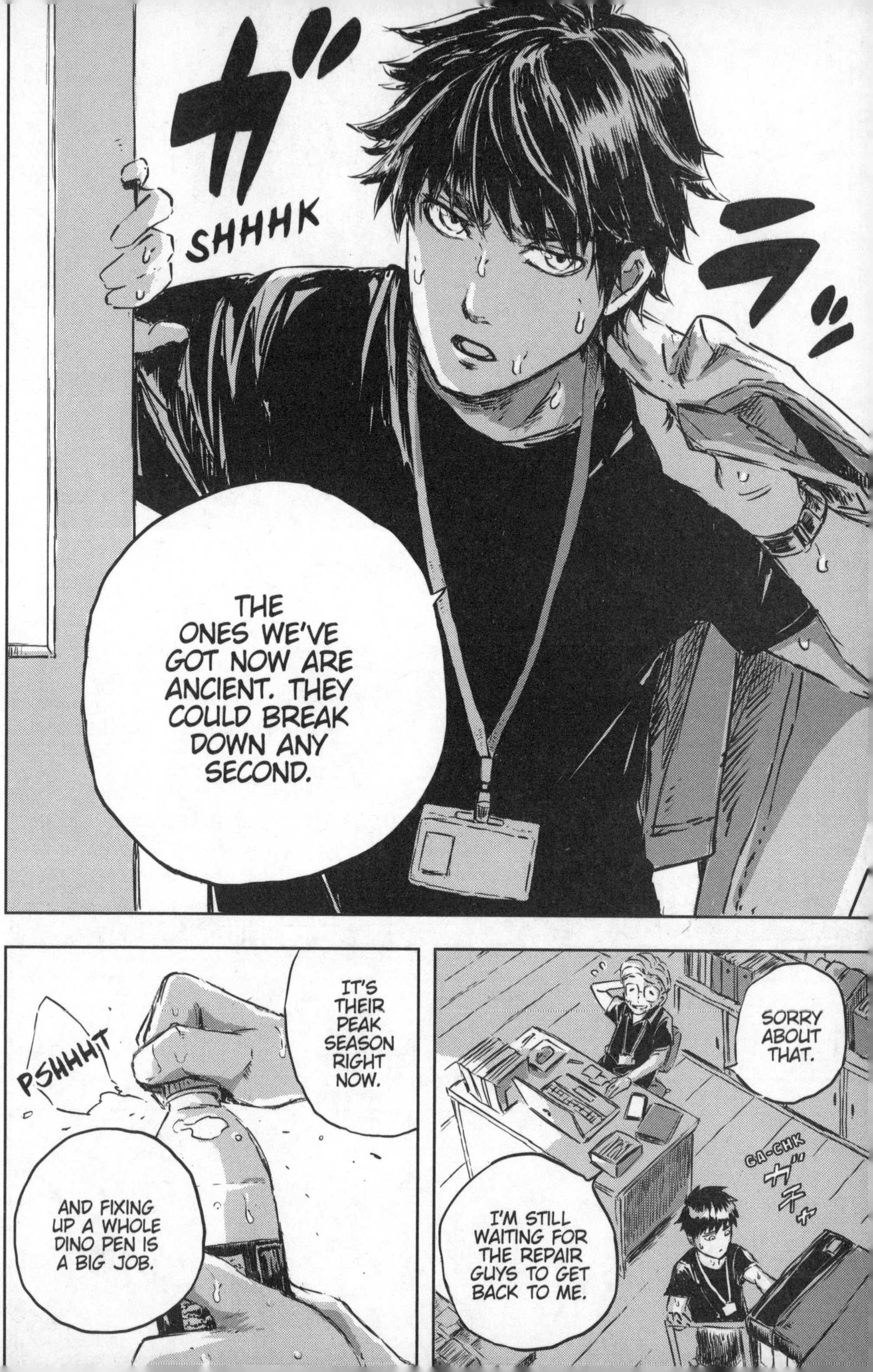
ガ
SHHHK
ラッ
THE ONES WE'VE GOT NOW ARE ANCIENT. THEY COULD BREAK DOWN ANY SECOND.
SORRY ABOUT THAT.
GA-CHK
ガチャ
I'M STILL WAITING FOR THE REPAIR GUYS TO GET BACK TO ME.
IT'S THEIR PEAK SEASON RIGHT NOW.
PSHHHT
AND FIXING UP A WHOLE DINO PEN IS A BIG JOB.

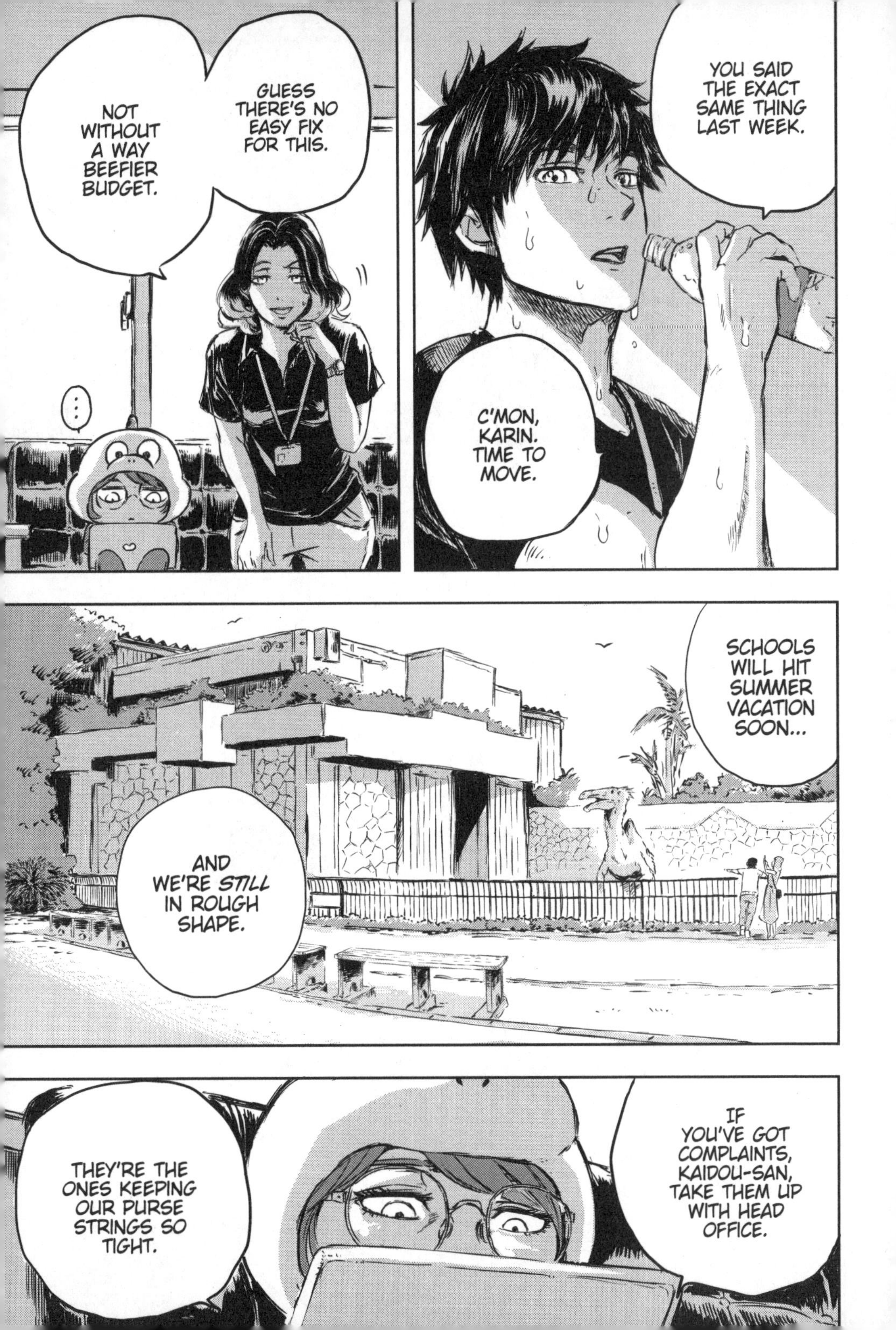
YOU SAID THE EXACT SAME THING LAST WEEK.
C'MON, KARIN. TIME TO MOVE.
GUESS THERE'S NO EASY FIX FOR THIS.
NOT WITHOUT A WAY BEEFIER BUDGET.
...
SCHOOLS WILL HIT SUMMER VACATION SOON...
AND WE'RE *STILL* IN ROUGH SHAPE.
IF YOU'VE GOT COMPLAINTS, KAIDOU-SAN, TAKE THEM UP WITH HEAD OFFICE.
THEY'RE THE ONES KEEPING OUR PURSE STRINGS SO TIGHT.

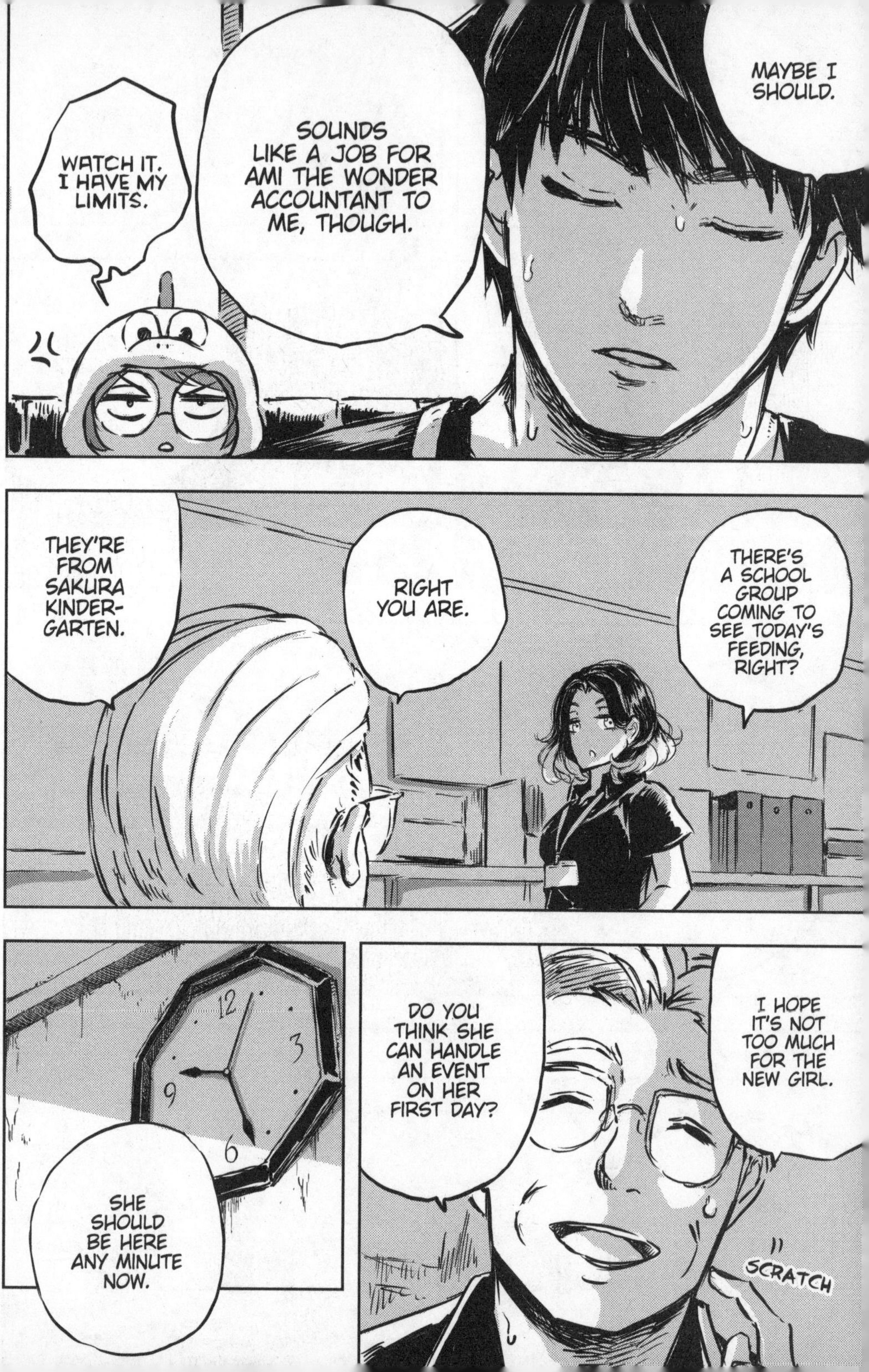
MAYBE I SHOULD.
SOUNDS LIKE A JOB FOR AMI THE WONDER ACCOUNTANT TO ME, THOUGH.
WATCH IT. I HAVE MY LIMITS.
THERE'S A SCHOOL GROUP COMING TO SEE TODAY'S FEEDING, RIGHT?
RIGHT YOU ARE.
THEY'RE FROM SAKURA KINDER-GARTEN.
I HOPE IT'S NOT TOO MUCH FOR THE NEW GIRL.
DO YOU THINK SHE CAN HANDLE AN EVENT ON HER FIRST DAY?
SCRATCH
SHE SHOULD BE HERE ANY MINUTE NOW.

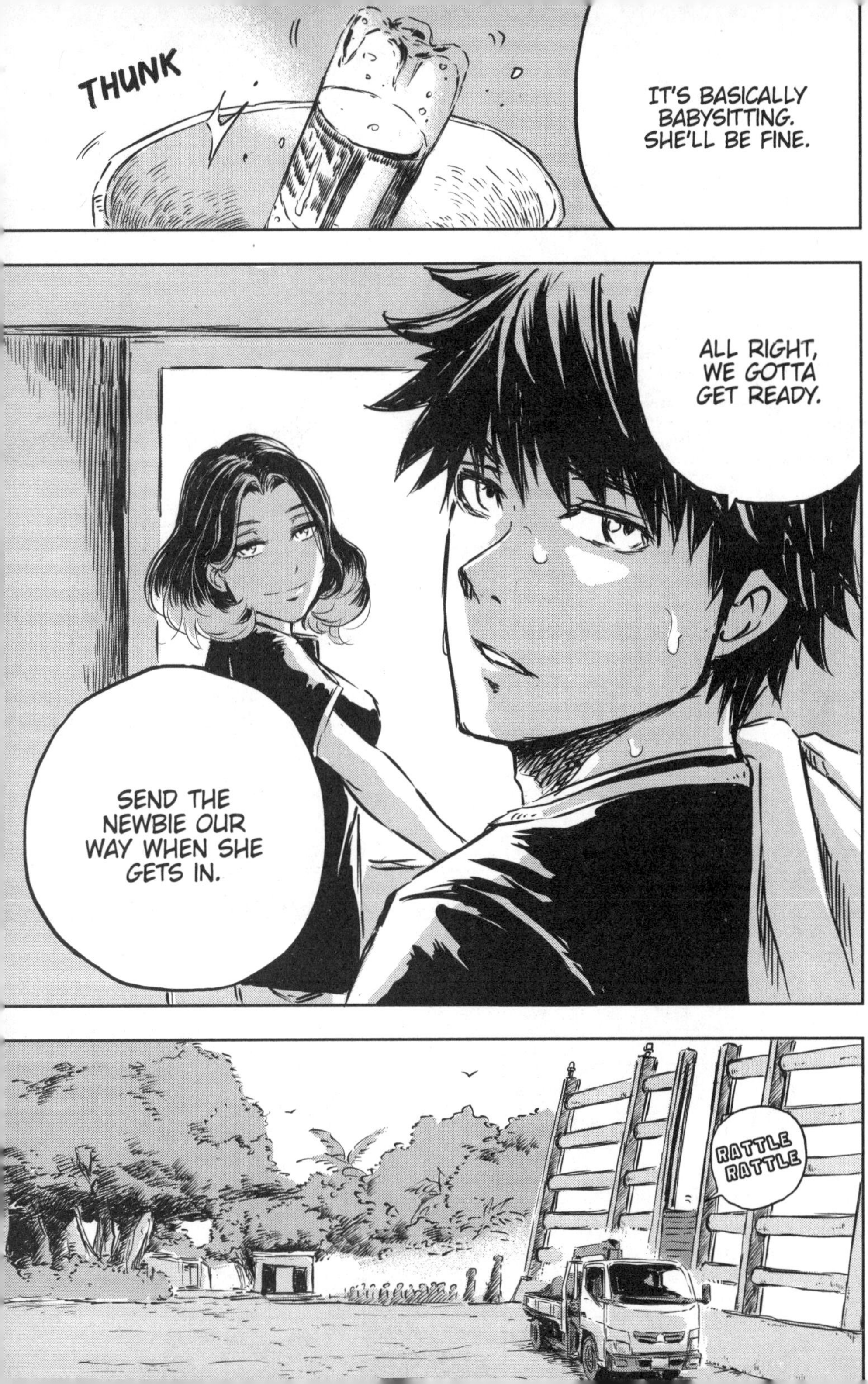
IT'S BASICALLY BABYSITTING. SHE'LL BE FINE.
THUNK
ALL RIGHT, WE GOTTA GET READY.
SEND THE NEWBIE OUR WAY WHEN SHE GETS IN.
RATTLE RATTLE

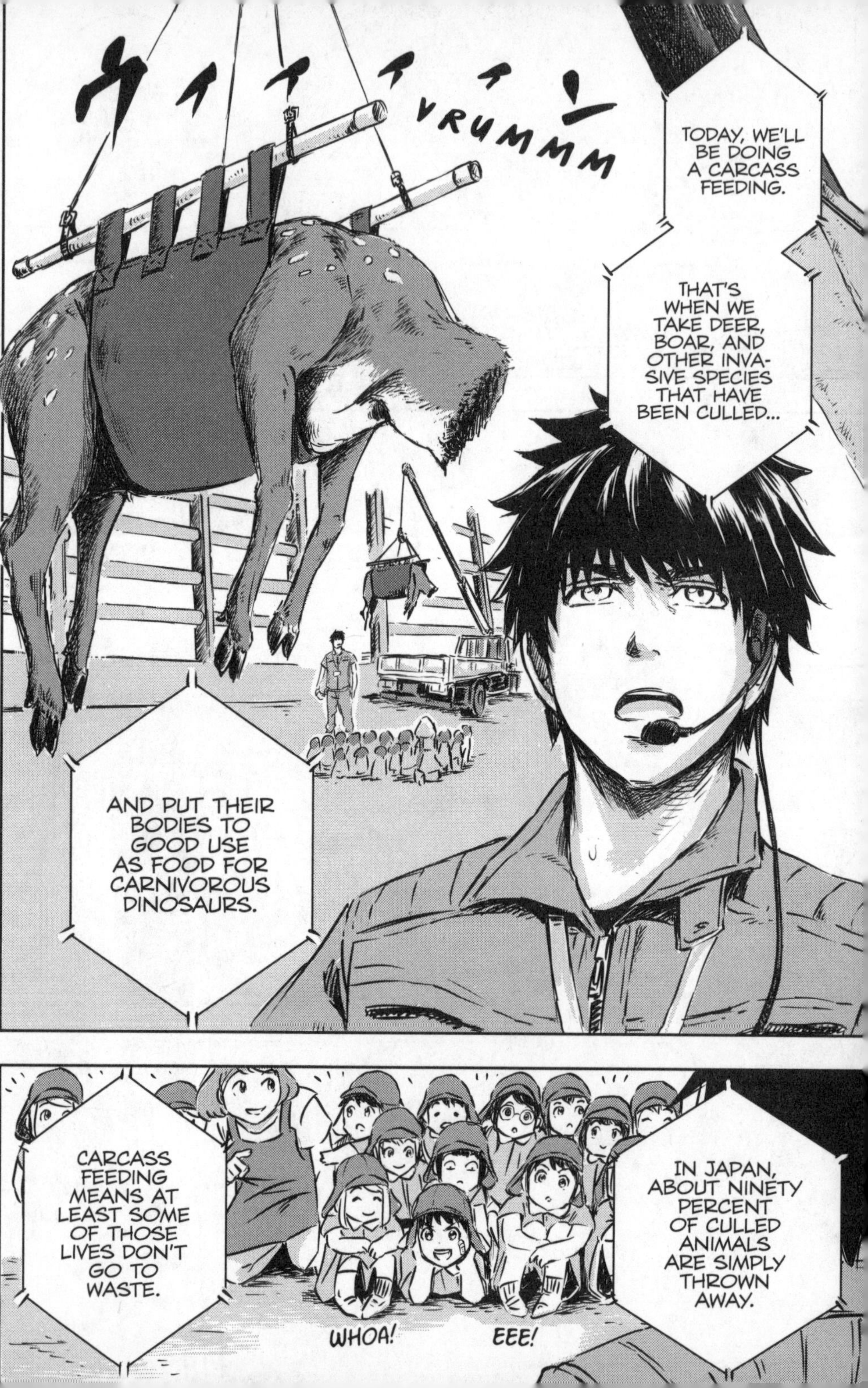
VRUMMM
TODAY, WE'LL BE DOING A CARCASS FEEDING.
THAT'S WHEN WE TAKE DEER, BOAR, AND OTHER INVASIVE SPECIES THAT HAVE BEEN CULLED...
AND PUT THEIR BODIES TO GOOD USE AS FOOD FOR CARNIVOROUS DINOSAURS.
IN JAPAN, ABOUT NINETY PERCENT OF CULLED ANIMALS ARE SIMPLY THROWN AWAY.
CARCASS FEEDING MEANS AT LEAST SOME OF THOSE LIVES DON'T GO TO WASTE.
EEE!
WHOA!

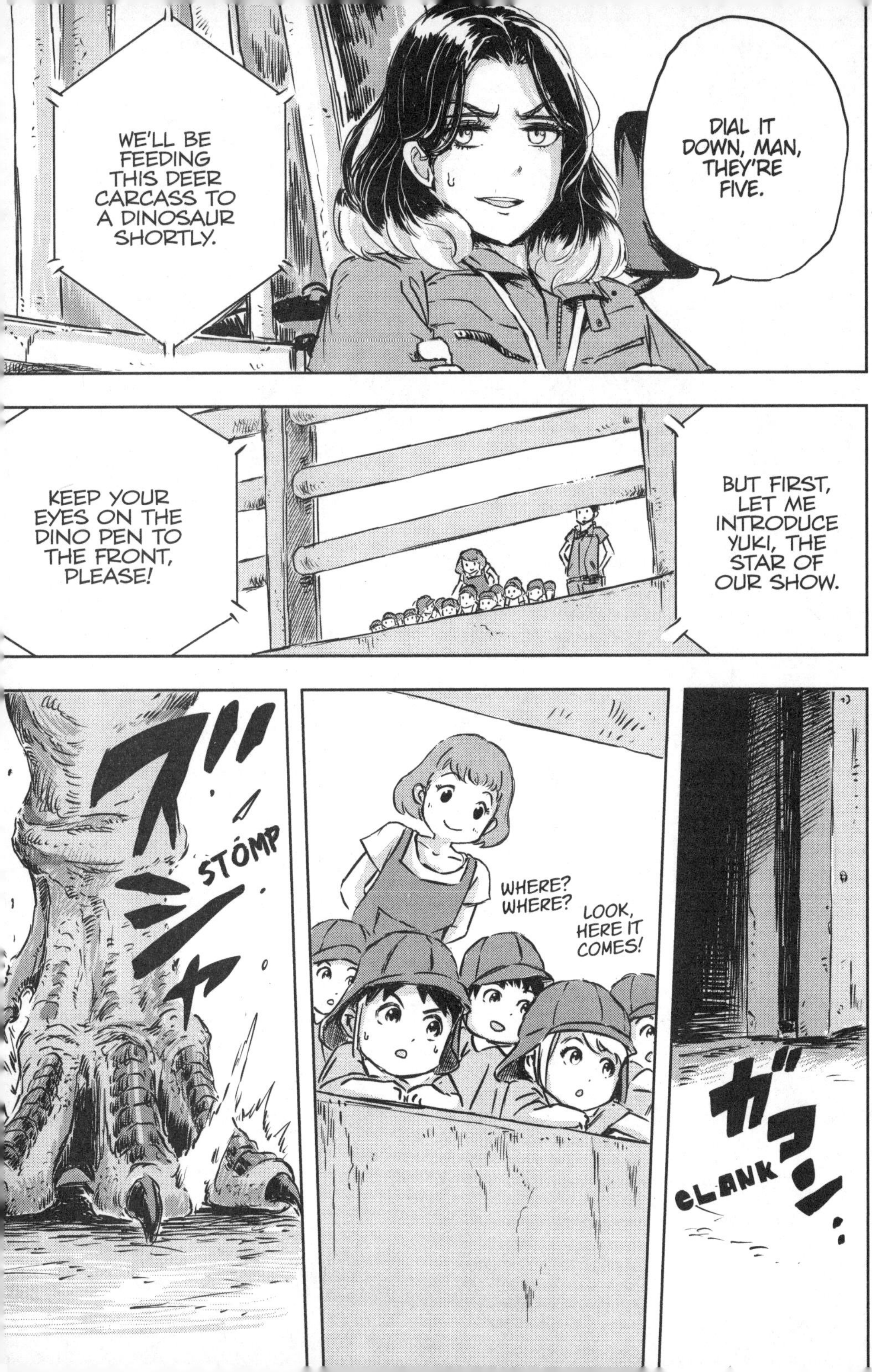
DIAL IT DOWN, MAN, THEY'RE FIVE.
WE'LL BE FEEDING THIS DEER CARCASS TO A DINOSAUR SHORTLY.
BUT FIRST, LET ME INTRODUCE YUKI, THE STAR OF OUR SHOW.
KEEP YOUR EYES ON THE DINO PEN TO THE FRONT, PLEASE!
CLANK
WHERE? WHERE?
LOOK, HERE IT COMES!
STOMP

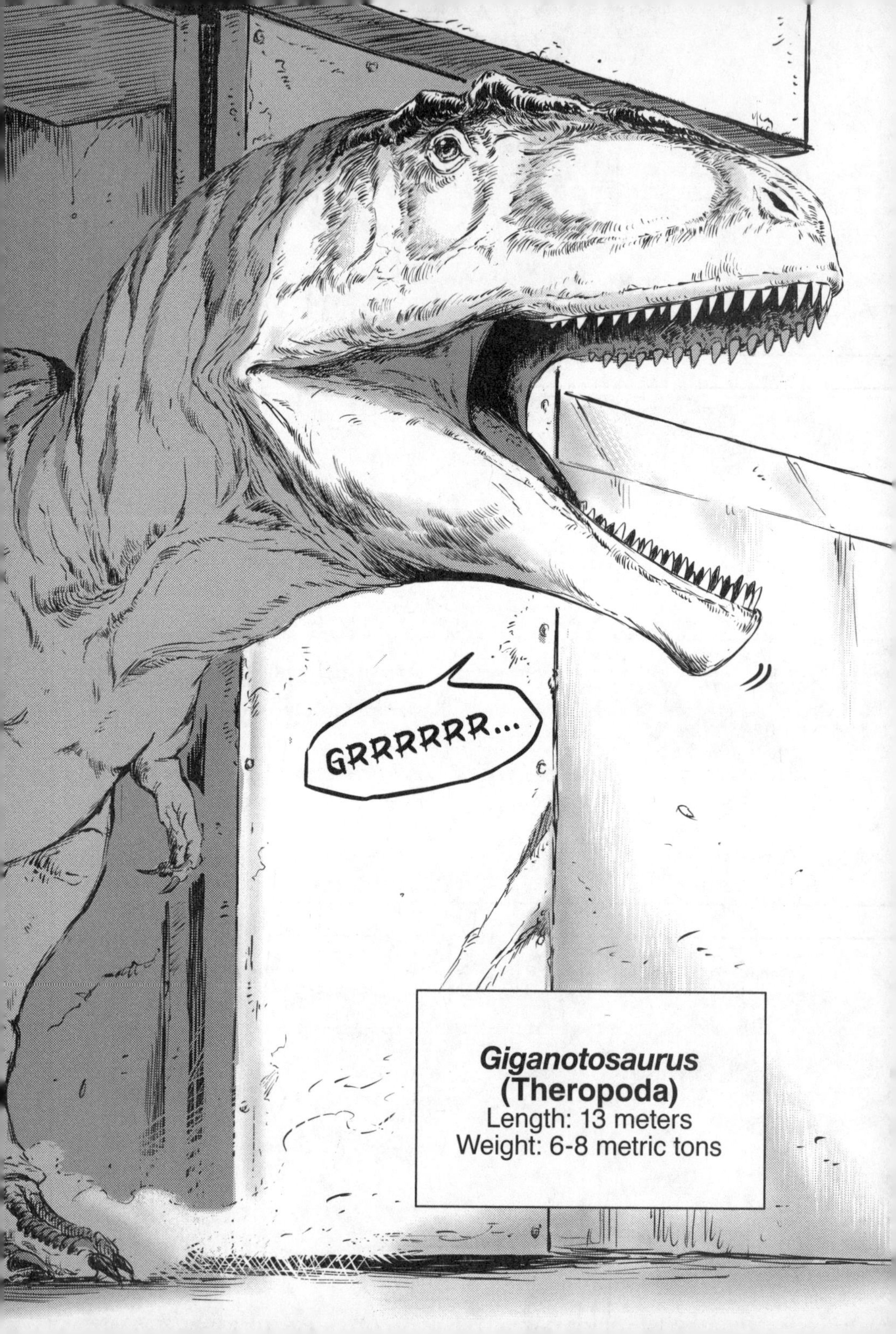
GRRRRRR...
Giganotosaurus (Theropoda)
Length: 13 meters
Weight: 6-8 metric tons

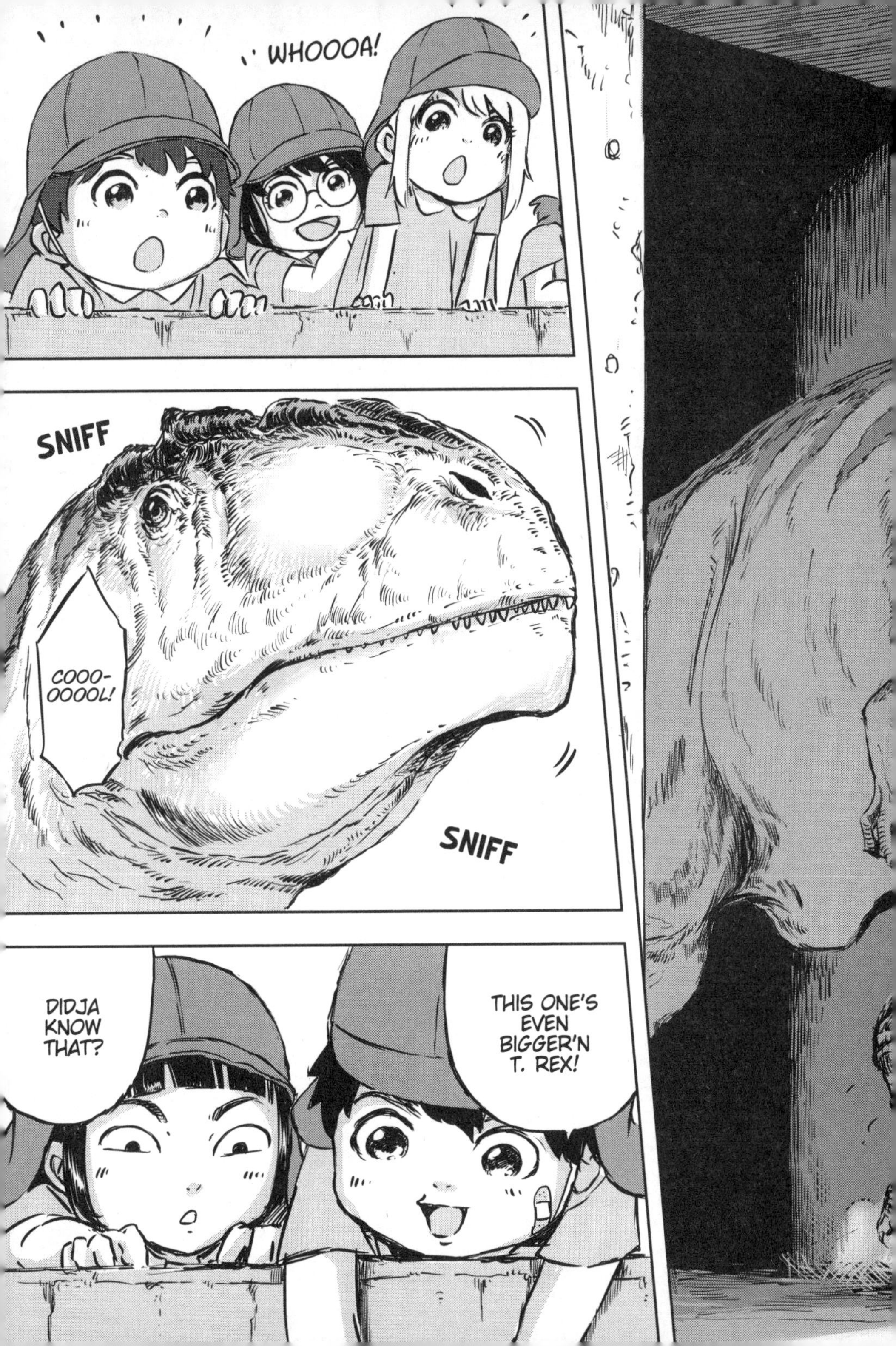
WHOOOA!
SNIFF
COOO-OOOOL!
SNIFF
THIS ONE'S EVEN BIGGER'N T. REX!
DIDJA KNOW THAT?

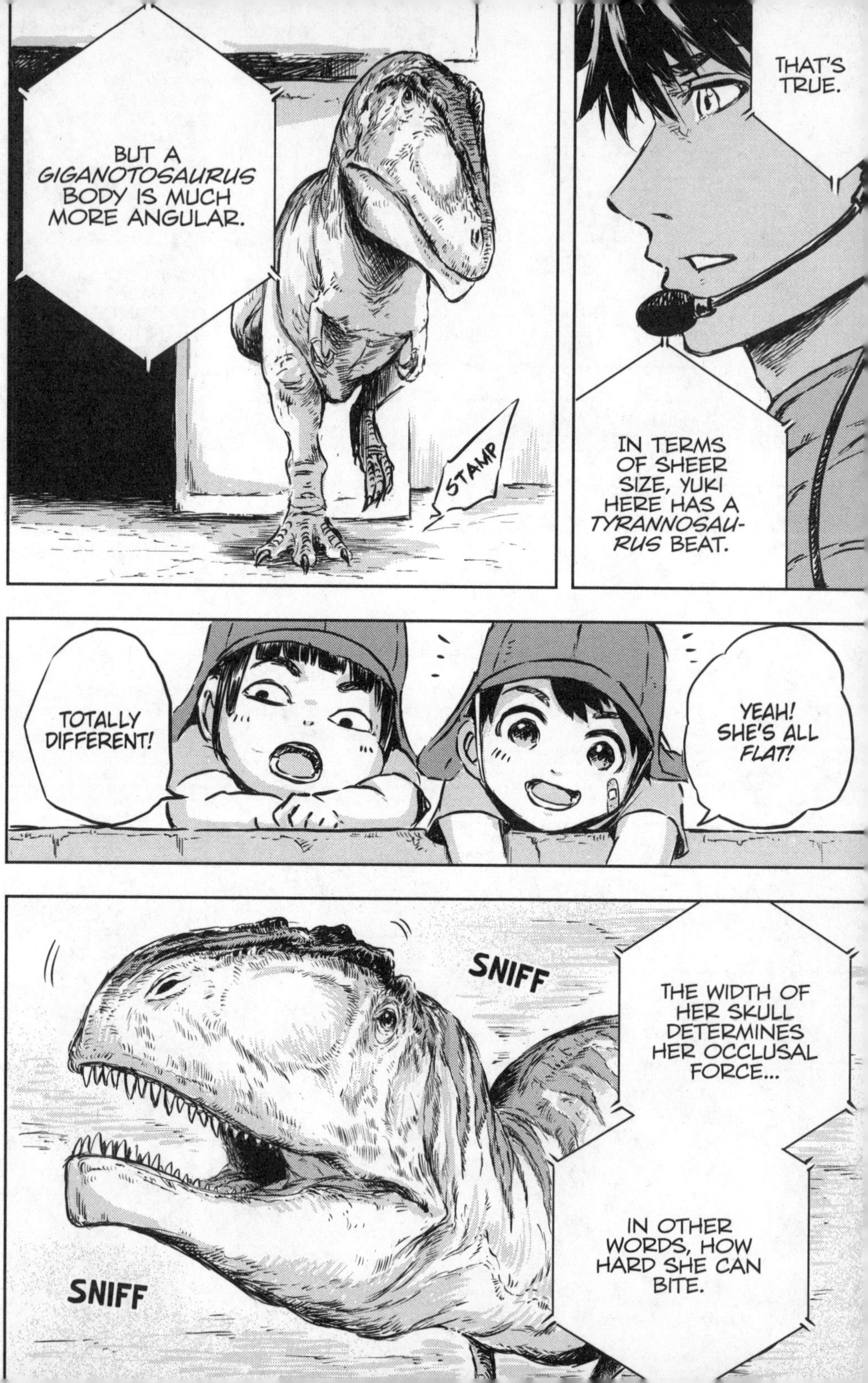
THAT'S TRUE.
IN TERMS OF SHEER SIZE, YUKI HERE HAS A TYRANNOSAURUS BEAT.
BUT A GIGANOTOSAURUS BODY IS MUCH MORE ANGULAR.
STAMP
YEAH! SHE'S ALL FLAT!
TOTALLY DIFFERENT!
THE WIDTH OF HER SKULL DETERMINES HER OCCLUSAL FORCE...
SNIFF
IN OTHER WORDS, HOW HARD SHE CAN BITE.
SNIFF

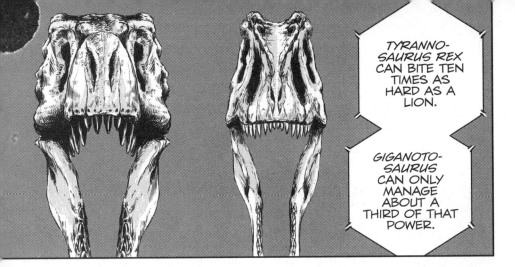

TYRANNOSAURUS REX CAN BITE TEN TIMES AS HARD AS A LION.
GIGANOTOSAURUS CAN ONLY MANAGE ABOUT A THIRD OF THAT POWER.
YUKI'S TEETH ALSO MAKE A DIFFERENCE THERE.
IF WE THINK OF T. REX'S TEETH AS THICK, STRONG HAMMERS THAT SHATTER BONE...
THEN YUKI'S TEETH ARE MORE LIKE SHARP KNIVES THAT SLICE THROUGH MEAT.

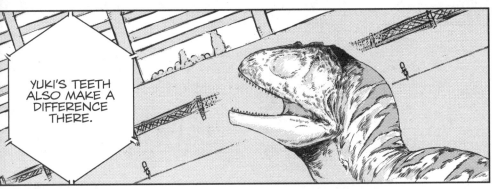

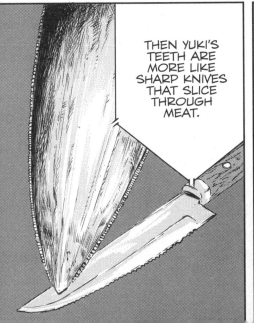

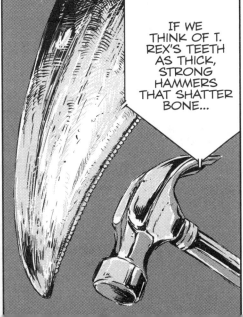

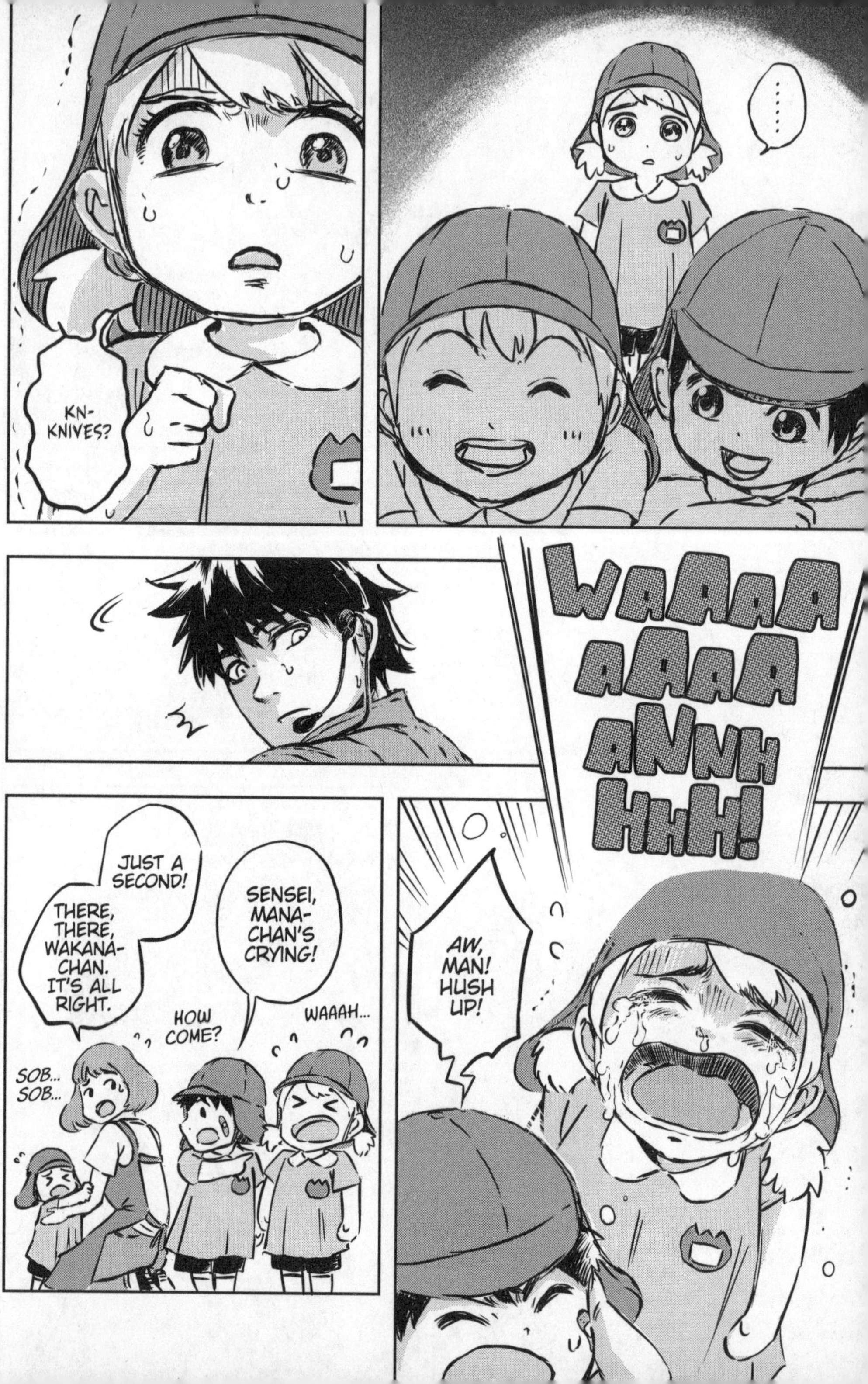
......
KN-KNIVES?
WAAAAAAAAANNHHHH!
AW, MAN! HUSH UP!
SENSEI, MANA-CHAN'S CRYING!
WAAAH...
HOW COME?
JUST A SECOND!
THERE, THERE, WAKANA-CHAN. IT'S ALL RIGHT.
SOB... SOB...

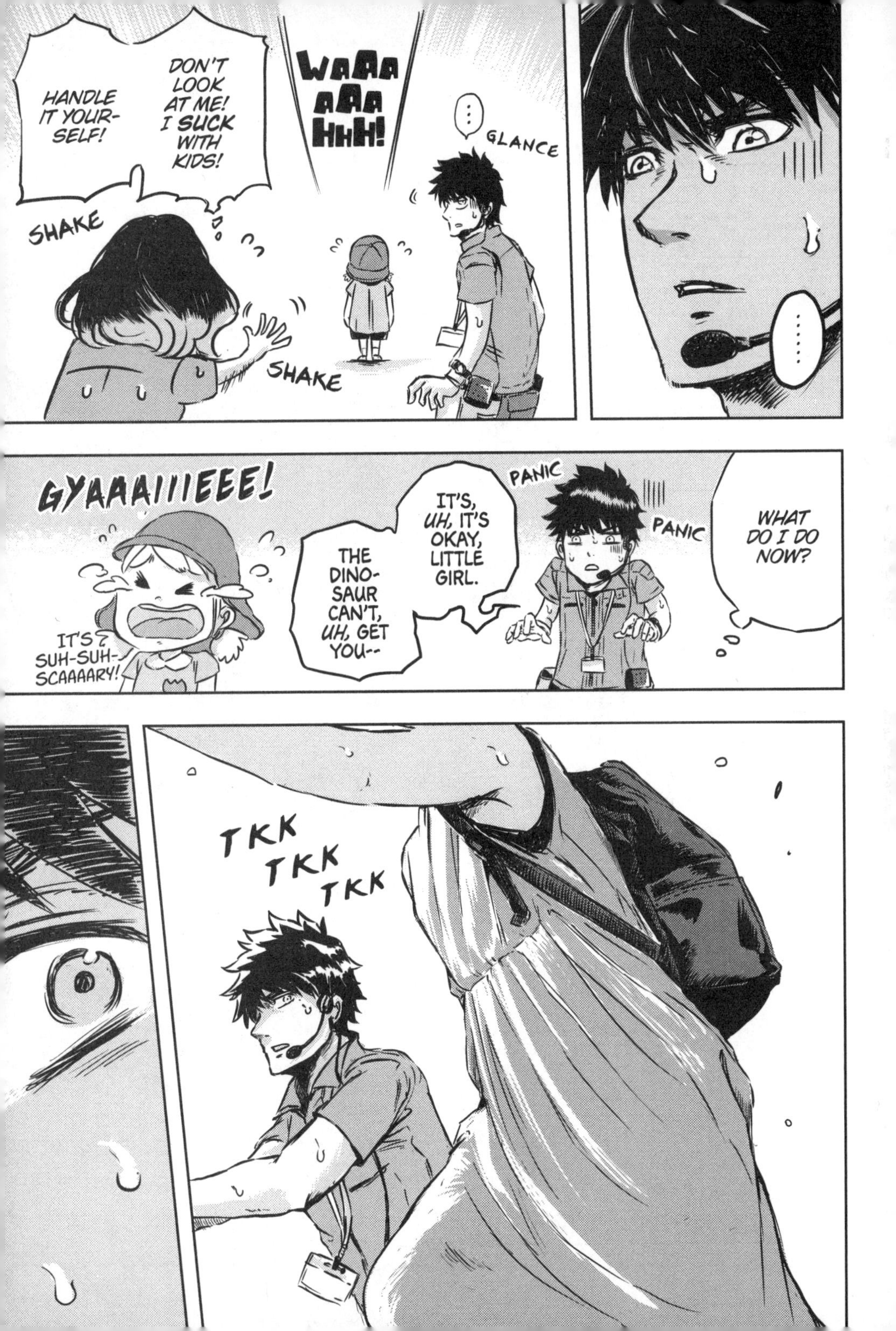
......
...
GLANCE
WAAAAAAHHH!
DON'T LOOK AT ME! I SUCK WITH KIDS!
HANDLE IT YOURSELF!
SHAKE
SHAKE
WHAT DO I DO NOW?
PANIC
PANIC
IT'S, UH, IT'S OKAY, LITTLE GIRL.
THE DINOSAUR CAN'T, UH, GET YOU--
GYAAAIIIEEE!
IT'S SUH-SUH-SCAAAARY!
TKK TKK TKK

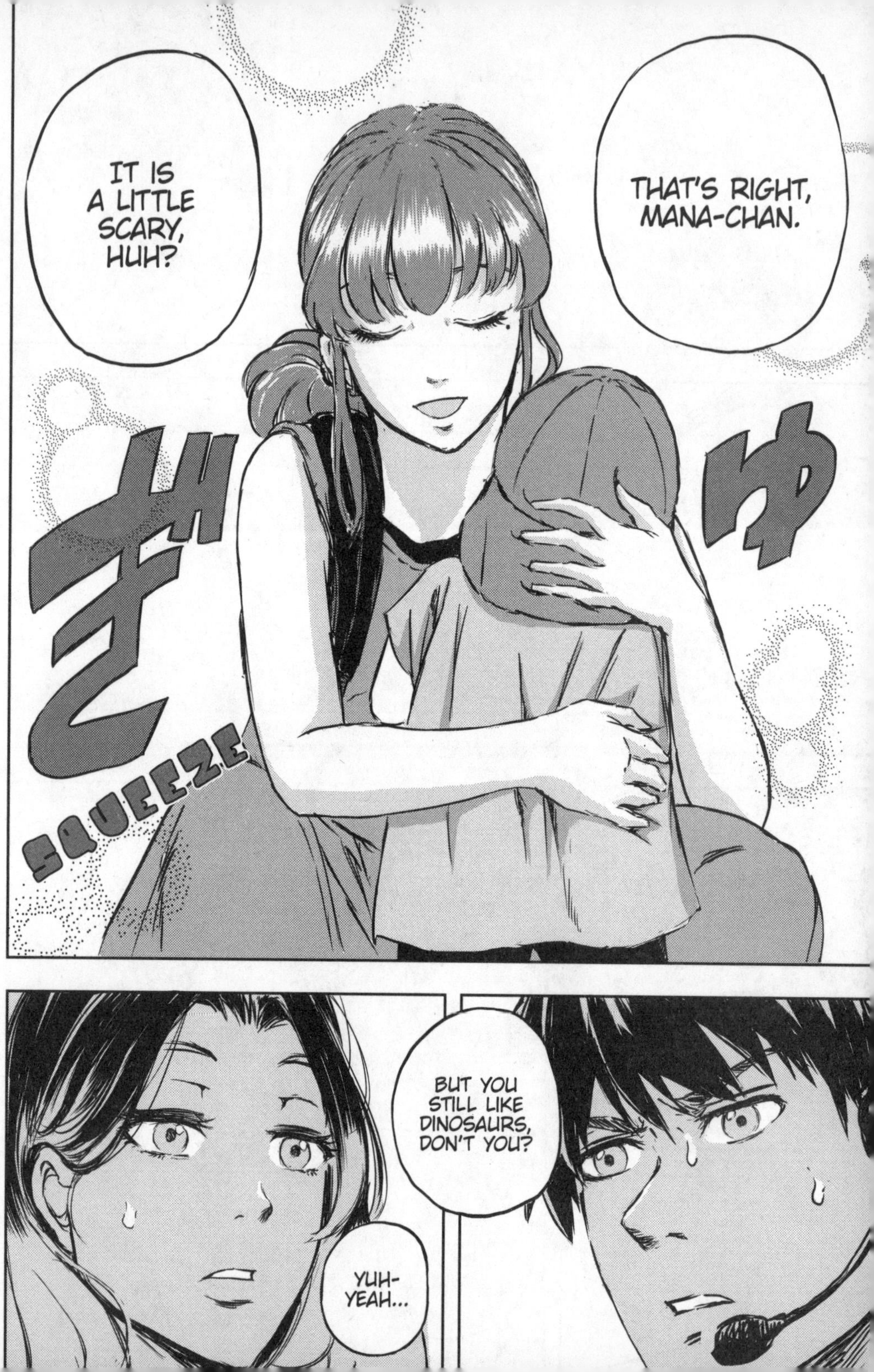
THAT'S RIGHT, MANA-CHAN.
IT IS A LITTLE SCARY, HUH?
ぎゅ
SQUEEZE
BUT YOU STILL LIKE DINOSAURS, DON'T YOU?
YUH-YEAH...

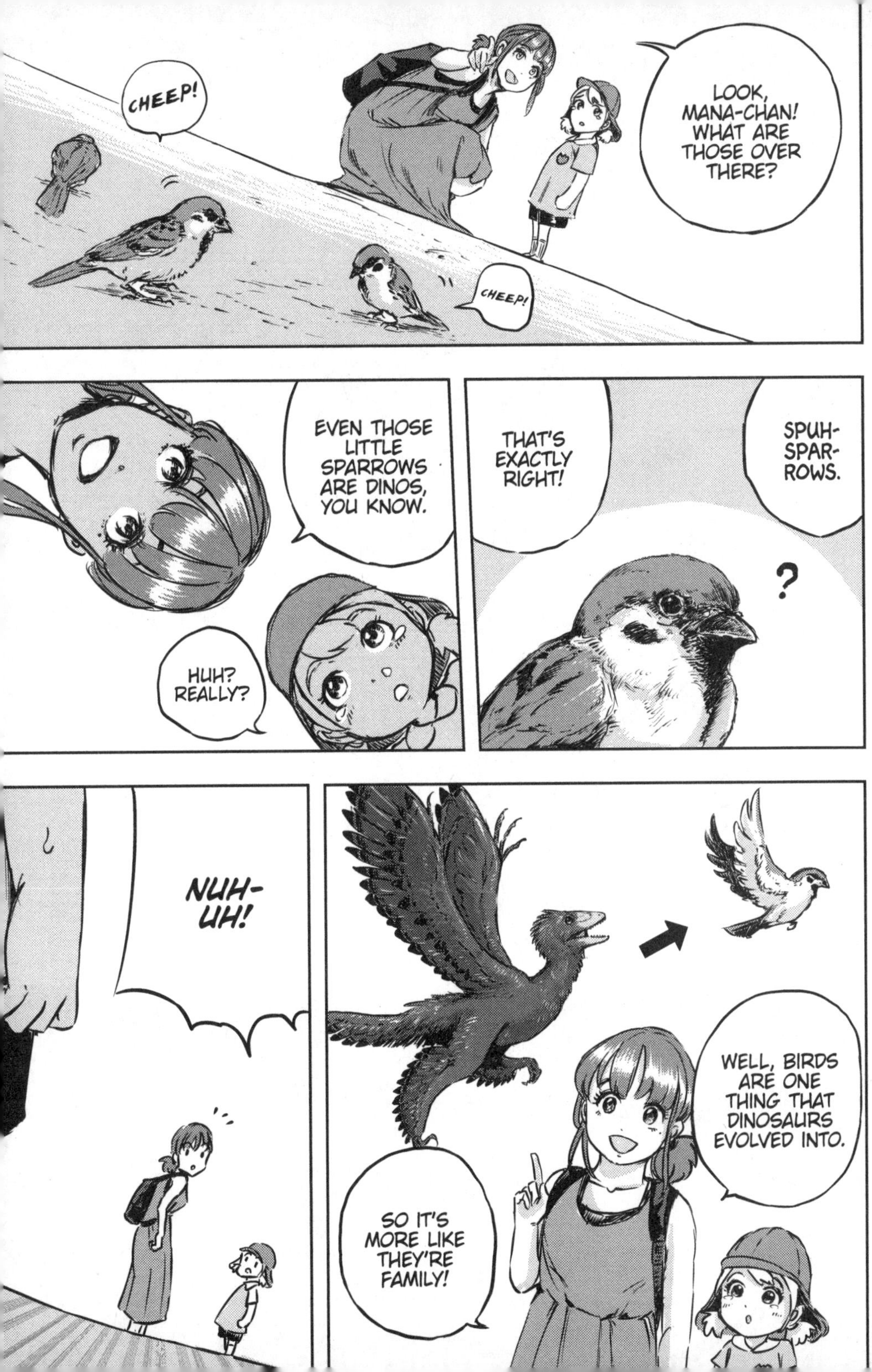
LOOK, MANA-CHAN! WHAT ARE THOSE OVER THERE?
CHEEP!
CHEEP!
SPUH-SPARROWS.
THAT'S EXACTLY RIGHT!
?
EVEN THOSE LITTLE SPARROWS ARE DINOS, YOU KNOW.
HUH? REALLY?
WELL, BIRDS ARE ONE THING THAT DINOSAURS EVOLVED INTO.
SO IT'S MORE LIKE THEY'RE FAMILY!
NUH-UH!

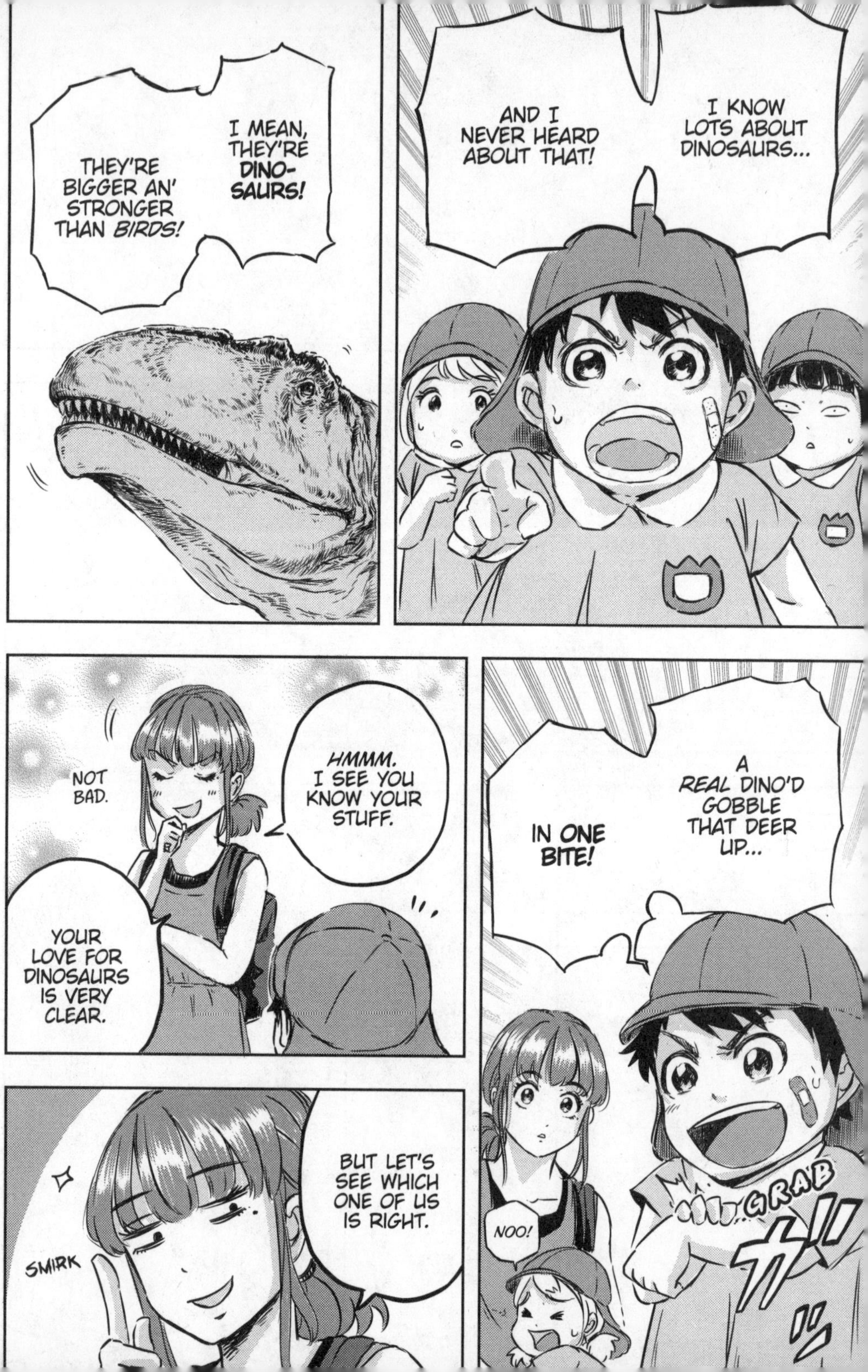
I KNOW LOTS ABOUT DINOSAURS...
AND I NEVER HEARD ABOUT THAT!
I MEAN, THEY'RE DINO-SAURS!
THEY'RE BIGGER AN' STRONGER THAN BIRDS!
A REAL DINO'D GOBBLE THAT DEER UP...
IN ONE BITE!
NOO!
GRAB
ガッ
HMMM. I SEE YOU KNOW YOUR STUFF.
NOT BAD.
YOUR LOVE FOR DINOSAURS IS VERY CLEAR.
BUT LET'S SEE WHICH ONE OF US IS RIGHT.
SMIRK

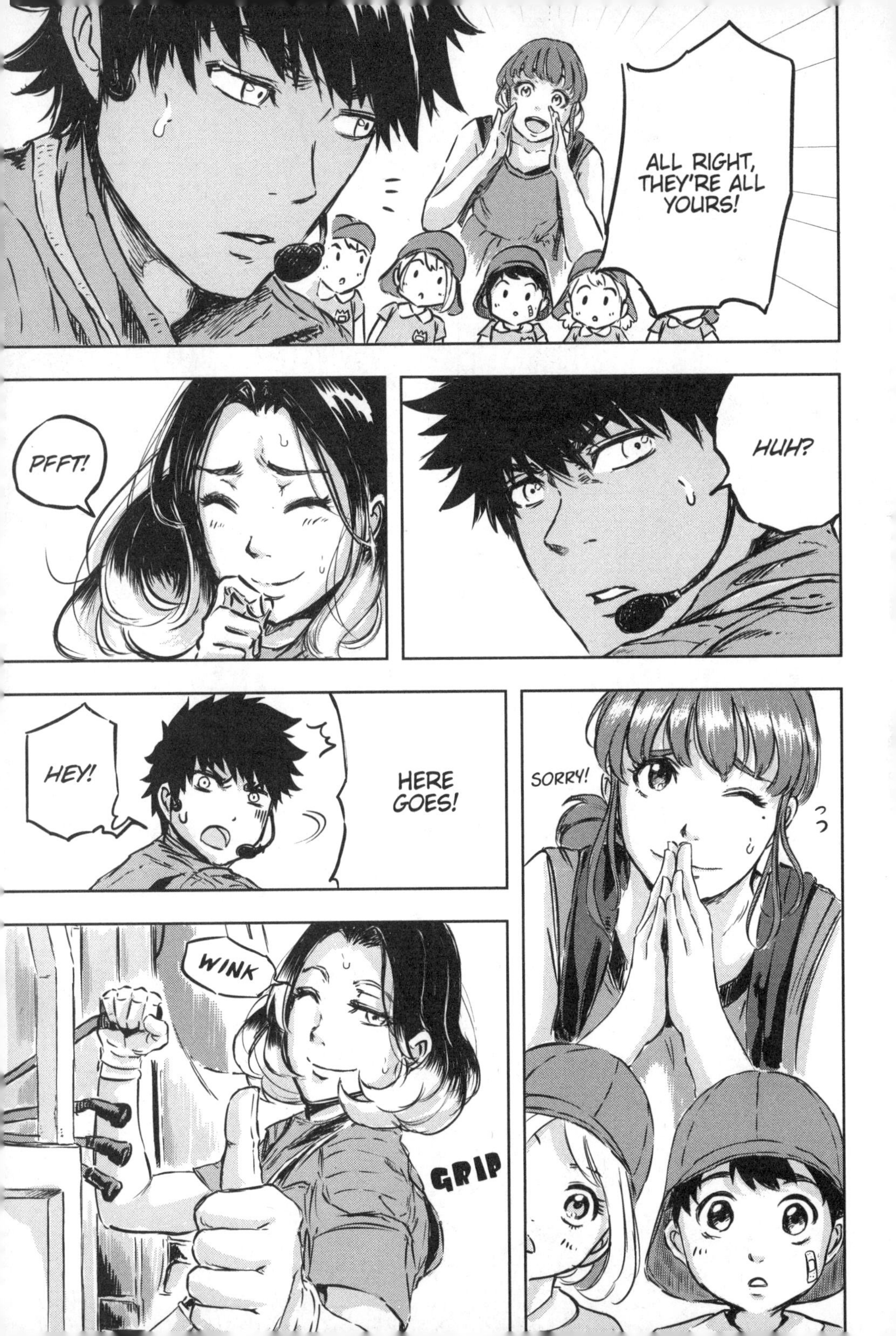
ALL RIGHT, THEY'RE ALL YOURS!
HUH?
PFFT!
SORRY!
HERE GOES!
HEY!
WINK
GRIP

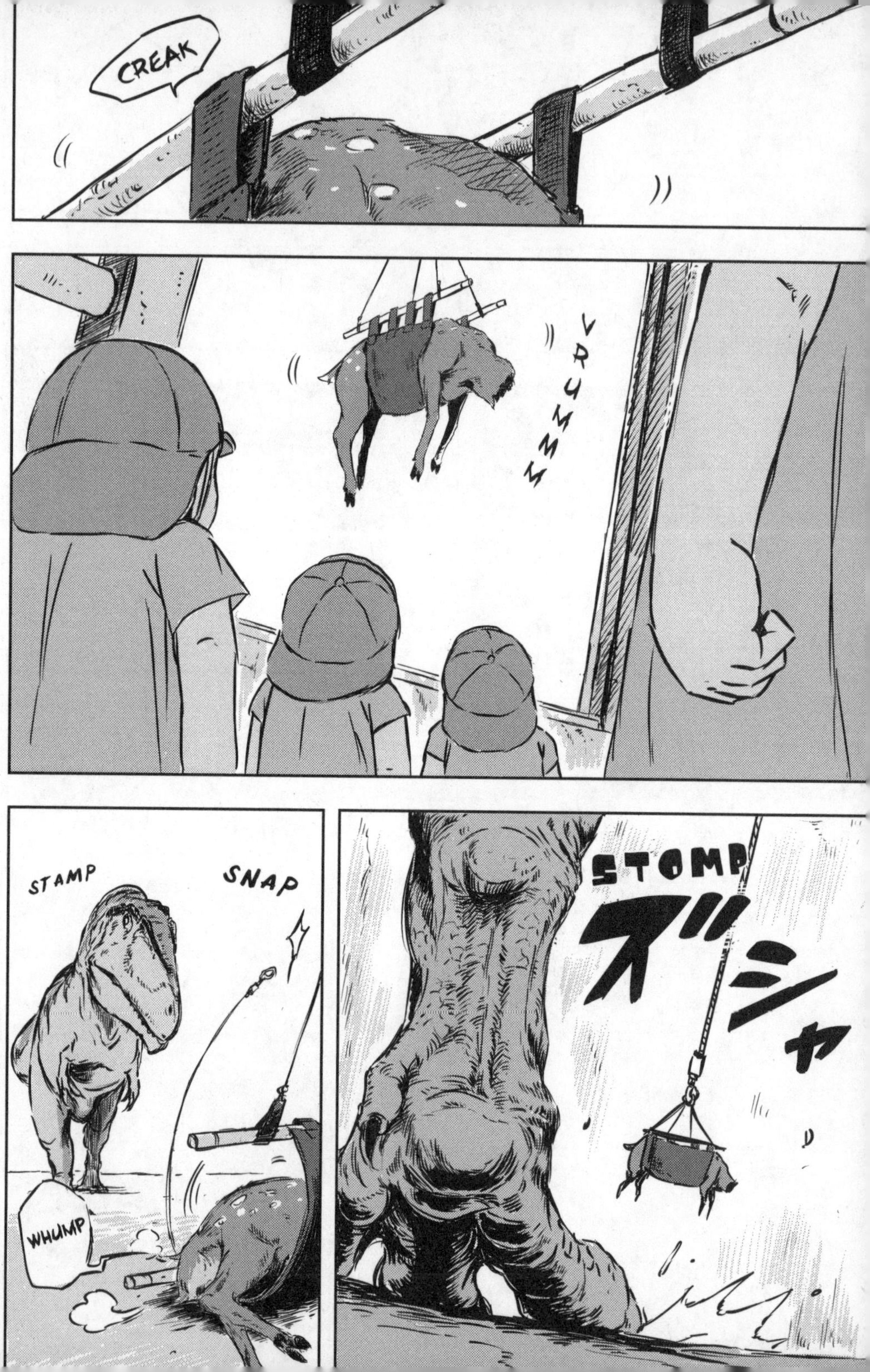
CREAK
VRUMMM
STOMP
ズシャ
SNAP
STAMP
WHUMP

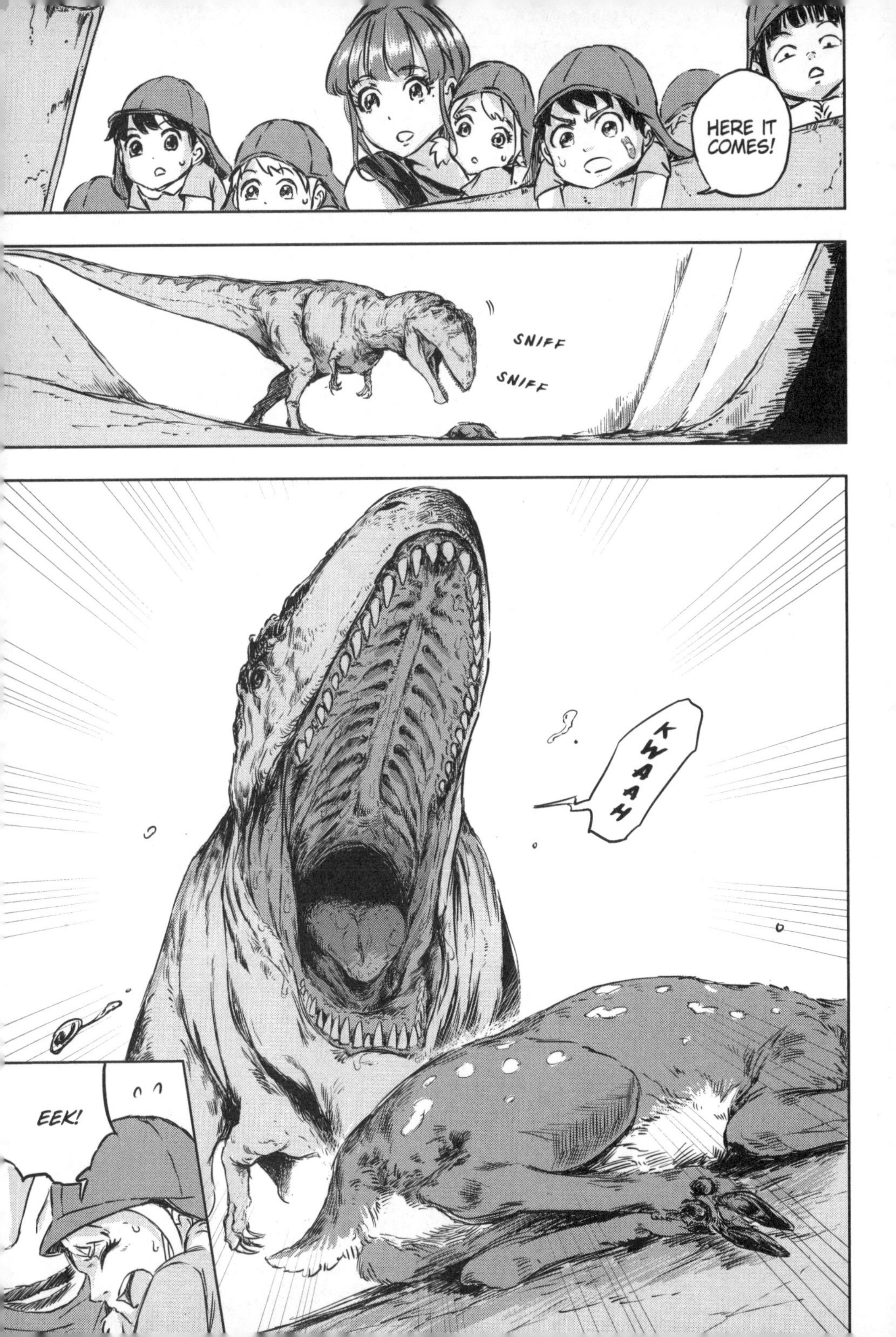
HERE IT COMES!
SNIFF
SNIFF
KWAAH
EEK!

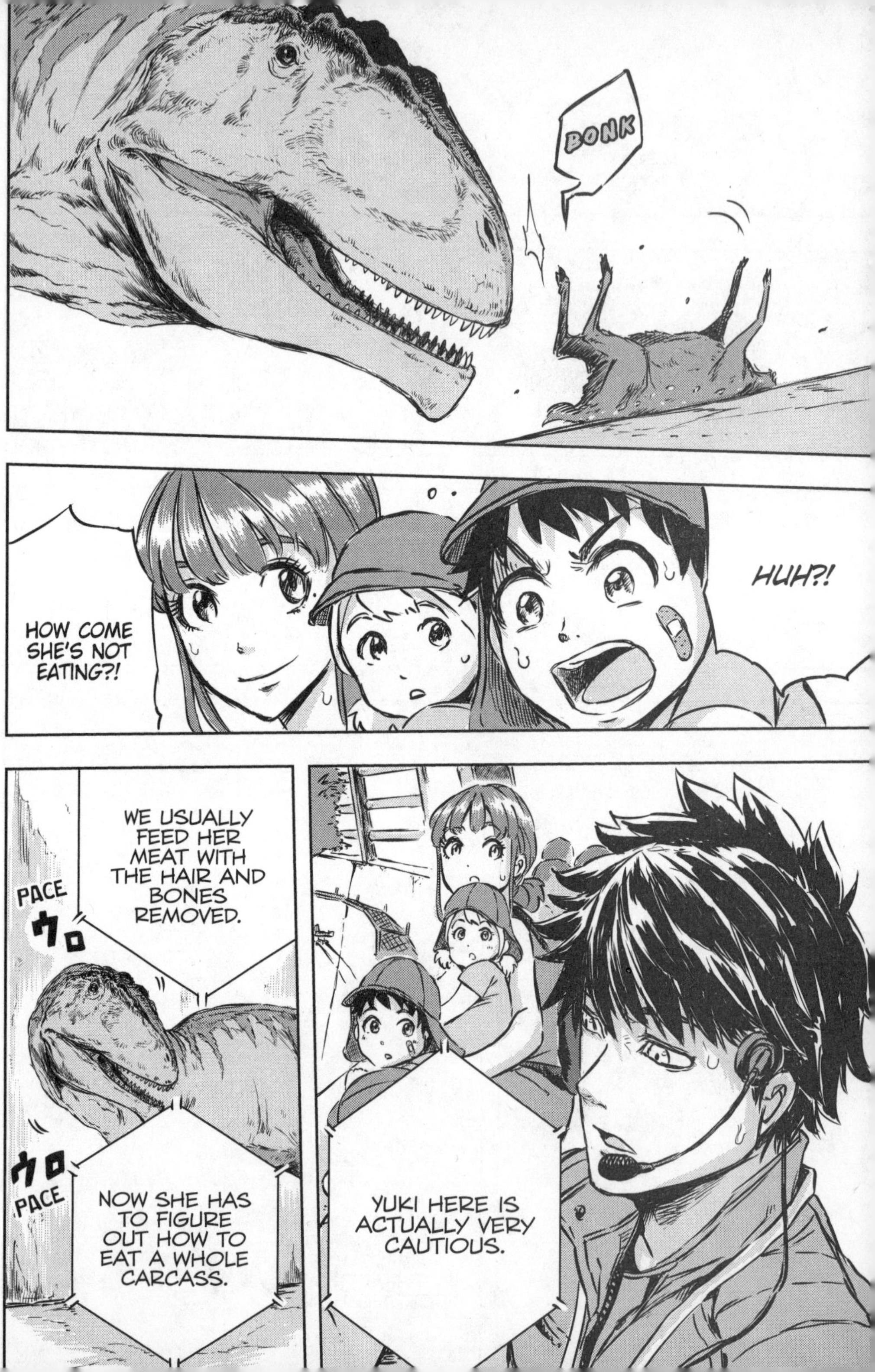
BONK
HUH?!
HOW COME SHE'S NOT EATING?!
YUKI HERE IS ACTUALLY VERY CAUTIOUS.
WE USUALLY FEED HER MEAT WITH THE HAIR AND BONES REMOVED.
PACE ウロ
ウロ PACE
NOW SHE HAS TO FIGURE OUT HOW TO EAT A WHOLE CARCASS.

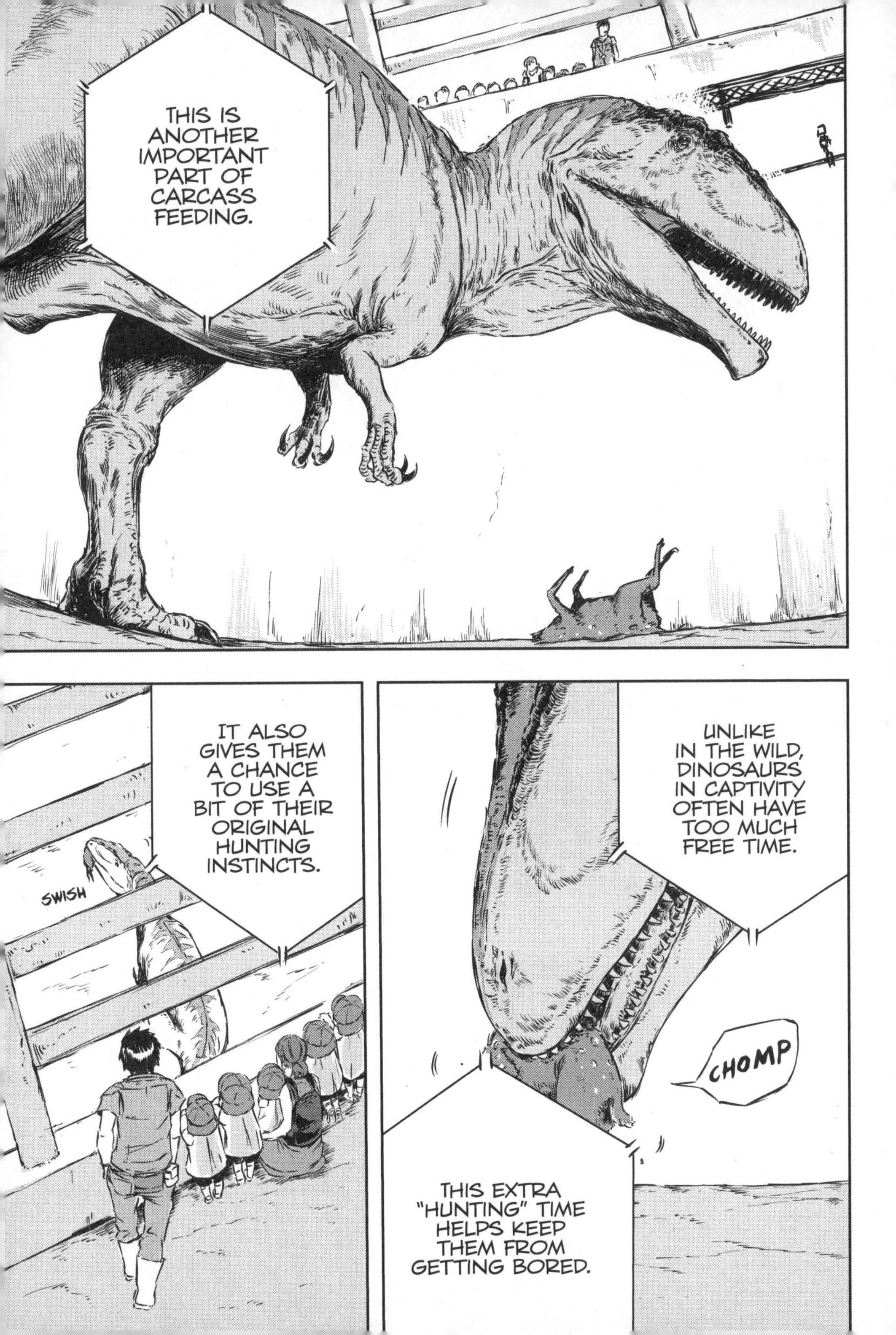
THIS IS ANOTHER IMPORTANT PART OF CARCASS FEEDING.
UNLIKE IN THE WILD, DINOSAURS IN CAPTIVITY OFTEN HAVE TOO MUCH FREE TIME.
CHOMP
THIS EXTRA "HUNTING" TIME HELPS KEEP THEM FROM GETTING BORED.
IT ALSO GIVES THEM A CHANCE TO USE A BIT OF THEIR ORIGINAL HUNTING INSTINCTS.
SWISH

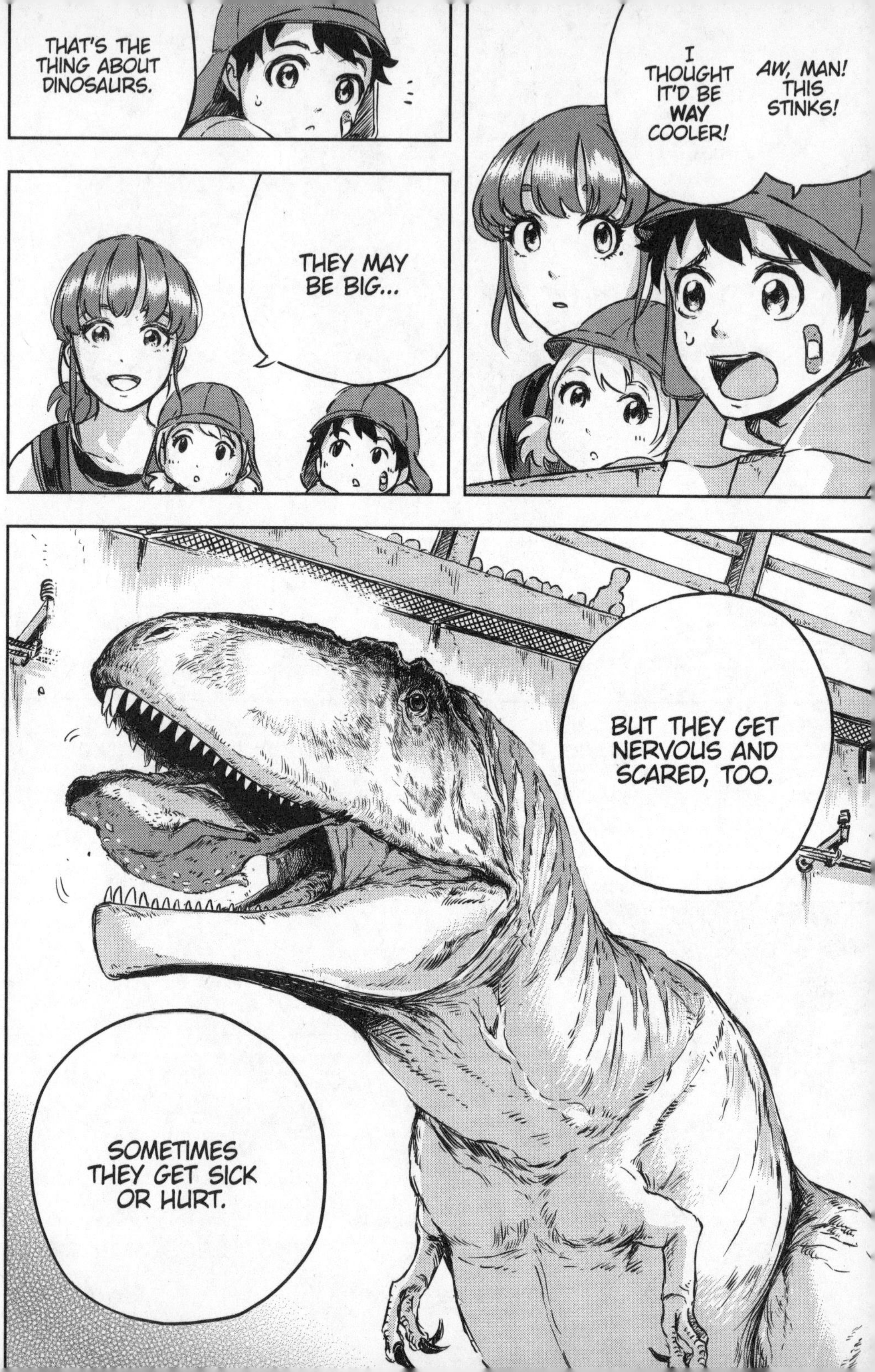
AW, MAN! THIS STINKS!
I THOUGHT IT'D BE WAY COOLER!
THAT'S THE THING ABOUT DINOSAURS.
THEY MAY BE BIG...
BUT THEY GET NERVOUS AND SCARED, TOO.
SOMETIMES THEY GET SICK OR HURT.

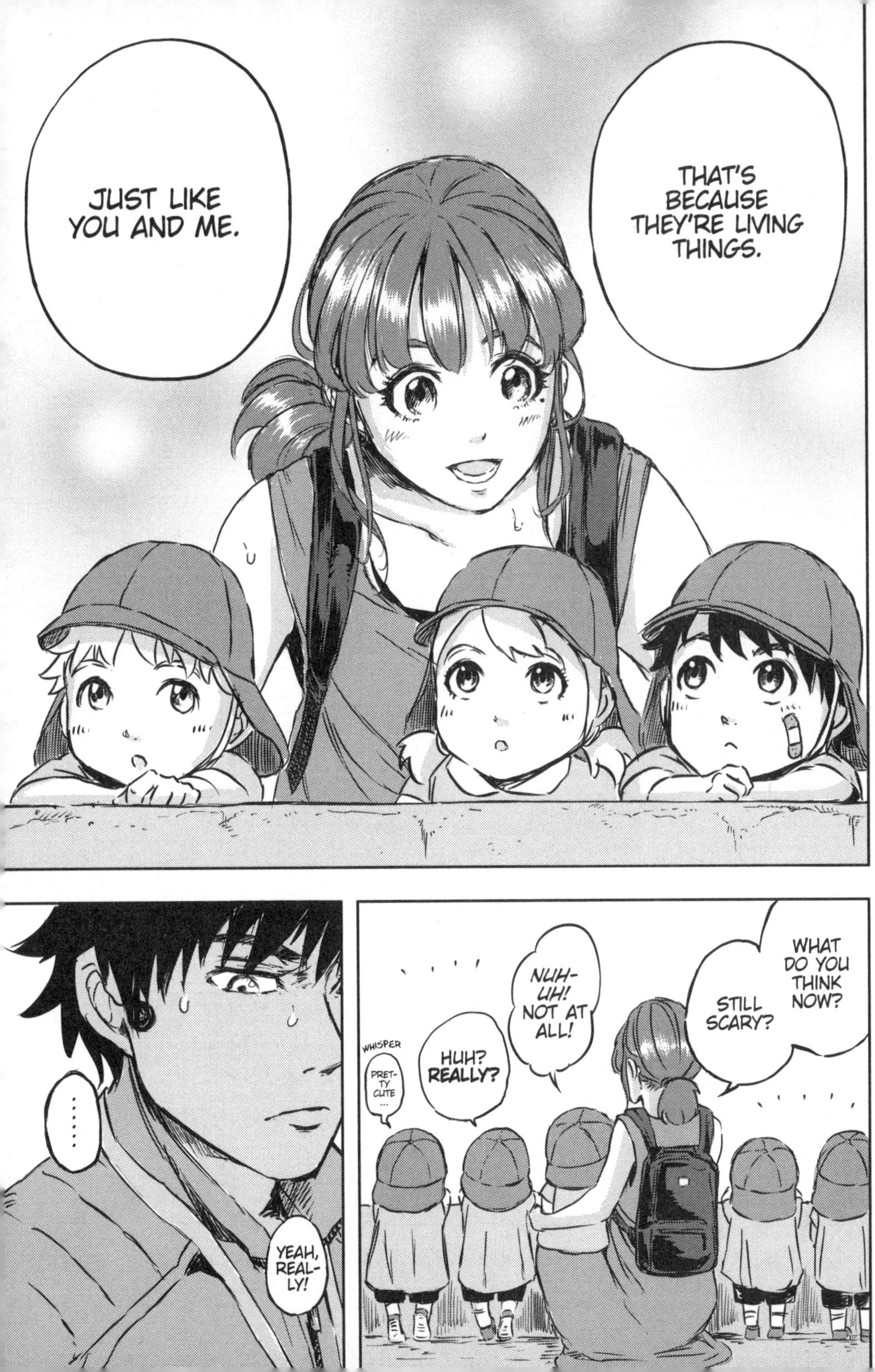
THAT'S BECAUSE THEY'RE LIVING THINGS.
JUST LIKE YOU AND ME.
WHAT DO YOU THINK NOW?
STILL SCARY?
NUH-UH! NOT AT ALL!
HUH? **REALLY?**
WHISPER
PRETTY CUTE...
......
YEAH, REALLY!

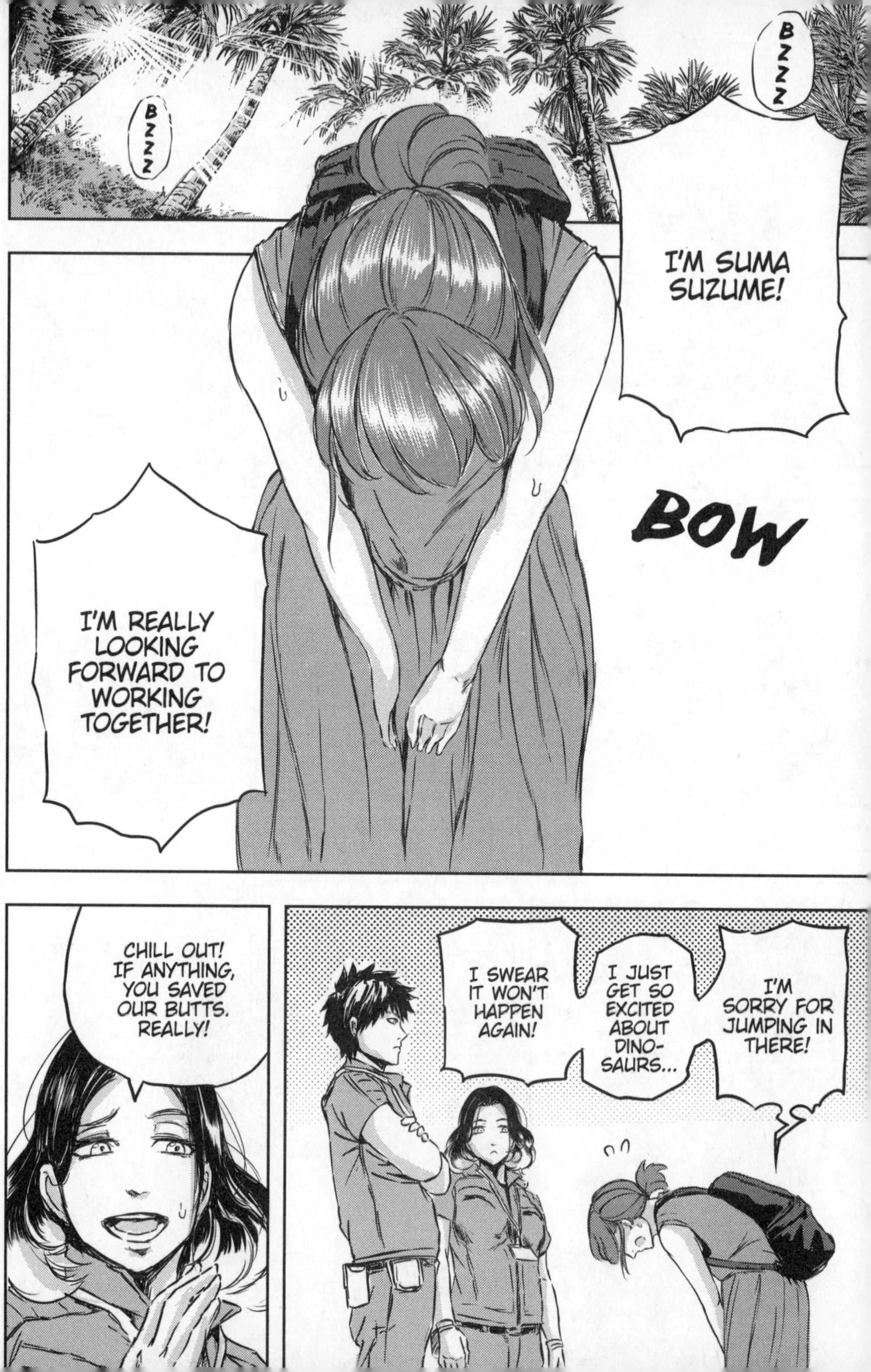
BZZZ
BZZZ
I'M SUMA SUZUME!
BOW
I'M REALLY LOOKING FORWARD TO WORKING TOGETHER!
I'M SORRY FOR JUMPING IN THERE!
I JUST GET SO EXCITED ABOUT DINO-SAURS...
I SWEAR IT WON'T HAPPEN AGAIN!
CHILL OUT! IF ANYTHING, YOU SAVED OUR BUTTS. REALLY!

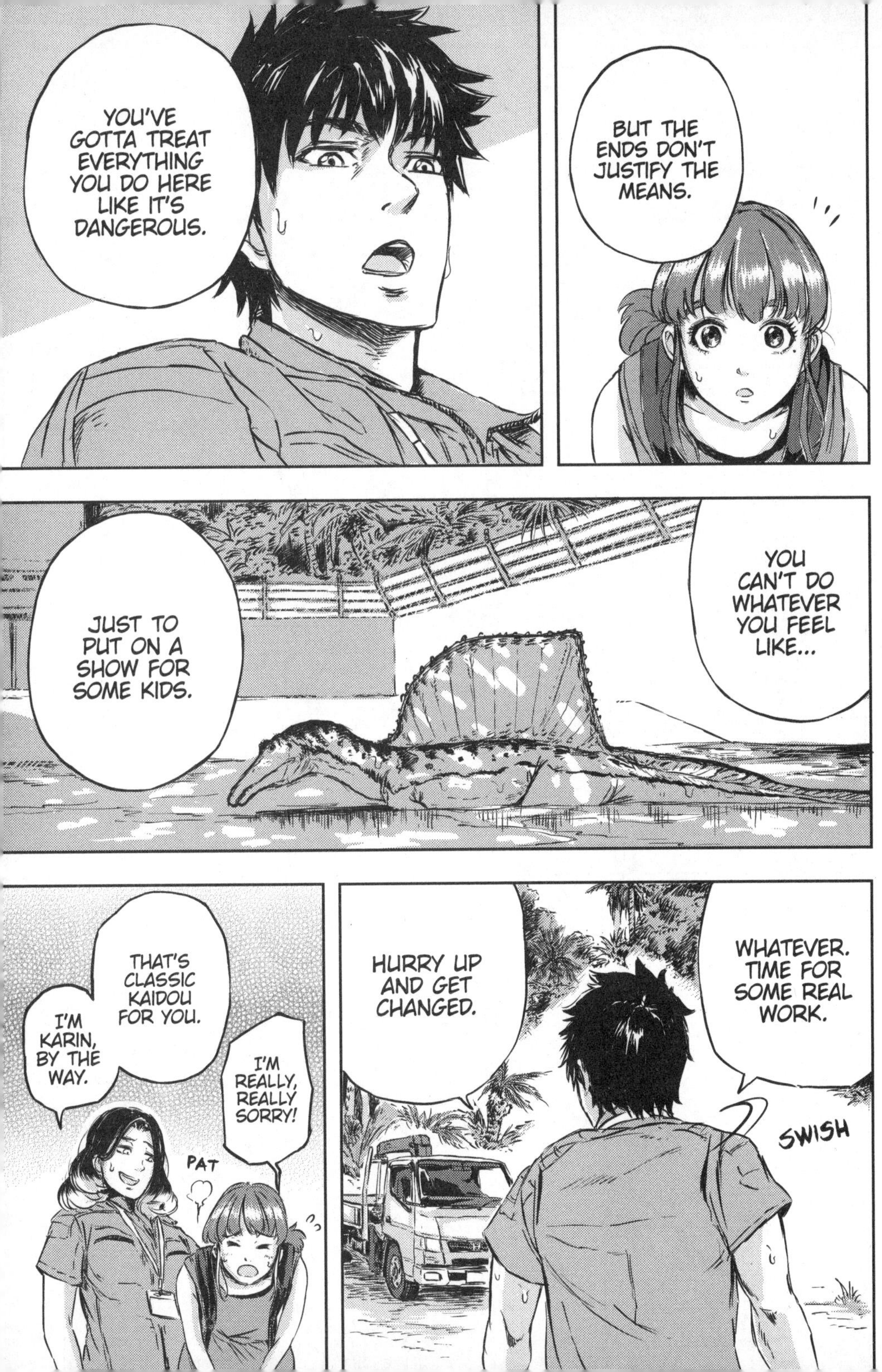
BUT THE ENDS DON'T JUSTIFY THE MEANS.
YOU'VE GOTTA TREAT EVERYTHING YOU DO HERE LIKE IT'S DANGEROUS.
YOU CAN'T DO WHATEVER YOU FEEL LIKE...
JUST TO PUT ON A SHOW FOR SOME KIDS.
WHATEVER. TIME FOR SOME REAL WORK.
HURRY UP AND GET CHANGED.
SWISH
THAT'S CLASSIC KAIDOU FOR YOU.
I'M REALLY, REALLY SORRY!
I'M KARIN, BY THE WAY.
PAT

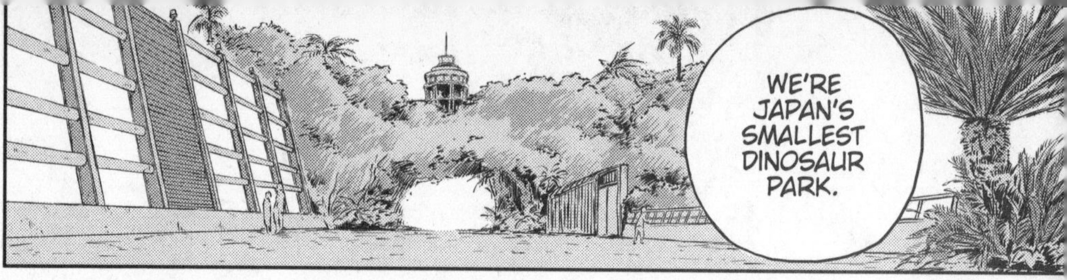
WE'RE JAPAN'S SMALLEST DINOSAUR PARK.

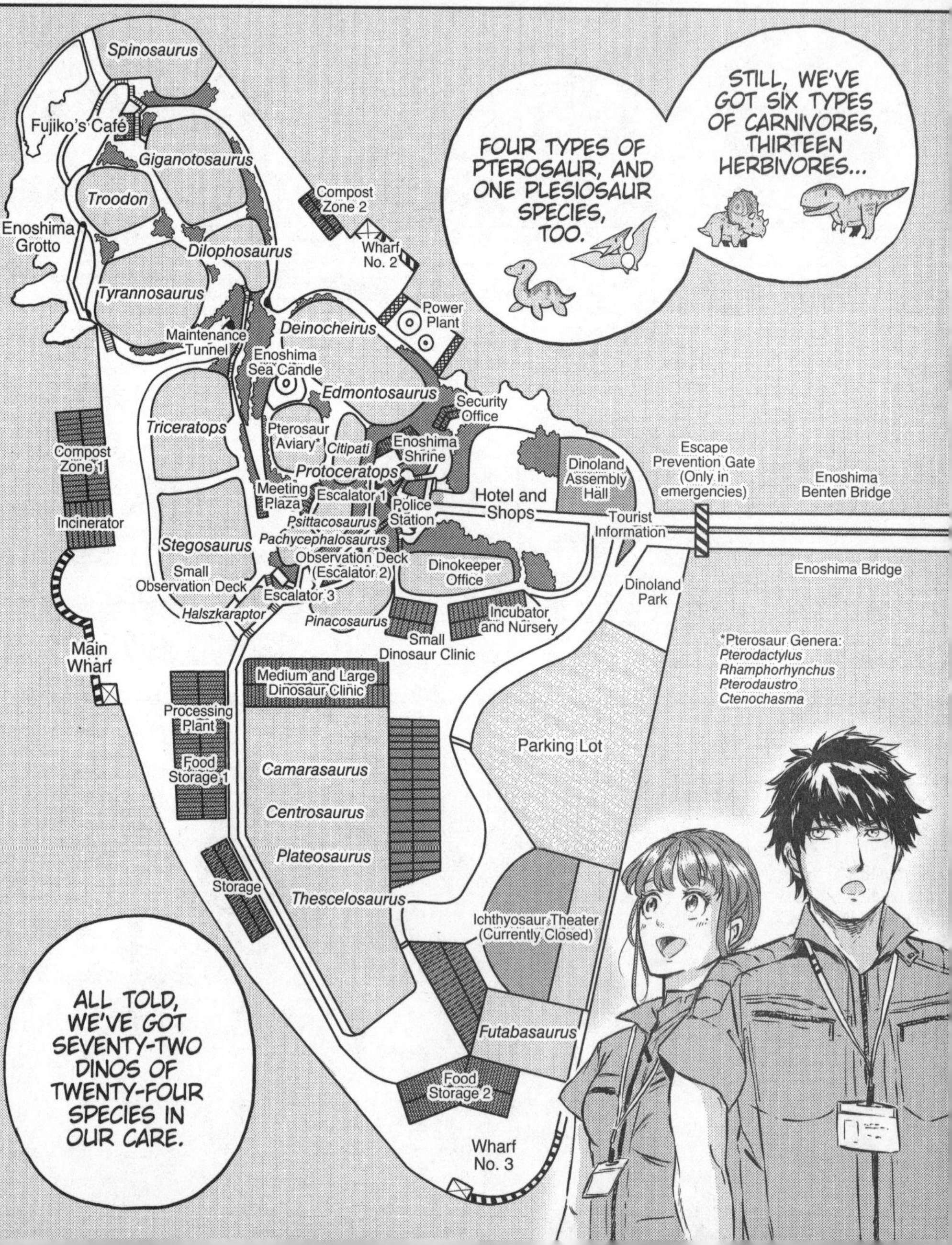
STILL, WE'VE GOT SIX TYPES OF CARNIVORES, THIRTEEN HERBIVORES...
FOUR TYPES OF PTEROSAUR, AND ONE PLESIOSAUR SPECIES, TOO.
Spinosaurus
Fujiko's Café
Giganotosaurus
Troodon
Enoshima Grotto
Dilophosaurus
Tyrannosaurus
Compost Zone 2
Wharf No. 2
Power Plant
Maintenance Tunnel
Deinocheirus
Enoshima Sea Candle
Edmontosaurus
Security Office
Triceratops
Pterosaur Aviary*
Citipati
Enoshima Shrine
Compost Zone 1
Protoceratops
Meeting Plaza
Escalator 1
Police Station
Hotel and Shops
Dinoland Assembly Hall
Escape Prevention Gate (Only in emergencies)
Enoshima Benten Bridge
Incinerator
Psittacosaurus
Pachycephalosaurus
Tourist Information
Stegosaurus
Observation Deck (Escalator 2)
Dinokeeper Office
Enoshima Bridge
Small Observation Deck
Escalator 3
Dinoland Park
Halszkaraptor
Pinacosaurus
Incubator and Nursery
Small Dinosaur Clinic
*Pterosaur Genera:
Pterodactylus
Rhamphorhynchus
Pterodaustro
Ctenochasma
Main Wharf
Medium and Large Dinosaur Clinic
Processing Plant
Parking Lot
Food Storage 1
Camarasaurus
Centrosaurus
Plateosaurus
Storage
Thescelosaurus
Ichthyosaur Theater (Currently Closed)
Futabasaurus
Food Storage 2
Wharf No. 3
ALL TOLD, WE'VE GOT SEVENTY-TWO DINOS OF TWENTY-FOUR SPECIES IN OUR CARE.

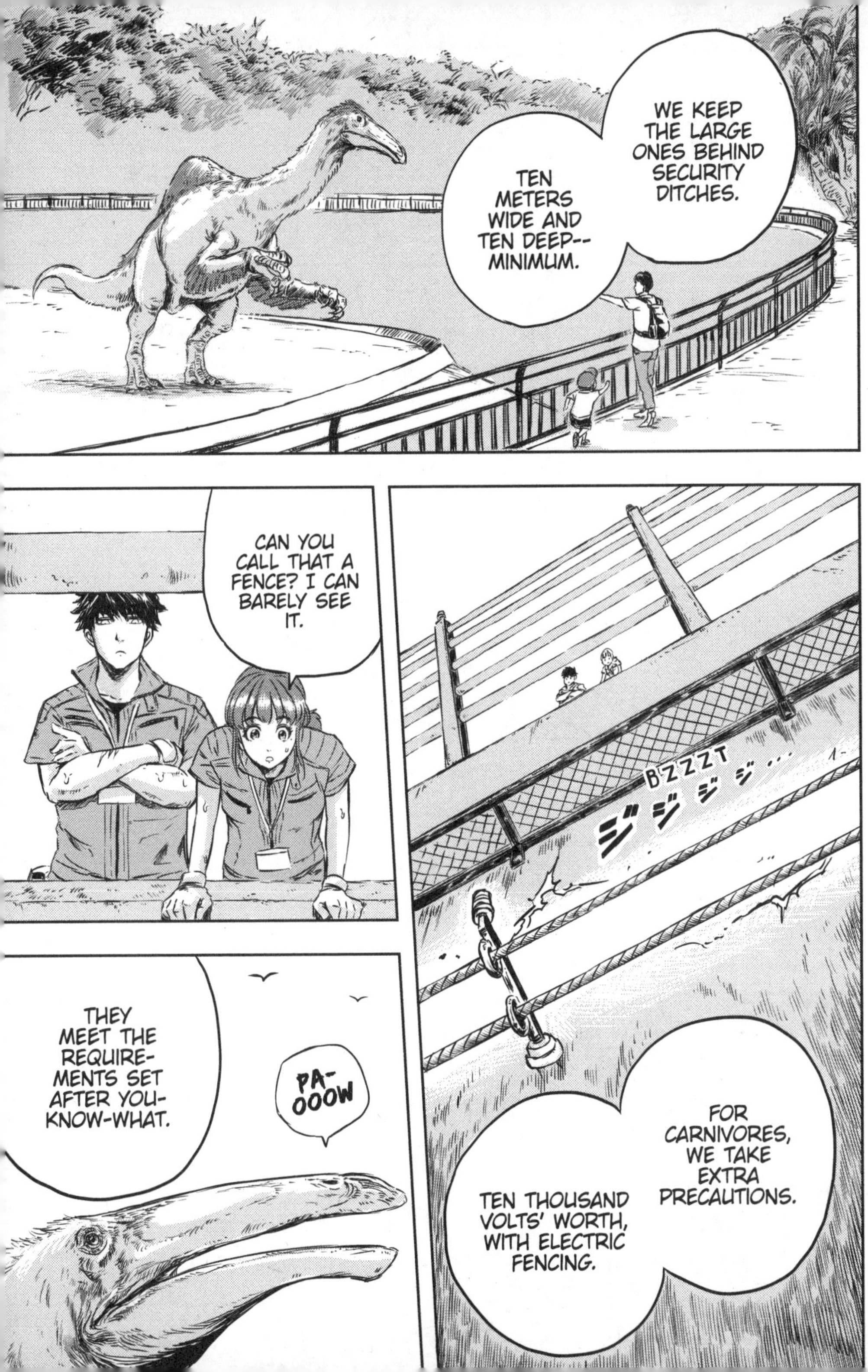
WE KEEP THE LARGE ONES BEHIND SECURITY DITCHES.
TEN METERS WIDE AND TEN DEEP--MINIMUM.
BZZZT
ジジジジ…
FOR CARNIVORES, WE TAKE EXTRA PRECAUTIONS.
TEN THOUSAND VOLTS' WORTH, WITH ELECTRIC FENCING.
CAN YOU CALL THAT A FENCE? I CAN BARELY SEE IT.
THEY MEET THE REQUIRE-MENTS SET AFTER YOU-KNOW-WHAT.
PA-OOOW

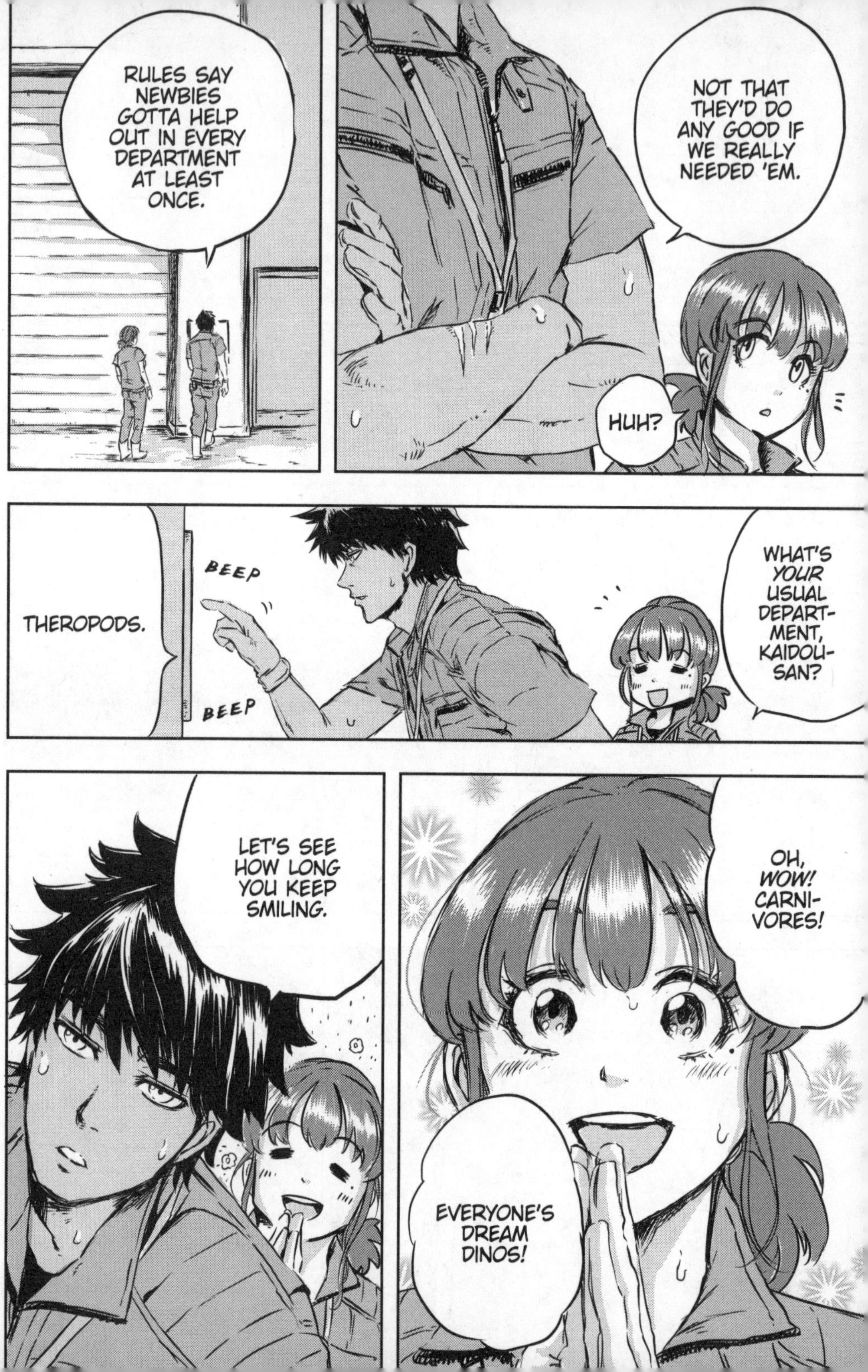
NOT THAT THEY'D DO ANY GOOD IF WE REALLY NEEDED 'EM.
HUH?
RULES SAY NEWBIES GOTTA HELP OUT IN EVERY DEPARTMENT AT LEAST ONCE.
WHAT'S YOUR USUAL DEPARTMENT, KAIDOU-SAN?
BEEP
BEEP
THEROPODS.
OH, WOW! CARNIVORES!
EVERYONE'S DREAM DINOS!
LET'S SEE HOW LONG YOU KEEP SMILING.

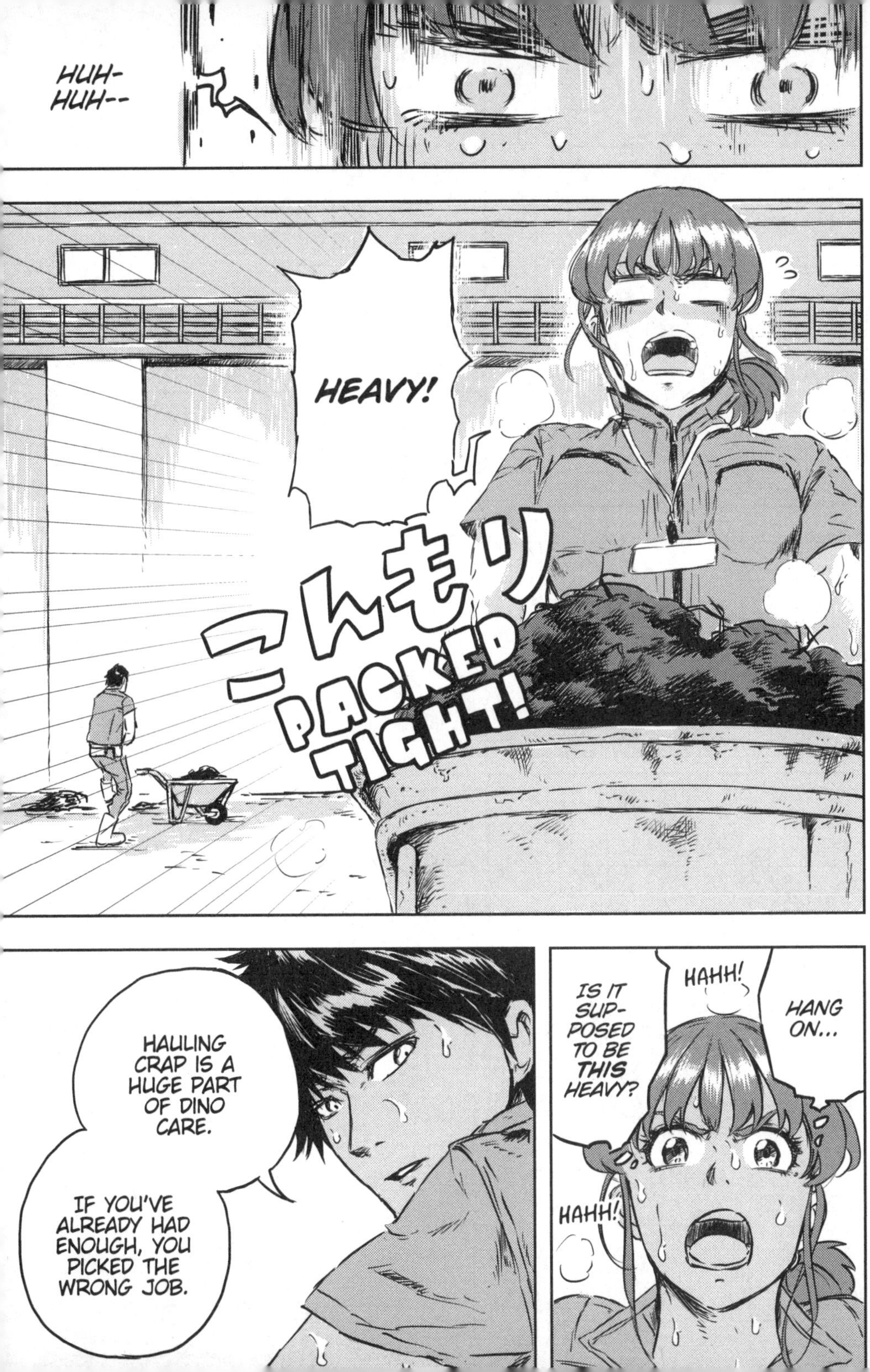
HUH-HUH--
HEAVY!
こんもり
PACKED TIGHT!
HANG ON...
HAHH!
IS IT SUP-POSED TO BE THIS HEAVY?
HAHH!
HAULING CRAP IS A HUGE PART OF DINO CARE.
IF YOU'VE ALREADY HAD ENOUGH, YOU PICKED THE WRONG JOB.

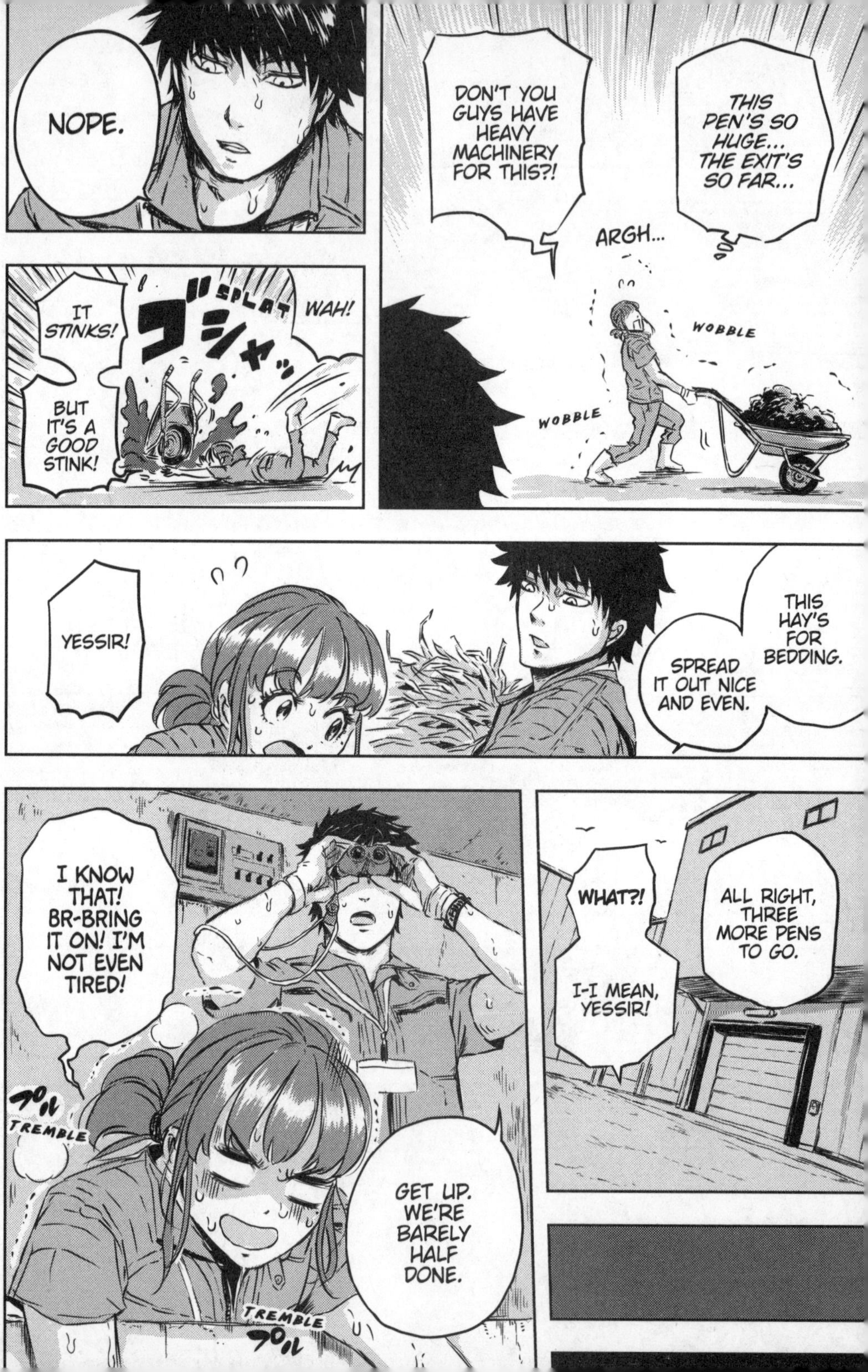
THIS PEN'S SO HUGE... THE EXIT'S SO FAR...
DON'T YOU GUYS HAVE HEAVY MACHINERY FOR THIS?!
ARGH...
WOBBLE
WOBBLE
NOPE.
WAH!
SPLAT
IT STINKS!
BUT IT'S A GOOD STINK!
THIS HAY'S FOR BEDDING.
SPREAD IT OUT NICE AND EVEN.
YESSIR!
ALL RIGHT, THREE MORE PENS TO GO.
WHAT?!
I-I MEAN, YESSIR!
GET UP. WE'RE BARELY HALF DONE.
I KNOW THAT! BR-BRING IT ON! I'M NOT EVEN TIRED!
TREMBLE
TREMBLE

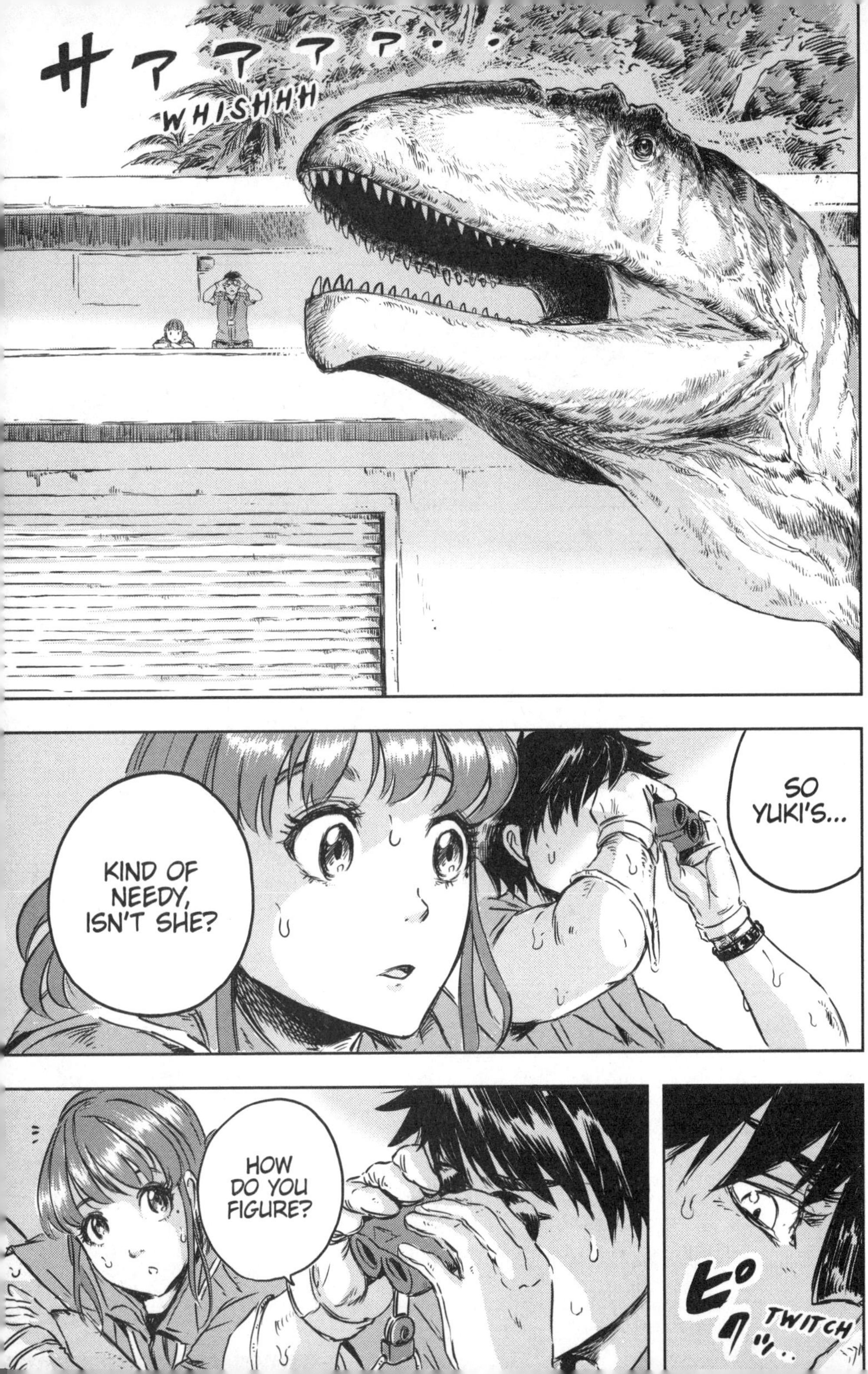
サァァァァ‥
WHISHHH
SO YUKI'S...
KIND OF NEEDY, ISN'T SHE?
ピクッ‥
TWITCH
HOW DO YOU FIGURE?

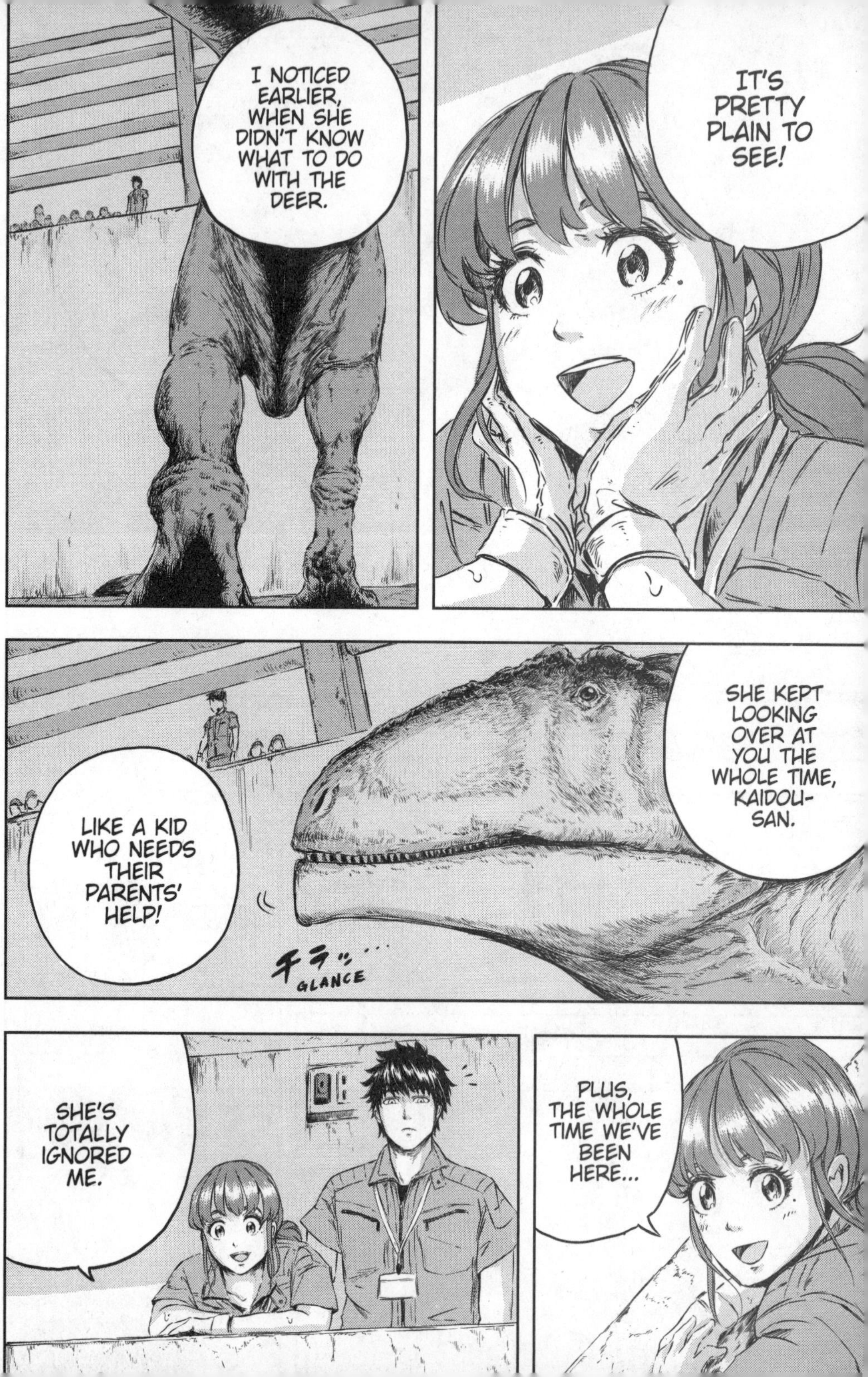
IT'S PRETTY PLAIN TO SEE!
I NOTICED EARLIER, WHEN SHE DIDN'T KNOW WHAT TO DO WITH THE DEER.
SHE KEPT LOOKING OVER AT YOU THE WHOLE TIME, KAIDOU-SAN.
LIKE A KID WHO NEEDS THEIR PARENTS' HELP!
チラッ…
GLANCE
PLUS, THE WHOLE TIME WE'VE BEEN HERE...
SHE'S TOTALLY IGNORED ME.

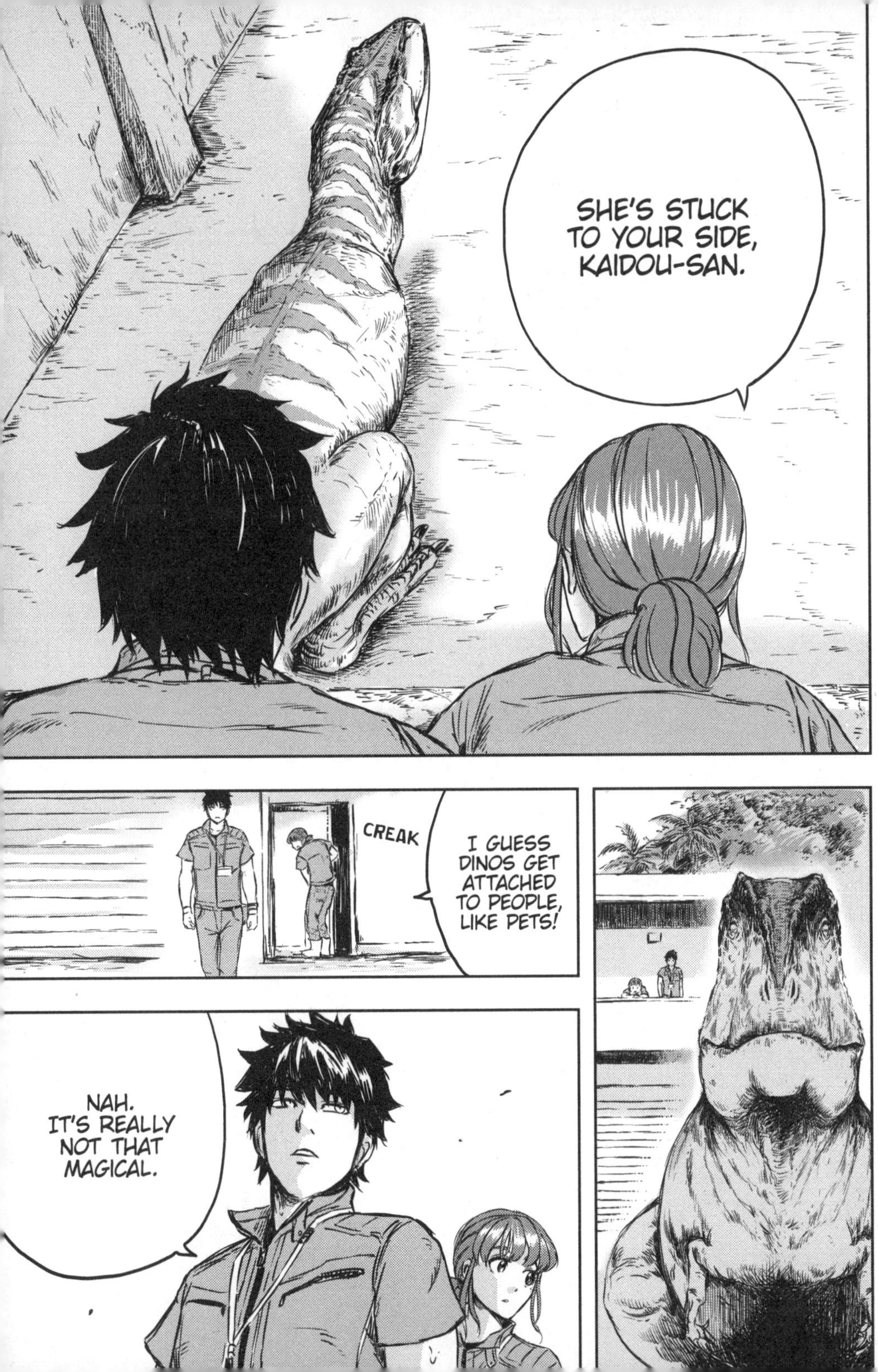
SHE'S STUCK TO YOUR SIDE, KAIDOU-SAN.
I GUESS DINOS GET ATTACHED TO PEOPLE, LIKE PETS!
CREAK
NAH. IT'S REALLY NOT THAT MAGICAL.

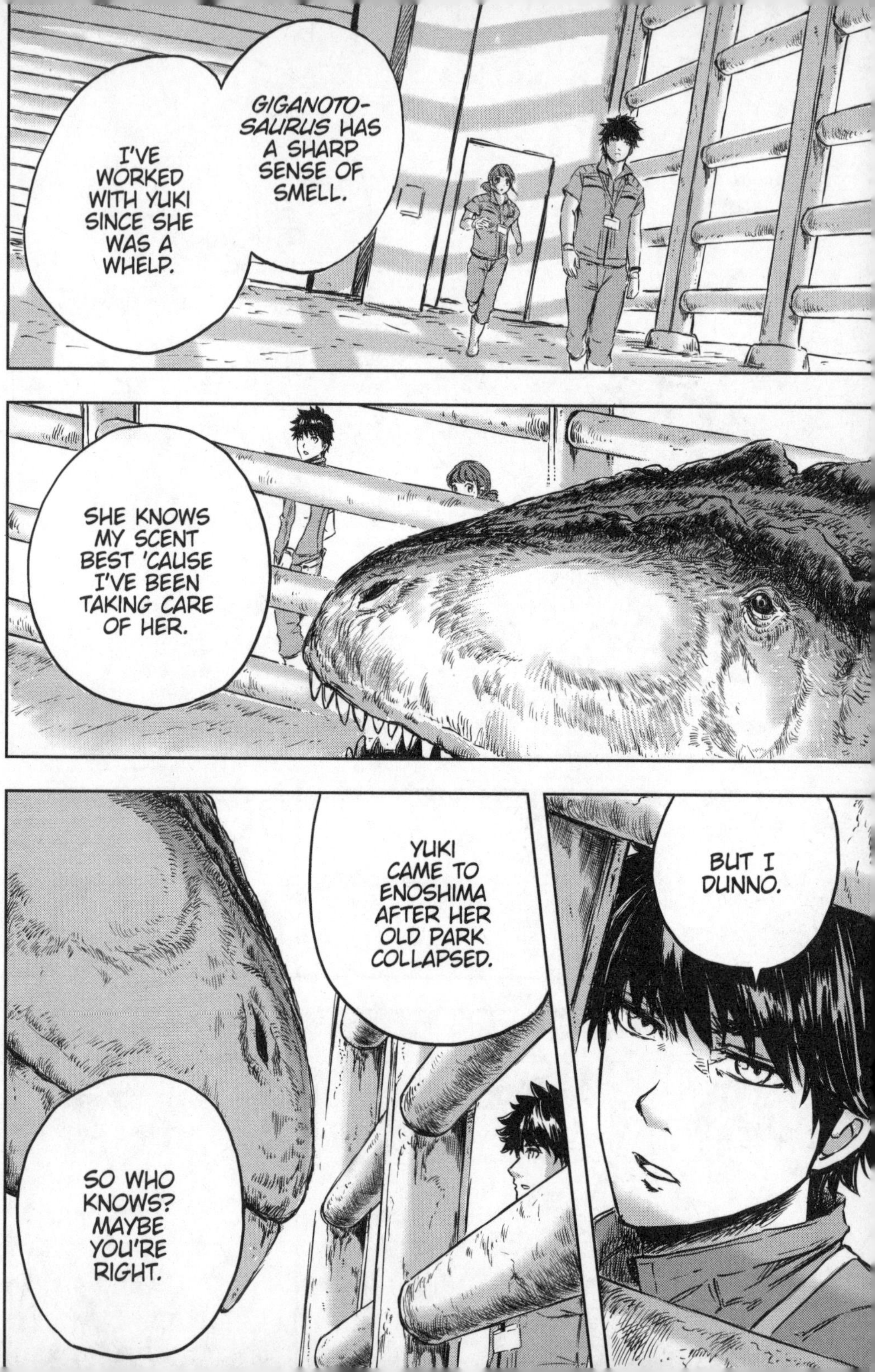
GIGANOTO-SAURUS HAS A SHARP SENSE OF SMELL.
I'VE WORKED WITH YUKI SINCE SHE WAS A WHELP.
SHE KNOWS MY SCENT BEST 'CAUSE I'VE BEEN TAKING CARE OF HER.
BUT I DUNNO.
YUKI CAME TO ENOSHIMA AFTER HER OLD PARK COLLAPSED.
SO WHO KNOWS? MAYBE YOU'RE RIGHT.

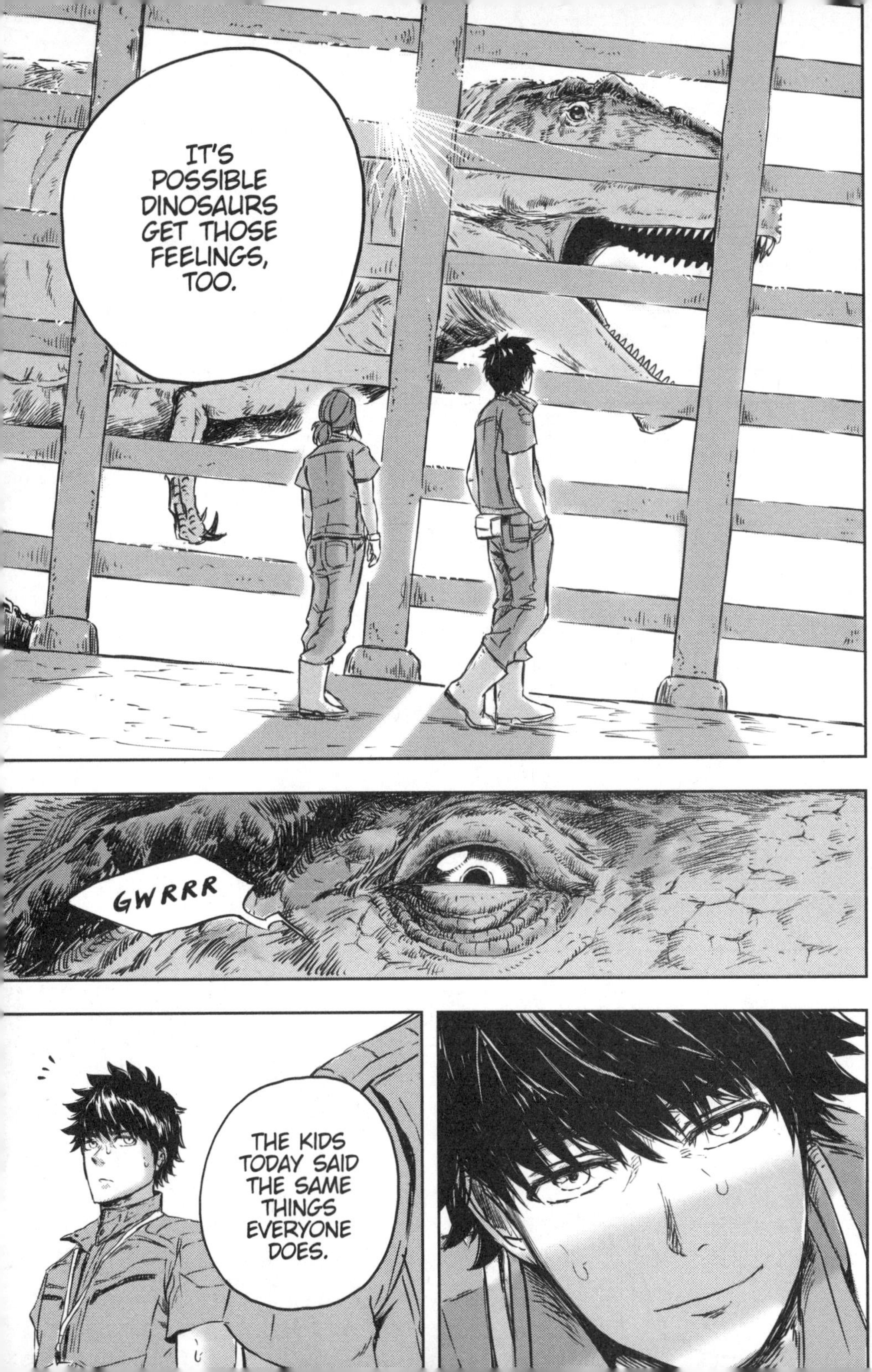
IT'S POSSIBLE DINOSAURS GET THOSE FEELINGS, TOO.
GWRRR
THE KIDS TODAY SAID THE SAME THINGS EVERYONE DOES.

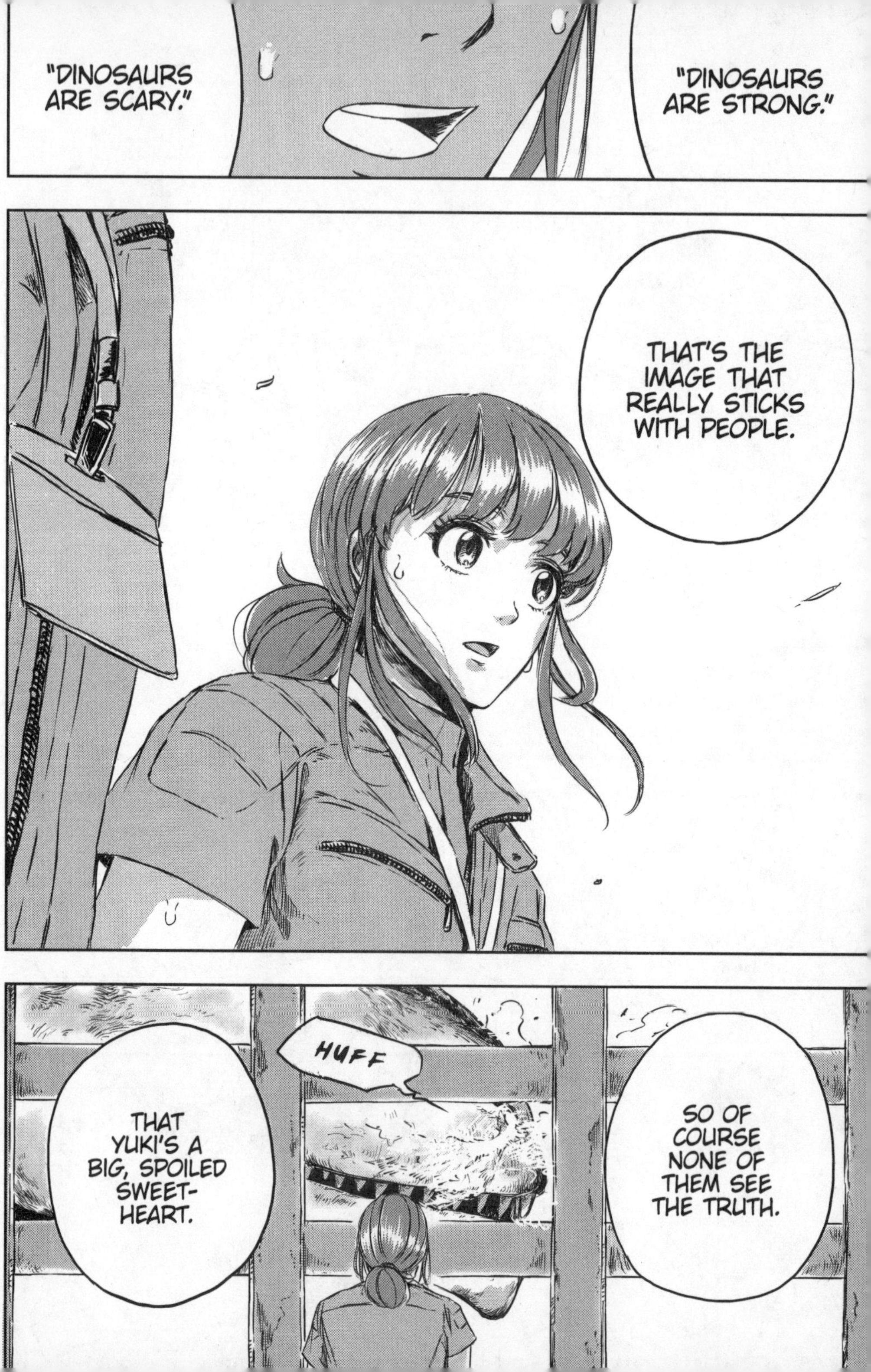
"DINOSAURS ARE STRONG."
"DINOSAURS ARE SCARY."
THAT'S THE IMAGE THAT REALLY STICKS WITH PEOPLE.
SO OF COURSE NONE OF THEM SEE THE TRUTH.
HUFF
THAT YUKI'S A BIG, SPOILED SWEET-HEART.

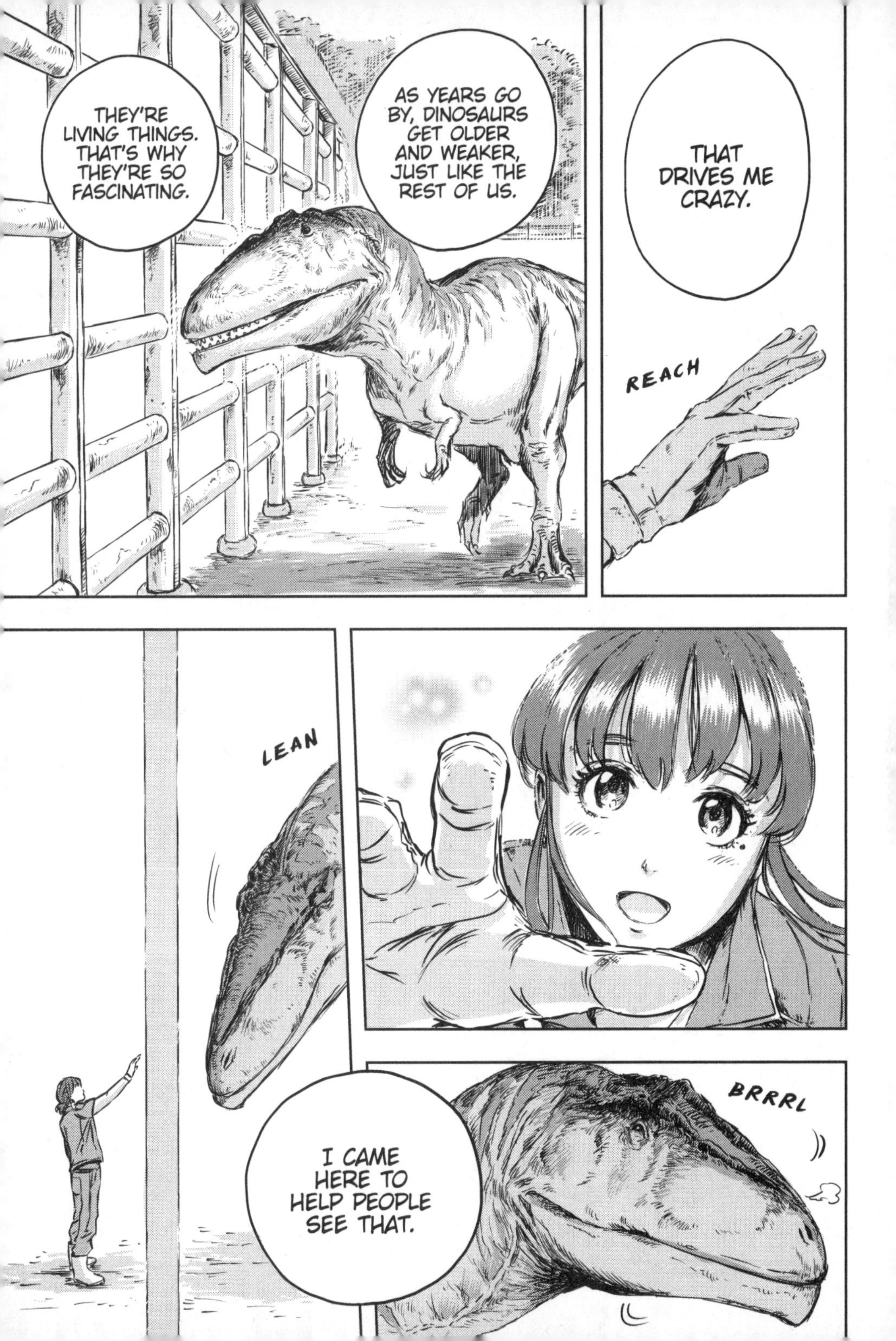
THAT DRIVES ME CRAZY.
REACH
AS YEARS GO BY, DINOSAURS GET OLDER AND WEAKER, JUST LIKE THE REST OF US.
THEY'RE LIVING THINGS. THAT'S WHY THEY'RE SO FASCINATING.
BRRRL
I CAME HERE TO HELP PEOPLE SEE THAT.
LEAN

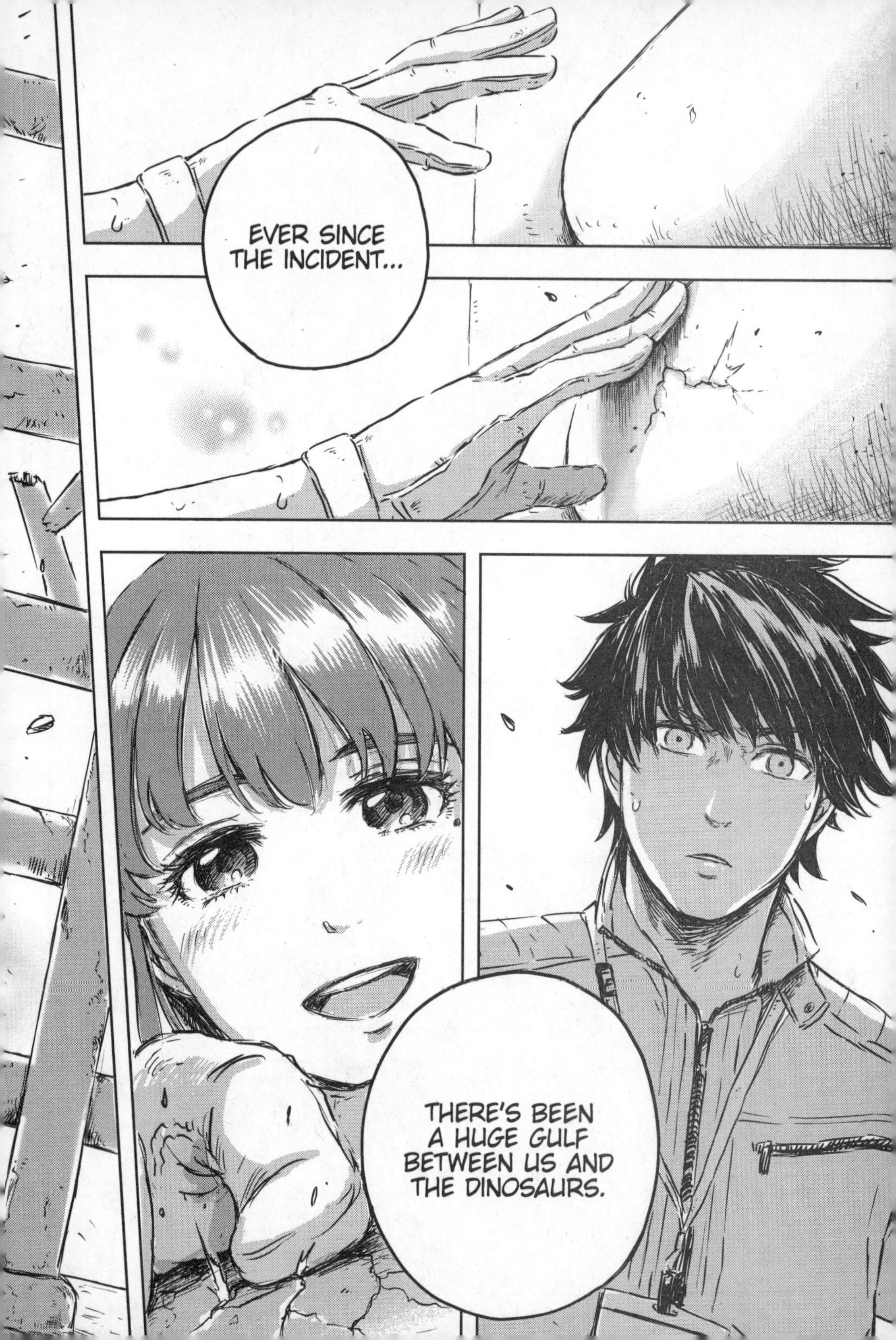
EVER SINCE THE INCIDENT...
THERE'S BEEN A HUGE GULF BETWEEN US AND THE DINOSAURS.

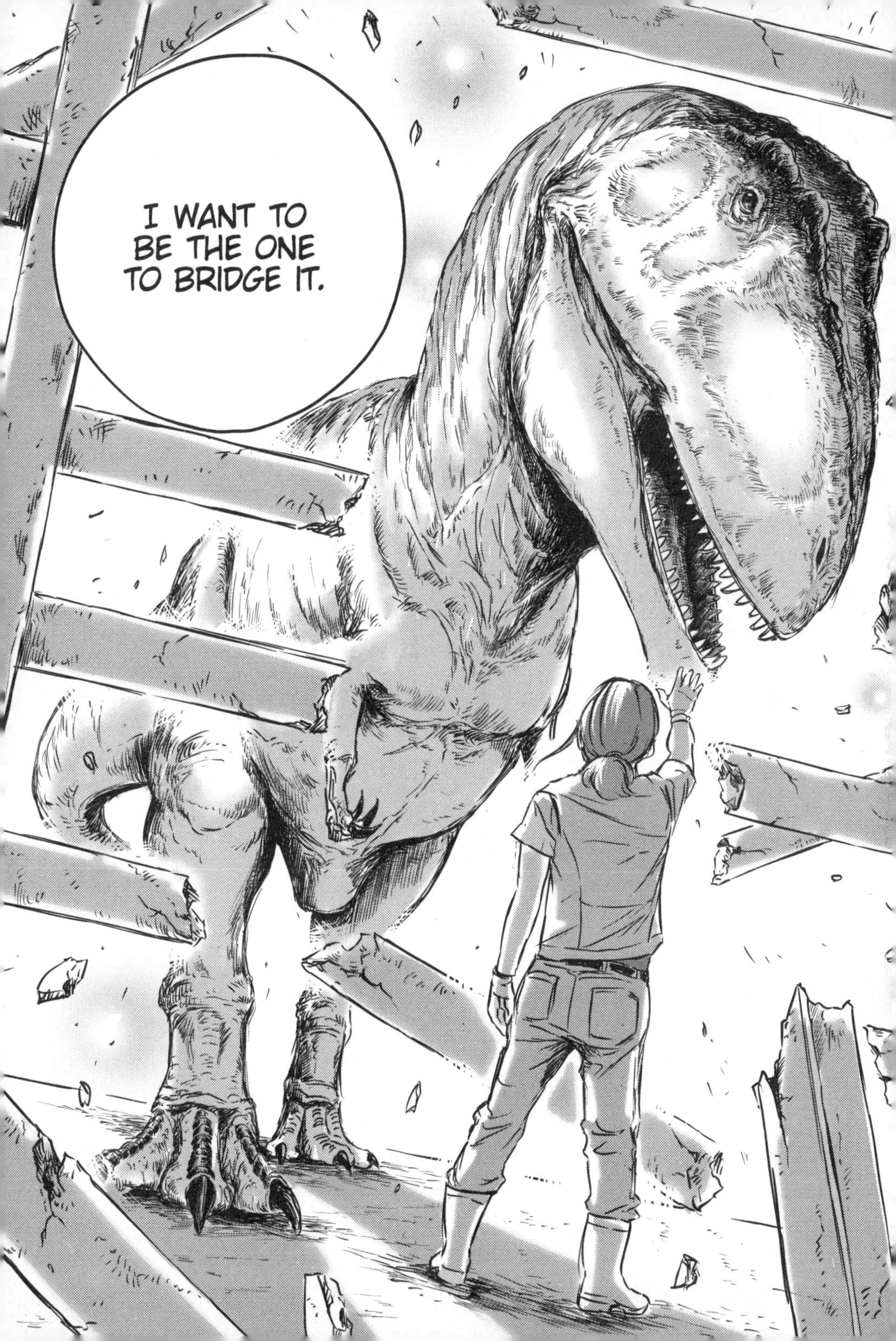
I WANT TO BE THE ONE TO BRIDGE IT.

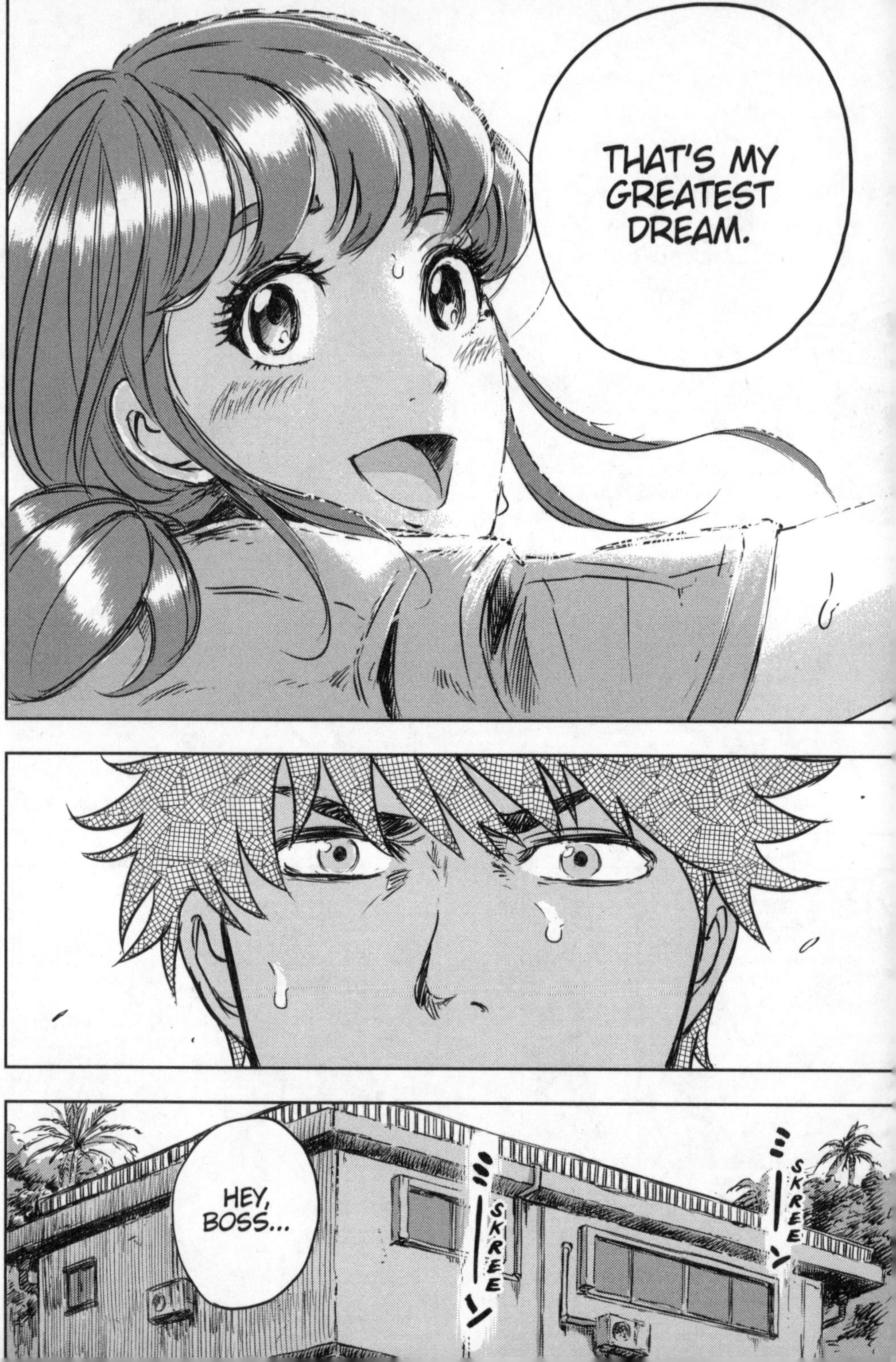
THAT'S MY GREATEST DREAM.
SKREE
SKREE
HEY, BOSS...

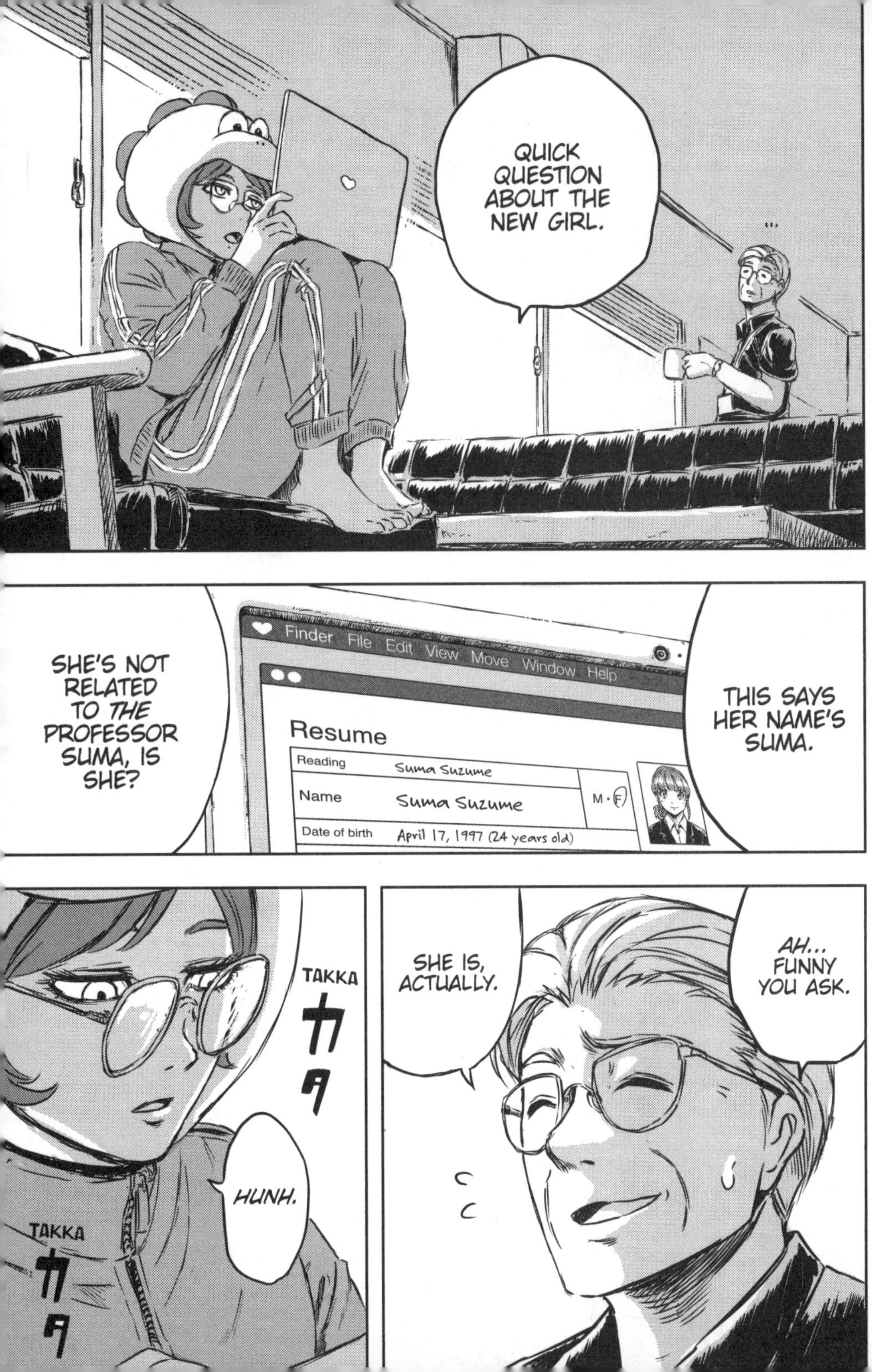
QUICK QUESTION ABOUT THE NEW GIRL.
...
THIS SAYS HER NAME'S SUMA.
Finder File Edit View Move Window Help
Resume
Reading Suma Suzume
Name Suma Suzume
M・F
Date of birth April 17, 1997 (24 years old)
SHE'S NOT RELATED TO *THE* PROFESSOR SUMA, IS SHE?
AH... FUNNY YOU ASK.
SHE IS, ACTUALLY.
TAKKA カタ
HUNH.
TAKKA カタ

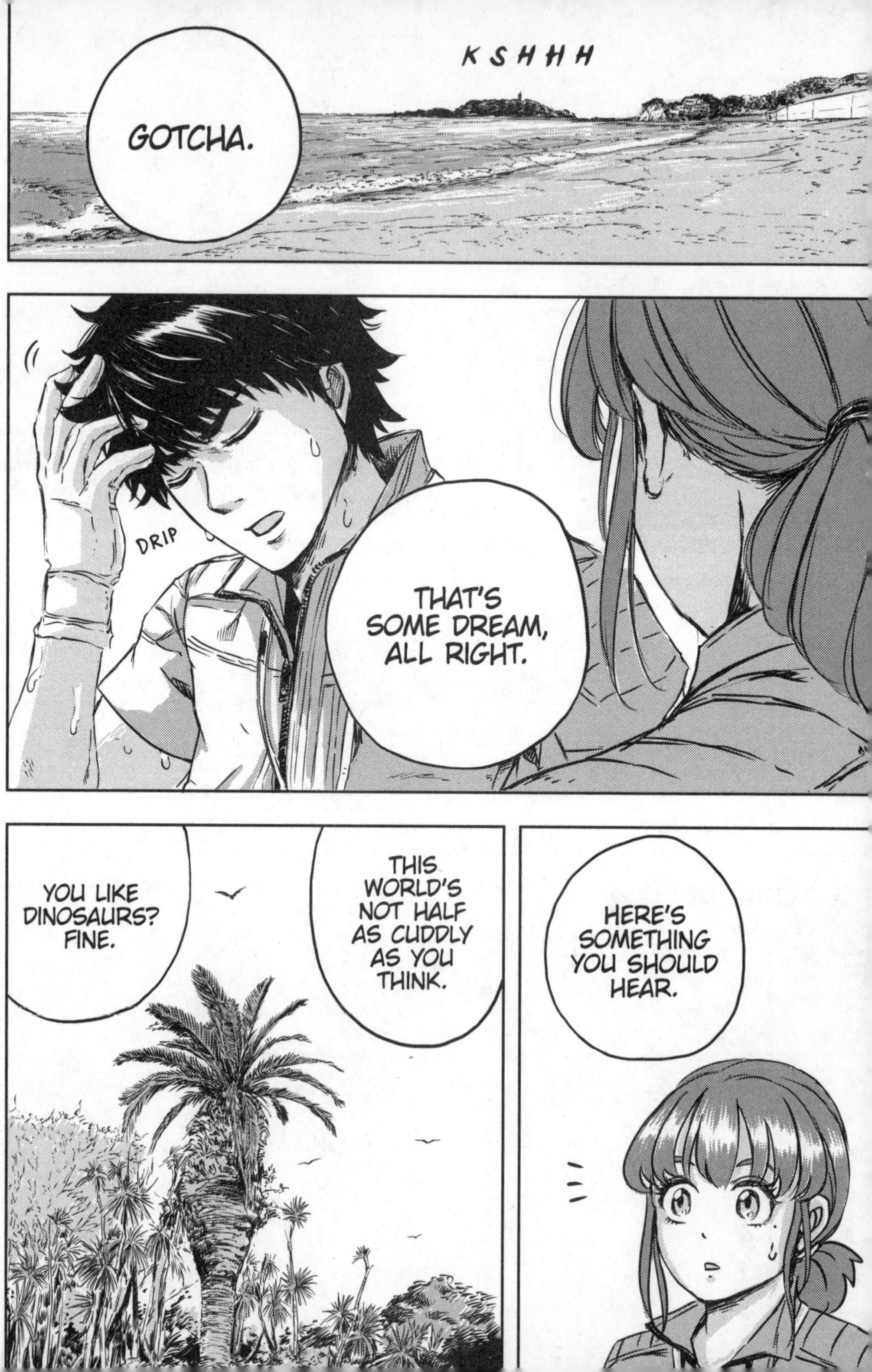
KSHHH
GOTCHA.
THAT'S SOME DREAM, ALL RIGHT.
DRIP
HERE'S SOMETHING YOU SHOULD HEAR.
THIS WORLD'S NOT HALF AS CUDDLY AS YOU THINK.
YOU LIKE DINOSAURS? FINE.

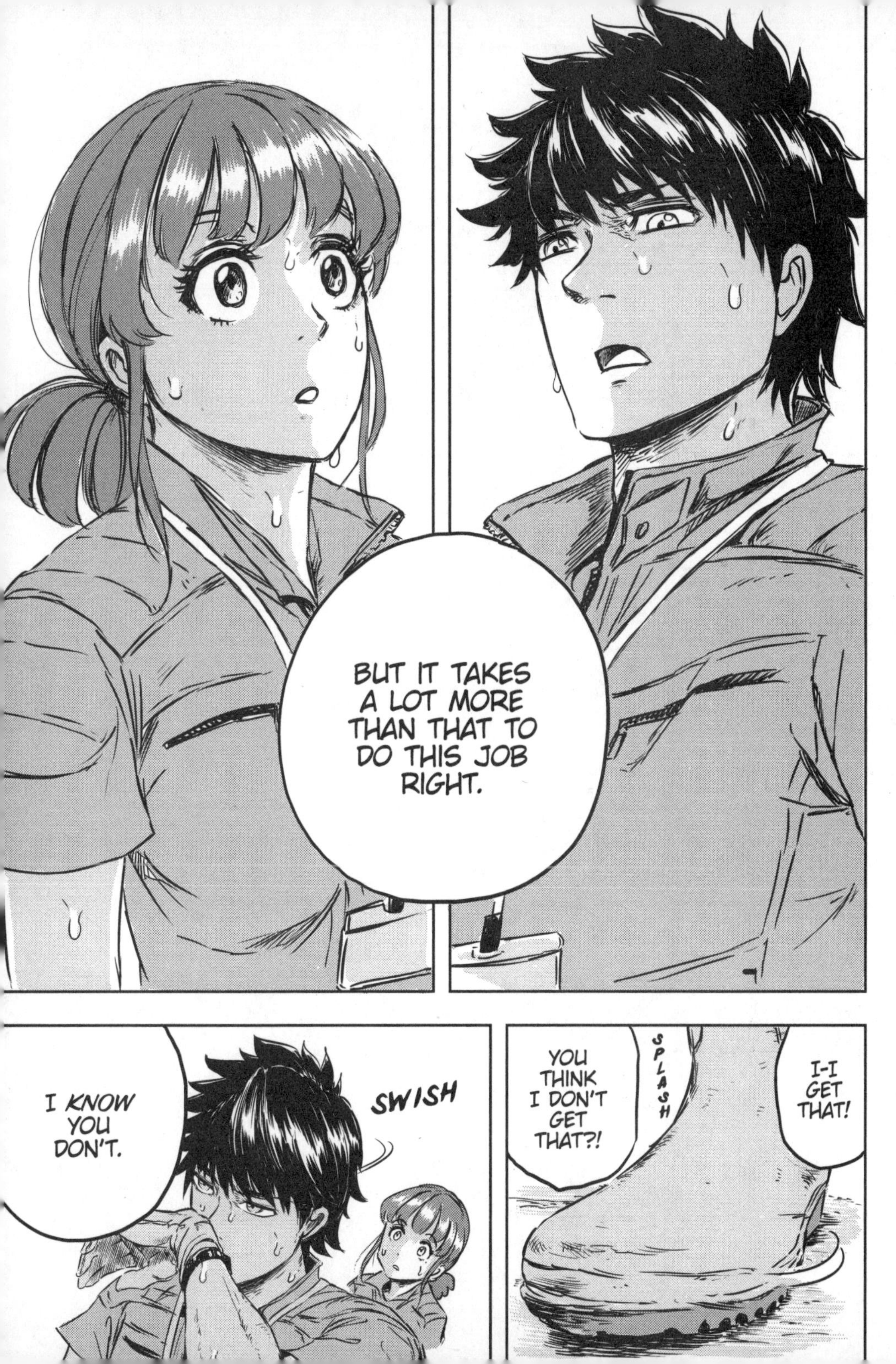
BUT IT TAKES A LOT MORE THAN THAT TO DO THIS JOB RIGHT.
I-I GET THAT!
SPLASH
YOU THINK I DON'T GET THAT?!
SWISH
I *KNOW* YOU DON'T.

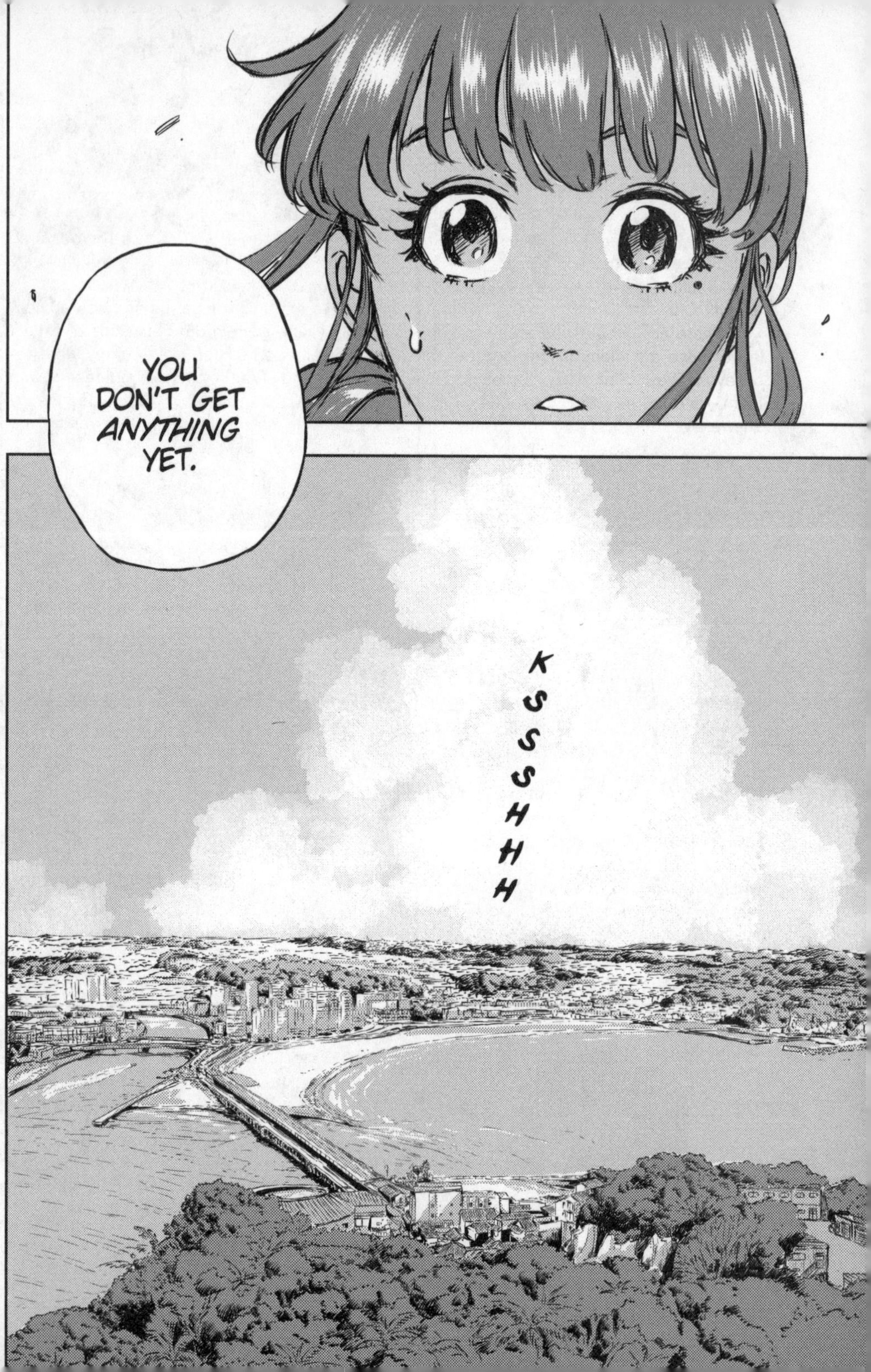
YOU DON'T GET ANYTHING YET.
KSSSHHH

Dr. Dino's Lab Log

FILE. 01 Finding Out What Dinosaurs *Really* Looked Like

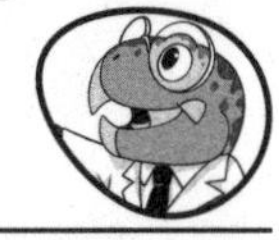

Have you ever wanted a dinosaur for a pet? The idea raises a lot of fun questions. How would it move around? What should I feed it?

There are people who aren't content to leave these questions in the land of make-believe. They think very seriously about them—and about how they can find the answers.

Before we go any further, I suppose I should introduce myself! My name is Shin-ichi Fujiwara. I'm a university researcher, and my research concerns those very questions: how extinct animals, like dinosaurs, looked and moved when they were alive.

Even among dinosaur scientists, there are different sorts of people. Some love to go out into the field and dig for fossils. Others prefer to imagine how the creatures that left those fossils behind looked. Even as a child, I was the latter type. Sure, I loved dinosaurs, but staring at fossils was never really my thing. Given the choice, I preferred going to the zoo or the aquarium to see living animals in motion. Now that I'm an adult, that still hasn't changed—and it plays a big part in my research! Every time I investigate an extinct animal, I start off by trying to figure out how it would have moved. You might be surprised to learn how many scientists started to develop their research styles when they were kids, just like I did!

So, how do we go about depicting what dinosaurs looked like when they were alive? Sadly, we'll never have the chance to see for ourselves and know for sure. On one hand, that means you've got total freedom when it comes to imagining their appearance—but without following the evidence, that's all it is: imagining. If you want your depiction to be truly convincing, it's crucial for it to make logical sense.

My research goal is to find as much of that information as I can. Once I've gathered a lot of potential evidence, I carefully choose the most rock-solid, certain parts of it. I believe that this will get us as close as possible to the truth in our depictions of extinct animals. In pursuit of this, I put my ideas together and share my thought processes with my fellow scientists. This pursuit, and the joy of making convincing new discoveries, are what science is all about.

Hey, a few pages back, did you notice how Yuki the *Giganotosaurus* rested in a strange, seated position? In large theropods like Yuki, the part of the pelvis called the pubic bone was thick and hard, and extended to around the knee. Meanwhile, though, their ribs were extremely fragile. Perhaps, then, whenever a theropod sat down, its pubic bone worked kind of like a built-in chair, keeping its chest and ribs from touching the ground so that they wouldn't break. In fact, there are fossils of theropod footprints that suggest their hind legs and pubic bones made contact with the ground as they sat!

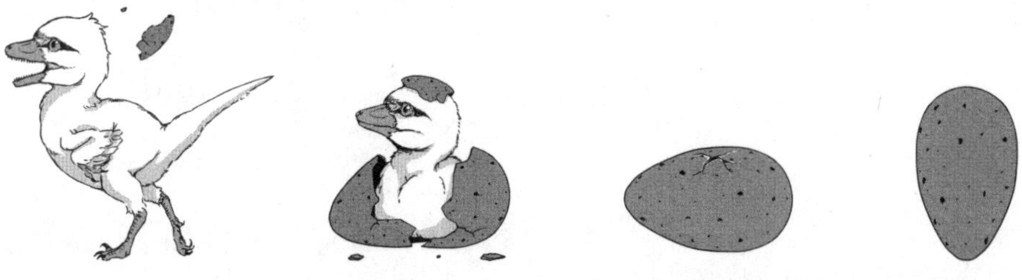

DINOSAUR SANCTUARY

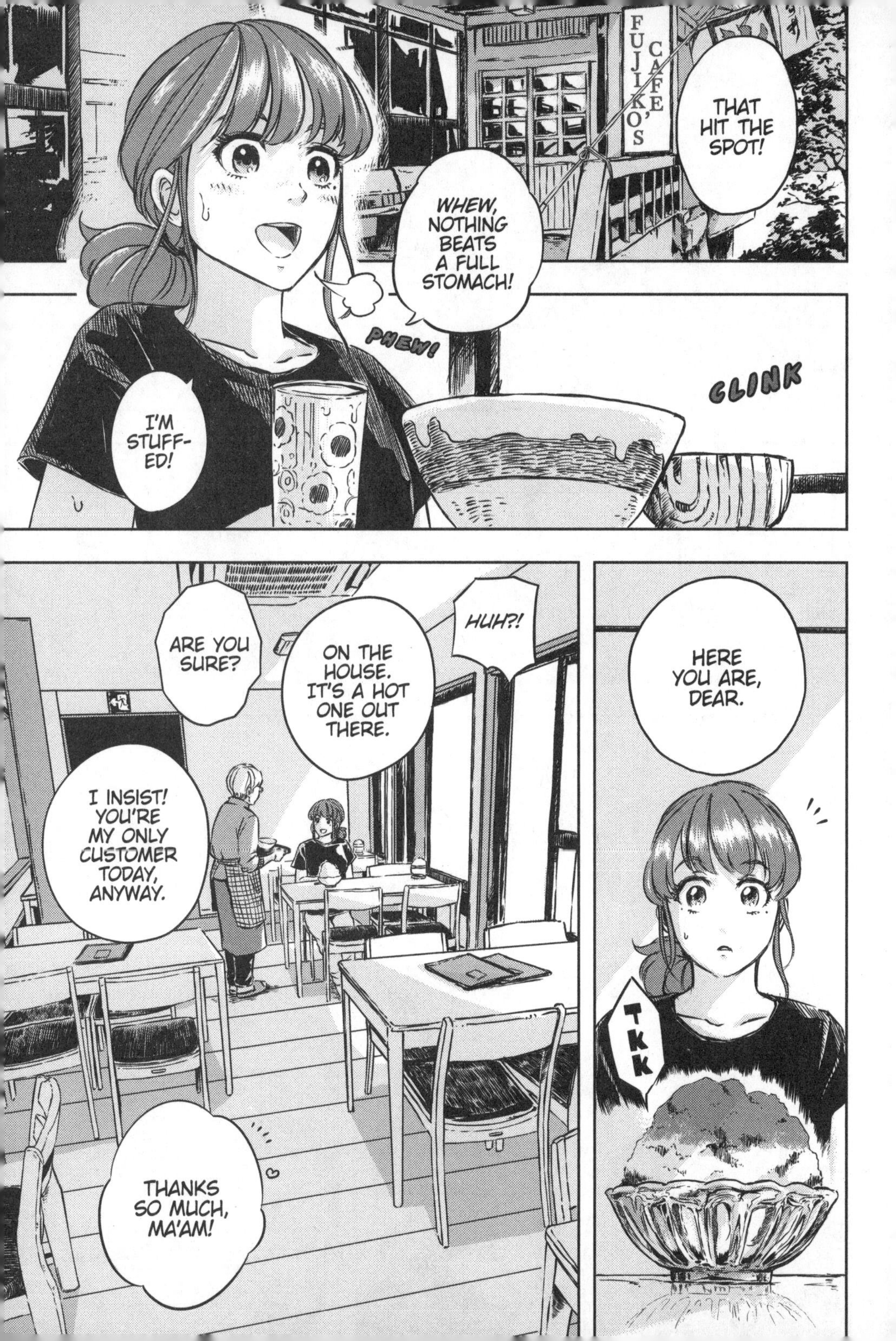
FUJIKO'S CAFE
THAT HIT THE SPOT!
WHEW, NOTHING BEATS A FULL STOMACH!
PHEW!
CLINK
I'M STUFFED-ED!
HERE YOU ARE, DEAR.
TKK
HUH?!
ON THE HOUSE. IT'S A HOT ONE OUT THERE.
ARE YOU SURE?
I INSIST! YOU'RE MY ONLY CUSTOMER TODAY, ANYWAY.
THANKS SO MUCH, MA'AM!

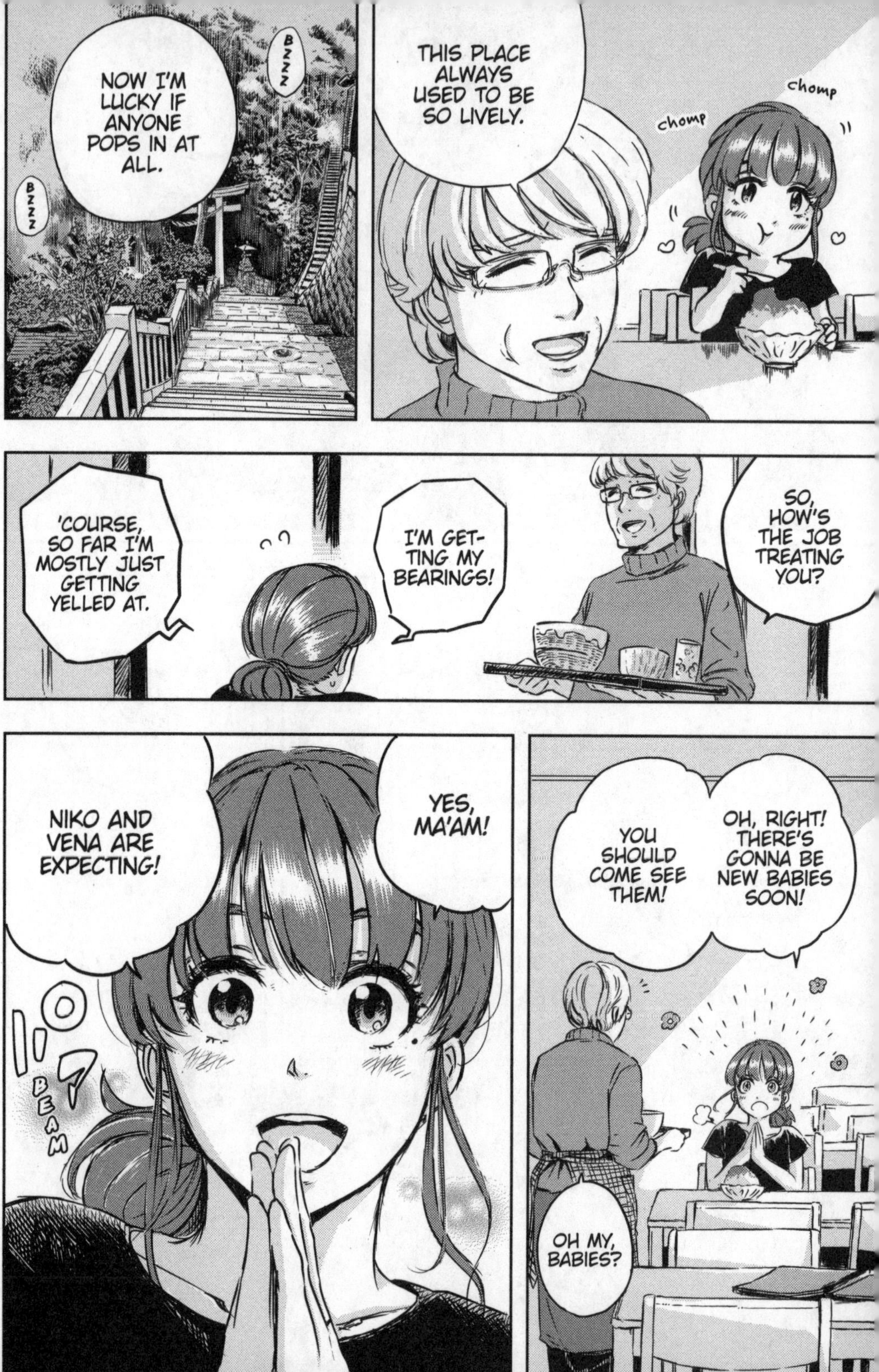
THIS PLACE ALWAYS USED TO BE SO LIVELY.
chomp
chomp
NOW I'M LUCKY IF ANYONE POPS IN AT ALL.
BZZZ
BZZZ
SO, HOW'S THE JOB TREATING YOU?
I'M GET-TING MY BEARINGS!
'COURSE, SO FAR I'M MOSTLY JUST GETTING YELLED AT.
OH, RIGHT! THERE'S GONNA BE NEW BABIES SOON!
YOU SHOULD COME SEE THEM!
OH MY, BABIES?
YES, MA'AM!
NIKO AND VENA ARE EXPECTING!
BEAM

CHAPTER 2 WELCOME TO FATHERHOOD, NIKO

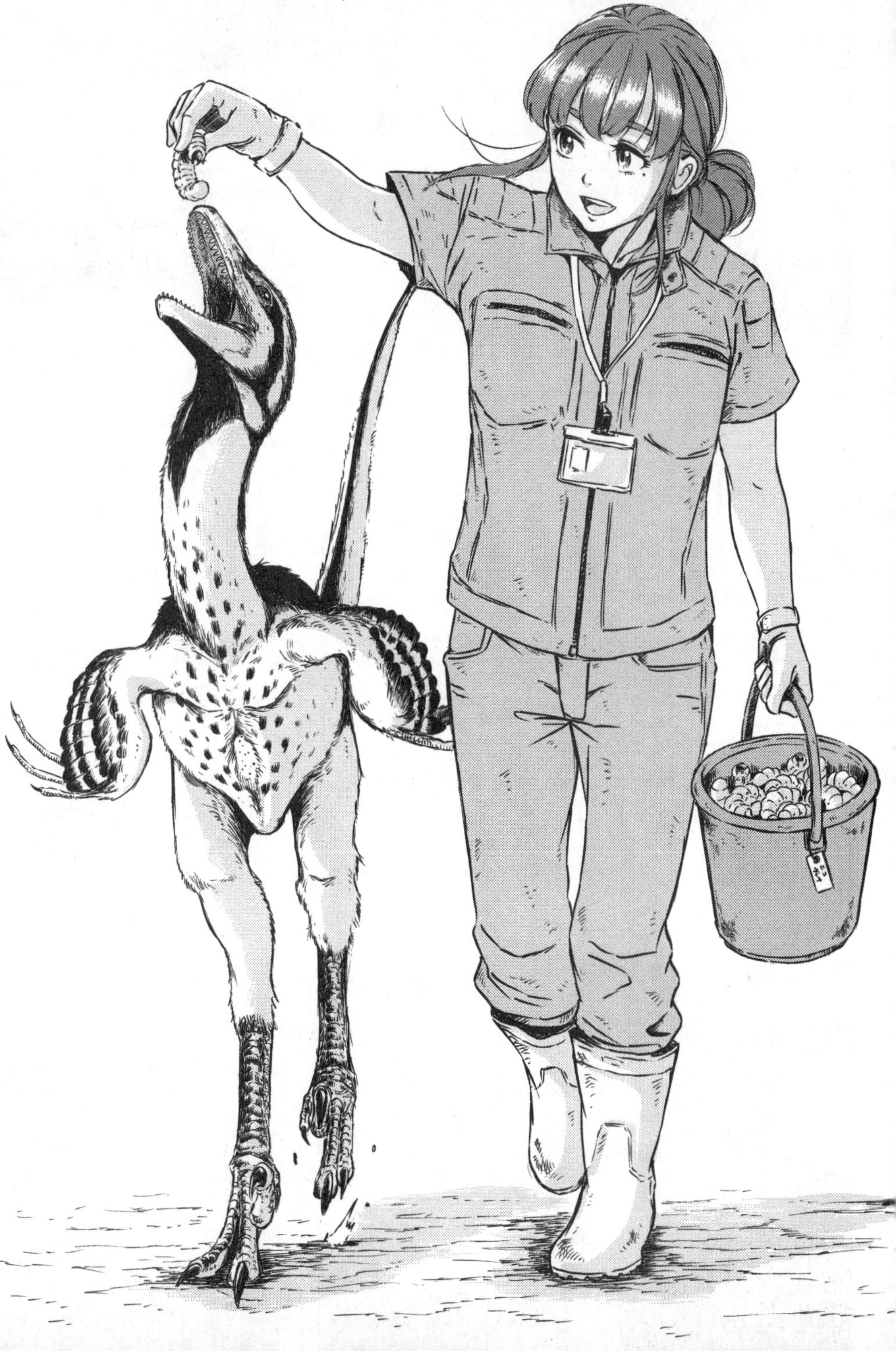

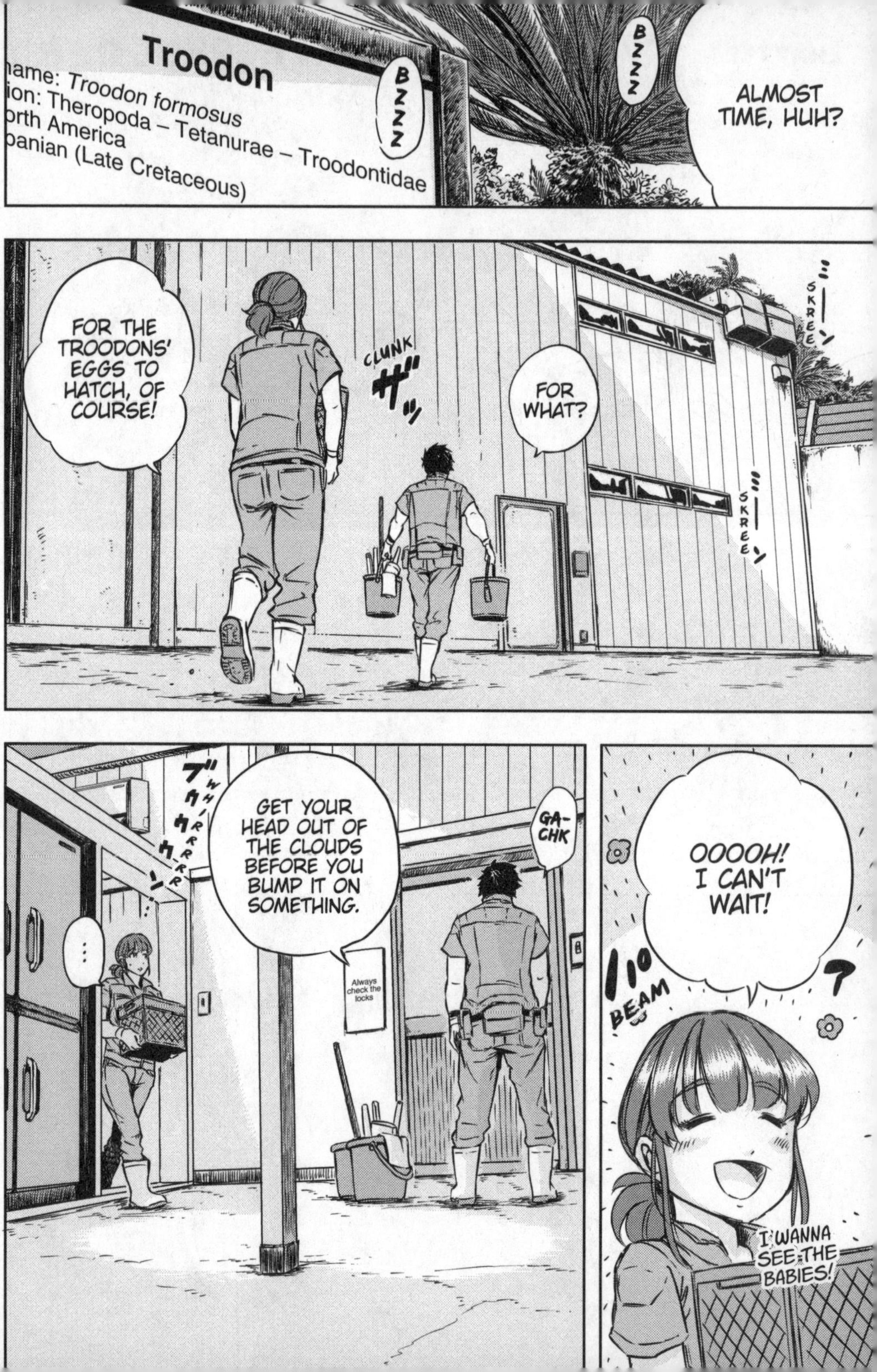
ALMOST TIME, HUH?
BZZZ
BZZZ
Troodon
name: Troodon formosus
ion: Theropoda – Tetanurae – Troodontidae
orth America
panian (Late Cretaceous)
SKREE
SKREE
FOR WHAT?
CLUNK
FOR THE TROODONS' EGGS TO HATCH, OF COURSE!
OOOOH! I CAN'T WAIT!
BEAM
I WANNA SEE THE BABIES!
GA-CHK
GET YOUR HEAD OUT OF THE CLOUDS BEFORE YOU BUMP IT ON SOMETHING.
Always check the locks
WHIRRR
...

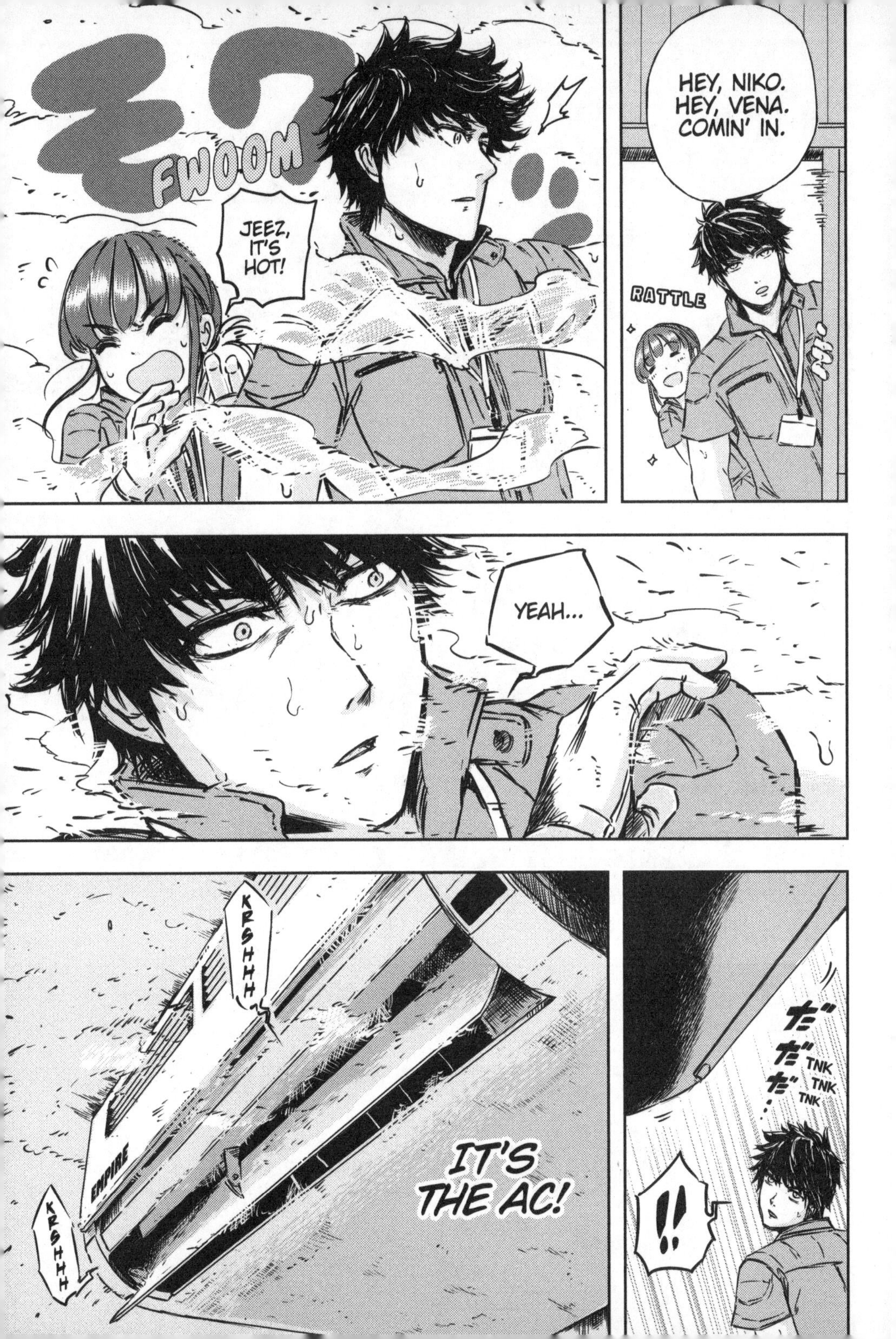

HEY, NIKO. HEY, VENA. COMIN' IN.
RATTLE
FWOOM
JEEZ, IT'S HOT!
YEAH...
TNK TNK TNK
!!
KRSHHH
EMPIRE
IT'S THE AC!
KRSHHH

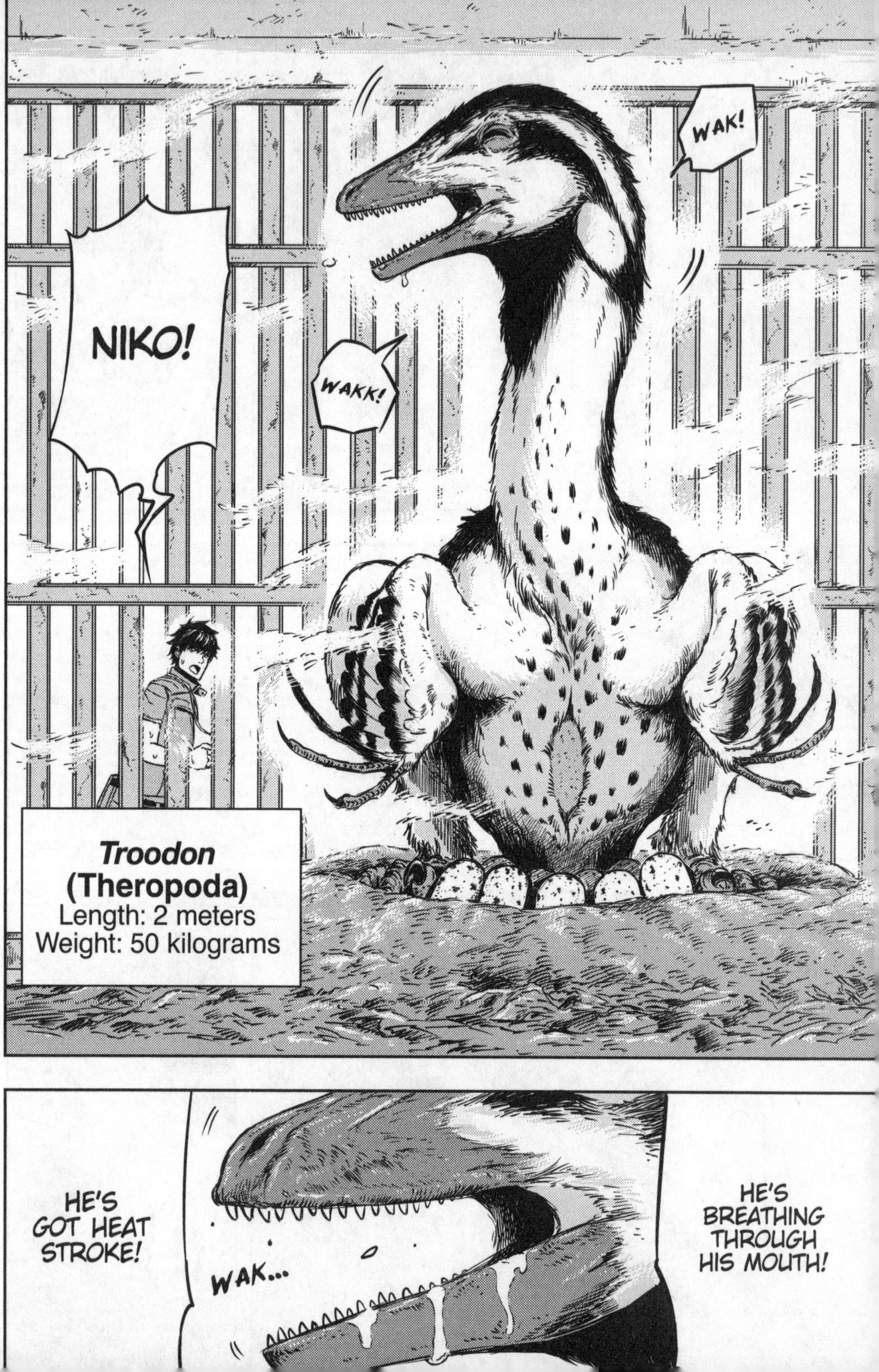
WAK!
NIKO!
WAKK!
Troodon
(Theropoda)
Length: 2 meters
Weight: 50 kilograms
HE'S BREATHING THROUGH HIS MOUTH!
WAK...
HE'S GOT HEAT STROKE!

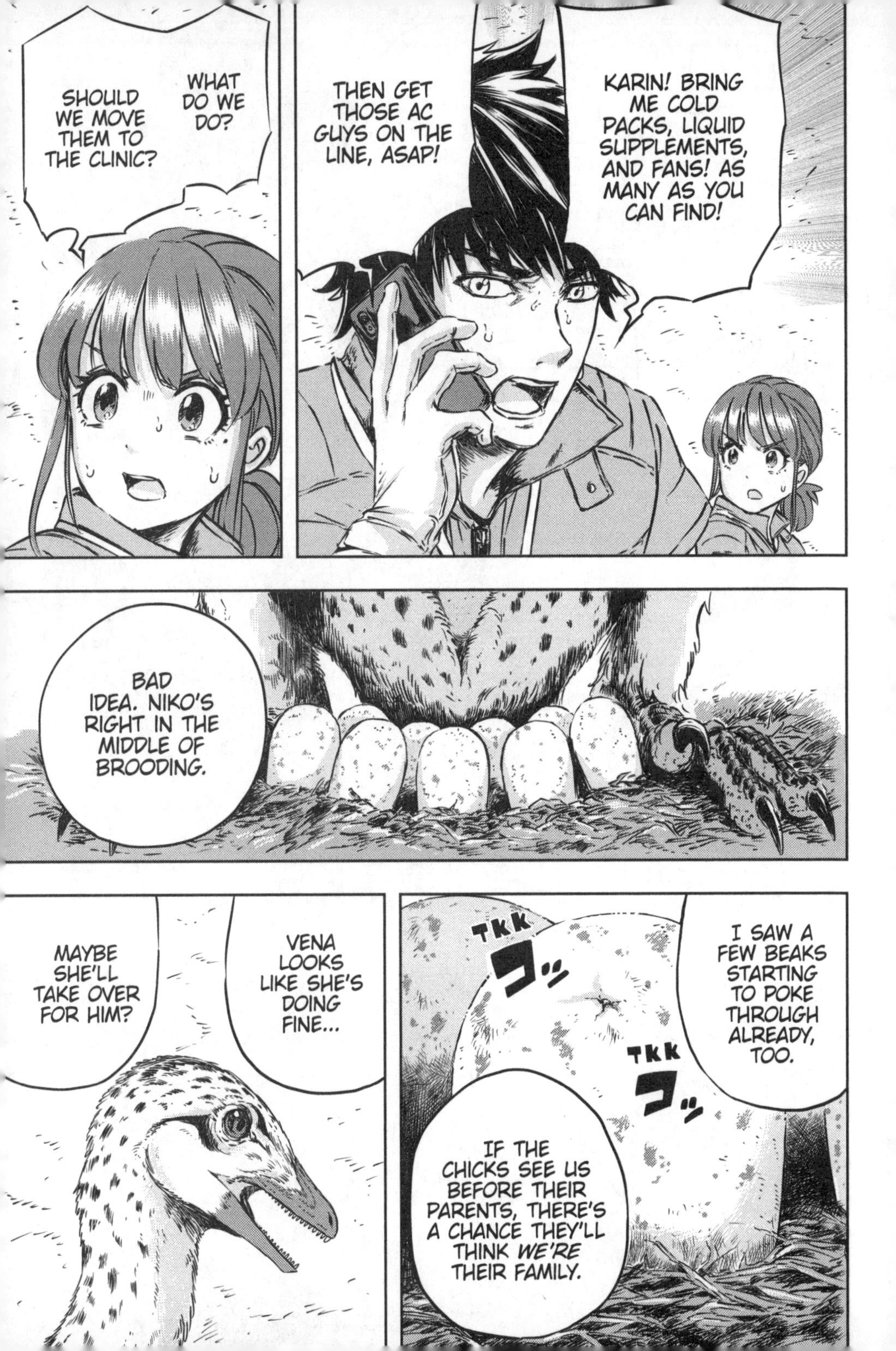
KARIN! BRING ME COLD PACKS, LIQUID SUPPLEMENTS, AND FANS! AS MANY AS YOU CAN FIND!
THEN GET THOSE AC GUYS ON THE LINE, ASAP!
WHAT DO WE DO?
SHOULD WE MOVE THEM TO THE CLINIC?
BAD IDEA. NIKO'S RIGHT IN THE MIDDLE OF BROODING.
I SAW A FEW BEAKS STARTING TO POKE THROUGH ALREADY, TOO.
TKK
TKK
IF THE CHICKS SEE US BEFORE THEIR PARENTS, THERE'S A CHANCE THEY'LL THINK *WE'RE* THEIR FAMILY.
VENA LOOKS LIKE SHE'S DOING FINE...
MAYBE SHE'LL TAKE OVER FOR HIM?

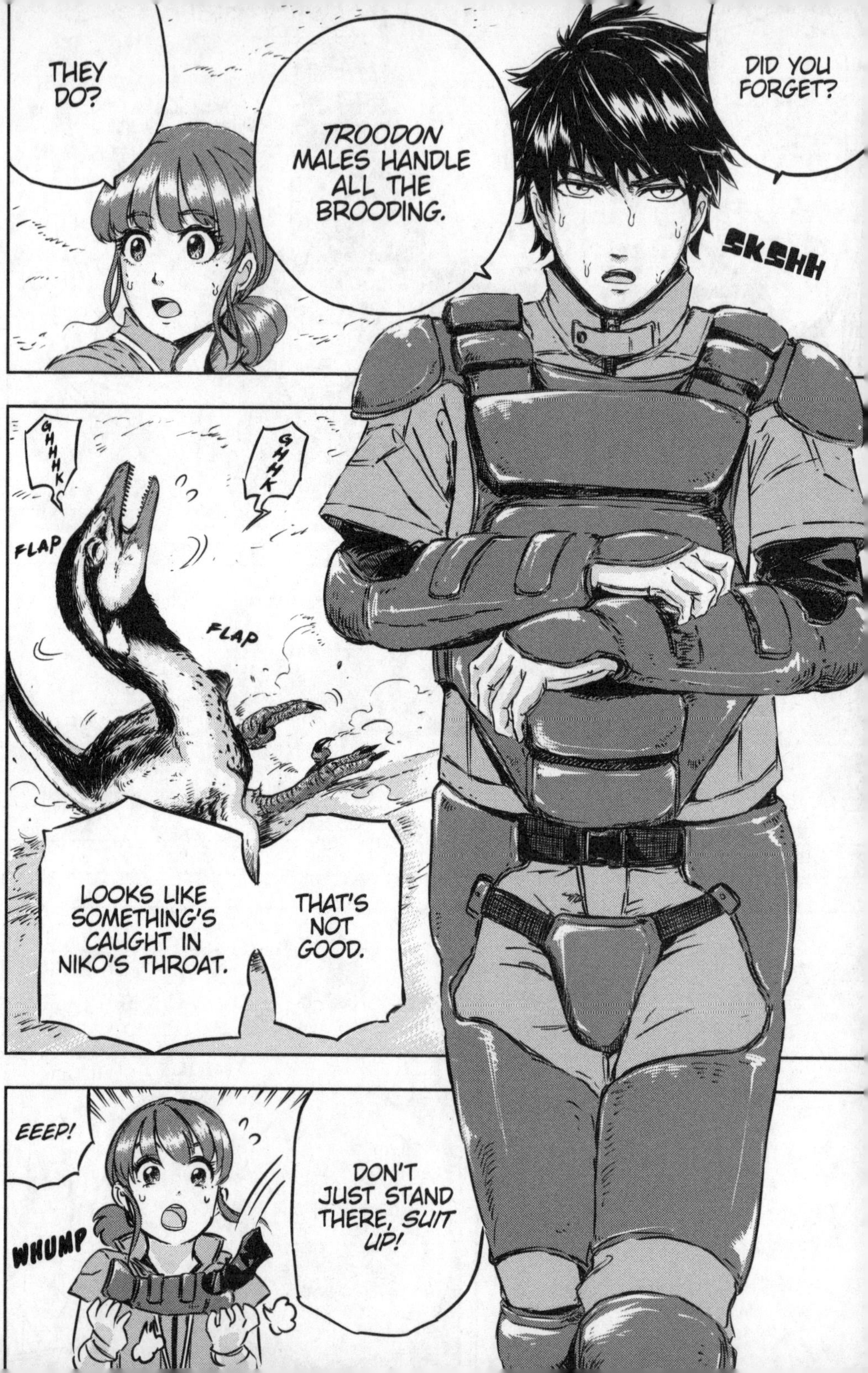
DID YOU FORGET?
TROODON MALES HANDLE ALL THE BROODING.
SKSHH
THEY DO?
GHHK
GHHHK
FLAP
FLAP
LOOKS LIKE SOMETHING'S CAUGHT IN NIKO'S THROAT.
THAT'S NOT GOOD.
DON'T JUST STAND THERE, SUIT UP!
EEEP!
WHUMP

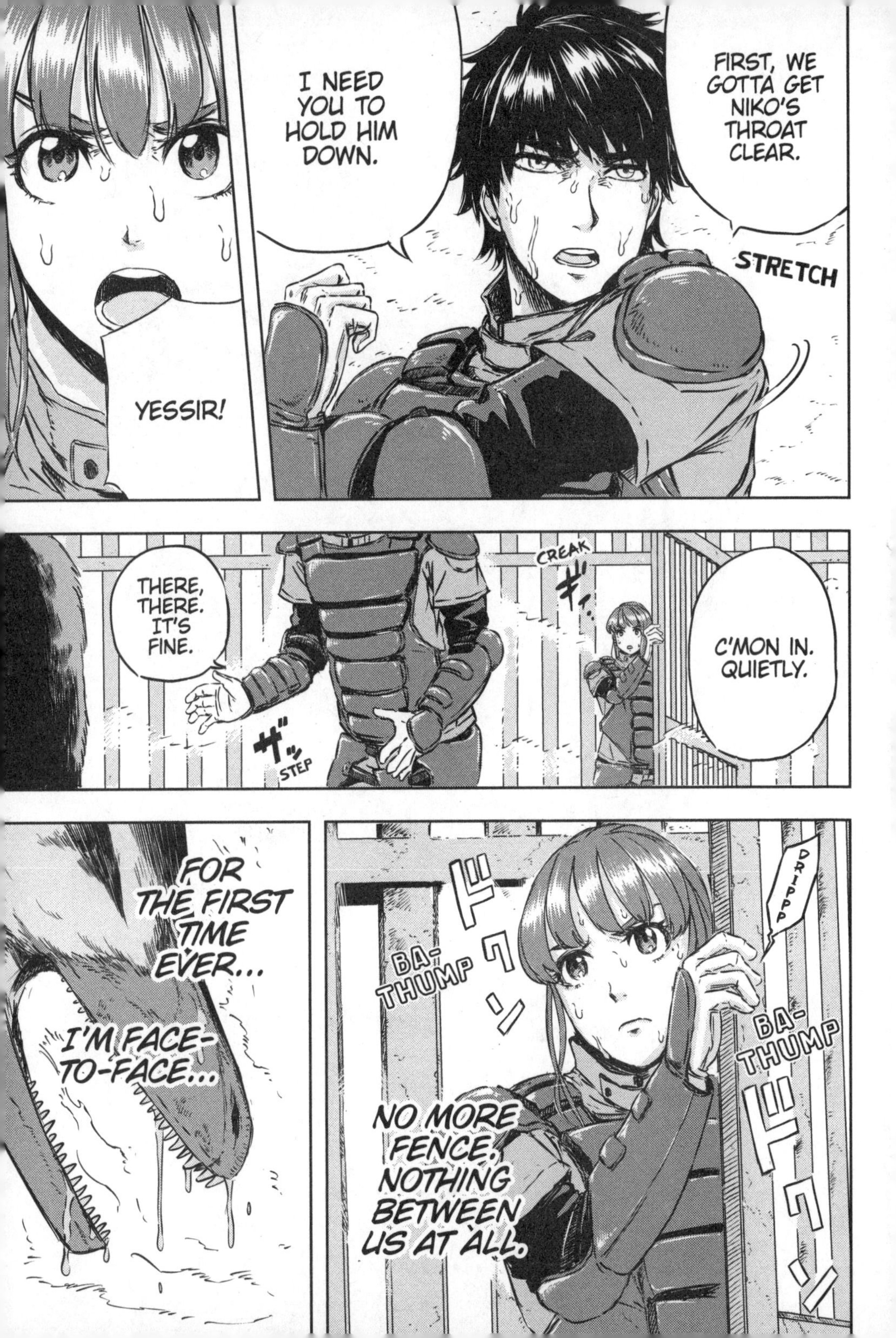
FIRST, WE GOTTA GET NIKO'S THROAT CLEAR.
STRETCH
I NEED YOU TO HOLD HIM DOWN.
YESSIR!
C'MON IN. QUIETLY.
CREAK
THERE, THERE. IT'S FINE.
STEP
DRIPPP
BA-THUMP
BA-THUMP
NO MORE FENCE. NOTHING BETWEEN US AT ALL.
FOR THE FIRST TIME EVER...
I'M FACE-TO-FACE...

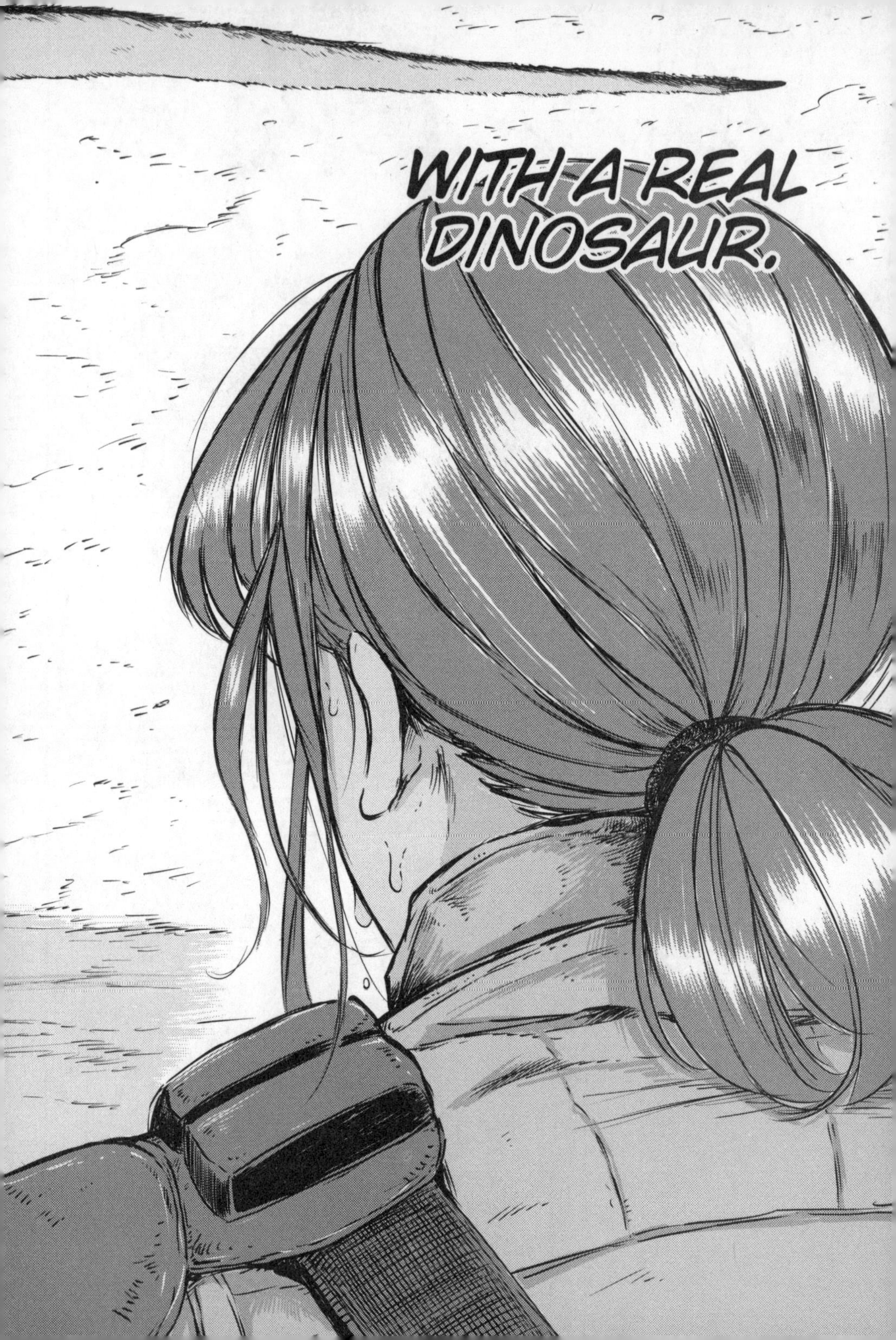
WITH A REAL DINOSAUR.

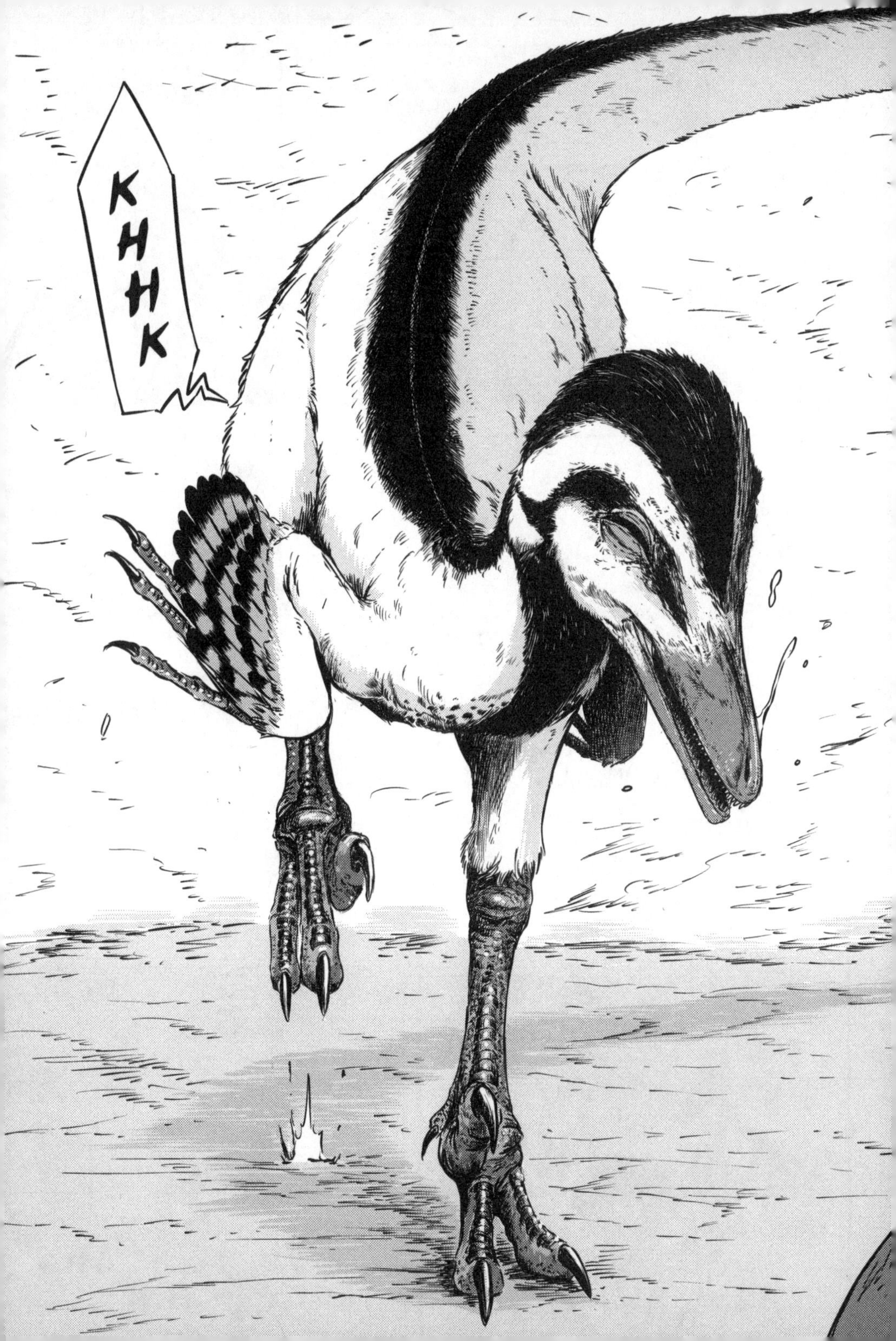
KHHK

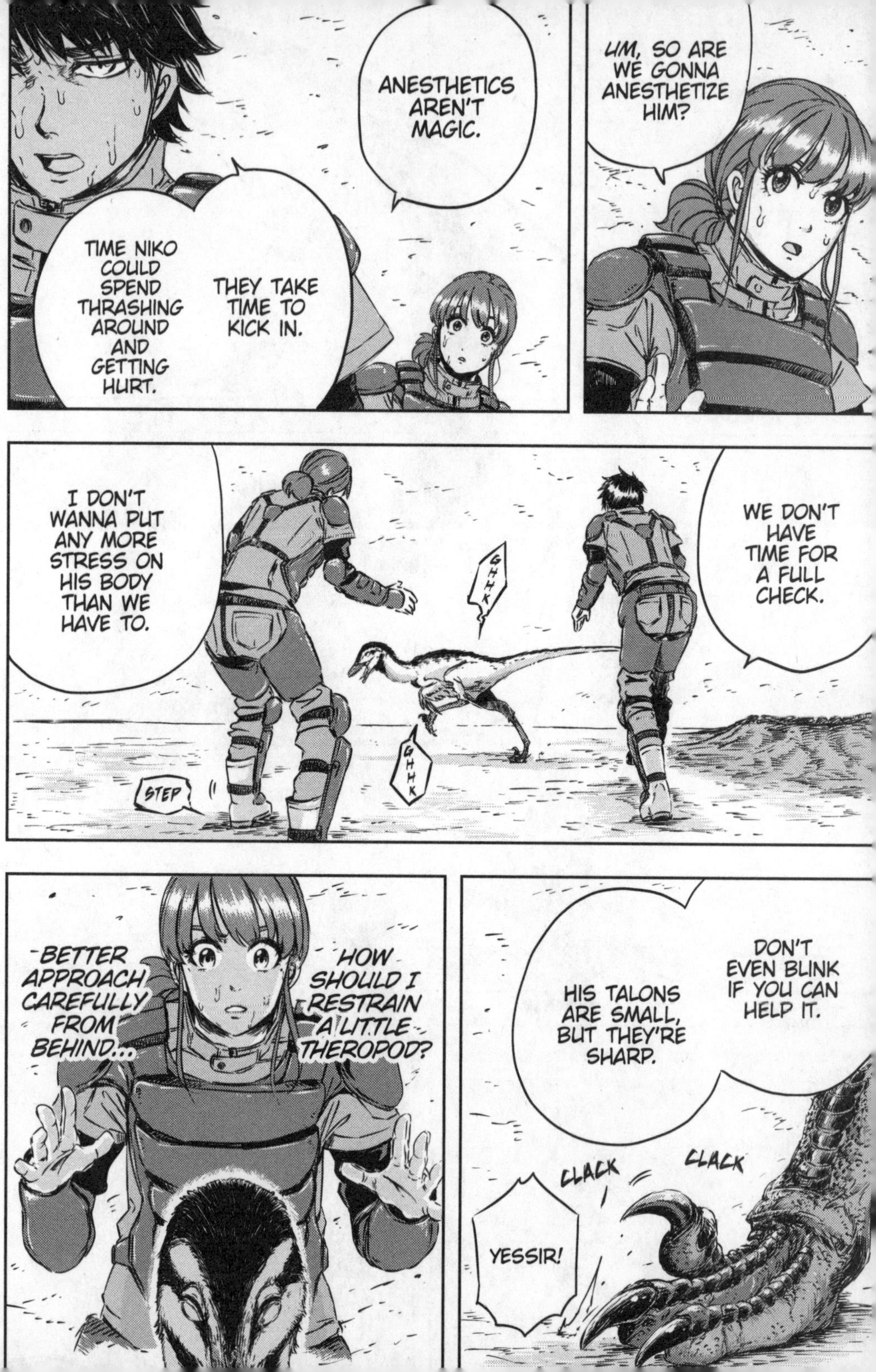
UM, SO ARE WE GONNA ANESTHETIZE HIM?
ANESTHETICS AREN'T MAGIC.
THEY TAKE TIME TO KICK IN.
TIME NIKO COULD SPEND THRASHING AROUND AND GETTING HURT.
WE DON'T HAVE TIME FOR A FULL CHECK.
GHHK
GHHK
I DON'T WANNA PUT ANY MORE STRESS ON HIS BODY THAN WE HAVE TO.
STEP
DON'T EVEN BLINK IF YOU CAN HELP IT.
HIS TALONS ARE SMALL, BUT THEY'RE SHARP.
CLACK
CLACK
YESSIR!
HOW SHOULD I RESTRAIN A LITTLE THEROPOD?
BETTER APPROACH CAREFULLY FROM BEHIND...

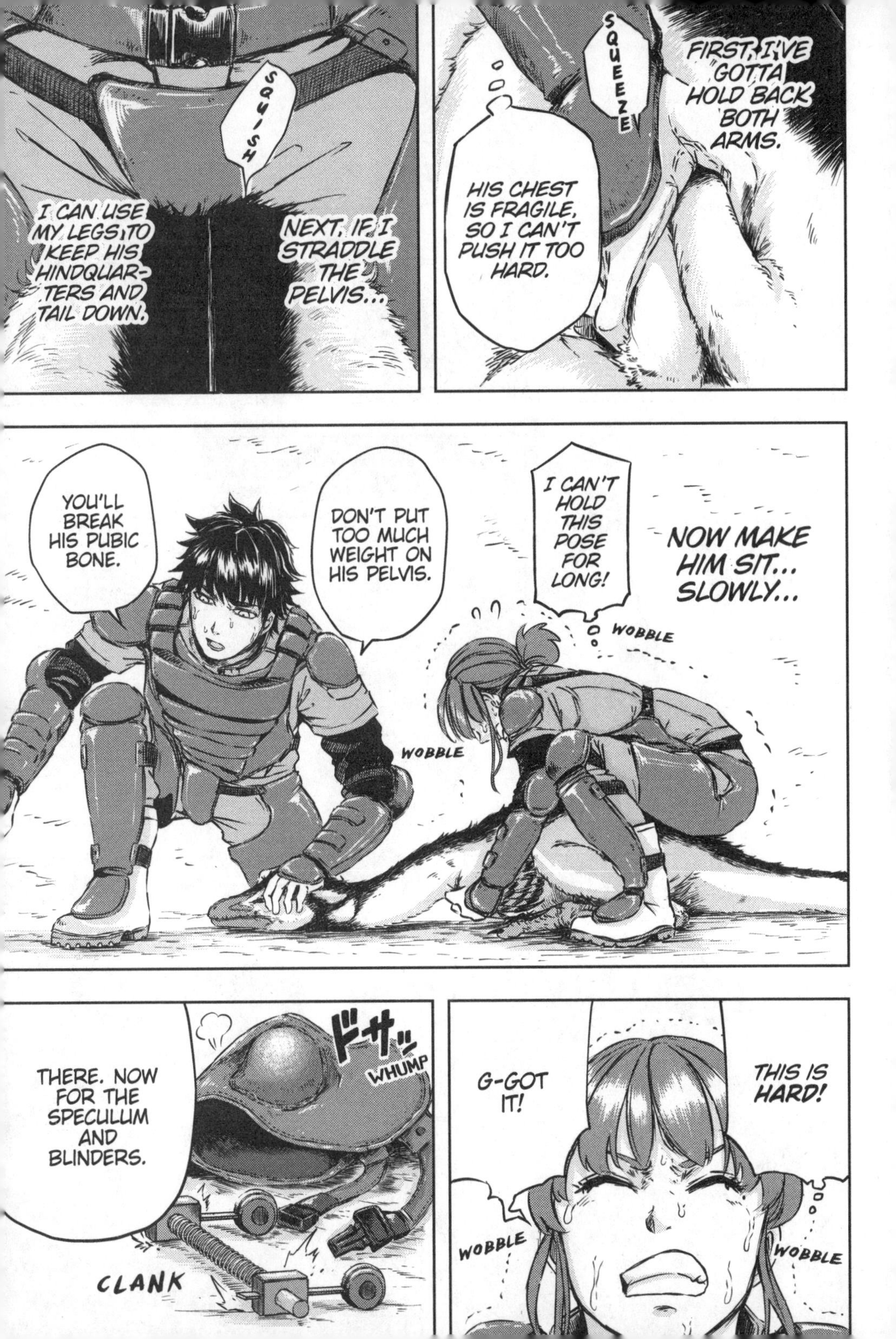
FIRST, I'VE GOTTA HOLD BACK BOTH ARMS.
SQUEEZE
HIS CHEST IS FRAGILE, SO I CAN'T PUSH IT TOO HARD.
SQUISH
NEXT, IF I STRADDLE THE PELVIS...
I CAN USE MY LEGS TO KEEP HIS HINDQUARTERS AND TAIL DOWN.
NOW MAKE HIM SIT... SLOWLY...
I CAN'T HOLD THIS POSE FOR LONG!
WOBBLE
DON'T PUT TOO MUCH WEIGHT ON HIS PELVIS.
YOU'LL BREAK HIS PUBIC BONE.
WOBBLE
THIS IS HARD!
G-GOT IT!
WOBBLE
WOBBLE
ドサッ
WHUMP
THERE. NOW FOR THE SPECULUM AND BLINDERS.
CLANK

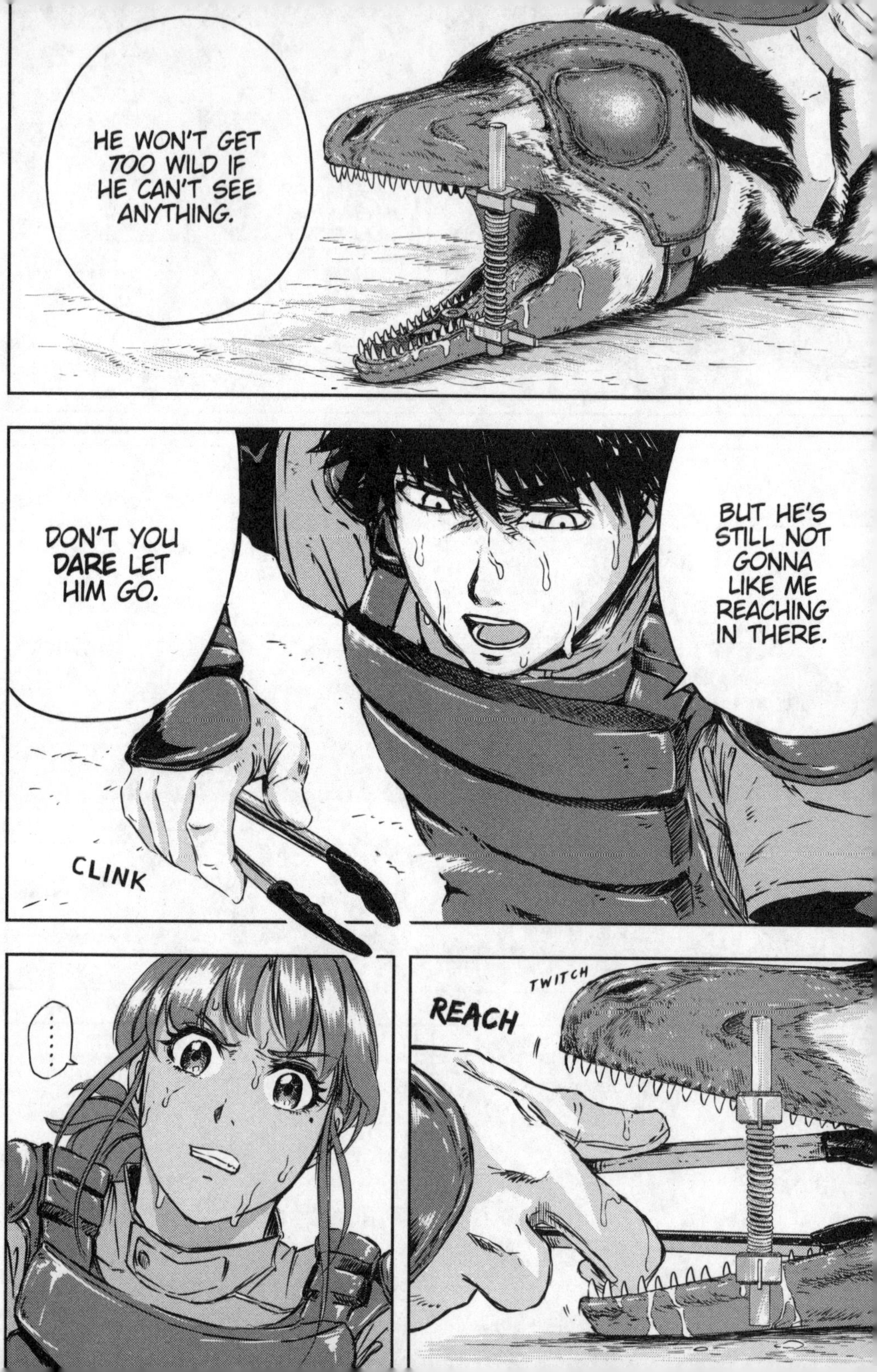
HE WON'T GET TOO WILD IF HE CAN'T SEE ANYTHING.
BUT HE'S STILL NOT GONNA LIKE ME REACHING IN THERE.
DON'T YOU DARE LET HIM GO.
CLINK
TWITCH
REACH
......

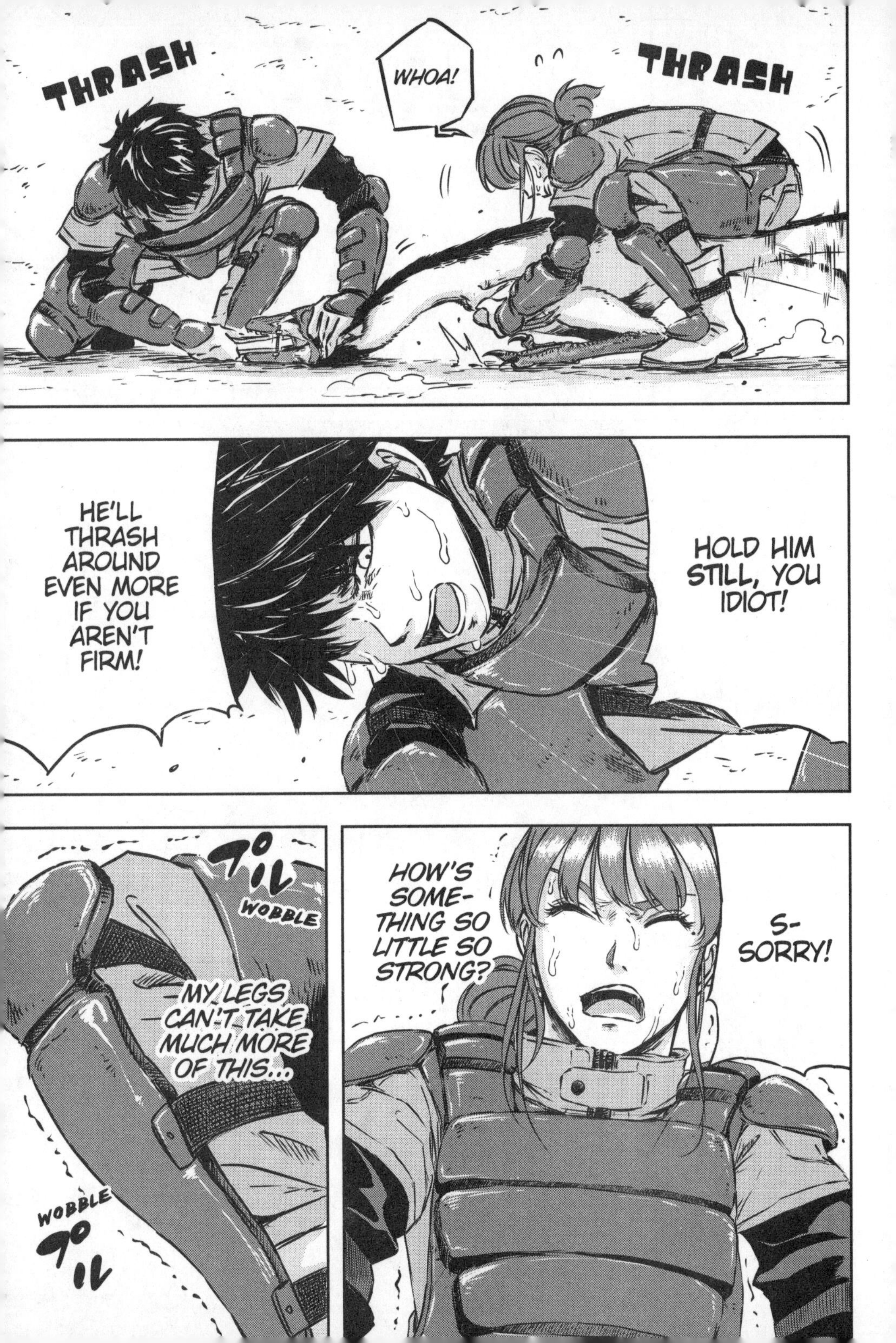
THRASH
WHOA!
THRASH
HOLD HIM STILL, YOU IDIOT!
HE'LL THRASH AROUND EVEN MORE IF YOU AREN'T FIRM!
S-SORRY!
HOW'S SOME-THING SO LITTLE SO STRONG?
プル
WOBBLE
MY LEGS CAN'T TAKE MUCH MORE OF THIS...
WOBBLE
プル

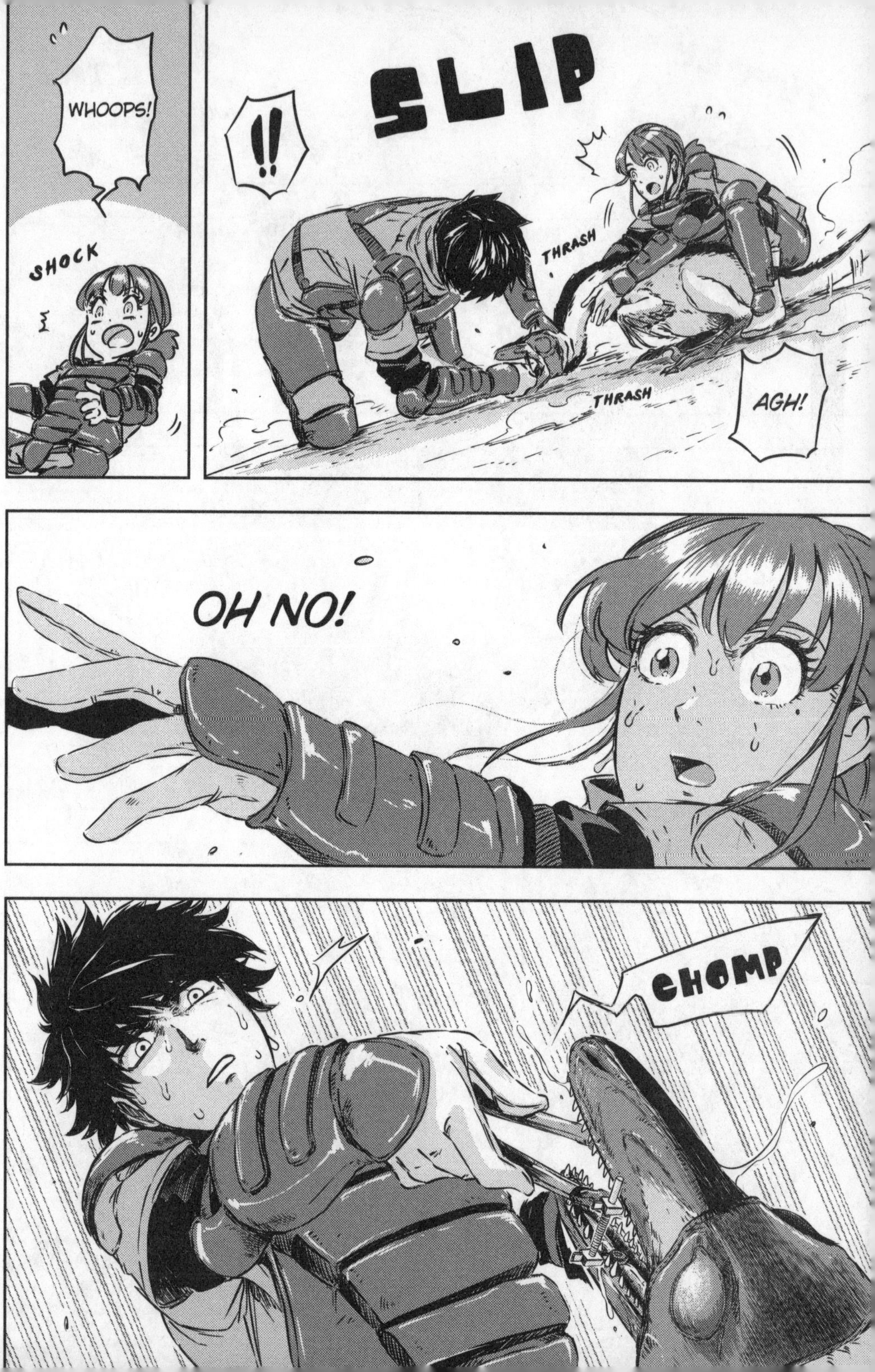
SLIP
!!
THRASH
AGH!
THRASH
WHOOPS!
SHOCK
OH NO!
CHOMP

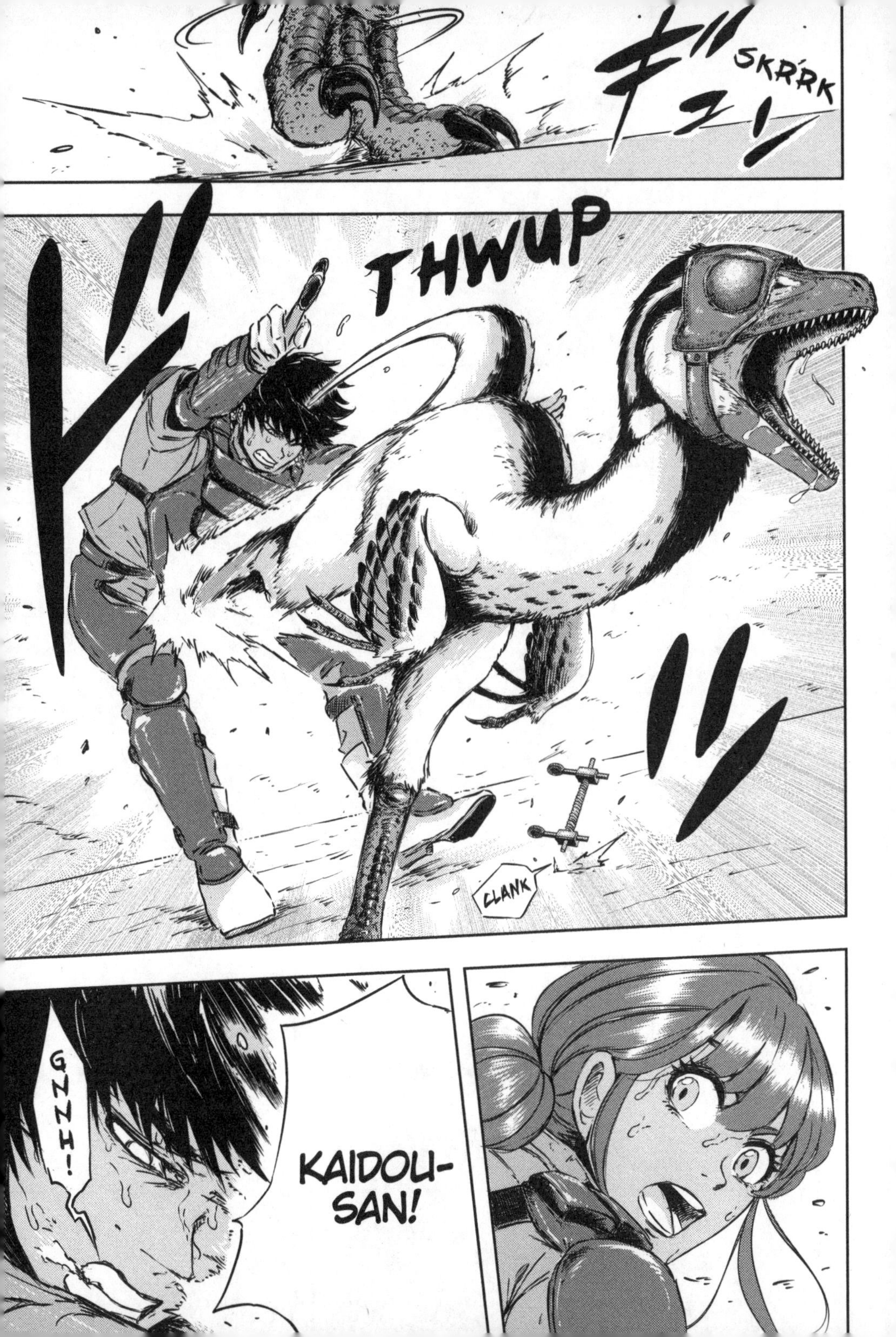
SKR'RK
THWUP
CLANK
KAIDOU-SAN!
GNNH!

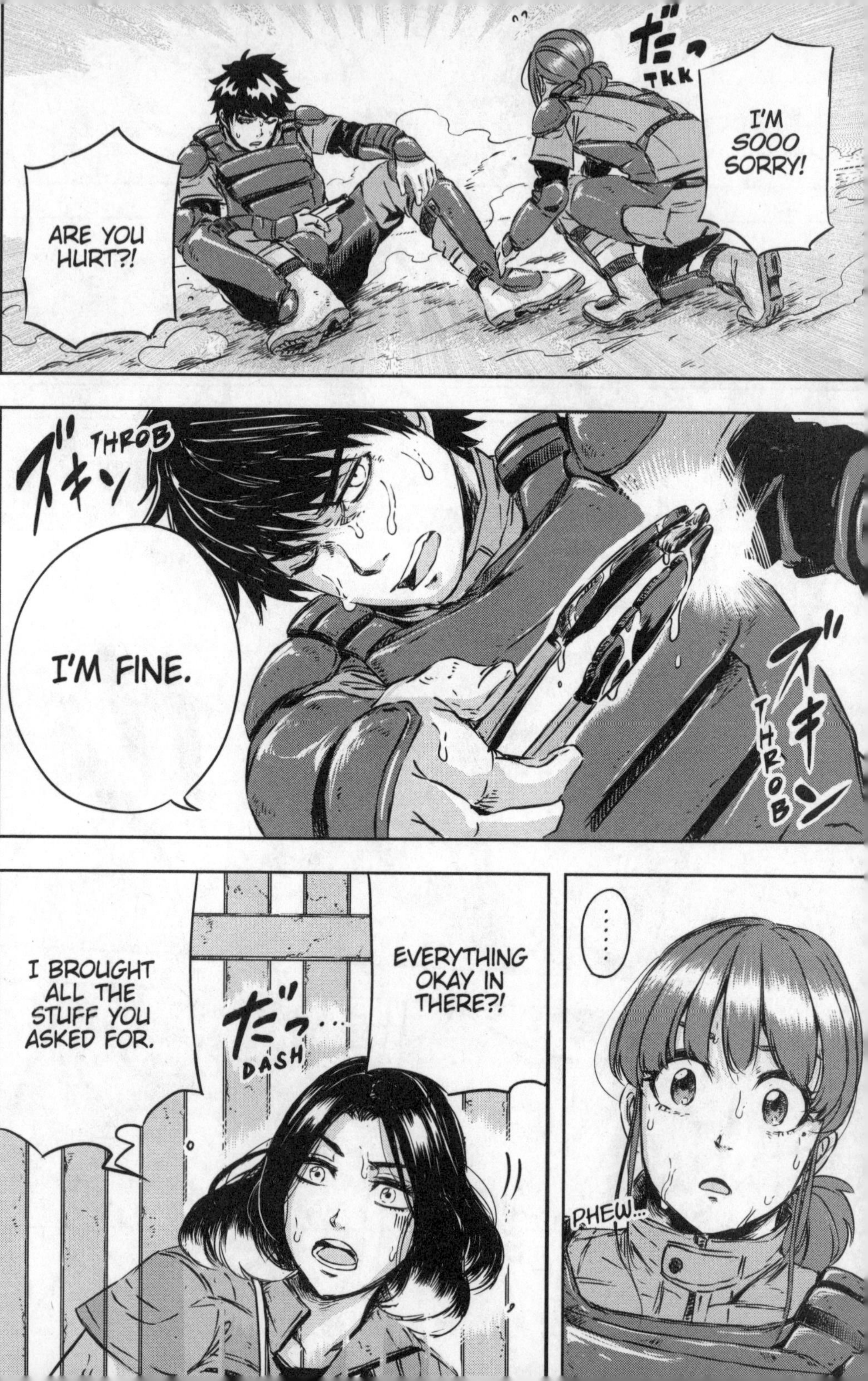
ダッ
TKK
I'M SOOO SORRY!
ARE YOU HURT?!
ズキン
THROB
I'M FINE.
ズキン
THROB
......
PHEW...
EVERYTHING OKAY IN THERE?!
だっ...
DASH
I BROUGHT ALL THE STUFF YOU ASKED FOR.

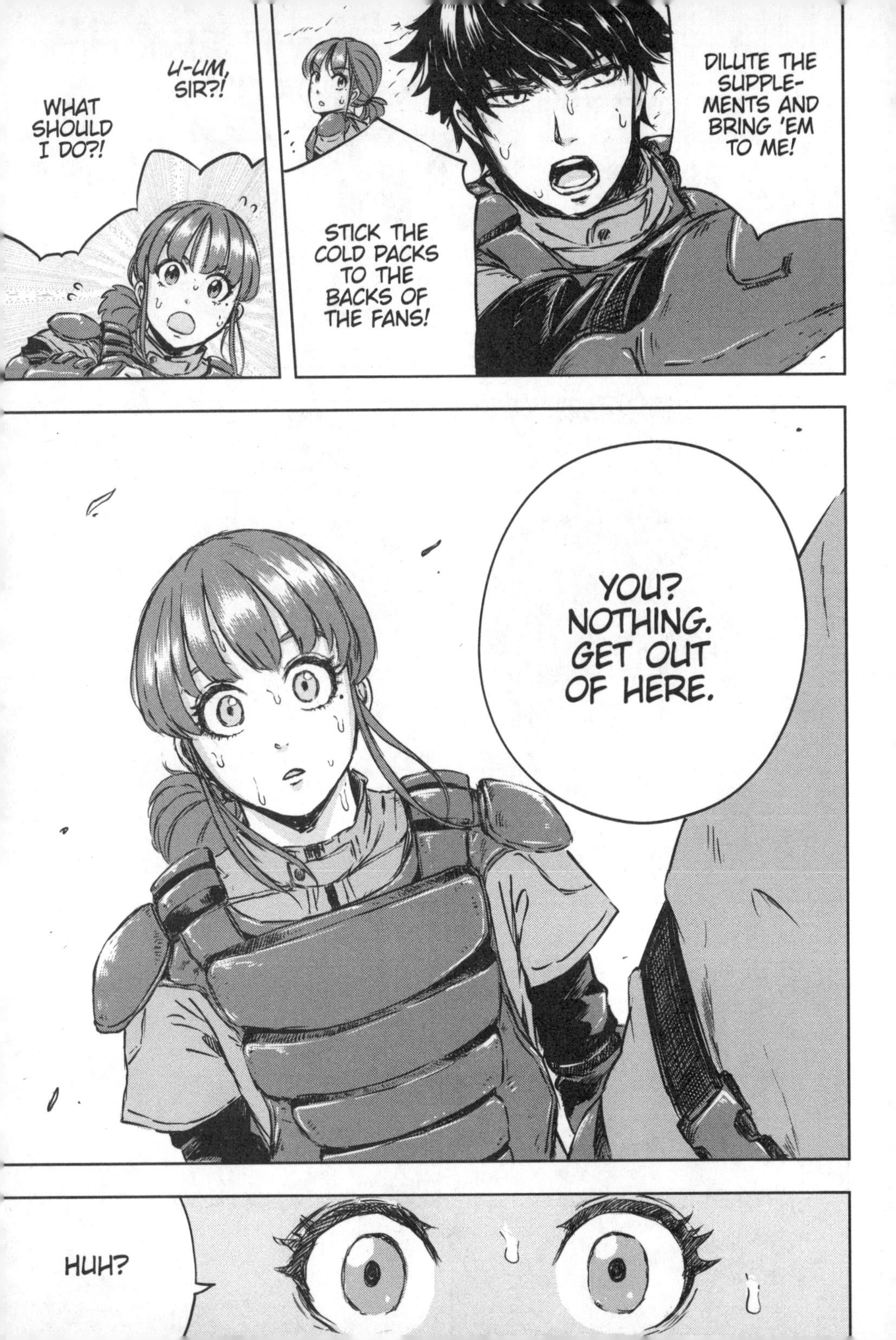
DILUTE THE SUPPLE-MENTS AND BRING 'EM TO ME!
STICK THE COLD PACKS TO THE BACKS OF THE FANS!
U-UM, SIR?!
WHAT SHOULD I DO?!
YOU? NOTHING. GET OUT OF HERE.
HUH?

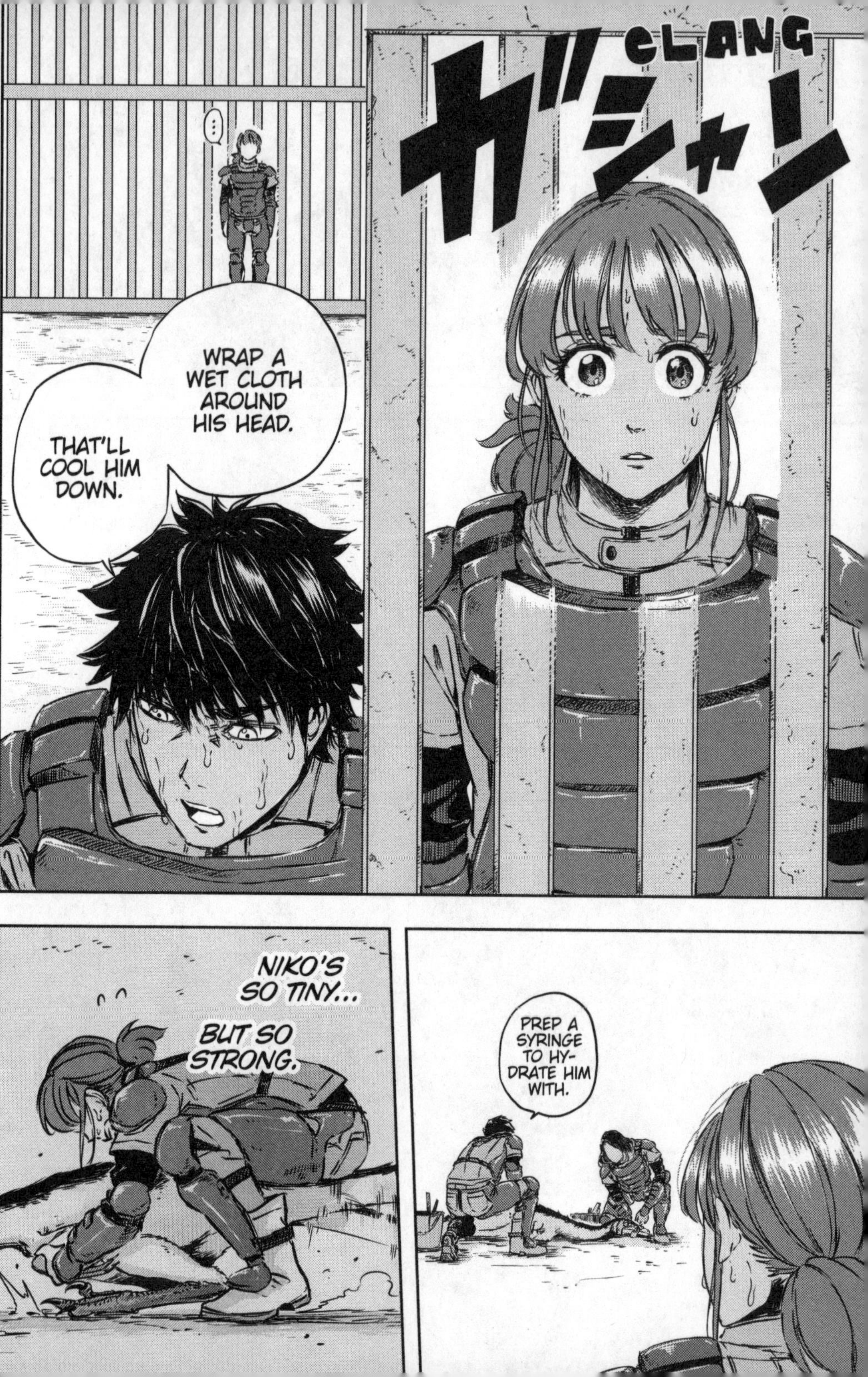
CLANG
ガシャン
...
WRAP A WET CLOTH AROUND HIS HEAD.
THAT'LL COOL HIM DOWN.
PREP A SYRINGE TO HY-DRATE HIM WITH.
NIKO'S SO TINY...
BUT SO STRONG.

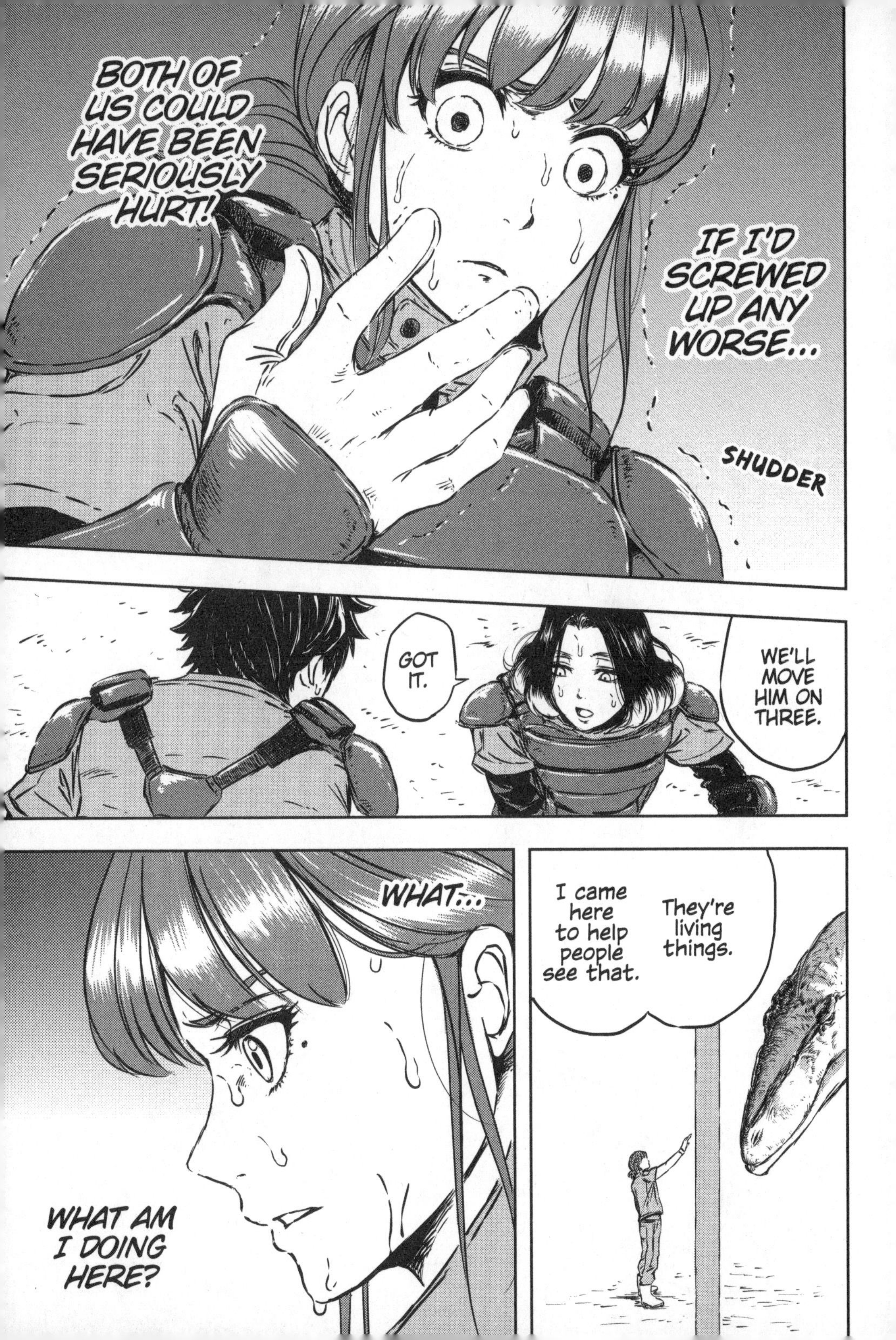
IF I'D SCREWED UP ANY WORSE...
BOTH OF US COULD HAVE BEEN SERIOUSLY HURT!
SHUDDER
WE'LL MOVE HIM ON THREE.
GOT IT.
They're living things.
I came here to help people see that.
WHAT...
WHAT AM I DOING HERE?

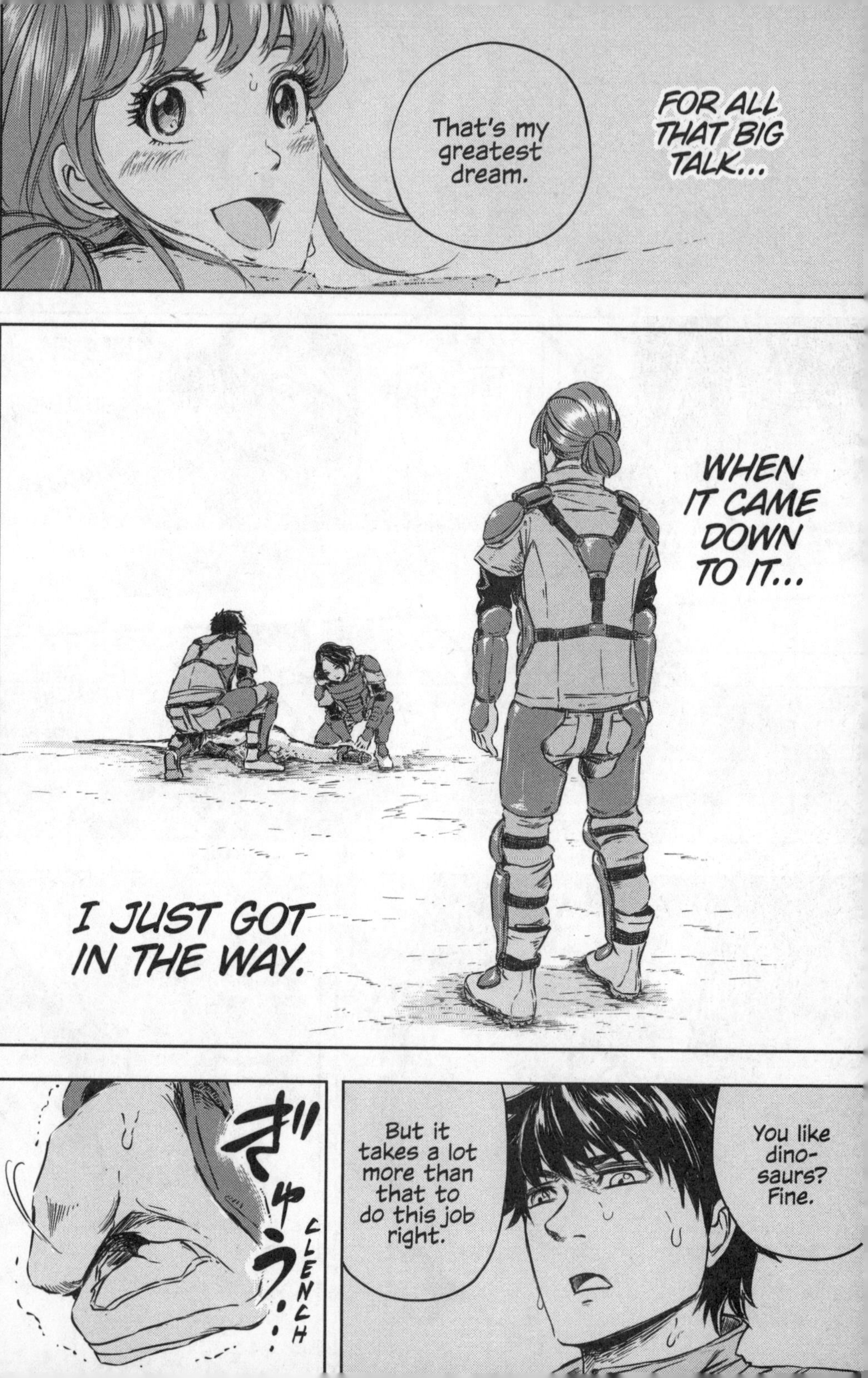

FOR ALL THAT BIG TALK...
That's my greatest dream.
WHEN IT CAME DOWN TO IT...
I JUST GOT IN THE WAY.
You like dino-saurs? Fine.
But it takes a lot more than that to do this job right.
ぎゅう…
CLENCH

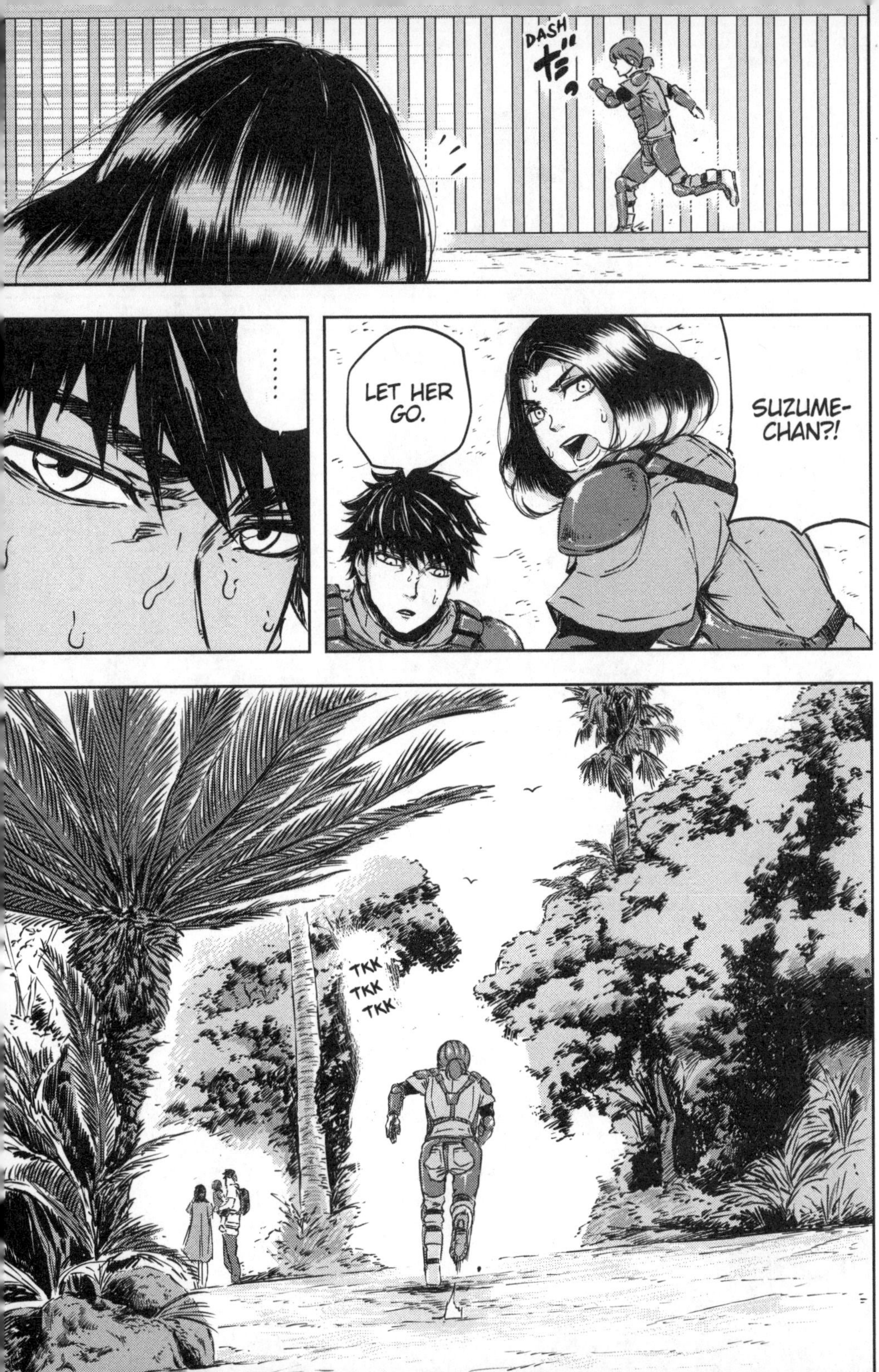
DASH
ダッ
SUZUME-CHAN?!
LET HER GO.
......
TKK
TKK
TKK

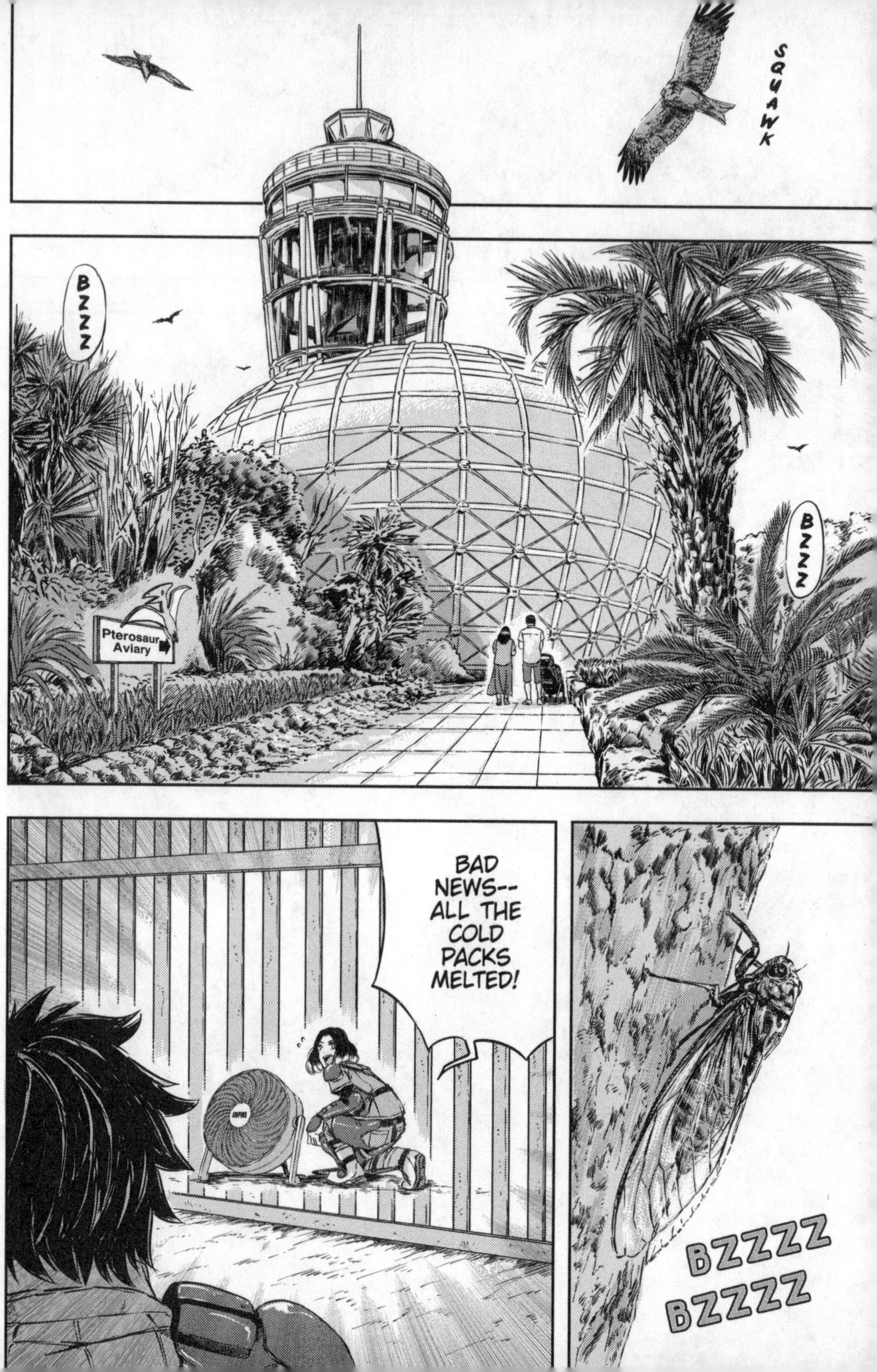
SQUAWK
BZZZ
BZZZ
Pterosaur Aviary
BZZZZZ BZZZZZ
BAD NEWS--ALL THE COLD PACKS MELTED!

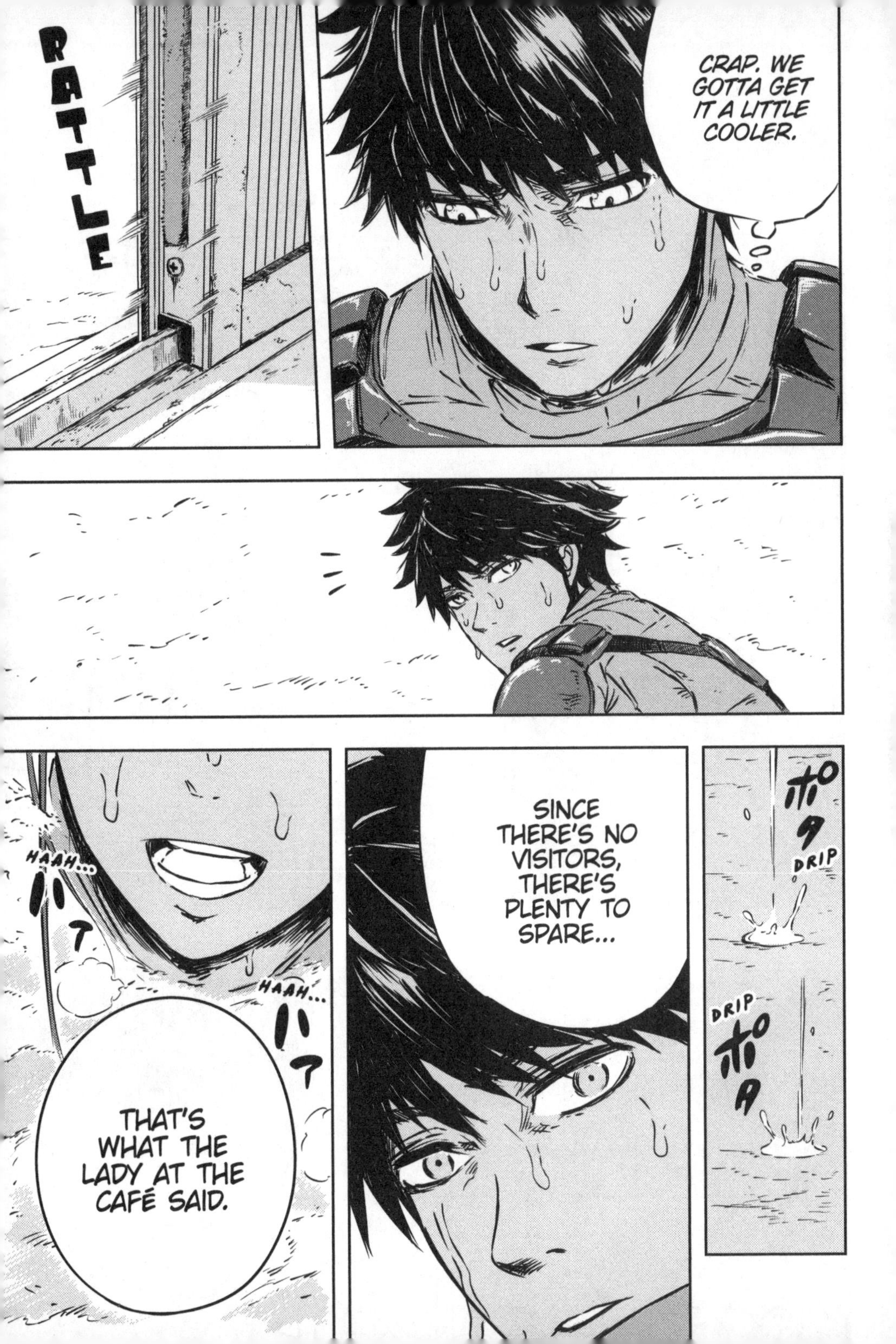
CRAP. WE GOTTA GET IT A LITTLE COOLER.
RATTLE
ポタ
DRIP
DRIP
ポタ
SINCE THERE'S NO VISITORS, THERE'S PLENTY TO SPARE...
HAAH...
ハァ
HAAH...
ハァ
THAT'S WHAT THE LADY AT THE CAFÉ SAID.

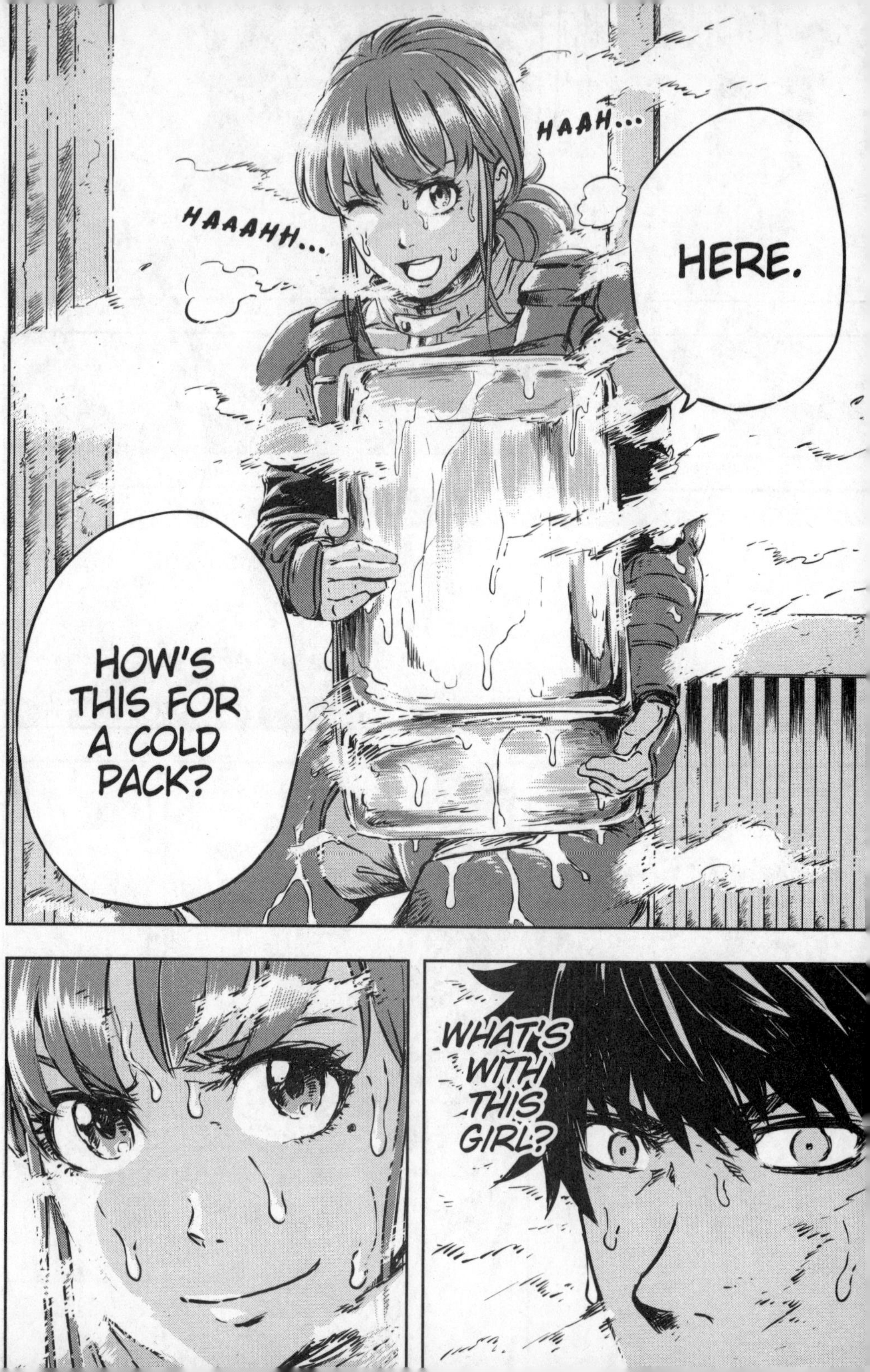
HERE.
HAAH...
HAAAHH...
HOW'S THIS FOR A COLD PACK?
WHAT'S WITH THIS GIRL?

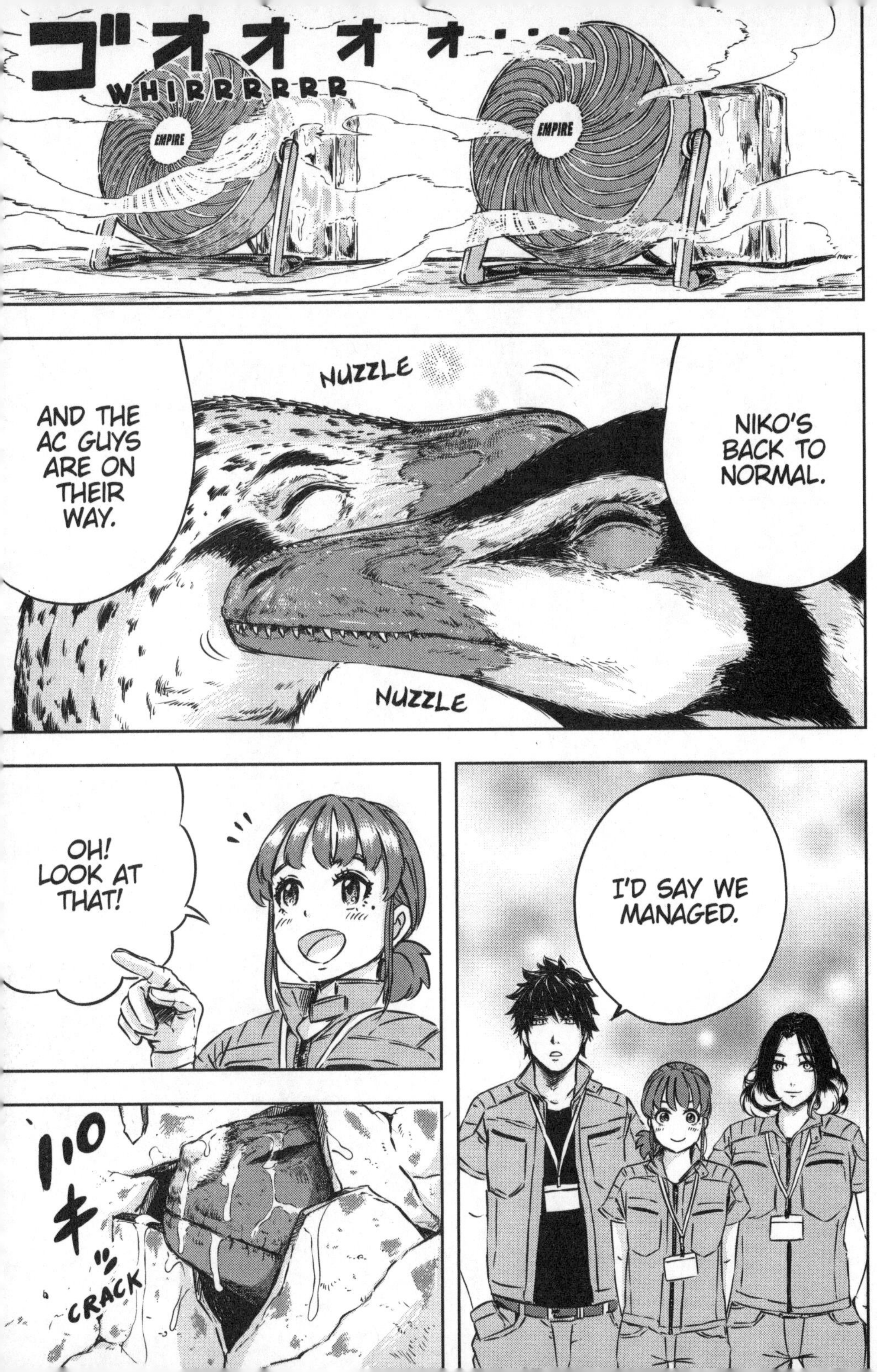
ゴオオオオ・・・
WHIRRRRRRR
NIKO'S BACK TO NORMAL.
NUZZLE
AND THE AC GUYS ARE ON THEIR WAY.
NUZZLE
I'D SAY WE MANAGED.
OH! LOOK AT THAT!
パキッ
CRACK

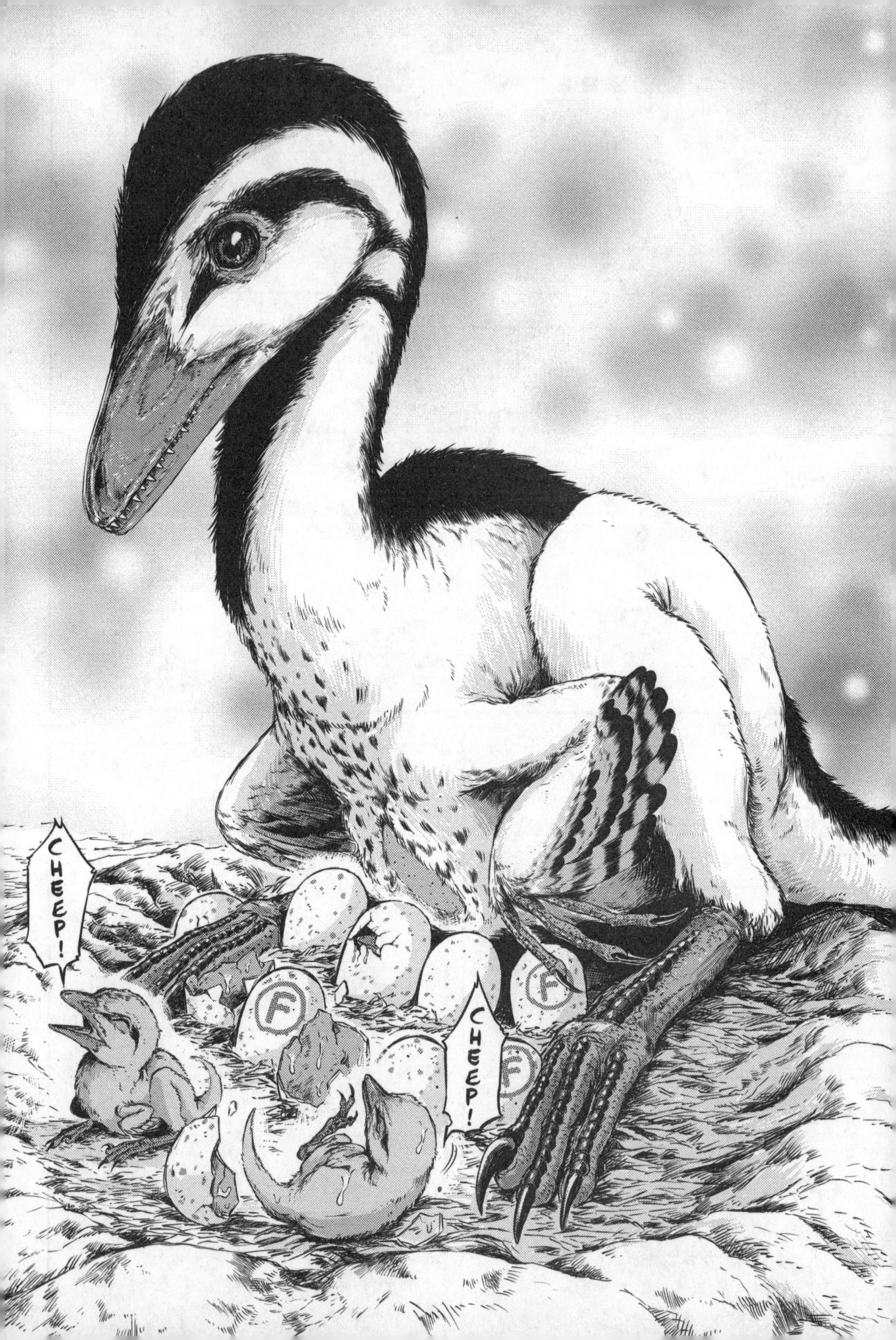
CHEEP!
CHEEP!

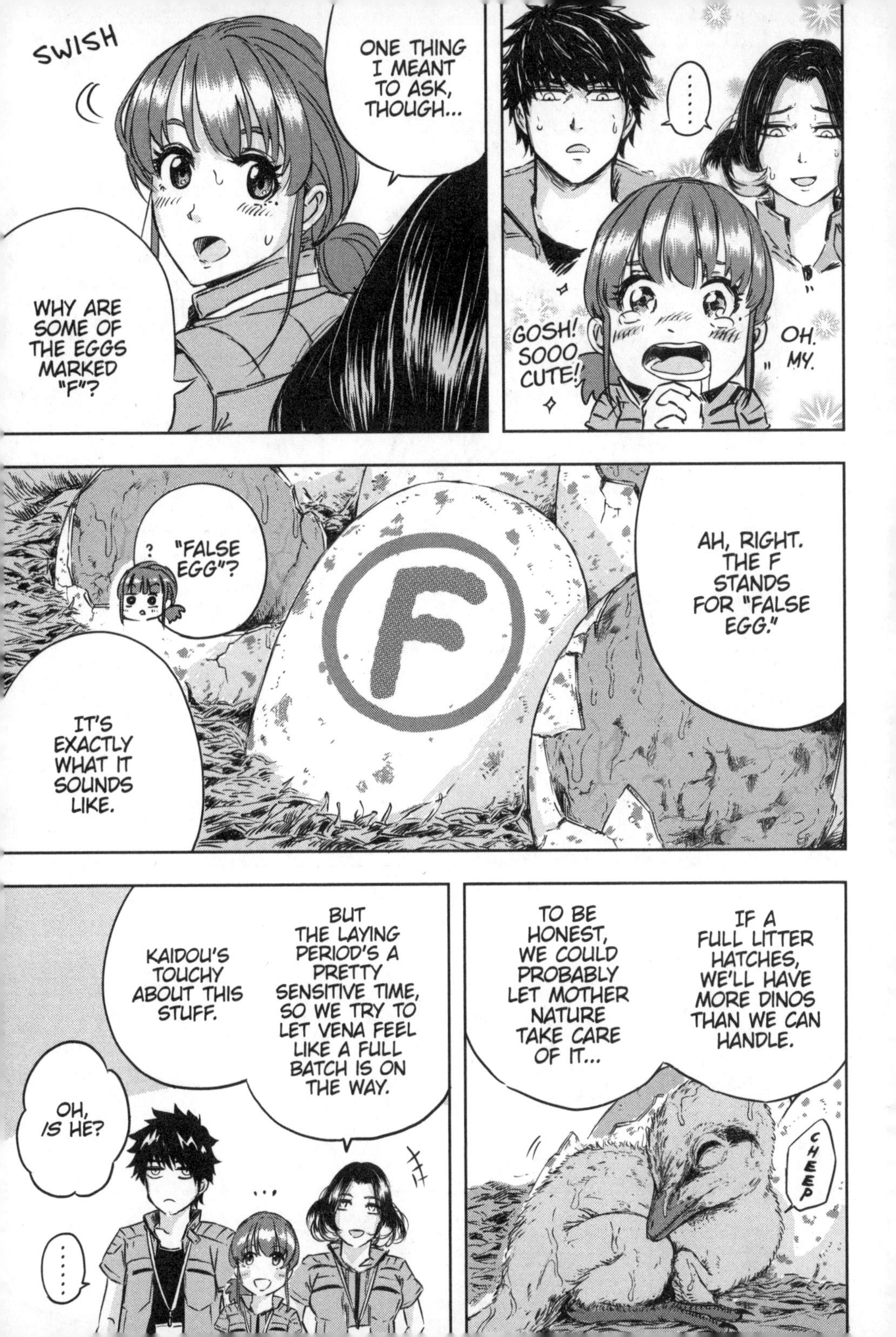
......
GOSH! SOOO CUTE!
OH. MY.
SWISH
ONE THING I MEANT TO ASK, THOUGH...
WHY ARE SOME OF THE EGGS MARKED "F"?
AH, RIGHT. THE F STANDS FOR "FALSE EGG."
"FALSE EGG"?
IT'S EXACTLY WHAT IT SOUNDS LIKE.
IF A FULL LITTER HATCHES, WE'LL HAVE MORE DINOS THAN WE CAN HANDLE.
TO BE HONEST, WE COULD PROBABLY LET MOTHER NATURE TAKE CARE OF IT...
CHEEP
BUT THE LAYING PERIOD'S A PRETTY SENSITIVE TIME, SO WE TRY TO LET VENA FEEL LIKE A FULL BATCH IS ON THE WAY.
KAIDOU'S TOUCHY ABOUT THIS STUFF.
OH, IS HE?
...
......

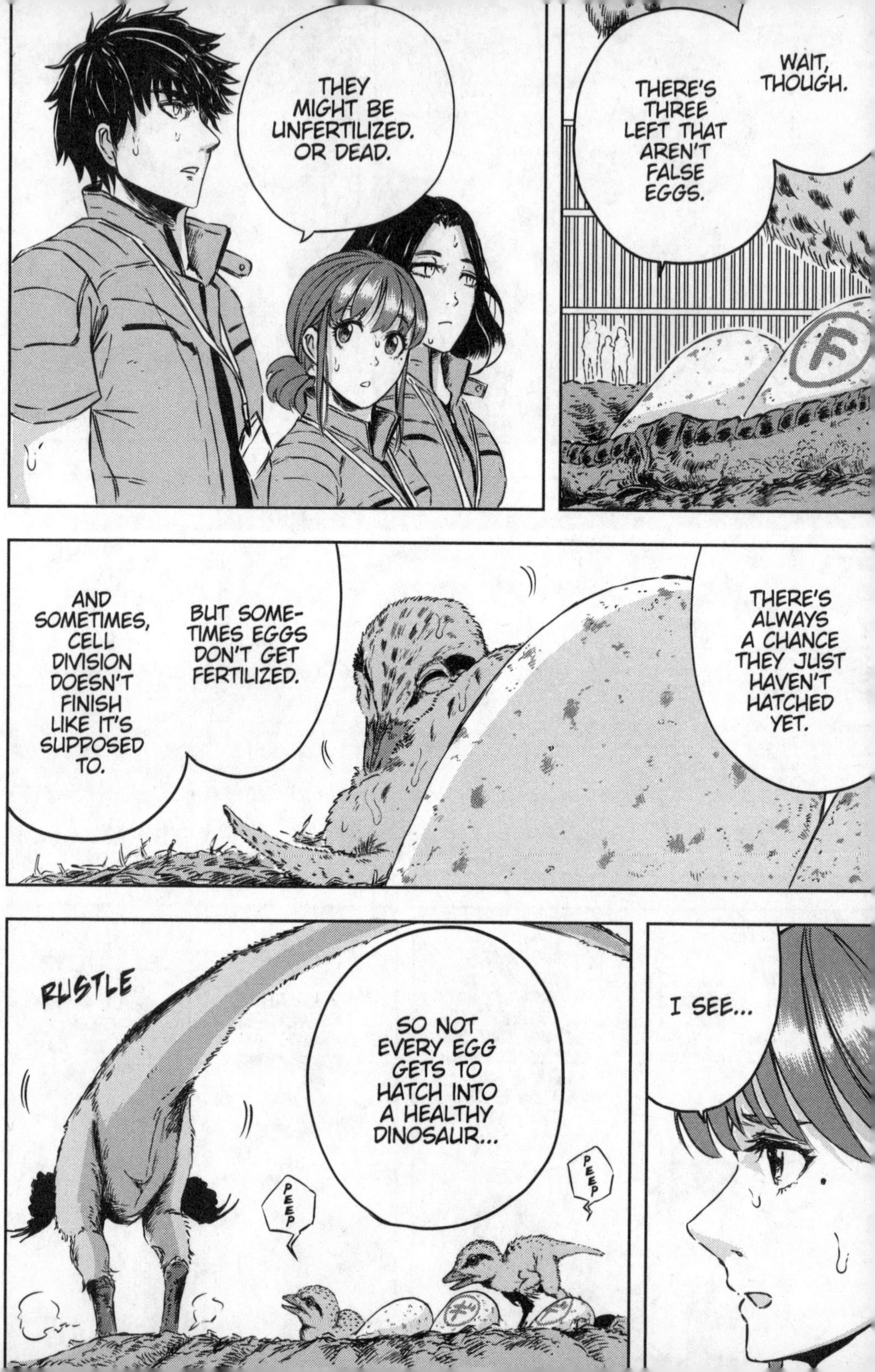
WAIT, THOUGH.
THERE'S THREE LEFT THAT AREN'T FALSE EGGS.
THEY MIGHT BE UNFERTILIZED. OR DEAD.
THERE'S ALWAYS A CHANCE THEY JUST HAVEN'T HATCHED YET.
BUT SOME-TIMES EGGS DON'T GET FERTILIZED.
AND SOMETIMES, CELL DIVISION DOESN'T FINISH LIKE IT'S SUPPOSED TO.
I SEE...
PEEP
SO NOT EVERY EGG GETS TO HATCH INTO A HEALTHY DINOSAUR...
PEEP
RUSTLE

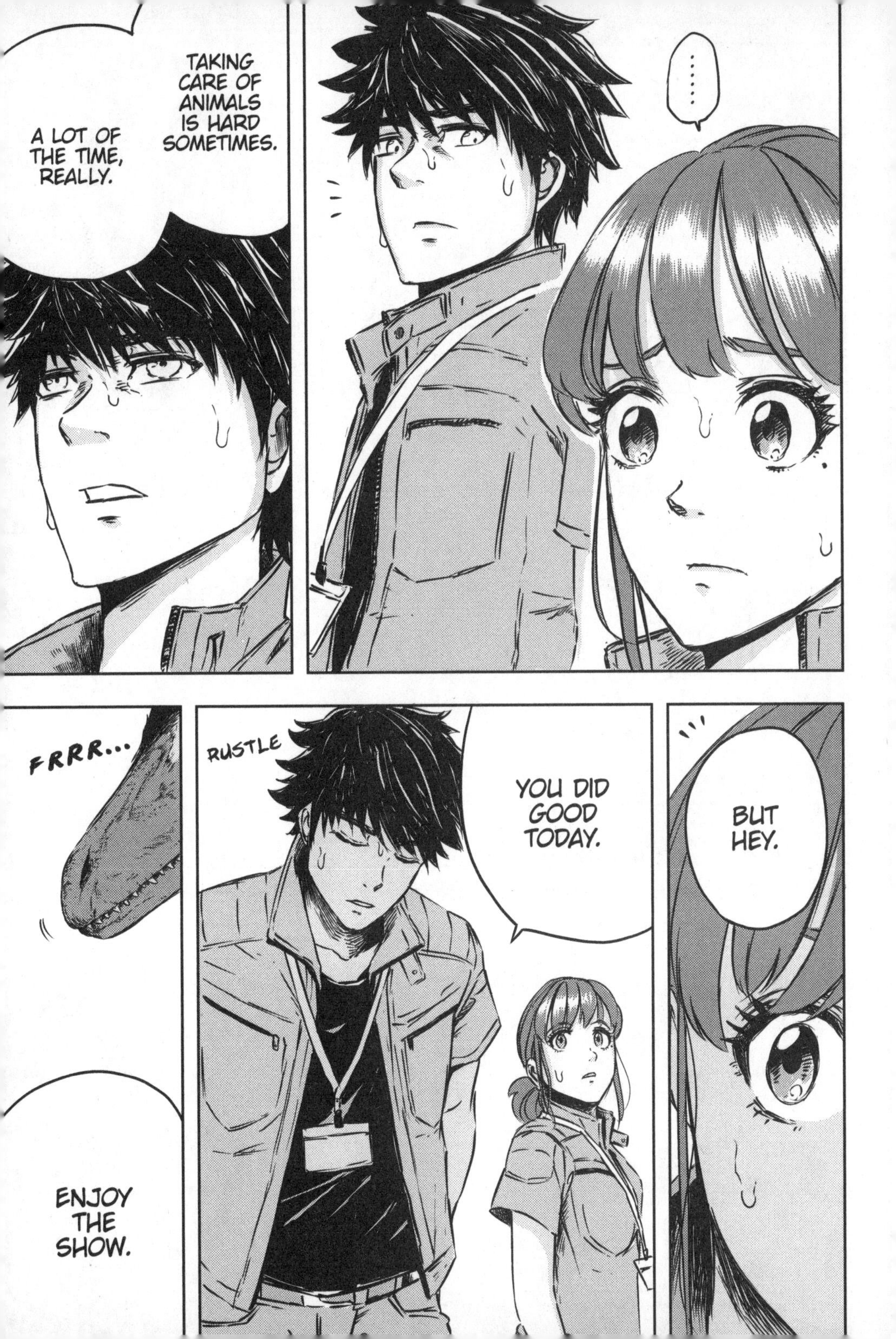
……
TAKING CARE OF ANIMALS IS HARD SOMETIMES.
A LOT OF THE TIME, REALLY.
BUT HEY.
YOU DID GOOD TODAY.
RUSTLE
FRRR...
ENJOY THE SHOW.

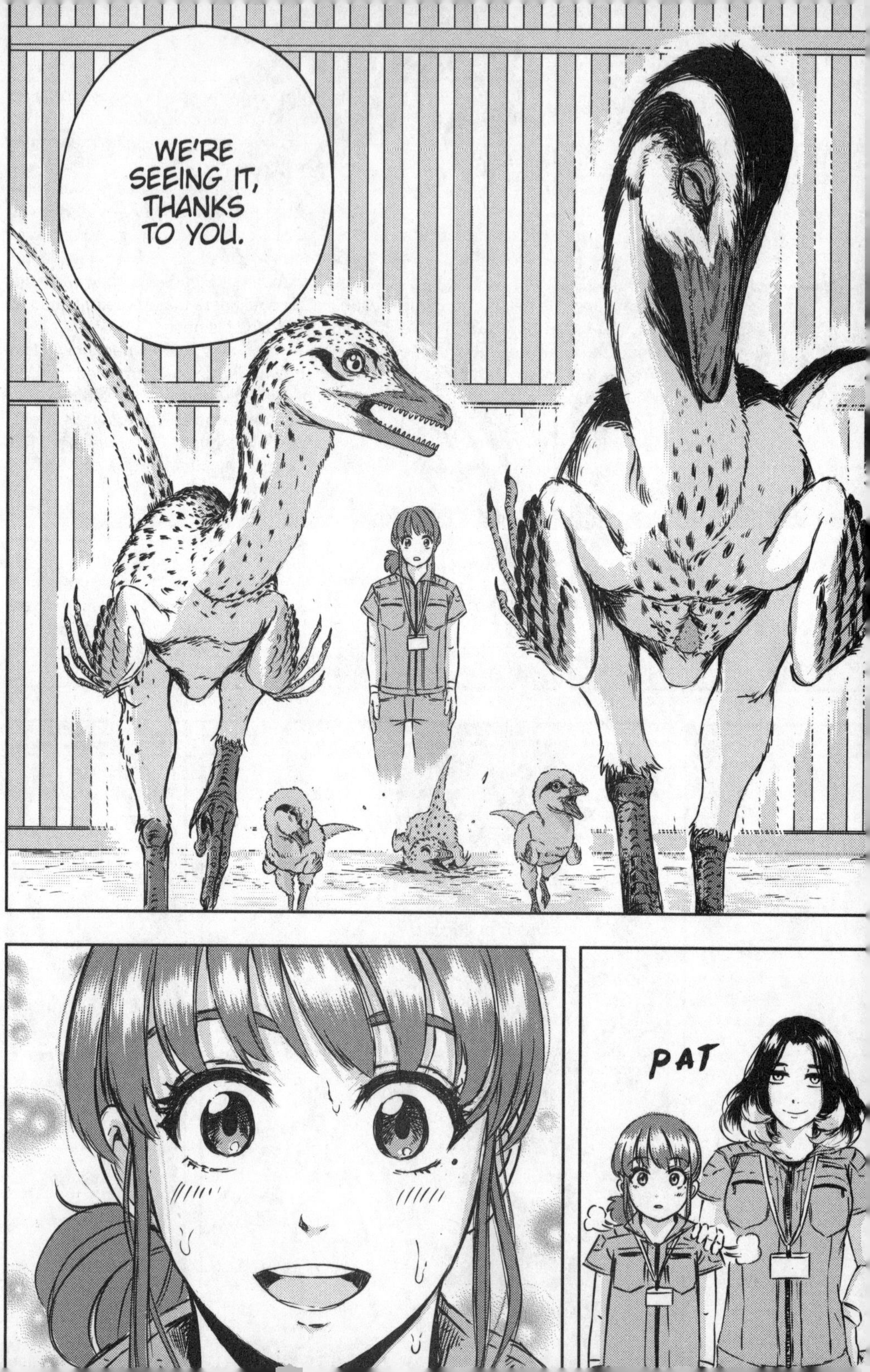
WE'RE SEEING IT, THANKS TO YOU.
PAT

Dr. Dino's Lab Log

FILE. 02 Finer Points of *Troodon* Hatching

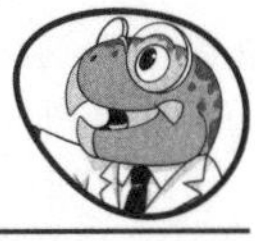

Take a look a few pages back, where the baby *Troodon* is born. Notice the little protrusion on the tip of its nose? From birds to alligators, lots of animals hatch from eggs with hard shells. The brand-new babies have to knock against the shell from the inside to break out. To do that, many of them use something called an "egg tooth." That's what you see on the baby *Troodon*! The egg tooth pops right off shortly after the hatching process, so you only ever see it on the newest of newborns.

Some birds, like chickens and ducks, start walking on their own immediately after they hatch. We call these *precocial*. Others, like sparrows and cuckoos, can't leave their nests at all for quite a while after they're born, and rely on their parents to bring them food. We call them *altricial*.

The key difference between precocial and altricial birds seems to be that the skeletons of precocial birds develop more fully while they're still in the embryonic stage—growing and waiting to be born inside the egg. Eggs that suggest that troodontid embryos had considerably developed skeletons have been reported. This tells us that *Troodons* were most likely precocial, and thus able to walk around on their own very shortly after hatching.

We have yet to discover a complete skeletal specimen of a *Troodon* itself. However, we *have* found several remarkably well-preserved fossils of its close relatives in the troodontids. These *Troodon* cousins are fairly unique among dinosaurs in that their eyes are positioned quite far to the fronts of their faces. That means they probably had excellent depth perception! Looking at a troodontid head-on, you could probably make proper eye contact!

In the chapter you just read, our dinokeepers put blinders over Niko's eyes. If they'd simply covered his eyes with a blindfold, Niko could probably have still seen something out of gaps to the front. That's why they needed a special set of blinders that were contoured to fit snugly around his head.

You may also remember how Niko struggled when Suzume straddled him to hold him still. Troodontids had sturdier ribs and breastbones than *Giganotosaurus* did, but they're still thought to be weaker than modern birds' skeletal structures. Putting pressure on a *Troodon's* chest to hold it down presents a risk of breaking its ribs. On the other hand, though, evidence suggests that *Troodons* had relatively sturdy pelvises. That's why Suzume tried to hold herself in a difficult half-seated position to hold him down with her weight. Remember how she wobbled and struggled? You'd probably have to be pretty strong to be a dinokeeper!

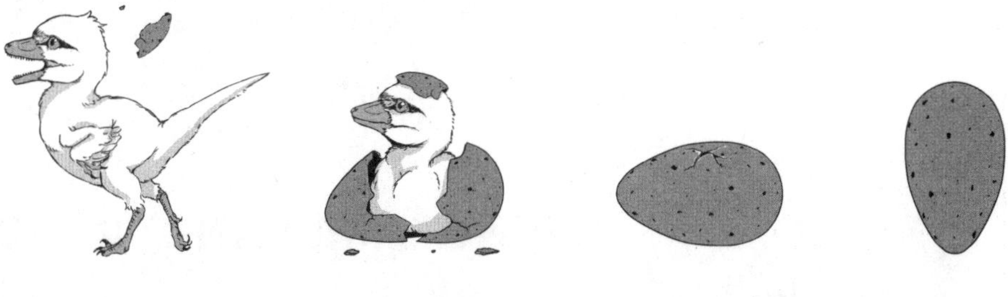

DINOSAUR SANCTUARY

CHAPTER 3 A PLACE FOR MASARU, PART 1

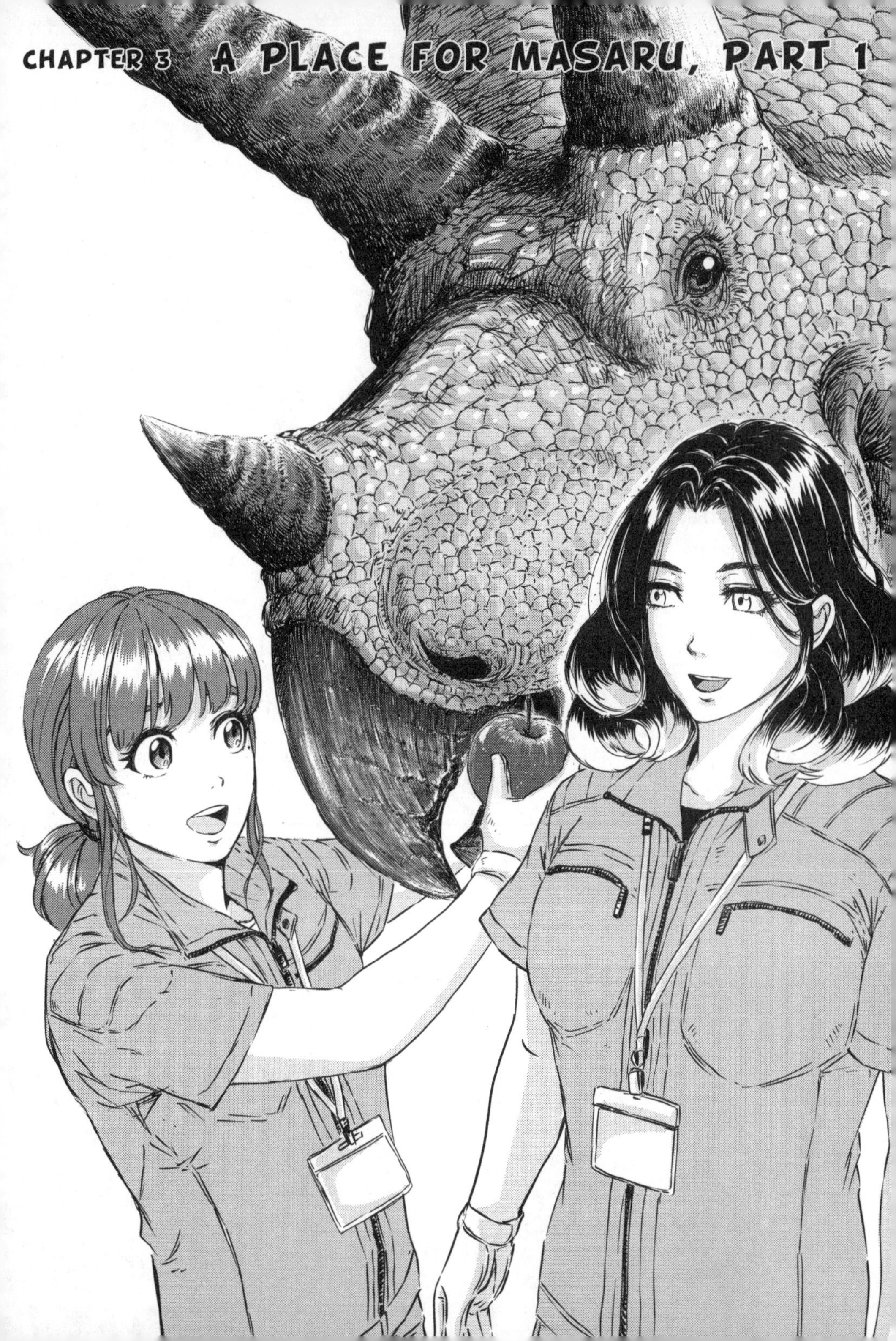

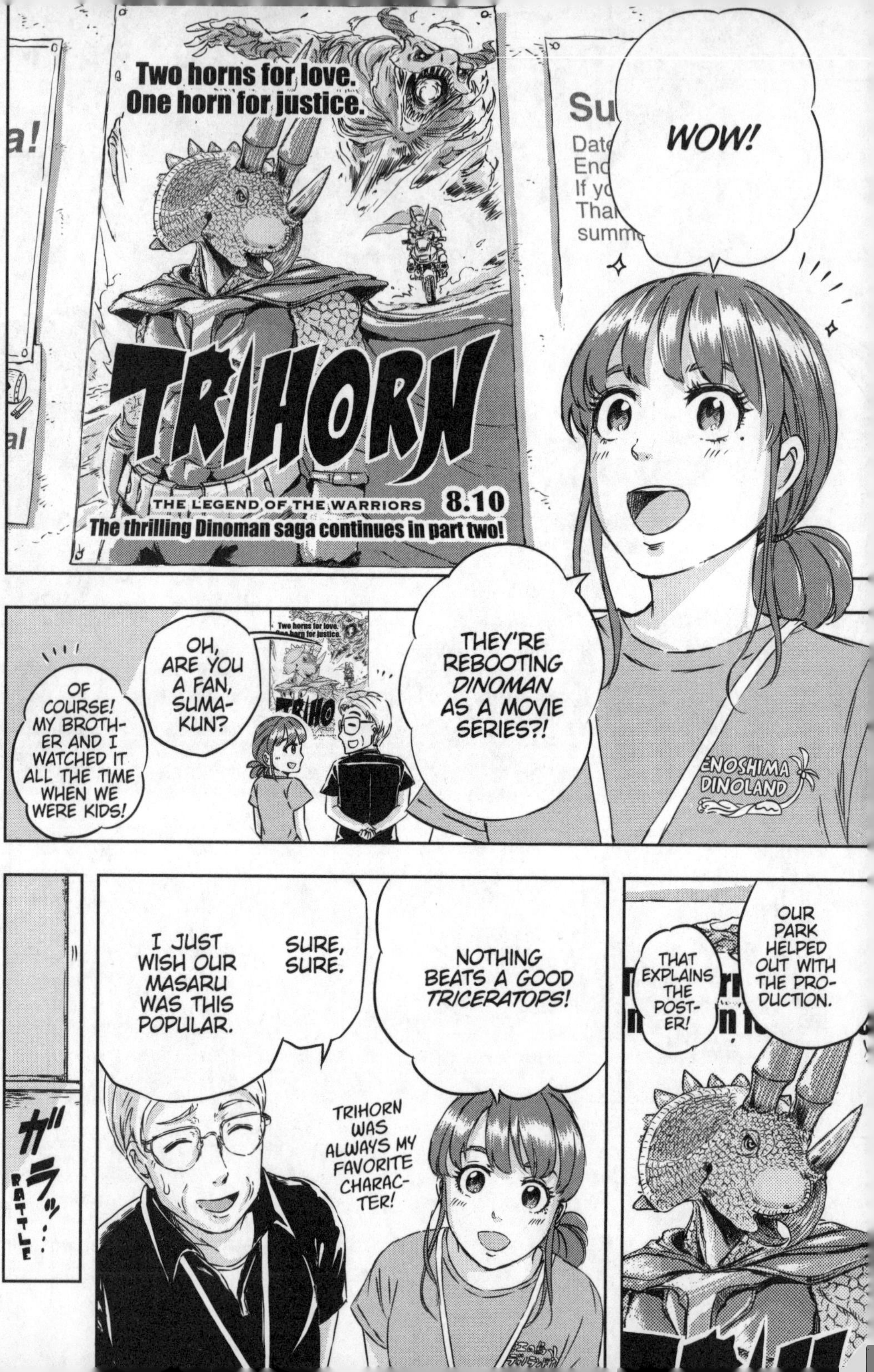
WOW!
Two horns for love. One horn for justice.
TRIHORN
THE LEGEND OF THE WARRIORS
8.10
The thrilling Dinoman saga continues in part two!
THEY'RE REBOOTING *DINOMAN* AS A MOVIE SERIES?!
ENOSHIMA DINOLAND
OH, ARE YOU A FAN, SUMA-KUN?
OF COURSE! MY BROTHER AND I WATCHED IT ALL THE TIME WHEN WE WERE KIDS!
OUR PARK HELPED OUT WITH THE PRODUCTION.
THAT EXPLAINS THE POSTER!
NOTHING BEATS A GOOD *TRICERATOPS*!
TRIHORN WAS ALWAYS MY FAVORITE CHARACTER!
SURE, SURE.
I JUST WISH OUR MASARU WAS THIS POPULAR.
RATTLE

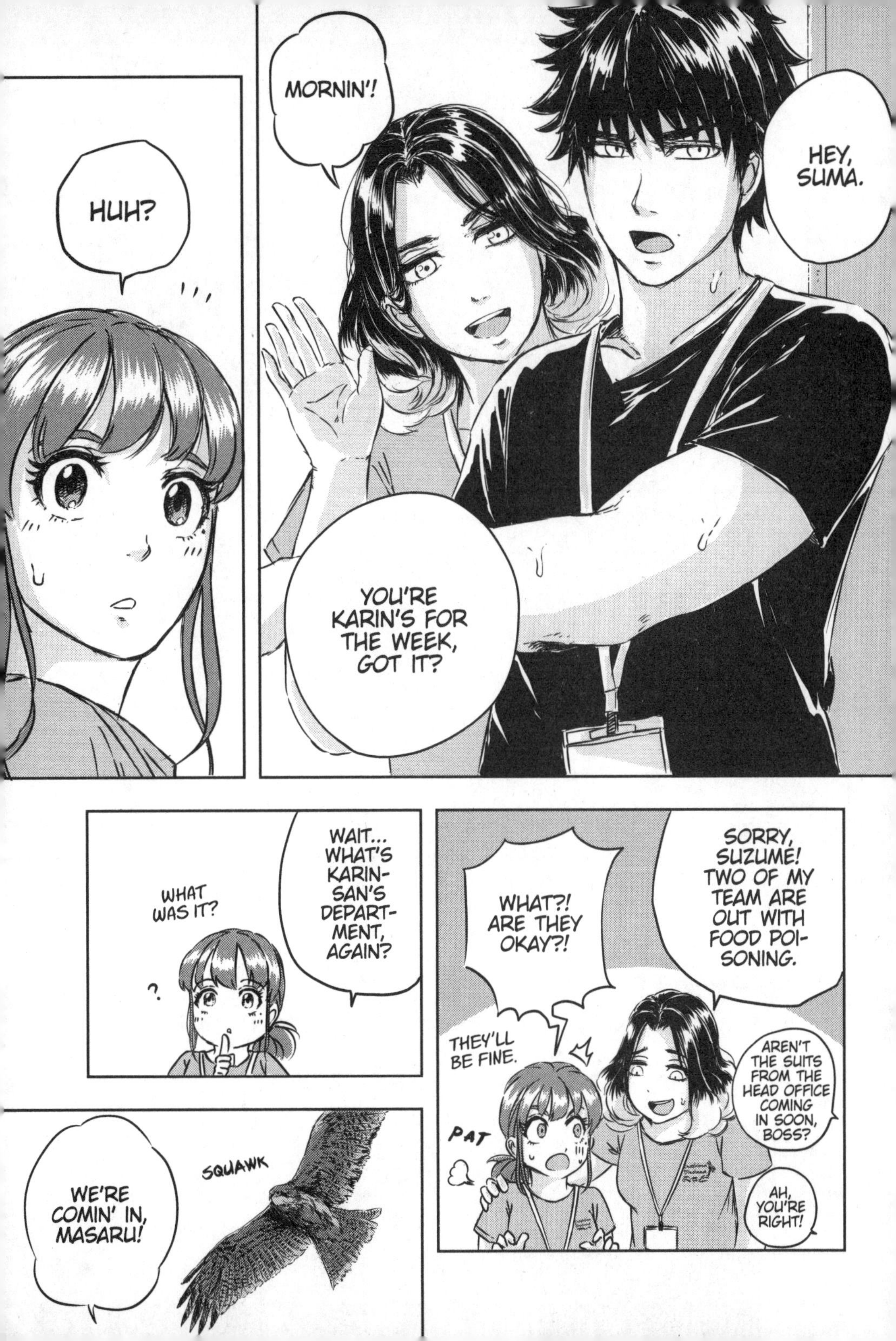
HEY, SUMA.
MORNIN'!
YOU'RE KARIN'S FOR THE WEEK, GOT IT?
HUH?
SORRY, SUZUME! TWO OF MY TEAM ARE OUT WITH FOOD POI-SONING.
WHAT?! ARE THEY OKAY?!
THEY'LL BE FINE.
PAT
AREN'T THE SUITS FROM THE HEAD OFFICE COMING IN SOON, BOSS?
AH, YOU'RE RIGHT!
WAIT... WHAT'S KARIN-SAN'S DEPART-MENT, AGAIN?
WHAT WAS IT?
SQUAWK
WE'RE COMIN' IN, MASARU!

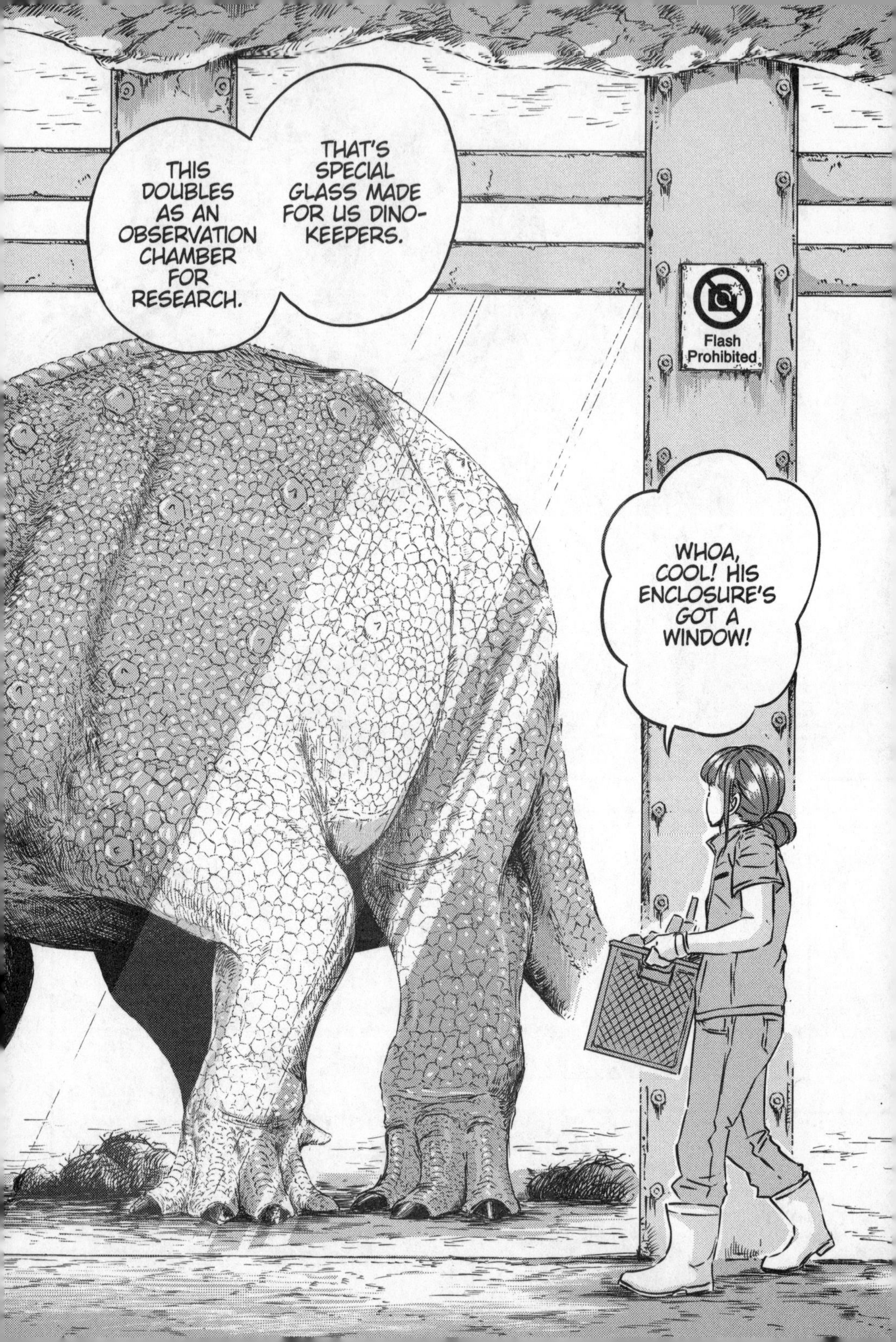

THAT'S SPECIAL GLASS MADE FOR US DINO-KEEPERS.
THIS DOUBLES AS AN OBSERVATION CHAMBER FOR RESEARCH.
Flash Prohibited
WHOA, COOL! HIS ENCLOSURE'S GOT A WINDOW!

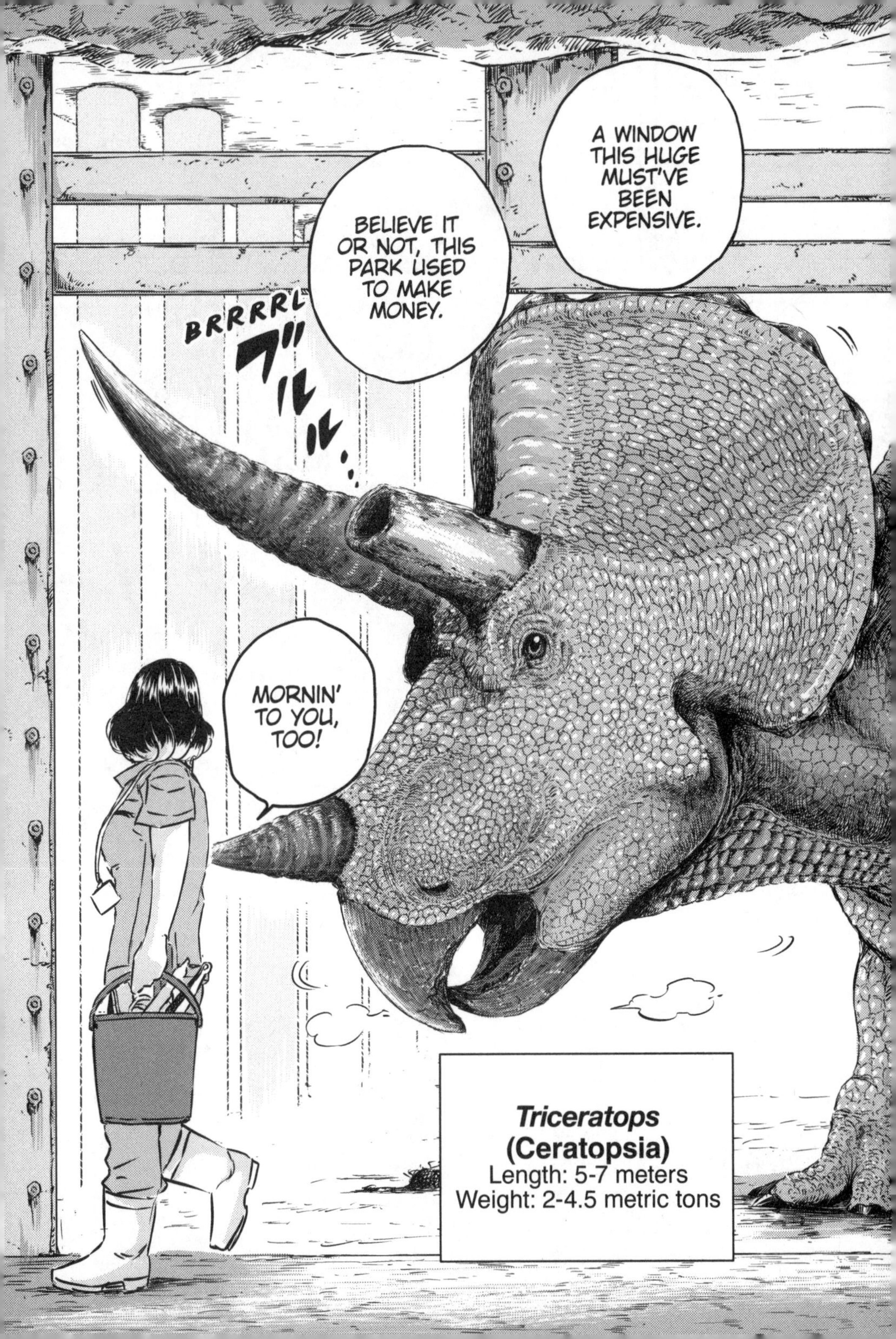
A WINDOW THIS HUGE MUST'VE BEEN EXPENSIVE.
BELIEVE IT OR NOT, THIS PARK USED TO MAKE MONEY.
BRRRRL
ブルル…
MORNIN' TO YOU, TOO!
Triceratops (Ceratopsia)
Length: 5-7 meters
Weight: 2-4.5 metric tons

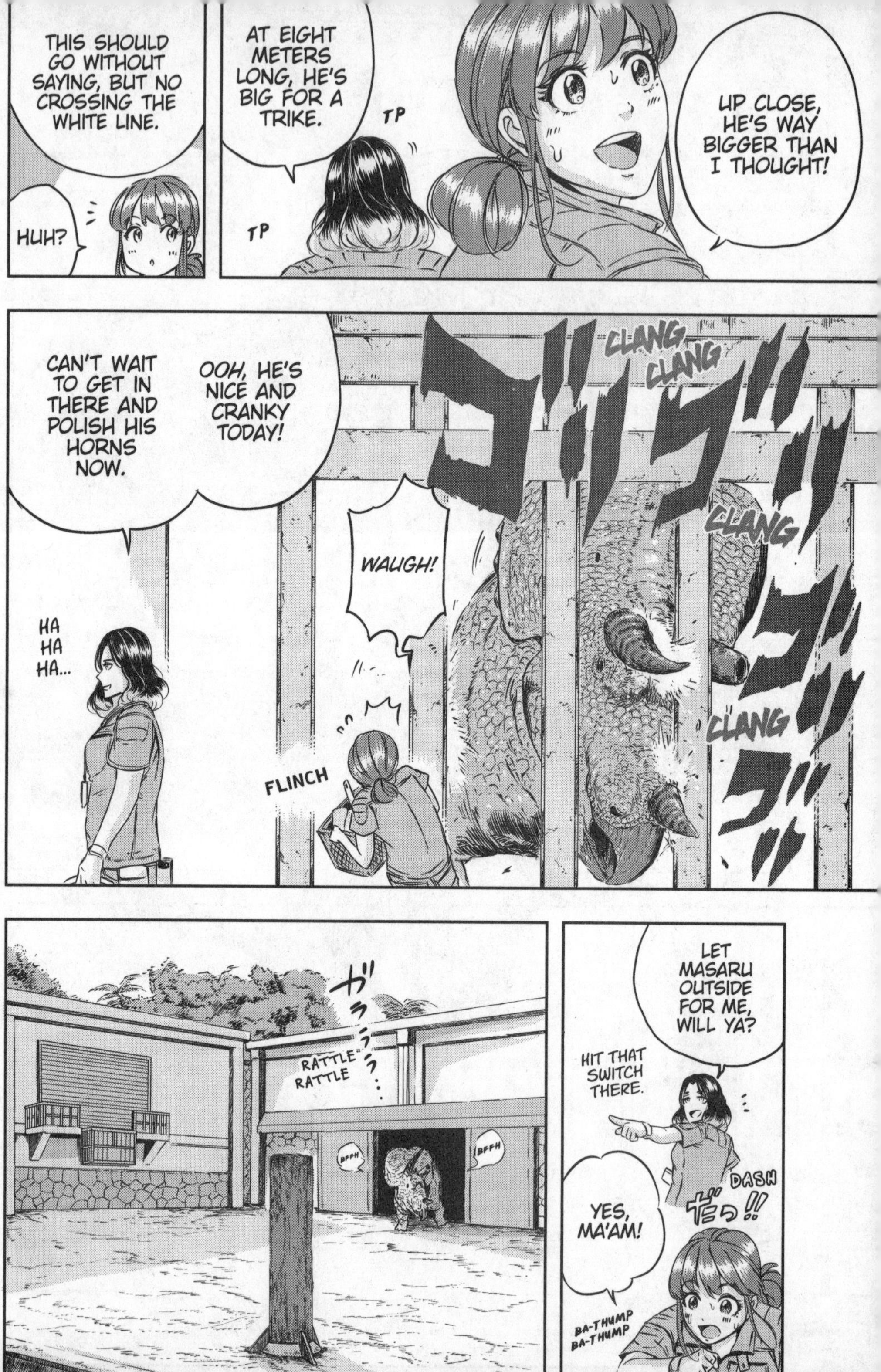
UP CLOSE, HE'S WAY BIGGER THAN I THOUGHT!
AT EIGHT METERS LONG, HE'S BIG FOR A TRIKE.
TP
TP
THIS SHOULD GO WITHOUT SAYING, BUT NO CROSSING THE WHITE LINE.
HUH?
CLANG CLANG
CLANG
CLANG
WAUGH!
FLINCH
OOH, HE'S NICE AND CRANKY TODAY!
CAN'T WAIT TO GET IN THERE AND POLISH HIS HORNS NOW.
HA HA HA...
LET MASARU OUTSIDE FOR ME, WILL YA?
HIT THAT SWITCH THERE.
DASH
YES, MA'AM!
BA-THUMP BA-THUMP
RATTLE RATTLE
BFFH
BFFH

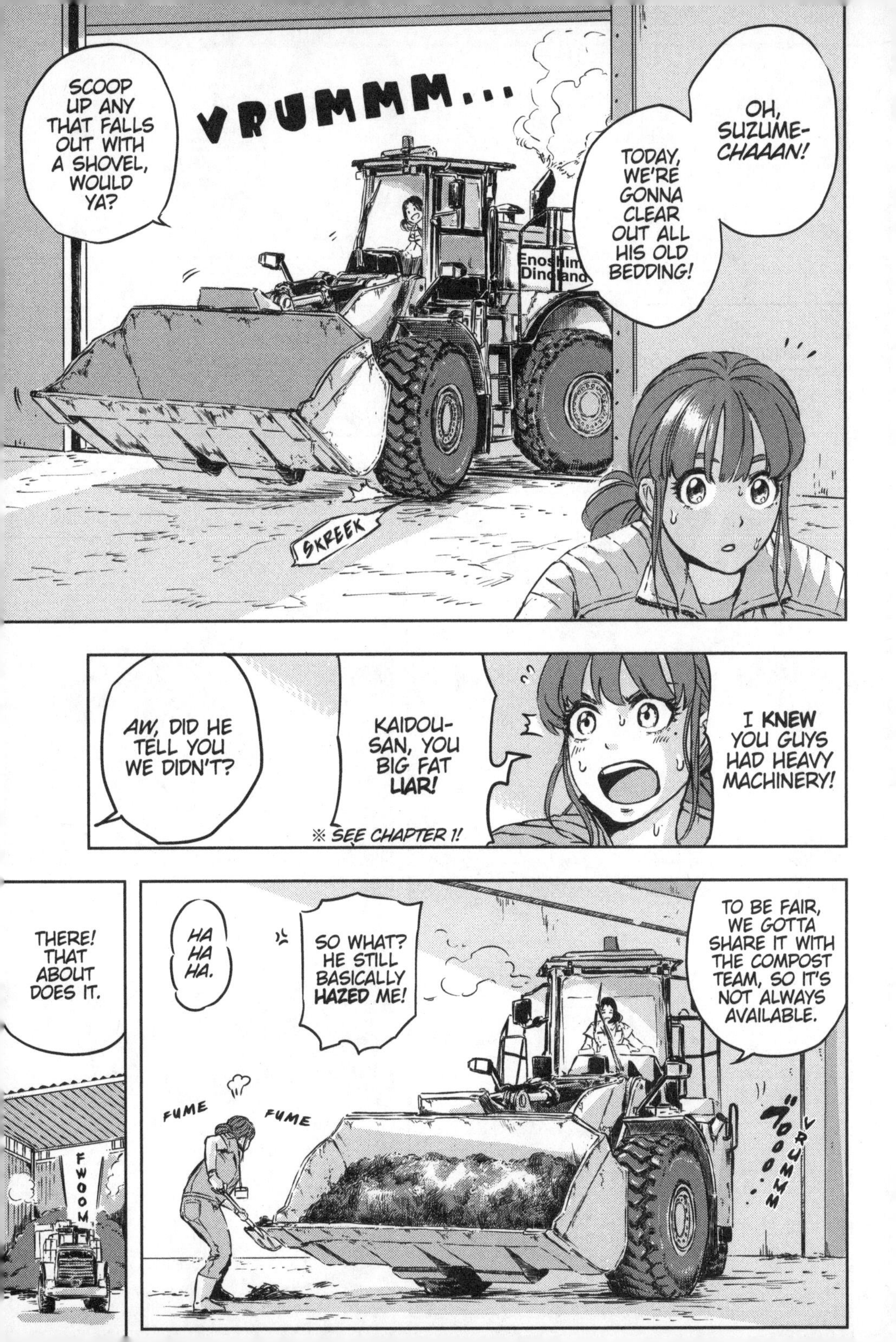
OH, SUZUME-CHAAAN!
TODAY, WE'RE GONNA CLEAR OUT ALL HIS OLD BEDDING!
VRUMMM...
SCOOP UP ANY THAT FALLS OUT WITH A SHOVEL, WOULD YA?
SKREEK
I KNEW YOU GUYS HAD HEAVY MACHINERY!
KAIDOU-SAN, YOU BIG FAT LIAR!
※ SEE CHAPTER 1!
AW, DID HE TELL YOU WE DIDN'T?
TO BE FAIR, WE GOTTA SHARE IT WITH THE COMPOST TEAM, SO IT'S NOT ALWAYS AVAILABLE.
SO WHAT? HE STILL BASICALLY HAZED ME!
HA HA HA.
FUME
FUME
THERE! THAT ABOUT DOES IT.
FWOOM

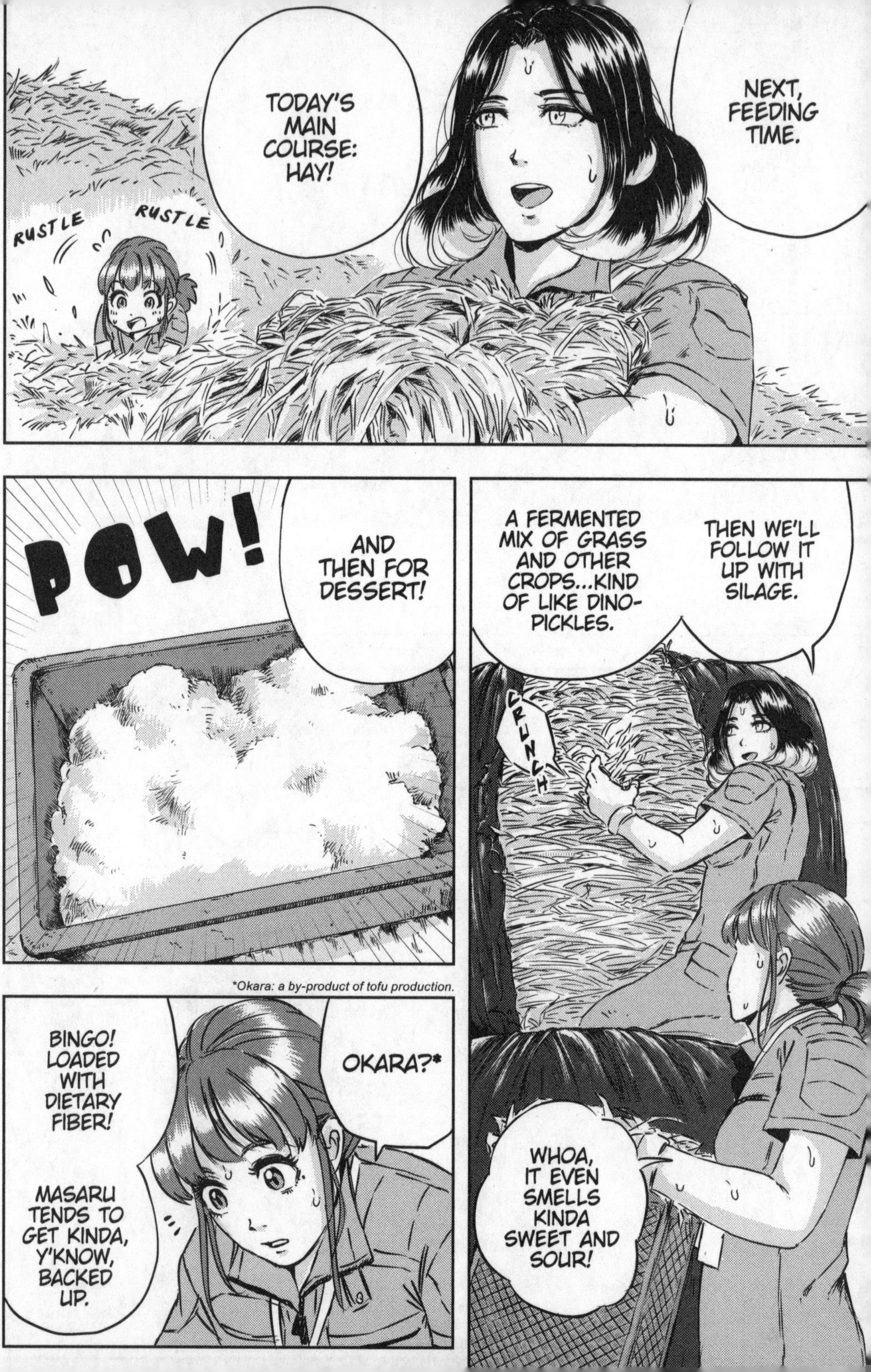
NEXT, FEEDING TIME.
TODAY'S MAIN COURSE: HAY!
RUSTLE RUSTLE
THEN WE'LL FOLLOW IT UP WITH SILAGE.
A FERMENTED MIX OF GRASS AND OTHER CROPS...KIND OF LIKE DINO-PICKLES.
CRUNCH
WHOA, IT EVEN SMELLS KINDA SWEET AND SOUR!
AND THEN FOR DESSERT!
POW!
OKARA?*
BINGO! LOADED WITH DIETARY FIBER!
MASARU TENDS TO GET KINDA, Y'KNOW, BACKED UP.
*Okara: a by-product of tofu production.

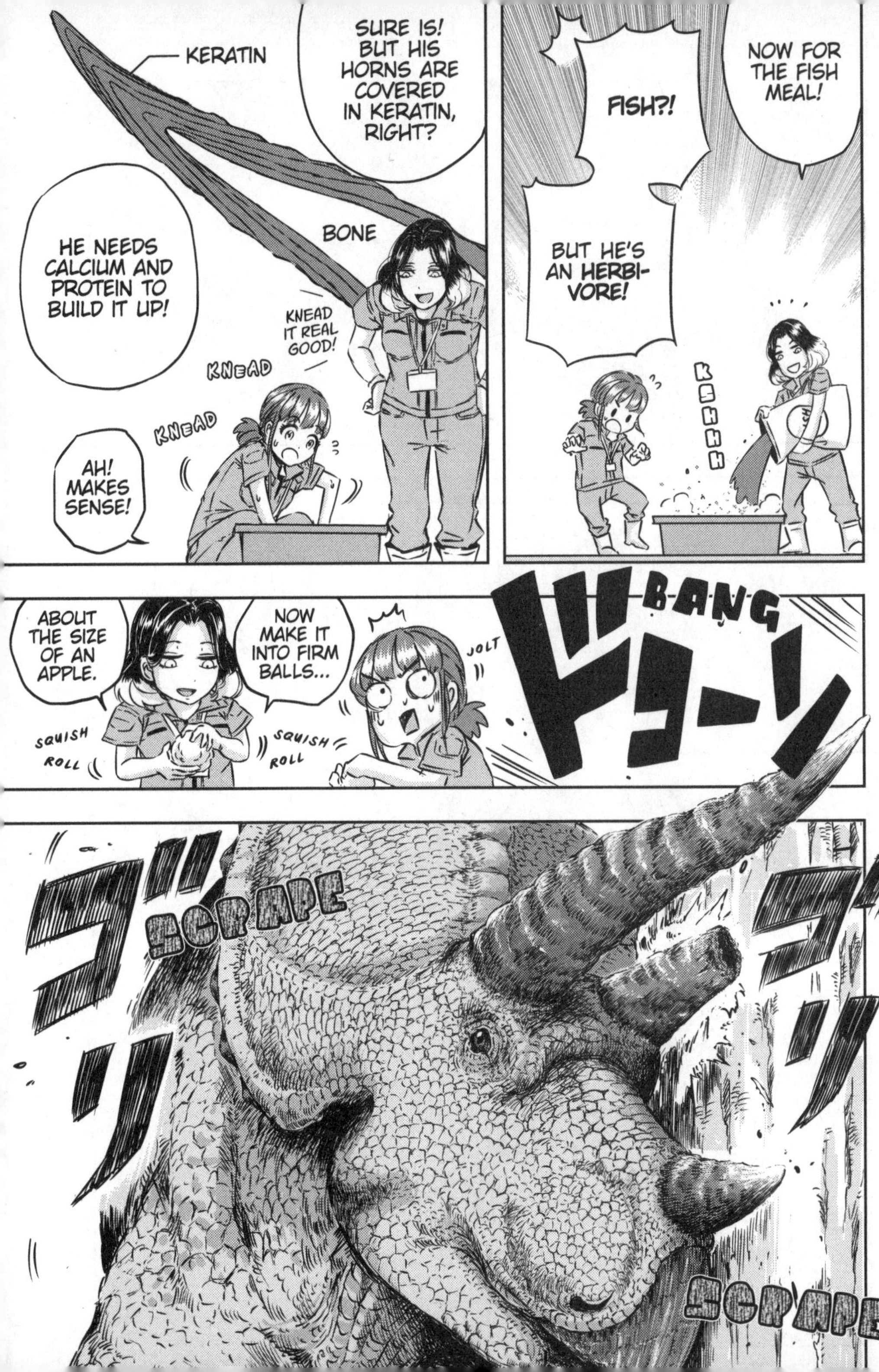
NOW FOR THE FISH MEAL!
FISH?!
BUT HE'S AN HERBIVORE!
KSHHHH
SURE IS! BUT HIS HORNS ARE COVERED IN KERATIN, RIGHT?
KERATIN
BONE
HE NEEDS CALCIUM AND PROTEIN TO BUILD IT UP!
KNEAD IT REAL GOOD!
KNEAD
KNEAD
AH! MAKES SENSE!
BANG
ドーン
JOLT
NOW MAKE IT INTO FIRM BALLS...
SQUISH
ROLL
ABOUT THE SIZE OF AN APPLE.
SQUISH
ROLL
SCRAPE
SCRAPE

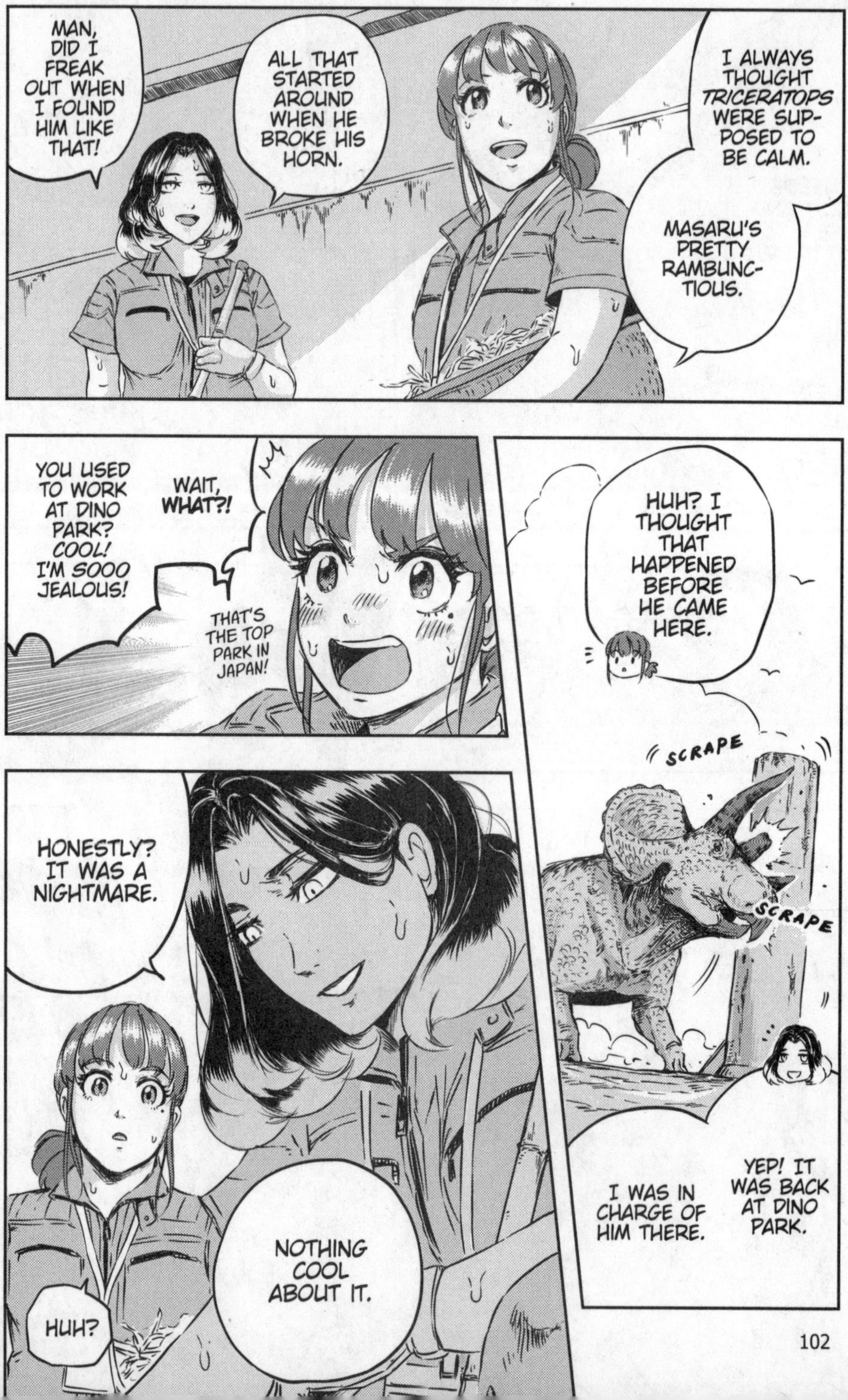
I ALWAYS THOUGHT *TRICERATOPS* WERE SUP-POSED TO BE CALM.
MASARU'S PRETTY RAMBUNC-TIOUS.
ALL THAT STARTED AROUND WHEN HE BROKE HIS HORN.
MAN, DID I FREAK OUT WHEN I FOUND HIM LIKE THAT!
HUH? I THOUGHT THAT HAPPENED BEFORE HE CAME HERE.
SCRAPE
SCRAPE
YEP! IT WAS BACK AT DINO PARK.
I WAS IN CHARGE OF HIM THERE.
WAIT, **WHAT?!**
YOU USED TO WORK AT DINO PARK? *COOL!* I'M *SOOO* JEALOUS!
THAT'S THE TOP PARK IN JAPAN!
HONESTLY? IT WAS A NIGHTMARE.
NOTHING COOL ABOUT IT.
HUH?

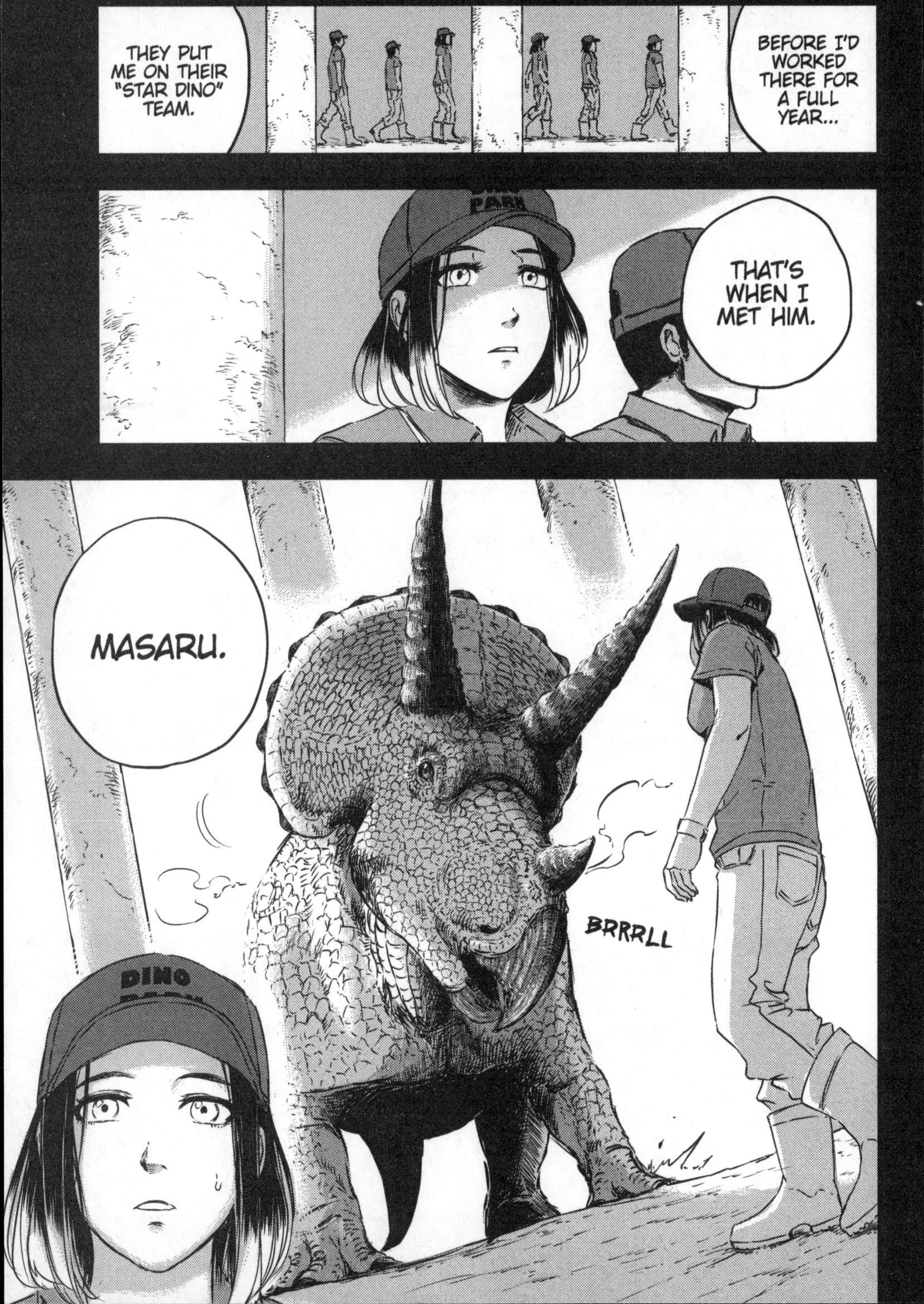
BEFORE I'D WORKED THERE FOR A FULL YEAR...
THEY PUT ME ON THEIR "STAR DINO" TEAM.
THAT'S WHEN I MET HIM.
MASARU.
BRRRLL
DINO

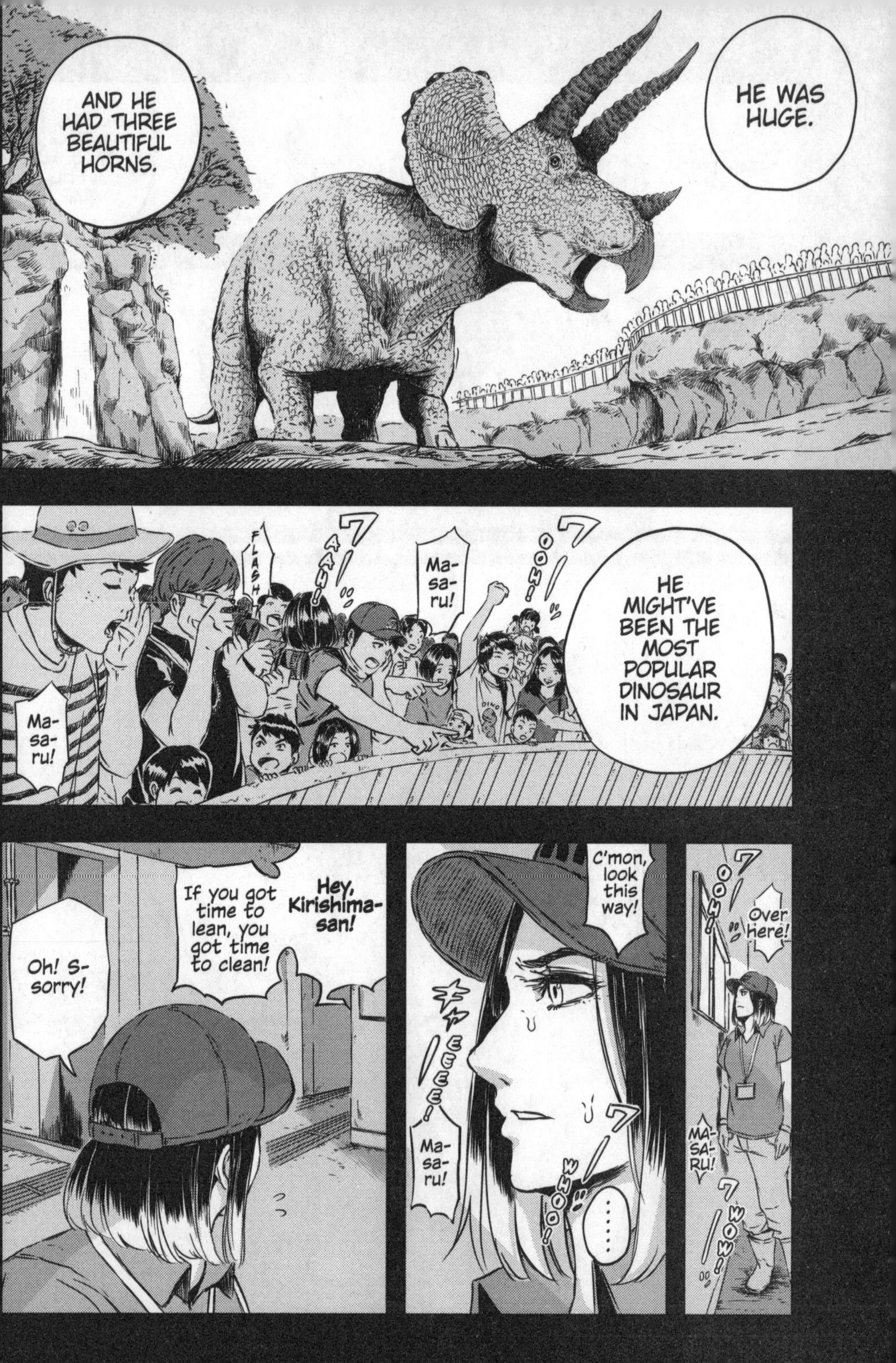
HE WAS HUGE.
AND HE HAD THREE BEAUTIFUL HORNS.
HE MIGHT'VE BEEN THE MOST POPULAR DINOSAUR IN JAPAN.
OOH!
Ma-sa-ru!
AAH!
FLASH
Ma-sa-ru!
OOH!
Over here!
MA-SA-RU!
WOW!
C'mon, look this way!
EEEE!
Ma-sa-ru!
WHOO!
......
Hey, Kirishima-san!
If you got time to lean, you got time to clean!
Oh! S-sorry!

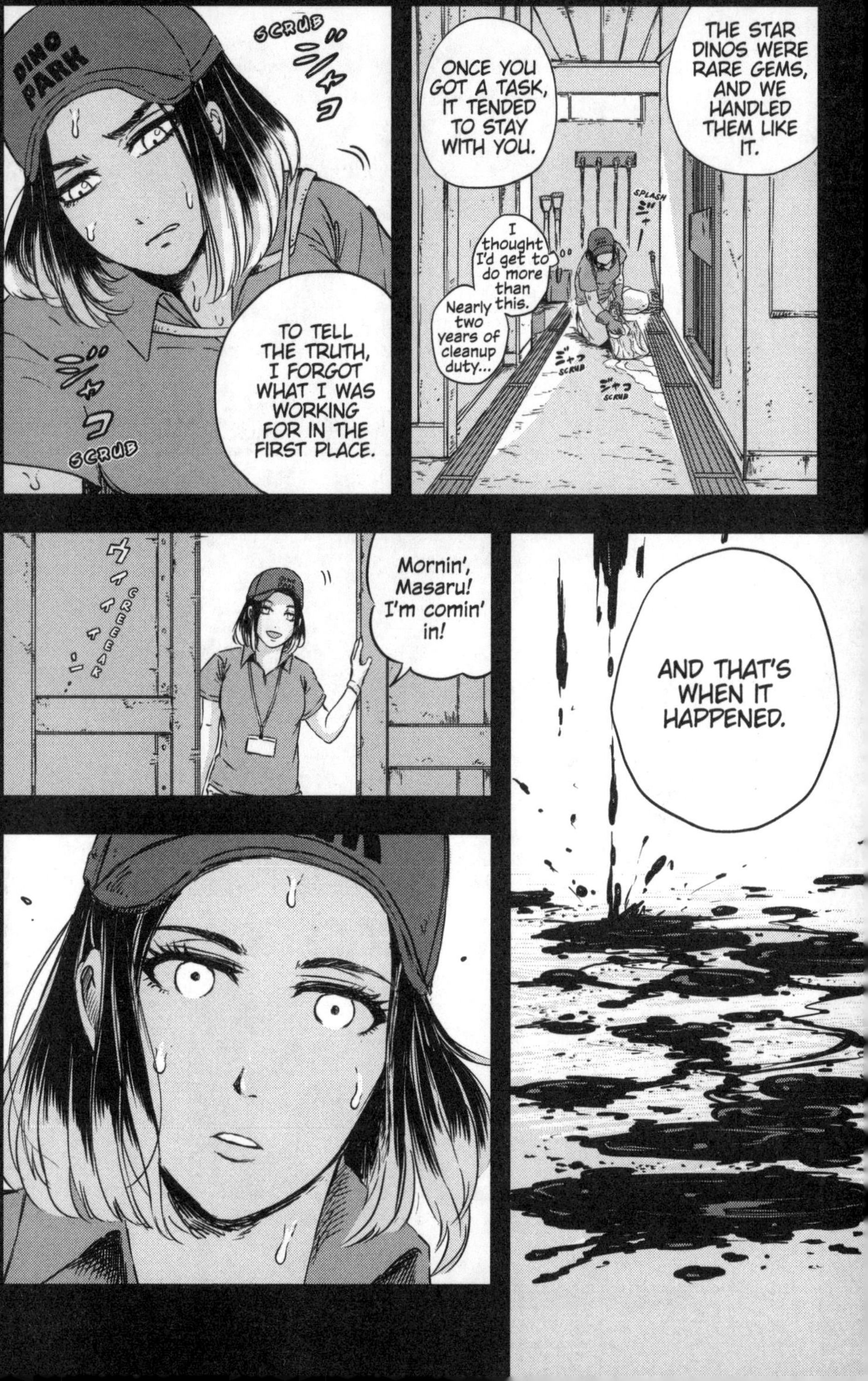
THE STAR DINOS WERE RARE GEMS, AND WE HANDLED THEM LIKE IT.
ONCE YOU GOT A TASK, IT TENDED TO STAY WITH YOU.
SPLASH
I thought I'd get to do more than this.
Nearly two years of cleanup duty...
SCRUB
SCRUB
SCRUB
TO TELL THE TRUTH, I FORGOT WHAT I WAS WORKING FOR IN THE FIRST PLACE.
SCRUB
AND THAT'S WHEN IT HAPPENED.
Mornin', Masaru! I'm comin' in!
CREEEAK

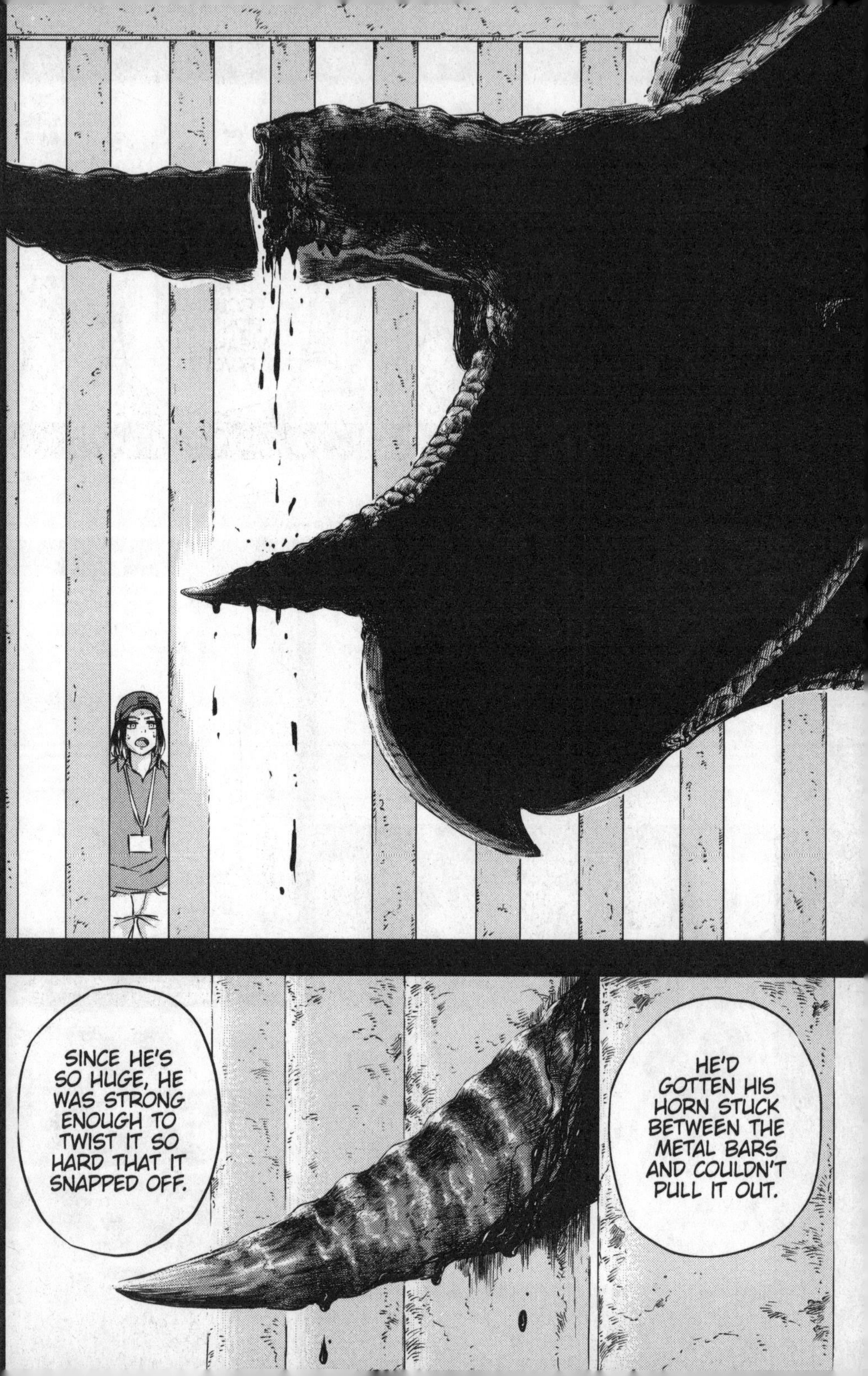
HE'D GOTTEN HIS HORN STUCK BETWEEN THE METAL BARS AND COULDN'T PULL IT OUT.
SINCE HE'S SO HUGE, HE WAS STRONG ENOUGH TO TWIST IT SO HARD THAT IT SNAPPED OFF.

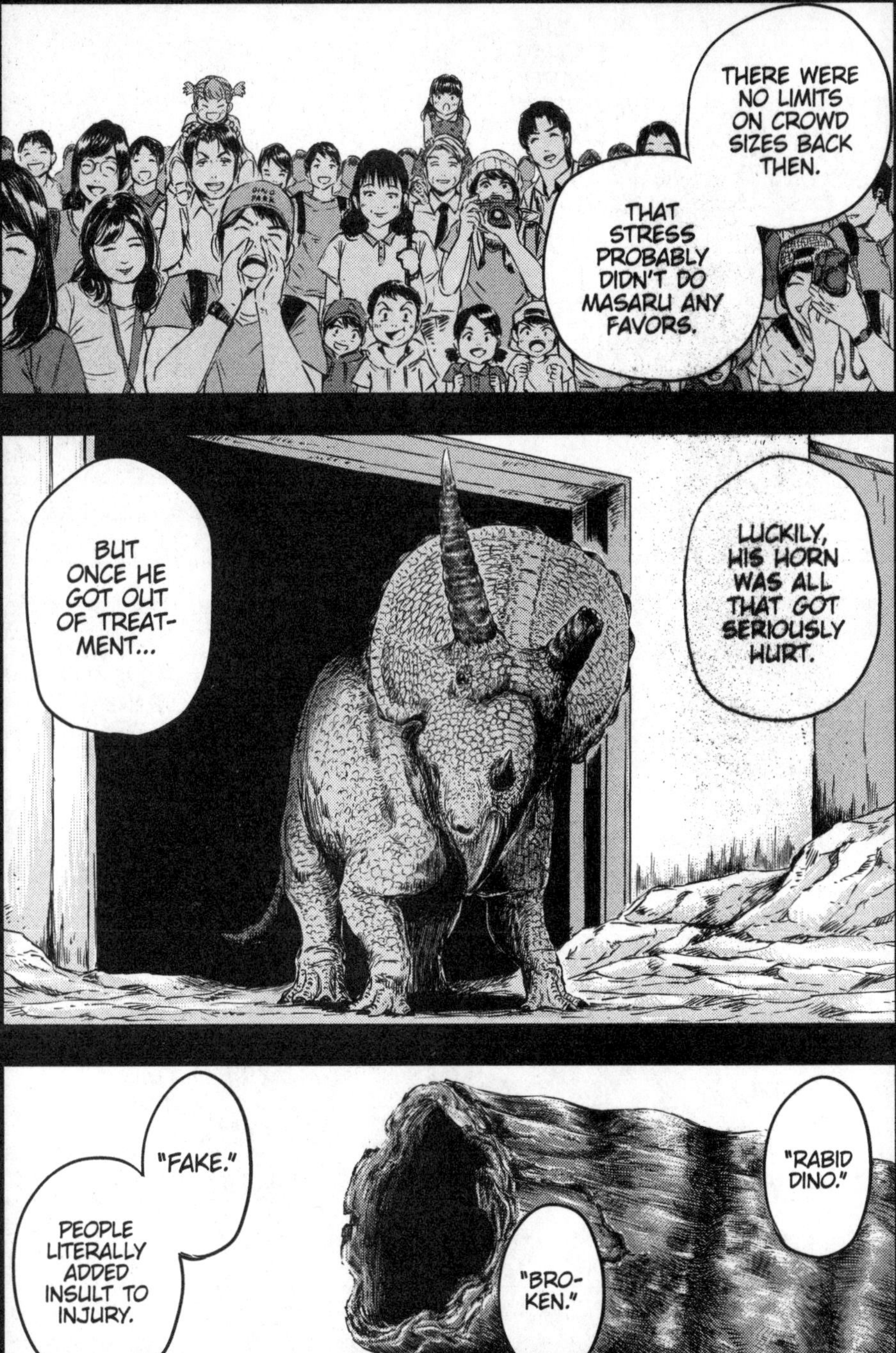
THERE WERE NO LIMITS ON CROWD SIZES BACK THEN.
THAT STRESS PROBABLY DIDN'T DO MASARU ANY FAVORS.
LUCKILY, HIS HORN WAS ALL THAT GOT SERIOUSLY HURT.
BUT ONCE HE GOT OUT OF TREAT-MENT...
"RABID DINO."
"FAKE."
"BRO-KEN."
PEOPLE LITERALLY ADDED INSULT TO INJURY.

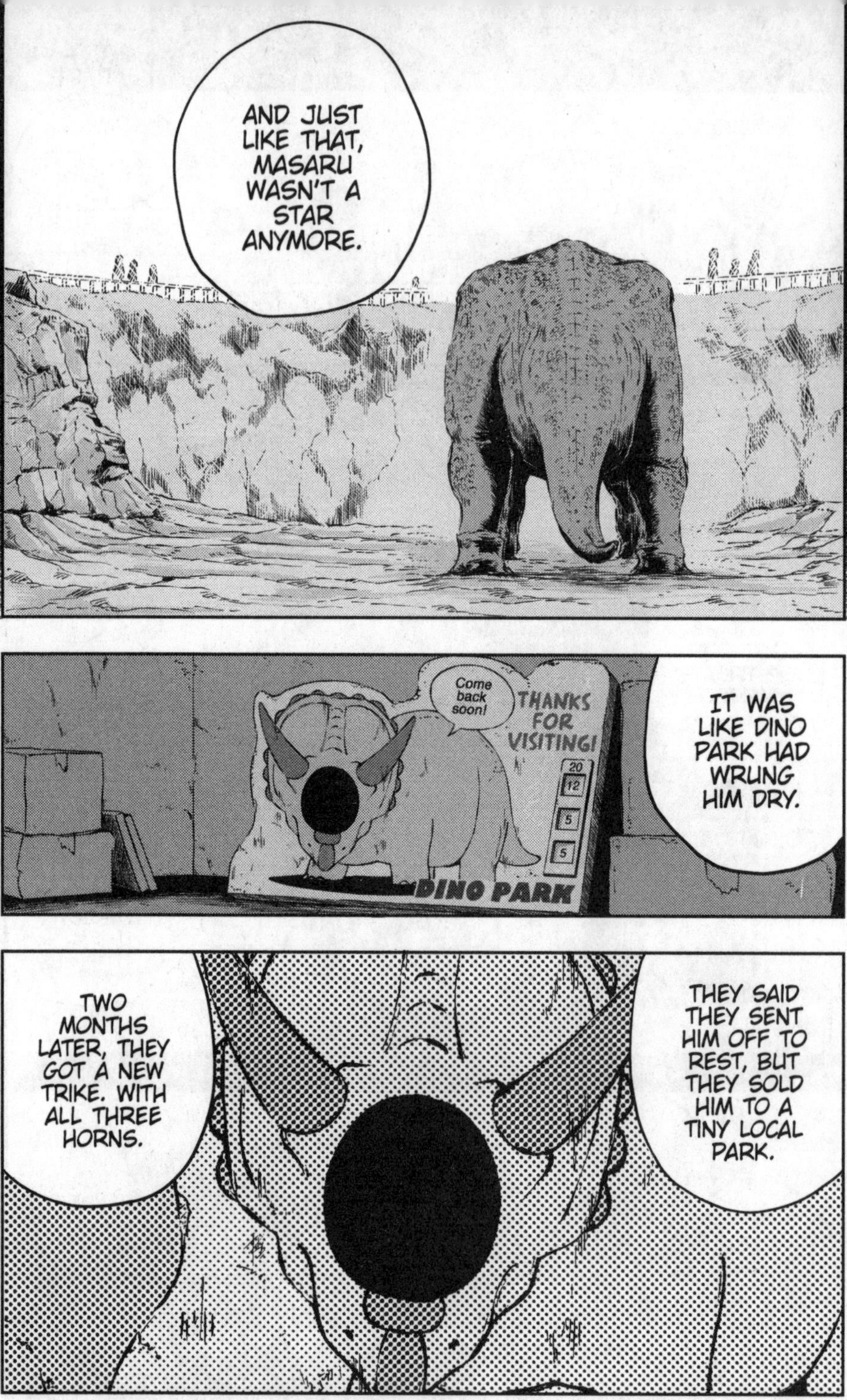
AND JUST LIKE THAT, MASARU WASN'T A STAR ANYMORE.
IT WAS LIKE DINO PARK HAD WRUNG HIM DRY.
THANKS FOR VISITING!
Come back soon!
DINO PARK
THEY SAID THEY SENT HIM OFF TO REST, BUT THEY SOLD HIM TO A TINY LOCAL PARK.
TWO MONTHS LATER, THEY GOT A NEW TRIKE. WITH ALL THREE HORNS.

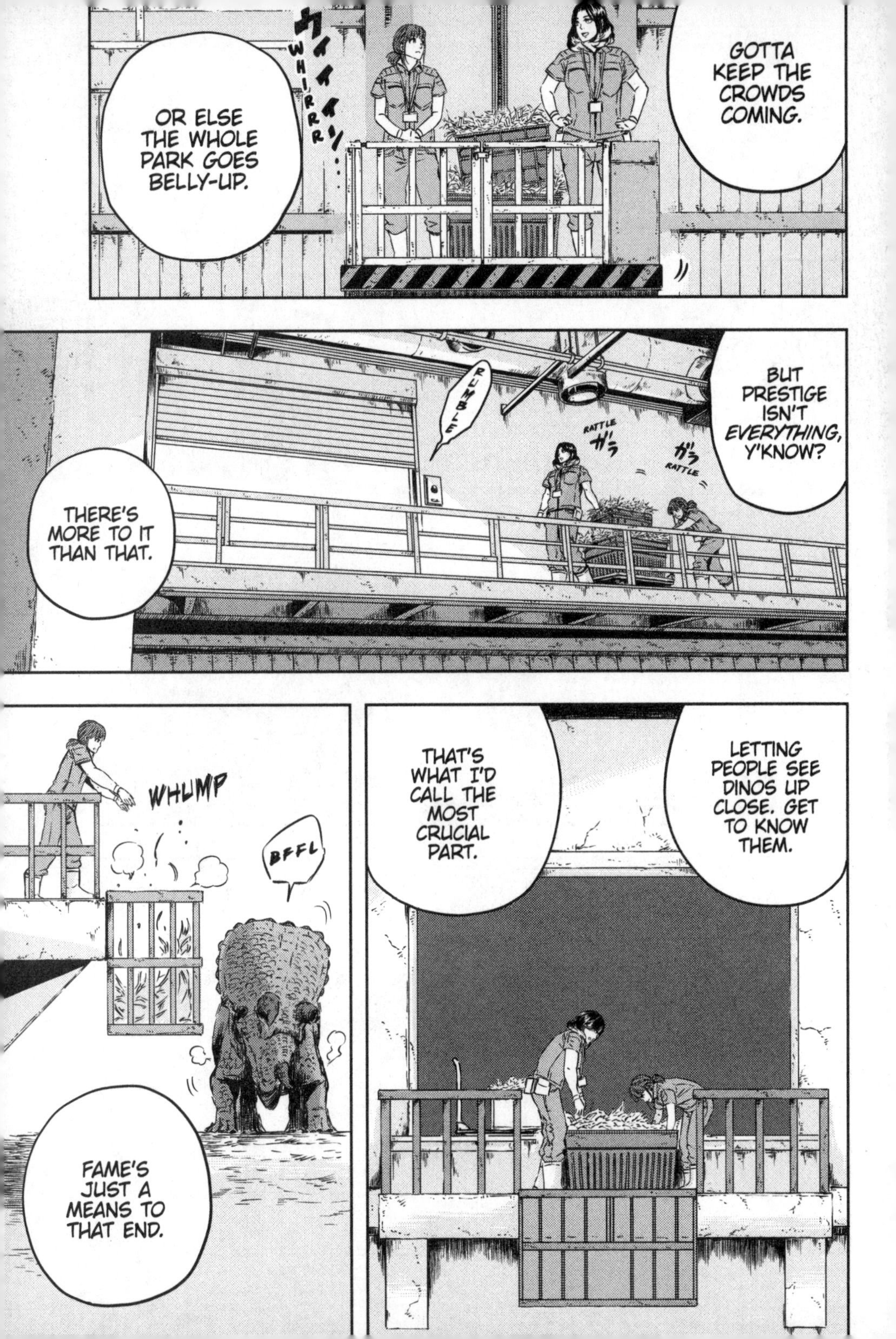
GOTTA KEEP THE CROWDS COMING.
WHIRRR
OR ELSE THE WHOLE PARK GOES BELLY-UP.
BUT PRESTIGE ISN'T *EVERYTHING*, Y'KNOW?
RATTLE
RUMBLE
RATTLE
THERE'S MORE TO IT THAN THAT.
LETTING PEOPLE SEE DINOS UP CLOSE. GET TO KNOW THEM.
THAT'S WHAT I'D CALL THE MOST CRUCIAL PART.
WHUMP
BFFL
FAME'S JUST A MEANS TO THAT END.

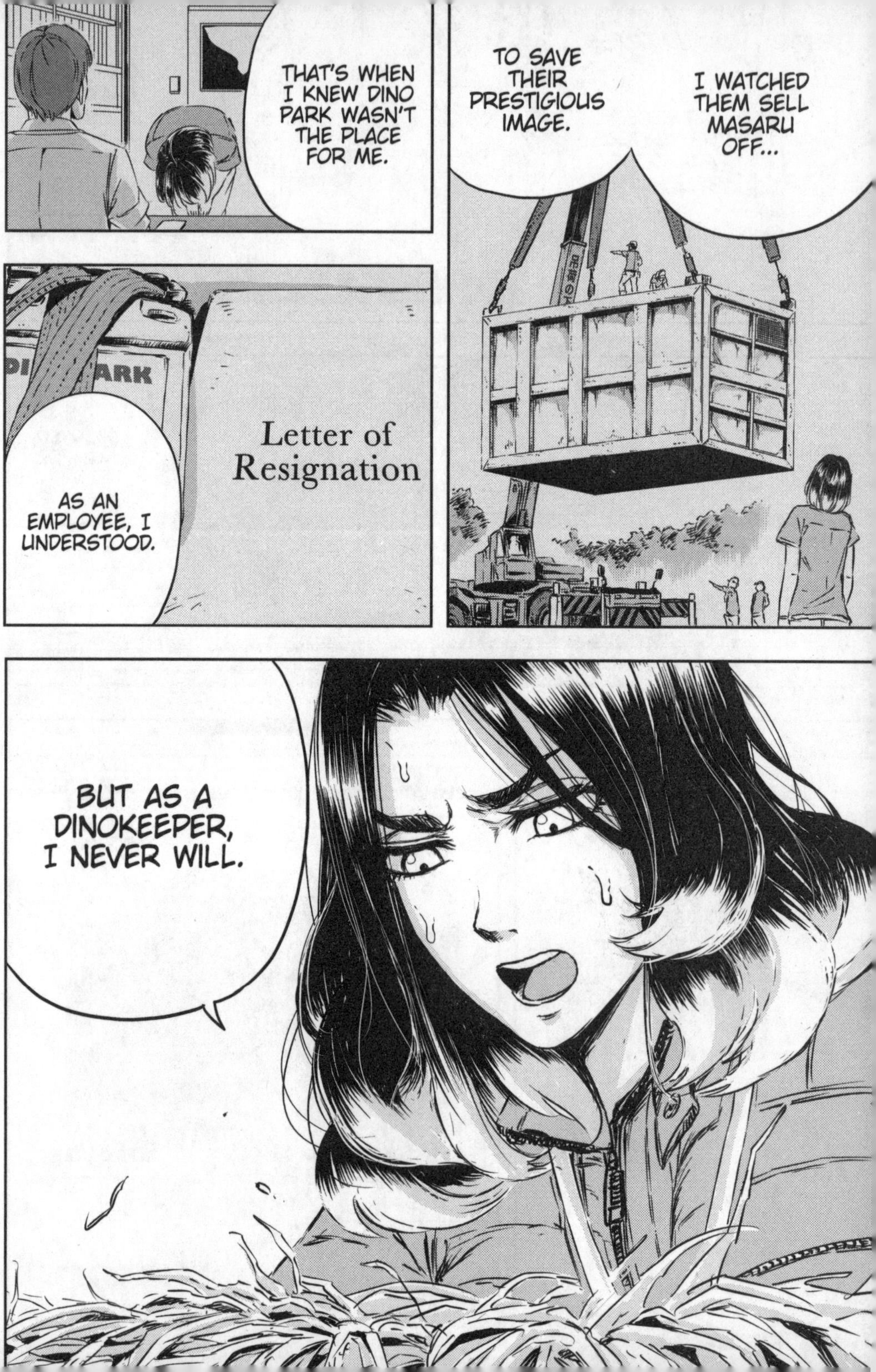
I WATCHED THEM SELL MASARU OFF...
TO SAVE THEIR PRESTIGIOUS IMAGE.
THAT'S WHEN I KNEW DINO PARK WASN'T THE PLACE FOR ME.
Letter of Resignation
AS AN EMPLOYEE, I UNDERSTOOD.
BUT AS A DINOKEEPER, I NEVER WILL.

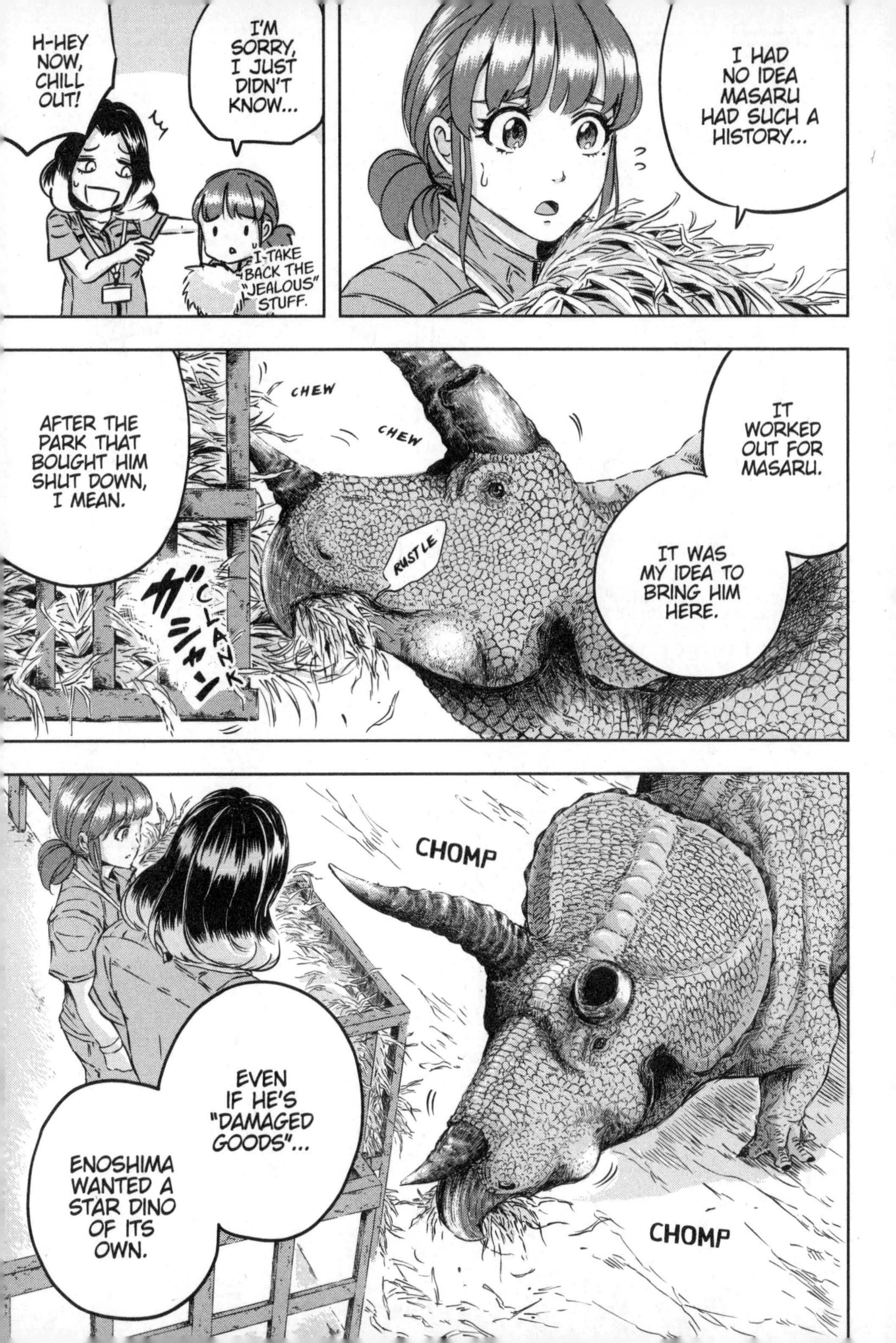
I HAD NO IDEA MASARU HAD SUCH A HISTORY...
I'M SORRY, I JUST DIDN'T KNOW...
H-HEY NOW, CHILL OUT!
I TAKE BACK THE "JEALOUS" STUFF.
IT WORKED OUT FOR MASARU.
IT WAS MY IDEA TO BRING HIM HERE.
CHEW
CHEW
RUSTLE
AFTER THE PARK THAT BOUGHT HIM SHUT DOWN, I MEAN.
ガシャン
CLANK
CHOMP
EVEN IF HE'S "DAMAGED GOODS"...
ENOSHIMA WANTED A STAR DINO OF ITS OWN.
CHOMP

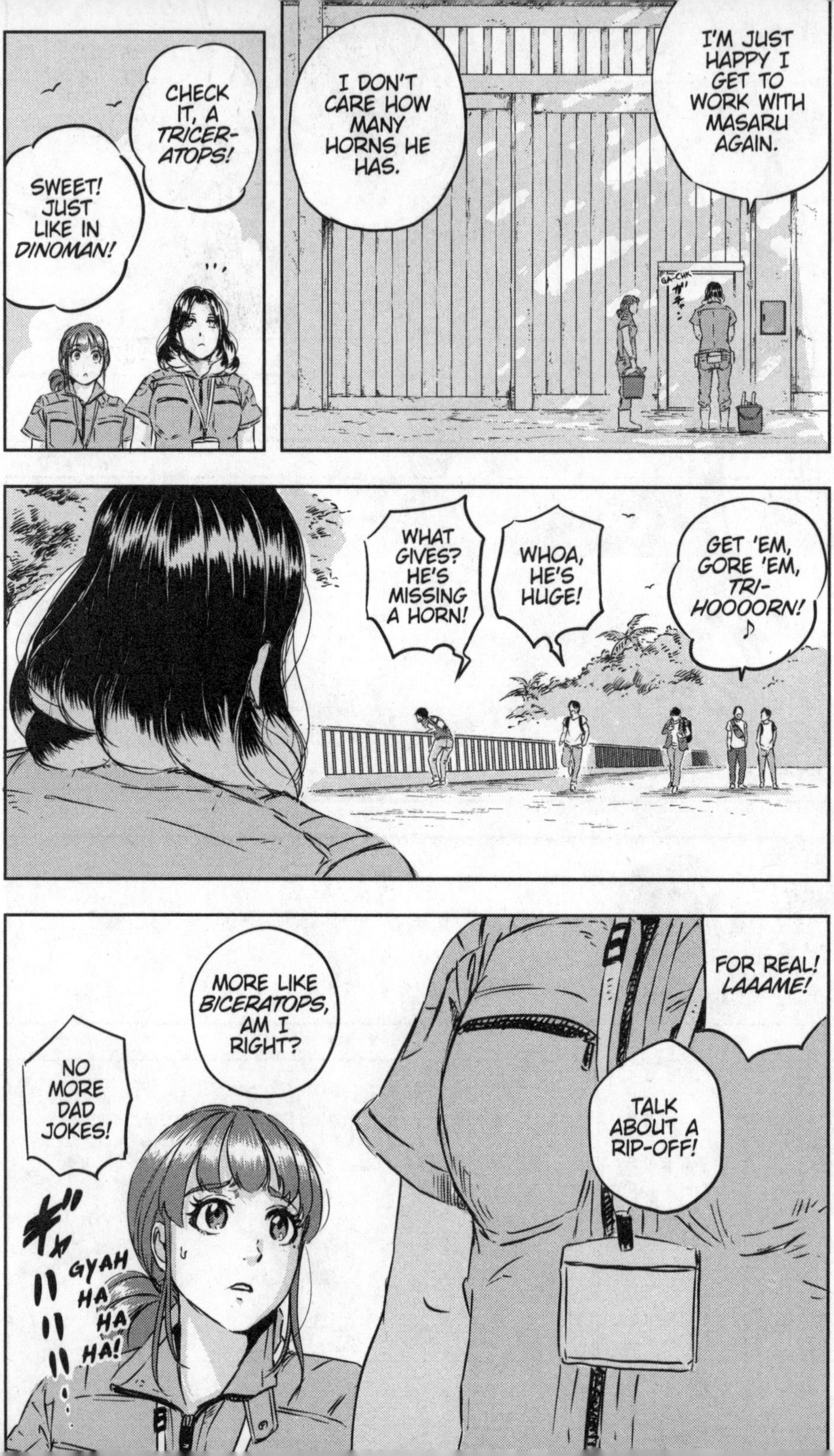

I'M JUST HAPPY I GET TO WORK WITH MASARU AGAIN.
I DON'T CARE HOW MANY HORNS HE HAS.
GA-CHK
CHECK IT, A *TRICERATOPS*!
SWEET! JUST LIKE IN *DINOMAN*!
GET 'EM, GORE 'EM, *TRI-HOOOORN*! ♪
WHOA, HE'S HUGE!
WHAT GIVES? HE'S MISSING A HORN!
FOR REAL! *LAAAME*!
TALK ABOUT A RIP-OFF!
MORE LIKE *BICERATOPS*, AM I RIGHT?
NO MORE DAD JOKES!
GYAH HA HA HA!

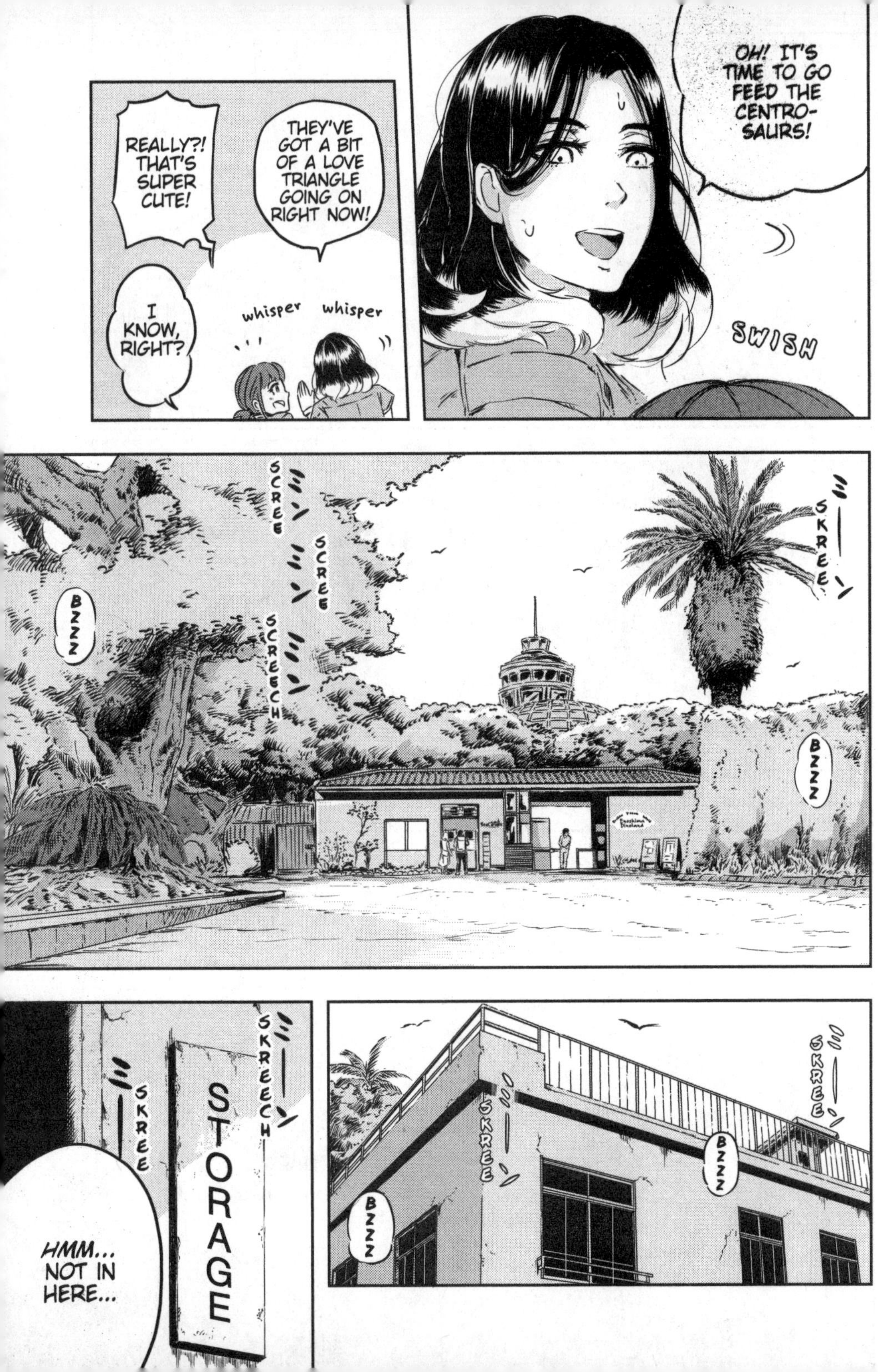
OH! IT'S TIME TO GO FEED THE CENTRO-SAURS!
SWISH
THEY'VE GOT A BIT OF A LOVE TRIANGLE GOING ON RIGHT NOW!
REALLY?! THAT'S SUPER CUTE!
whisper
whisper
I KNOW, RIGHT?
SKREE
SCREE
SCREE
SCREECH
BZZZ
BZZZ
SKREE
BZZZ
SKREE
BZZZ
SKREECH
STORAGE
SKREE
HMM... NOT IN HERE...

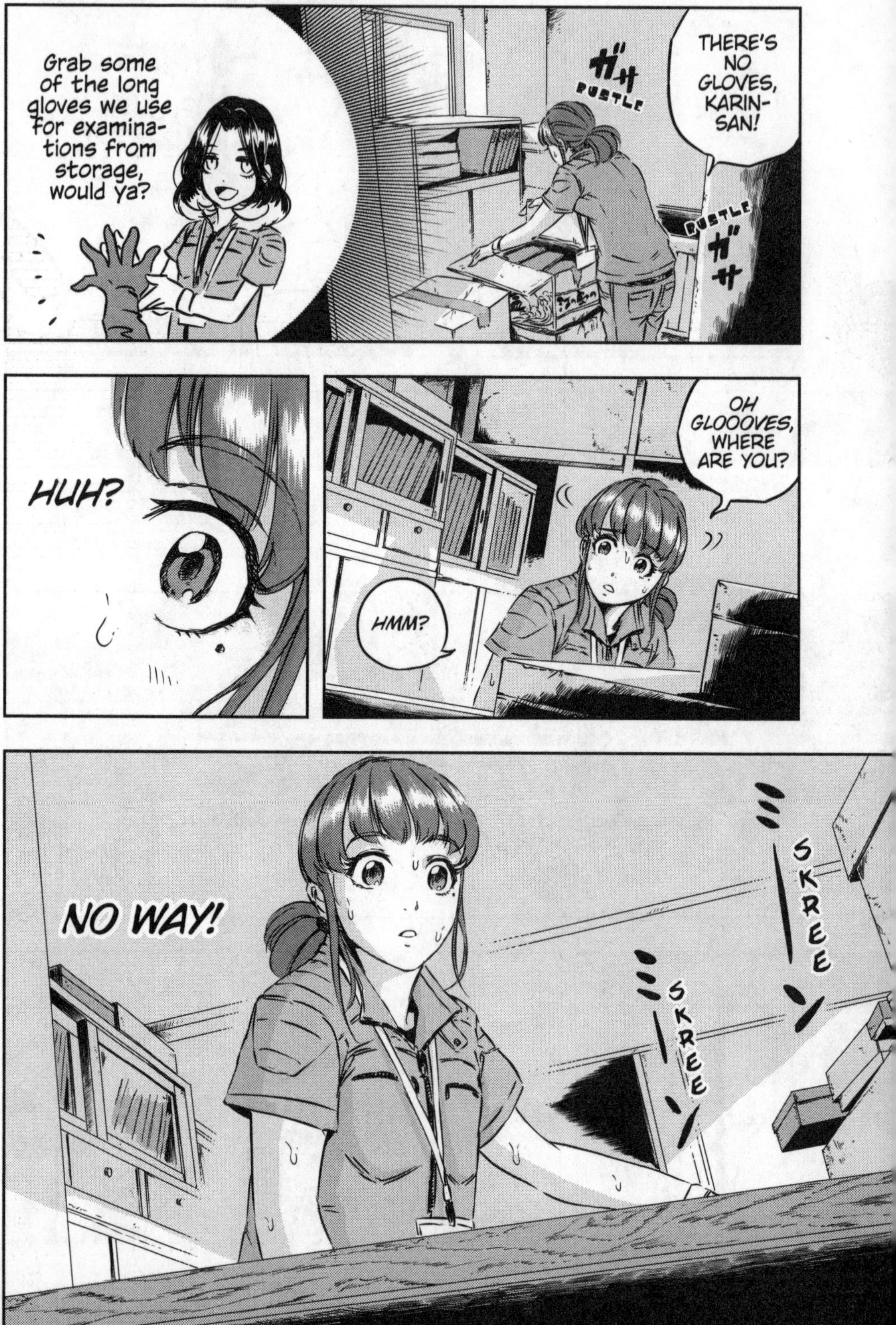
THERE'S NO GLOVES, KARIN-SAN!
ガサ RUSTLE
RUSTLE ガサ
Grab some of the long gloves we use for examinations from storage, would ya?
OH GLOOOVES, WHERE ARE YOU?
HMM?
HUH?
SKREE
SKREE
NO WAY!

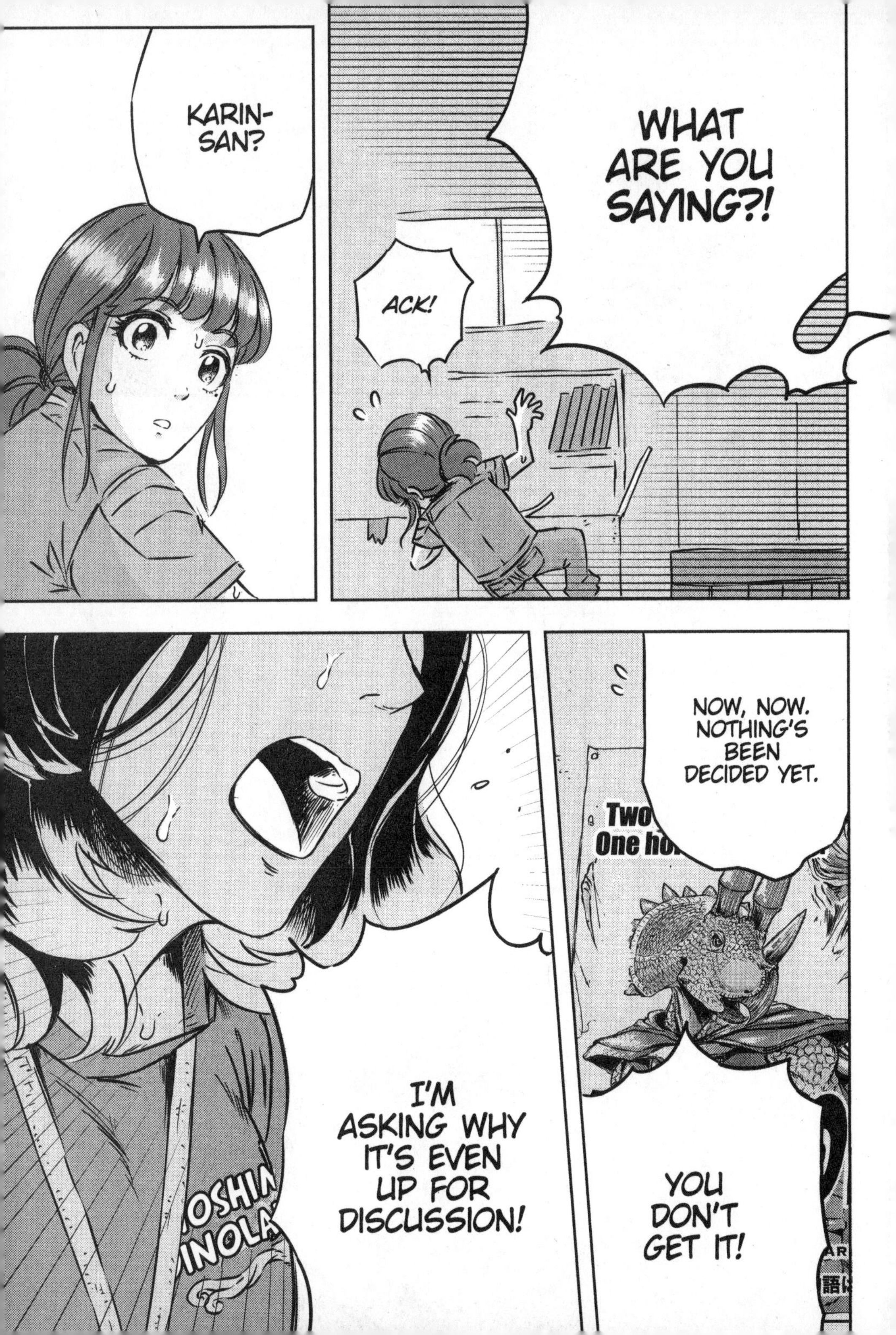
WHAT ARE YOU SAYING?!
ACK!
KARIN-SAN?
NOW, NOW. NOTHING'S BEEN DECIDED YET.
YOU DON'T GET IT!
I'M ASKING WHY IT'S EVEN UP FOR DISCUSSION!

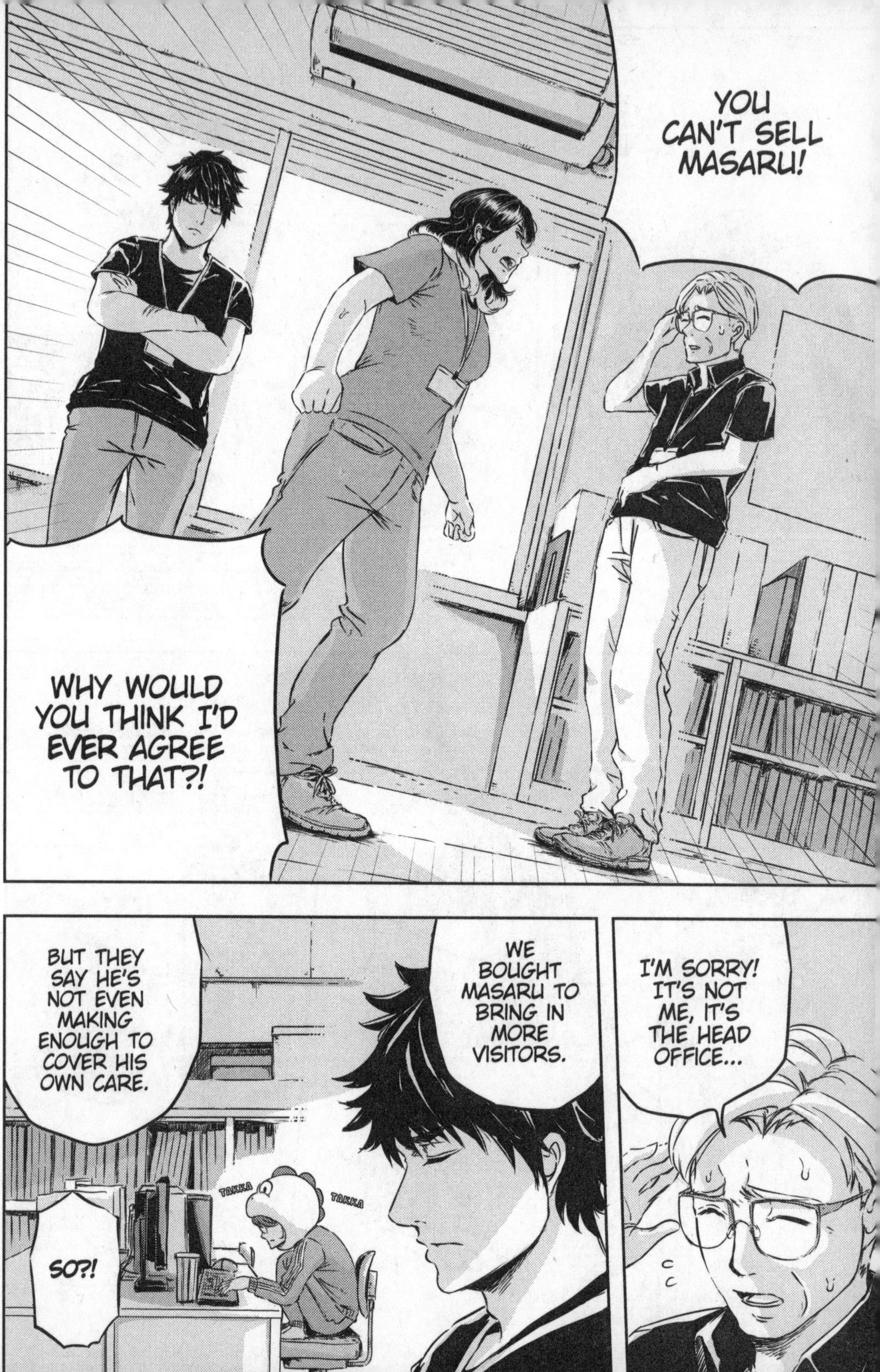
YOU CAN'T SELL MASARU!
WHY WOULD YOU THINK I'D EVER AGREE TO THAT?!
I'M SORRY! IT'S NOT ME, IT'S THE HEAD OFFICE...
WE BOUGHT MASARU TO BRING IN MORE VISITORS.
BUT THEY SAY HE'S NOT EVEN MAKING ENOUGH TO COVER HIS OWN CARE.
TAKKA
TAKKA
SO?!

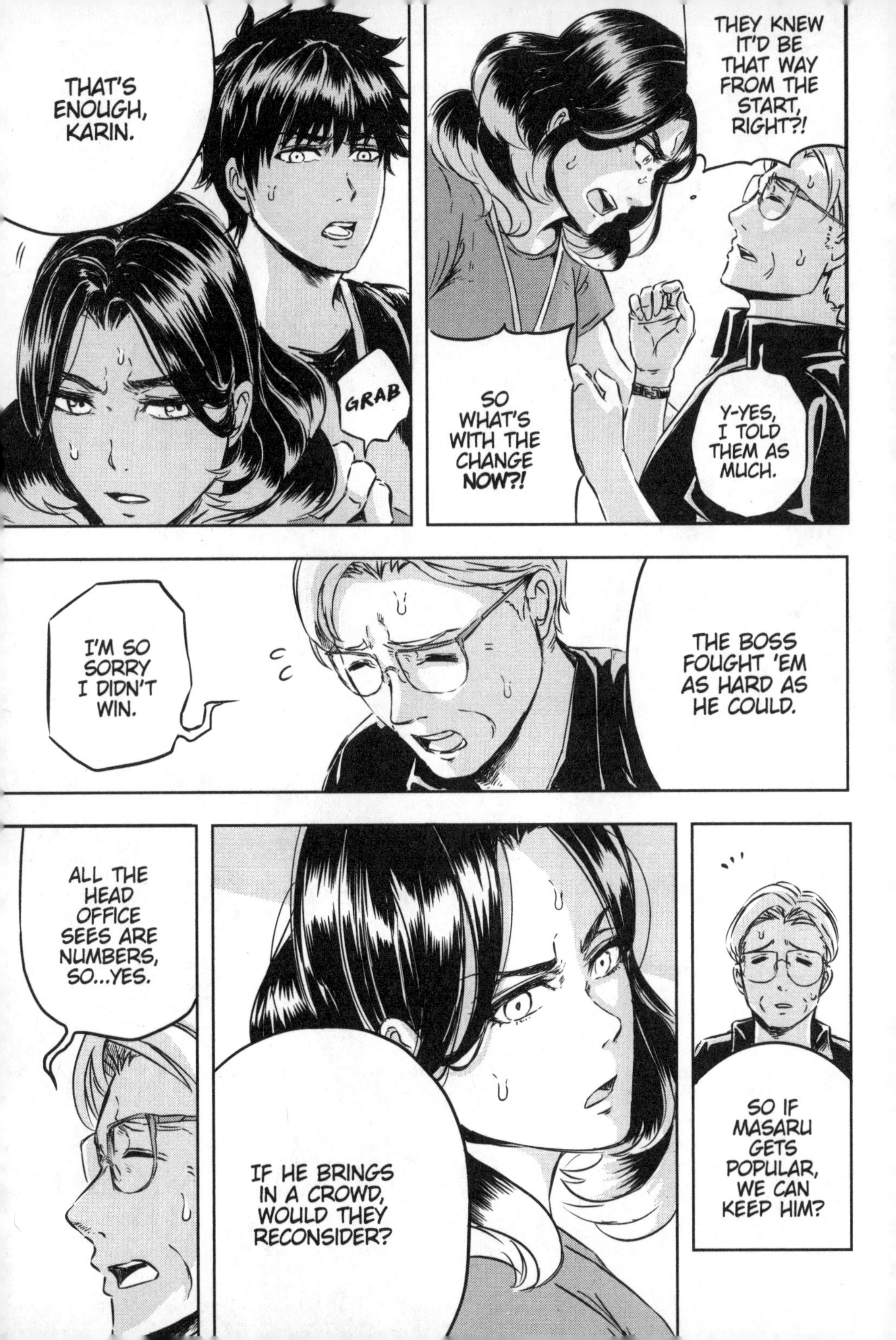
THEY KNEW IT'D BE THAT WAY FROM THE START, RIGHT?!
Y-YES, I TOLD THEM AS MUCH.
SO WHAT'S WITH THE CHANGE NOW?!
THAT'S ENOUGH, KARIN.
GRAB
THE BOSS FOUGHT 'EM AS HARD AS HE COULD.
I'M SO SORRY I DIDN'T WIN.
SO IF MASARU GETS POPULAR, WE CAN KEEP HIM?
IF HE BRINGS IN A CROWD, WOULD THEY RECONSIDER?
ALL THE HEAD OFFICE SEES ARE NUMBERS, SO...YES.

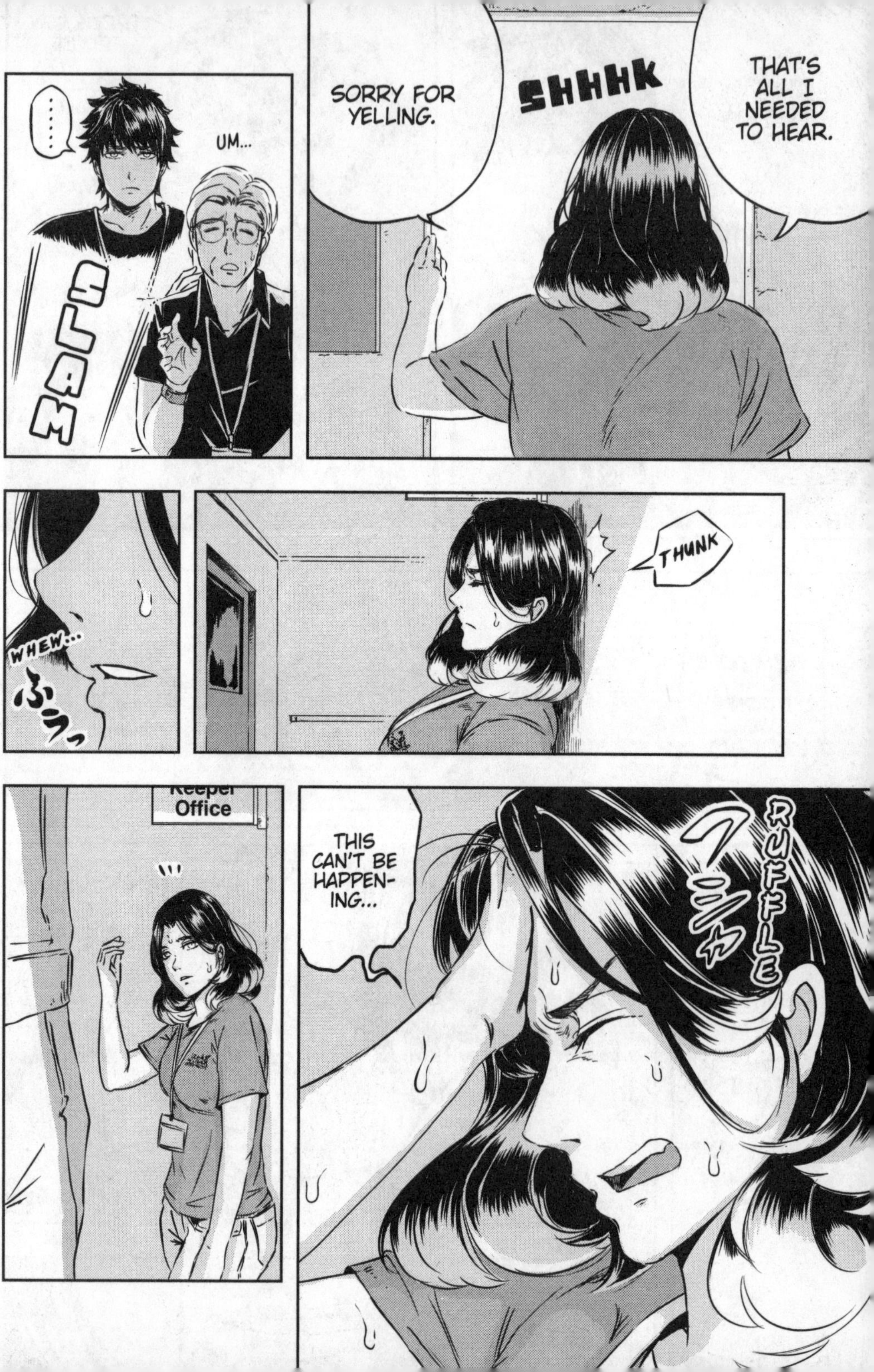
THAT'S ALL I NEEDED TO HEAR.
SHHHK
SORRY FOR YELLING.
UM...
......
SLAM
THUNK
WHEW...
ふうっ
RUFFLE
THIS CAN'T BE HAPPEN-ING...
Keeper Office

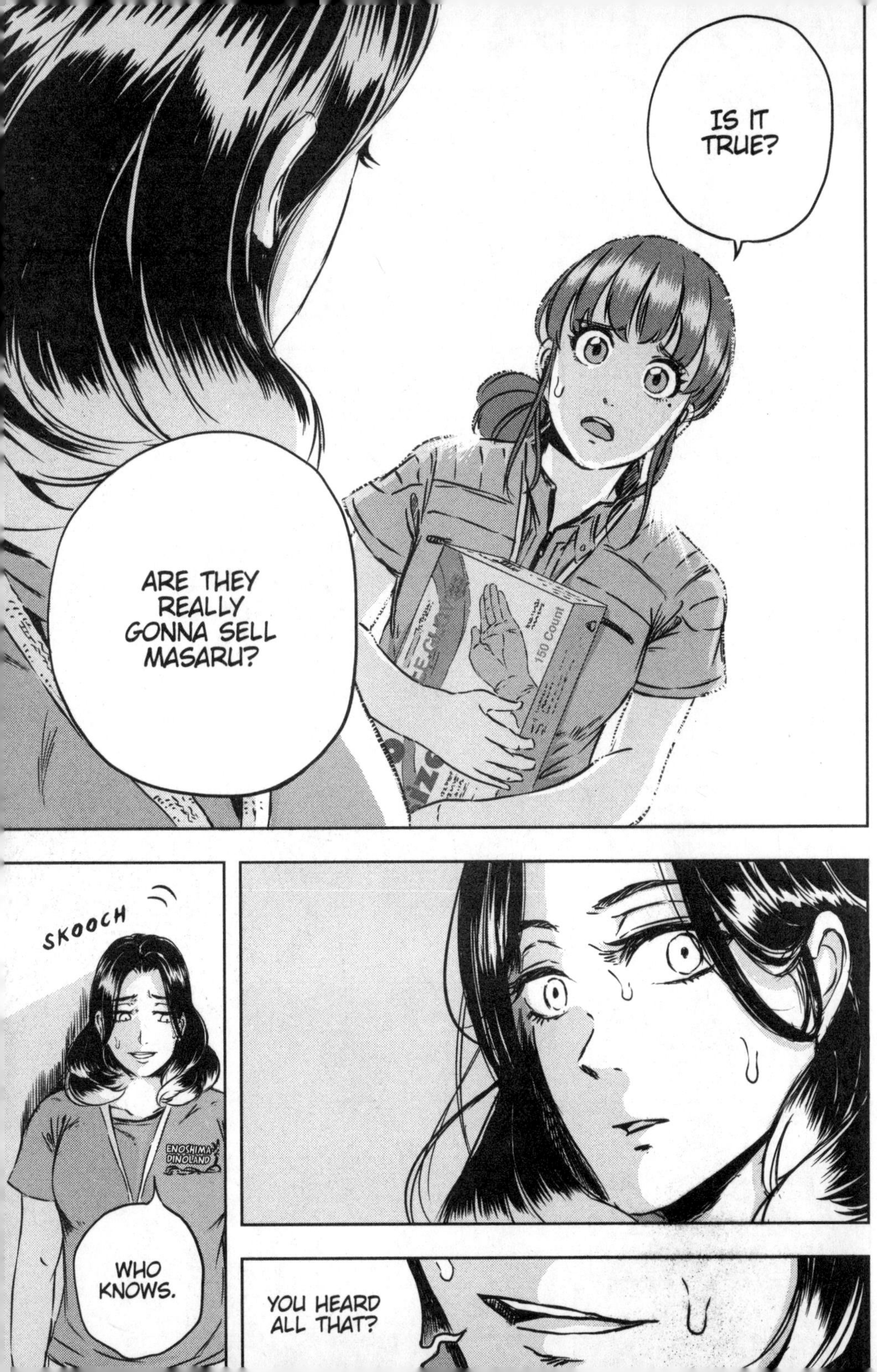
IS IT TRUE?
ARE THEY REALLY GONNA SELL MASARU?
150 Count
YOU HEARD ALL THAT?
SKOOCH
ENOSHIMA DINOLAND
WHO KNOWS.

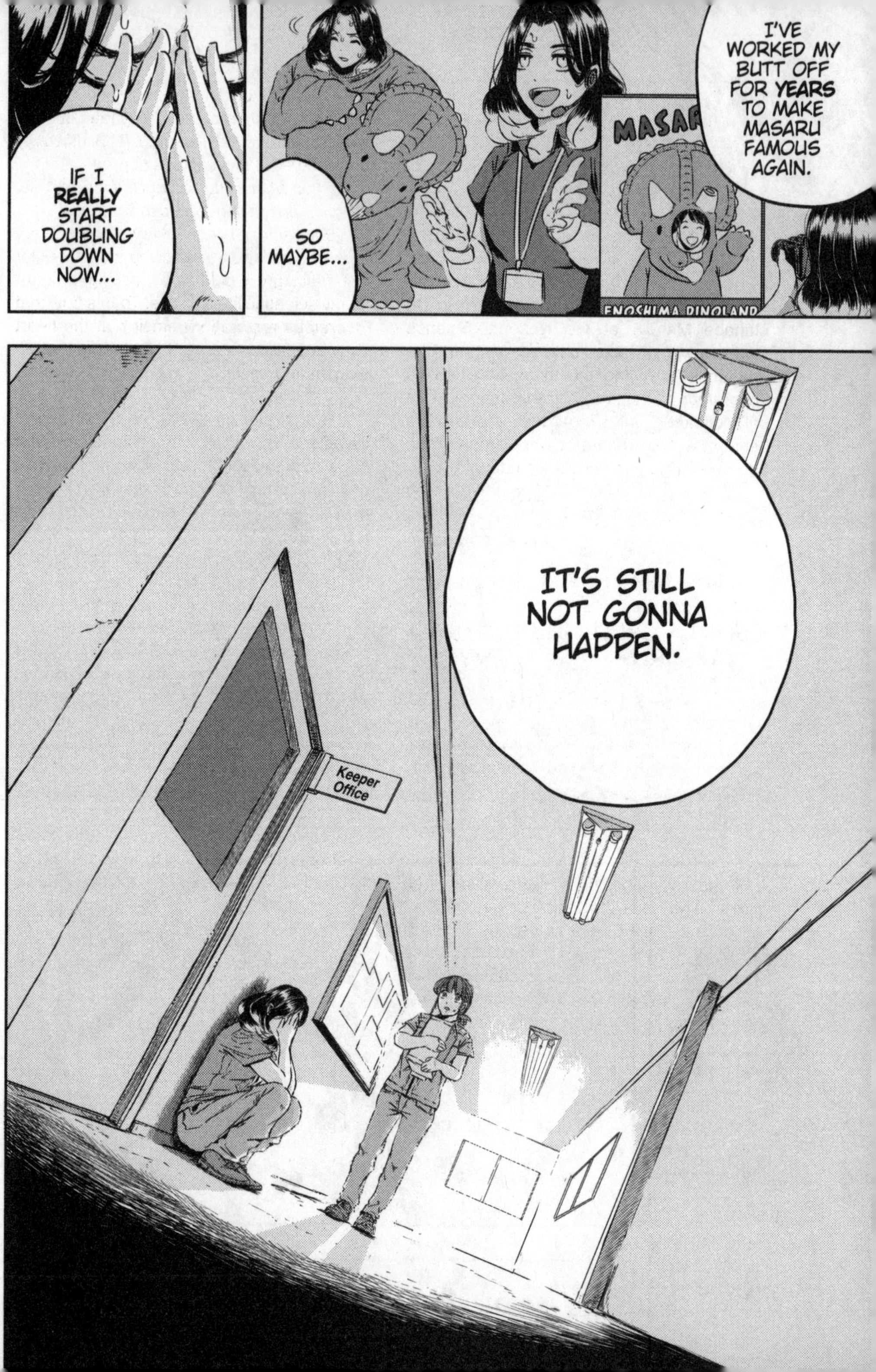
I'VE WORKED MY BUTT OFF FOR **YEARS** TO MAKE MASARU FAMOUS AGAIN.
MASAR
ENOSHIMA DINOLAND
SO MAYBE...
IF I **REALLY** START DOUBLING DOWN NOW...
IT'S STILL NOT GONNA HAPPEN.
Keeper Office

Dr. Dino's Lab Log

FILE. 03 A Firm Foundation for Research

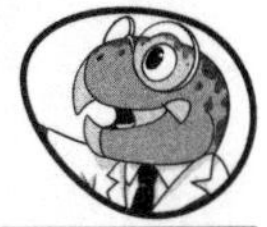

Triceratops is an especially precious dinosaur to me, and has been since back in 2003. That's when I began my university master's degree program. I went to Dr. Manabe Makoto at the National Science Museum with a rather bold request, and he granted it—allowing me to use the NSM's *Triceratops* specimen in my research. This particular dinosaur is regarded as the world's best-preserved *Triceratops* specimen! Thus began my career in vertebrate paleontology.

There were conflicting hypotheses over how to properly restore *Triceratops'* forelimb posture. Nobody at that point had been able to settle the issue with any certainty. Every Monday, when the National Science Museum is closed to the public, they let me into the exhibition room, where I stood face-to-face with their *Triceratops*. It stood there, almost taunting me, as I puzzled over it until my head hurt. I still can't thank Dr. Manabe enough for taking time out of his busy schedule to accompany me every single time I showed up. Thanks to him, I studied *Triceratops* to my heart's content.

What I learned, though, was this: *You can't learn anything just staring at fossils!*

Just as I was at my most bewildered, it hit me: I was looking at the remains of an animal. The bone structures of currently living animals might have something to teach me! As I observed them, I noticed that the orientations in which different animals' bones project explained the difference in their posture. Wouldn't that be useful, I thought, in reconstructing how *Triceratops'* limbs were positioned?

Once I had that stroke of inspiration, it was like a fountain of research ideas opened up and poured out all over me. It solidified my resolve to earn my master's degree.

If you want to learn about extinct animals, start with the animals that currently exist.

Everything I encountered during my *Triceratops* research, including that particular flash of insight, would be a blessing throughout my scientific life to come. To this day, that *Triceratops* restoration remains at the heart of my academic interest. It's a theme I return to again and again.

Horns, like on a cow or rhino; beaks; claws; scales... All of these animal parts are made up of multiple layers of keratin, stacked up on the surface of bone or skin. Keratin usually isn't left behind in the fossil record, but I expect that if you were to split a *Triceratops'* horn, you'd see that it was made up of layers, like a sort of keratin crepe.

Such layers are built up, little by little, from the outside of the bone beneath, and extend towards a tip—stacking up kind of like ice cream cones. Striations of keratin growth are visible from the outside, though sometimes there are lines that run parallel to the direction of growth, too. Just like you can see with your own fingernails, the keratin portion of a horn will continue to grow, even if the horn is broken. The tips of horns and other keratin parts that commonly rub against other objects will eventually grow smooth as they're polished away.

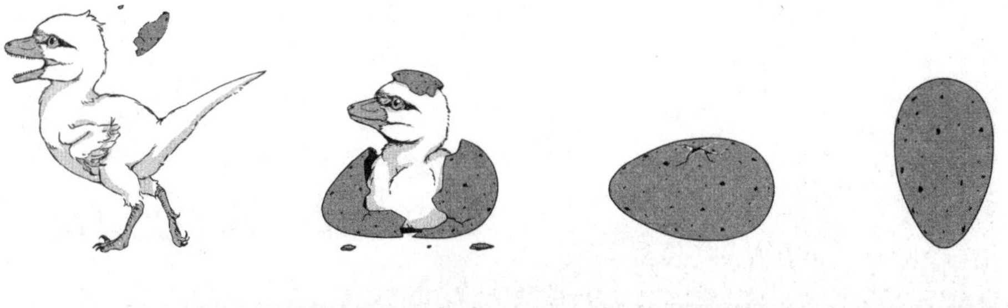

DINOSAUR SANCTUARY

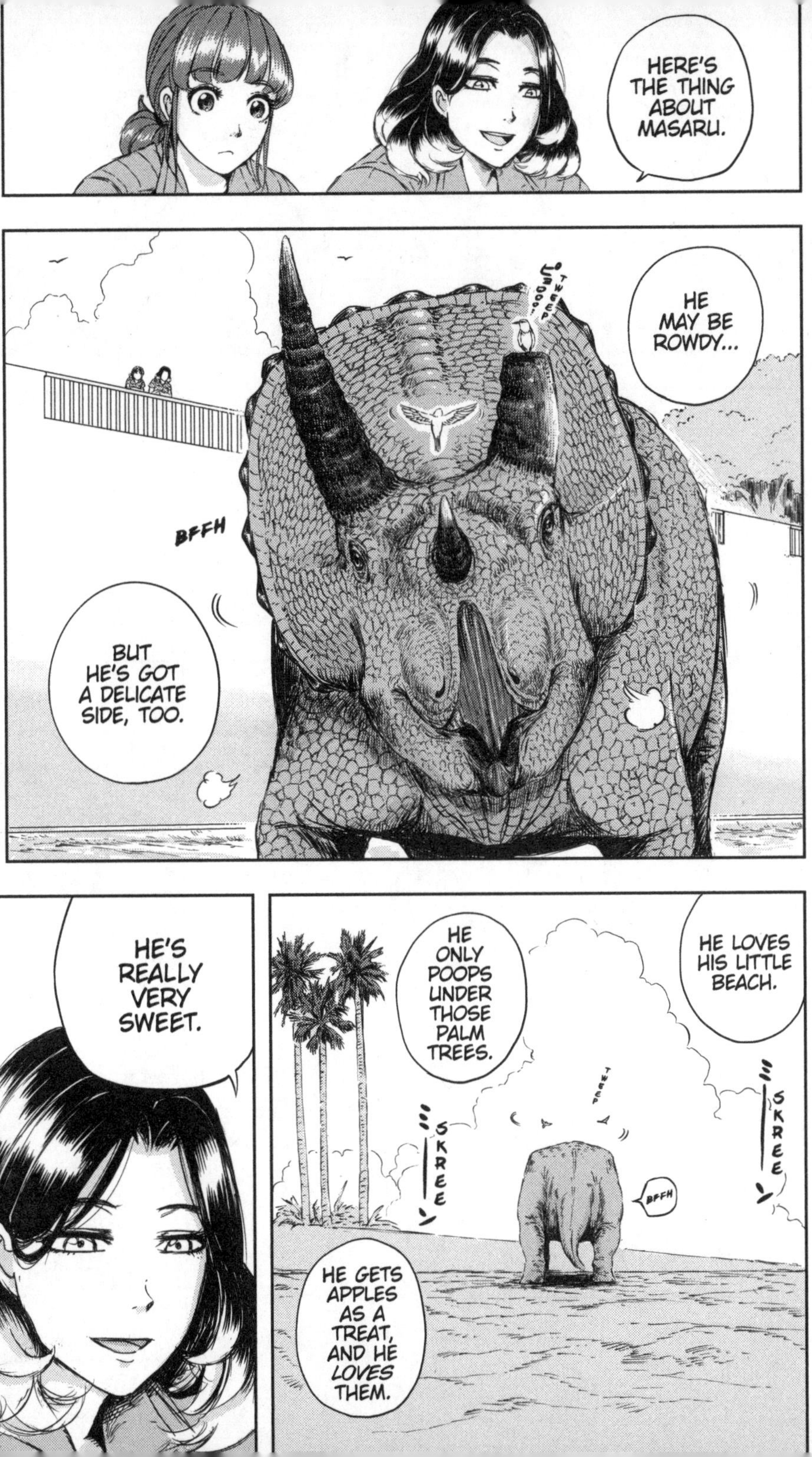
HERE'S THE THING ABOUT MASARU.
HE MAY BE ROWDY...
BFFH
BUT HE'S GOT A DELICATE SIDE, TOO.
HE LOVES HIS LITTLE BEACH.
HE ONLY POOPS UNDER THOSE PALM TREES.
SKREE
TWEEP
BFFH
SKREE
HE GETS APPLES AS A TREAT, AND HE LOVES THEM.
HE'S REALLY VERY SWEET.

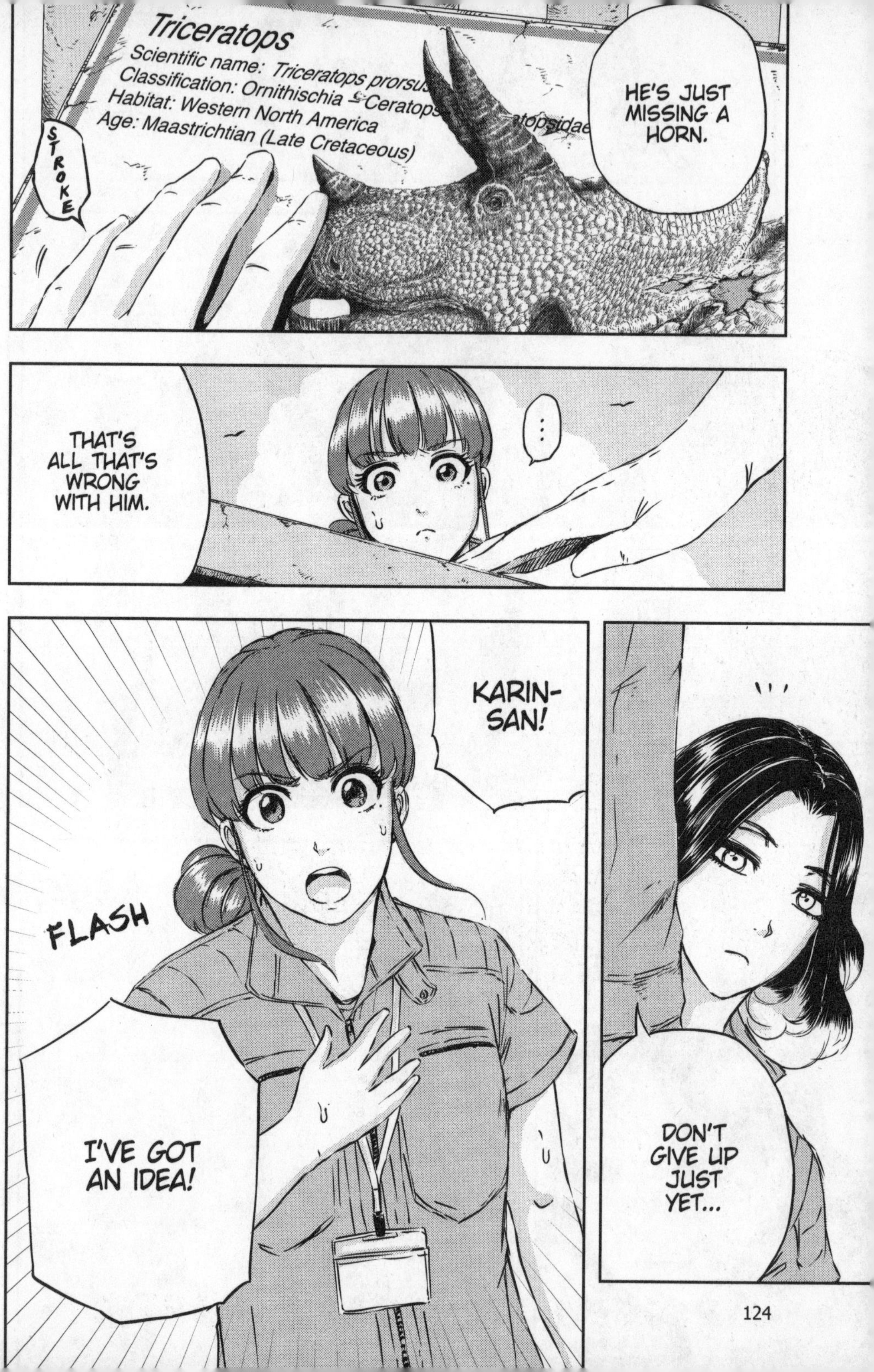
HE'S JUST MISSING A HORN.
Triceratops
Scientific name: Triceratops prorsu
Classification: Ornithischia – Ceratops
atopsidae
Habitat: Western North America
Age: Maastrichtian (Late Cretaceous)
STROKE
...
THAT'S ALL THAT'S WRONG WITH HIM.
!!
DON'T GIVE UP JUST YET...
KARIN-SAN!
FLASH
I'VE GOT AN IDEA!

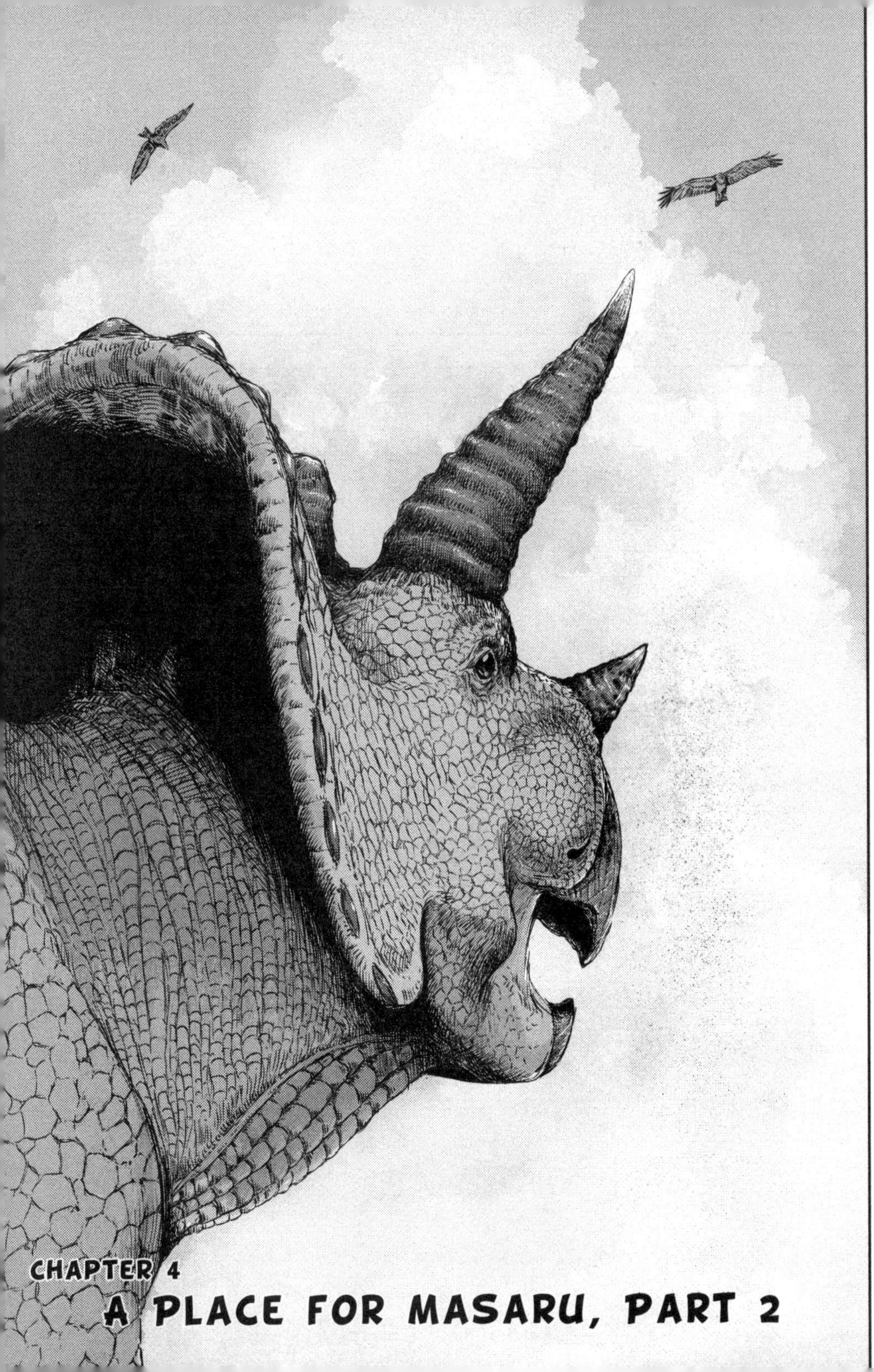

CHAPTER 4
A PLACE FOR MASARU, PART 2

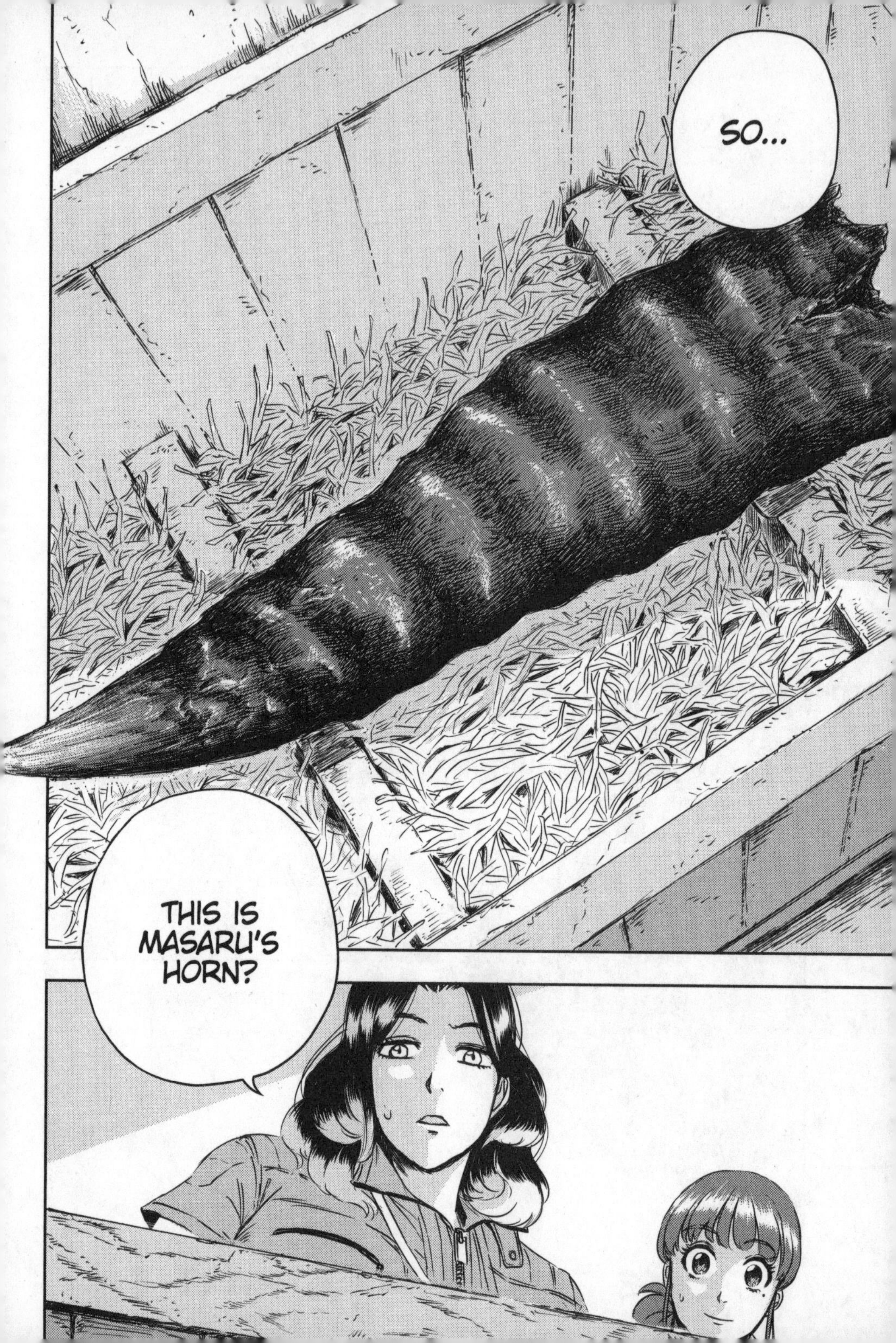
SO...
THIS IS MASARU'S HORN?

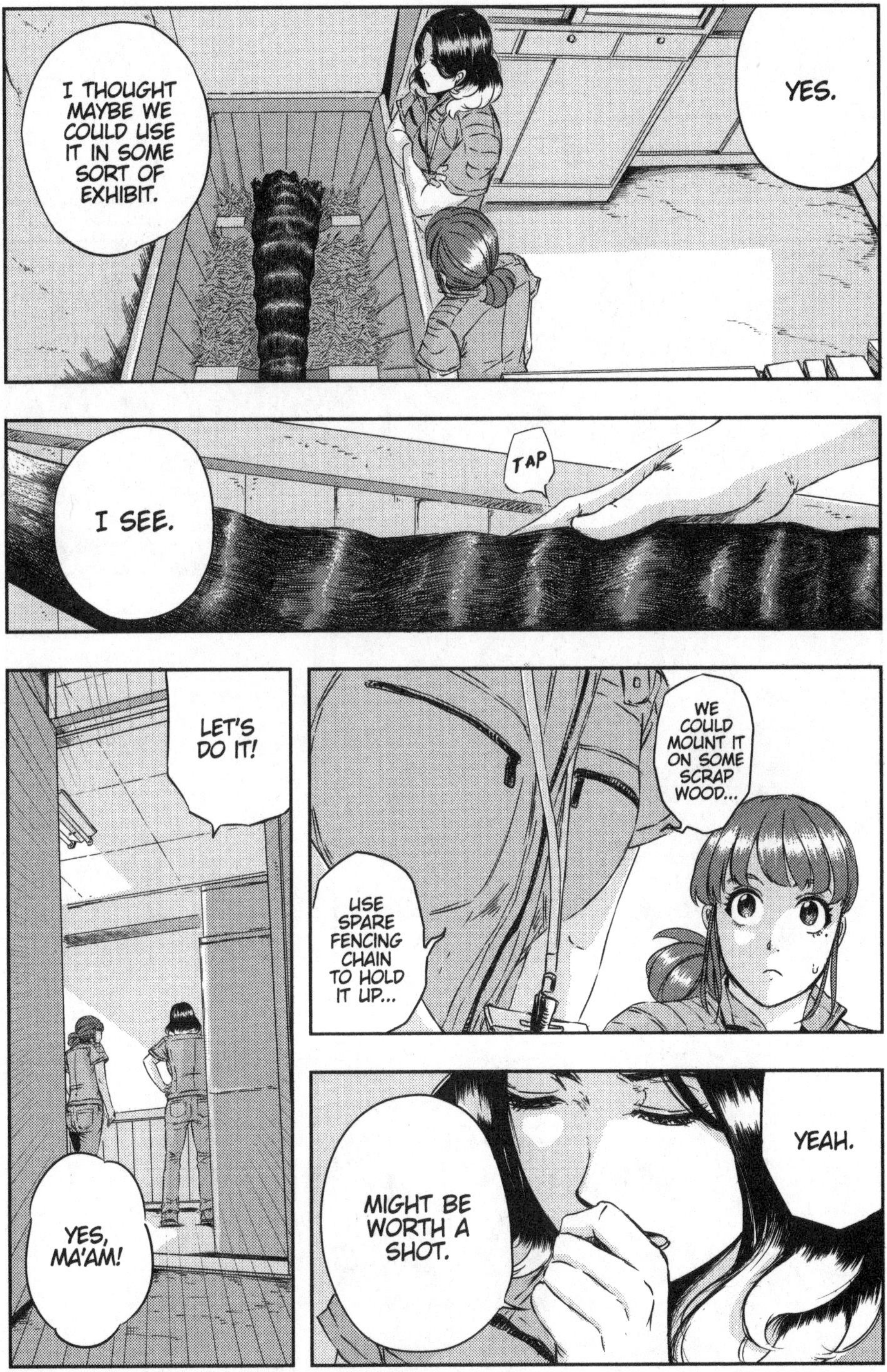
YES.
I THOUGHT MAYBE WE COULD USE IT IN SOME SORT OF EXHIBIT.
TAP
I SEE.
WE COULD MOUNT IT ON SOME SCRAP WOOD...
USE SPARE FENCING CHAIN TO HOLD IT UP...
YEAH.
MIGHT BE WORTH A SHOT.
LET'S DO IT!
YES, MA'AM!

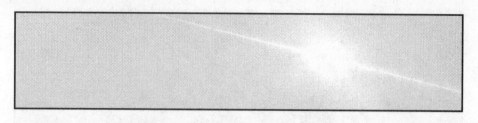

KCHHH

SCRUB

SCRUB

AH, HELLO, KAIDOU-KUN.

GA SHHK

HEY, BOSS.

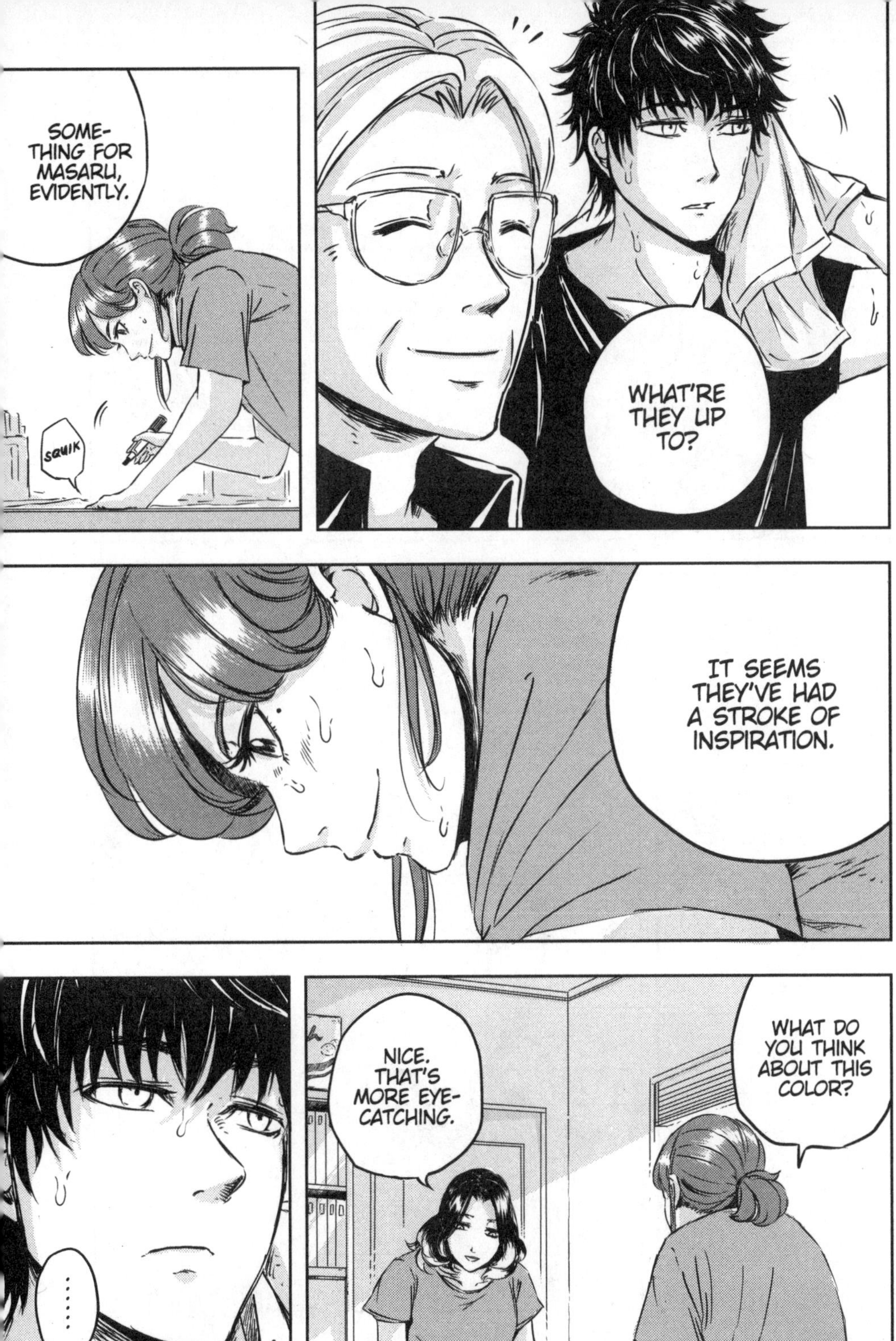
WHAT'RE THEY UP TO?
SOME-THING FOR MASARU, EVIDENTLY.
SQUIK
IT SEEMS THEY'VE HAD A STROKE OF INSPIRATION.
WHAT DO YOU THINK ABOUT THIS COLOR?
NICE. THAT'S MORE EYE-CATCHING.
......

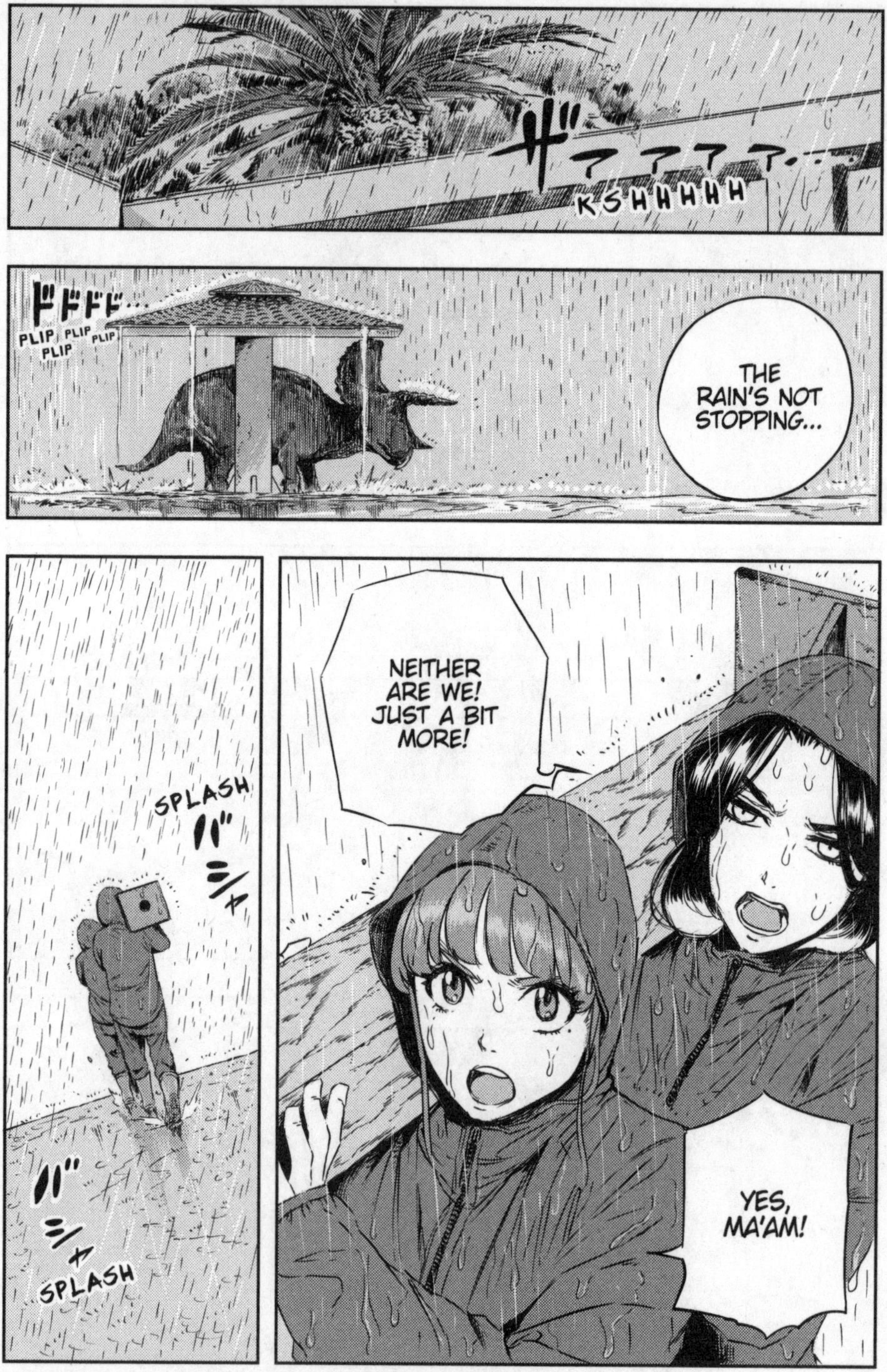
ザァァァァ…
KSHHHHH
ドドドド
PLIP PLIP PLIP PLIP
THE RAIN'S NOT STOPPING...
NEITHER ARE WE! JUST A BIT MORE!
YES, MA'AM!
SPLASH
バシャ
バシャ
SPLASH

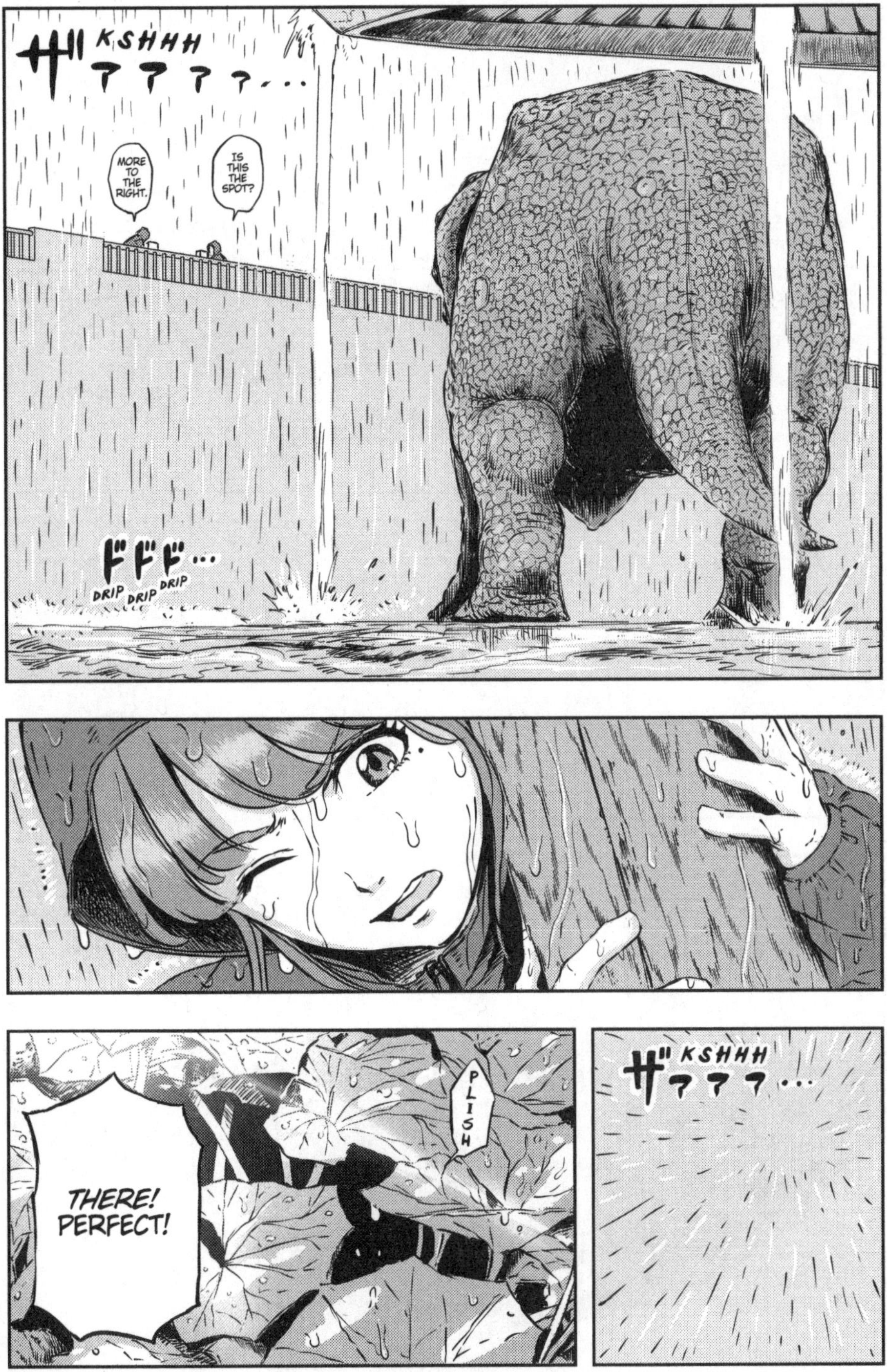
ザァァァァ… KSHHH
IS THIS THE SPOT?
MORE TO THE RIGHT.
ドドド… DRIP DRIP DRIP
ザァァァ… KSHHH
PLISH
THERE! PERFECT!

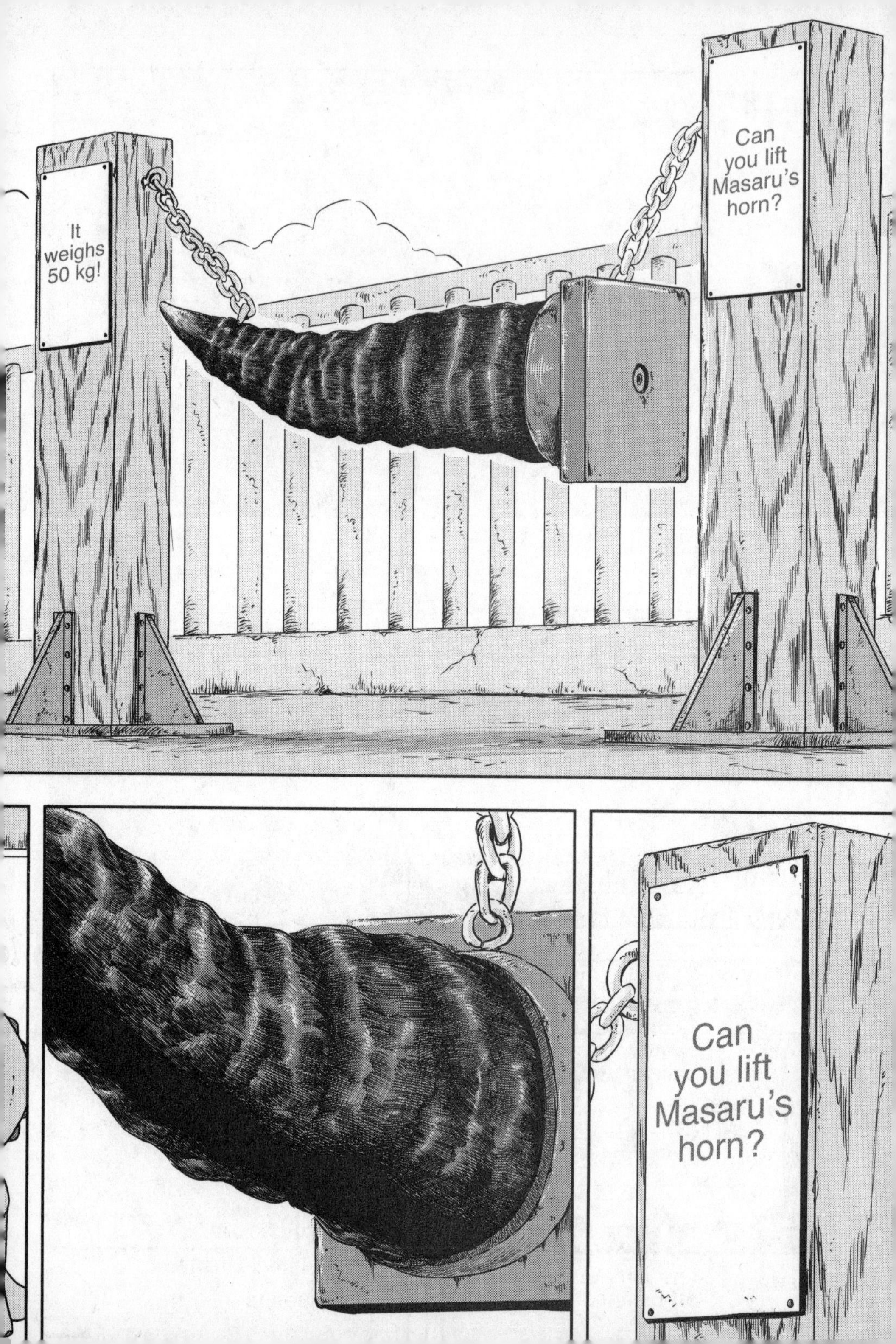
Can you lift Masaru's horn?
It weighs 50 kg!
Can you lift Masaru's horn?

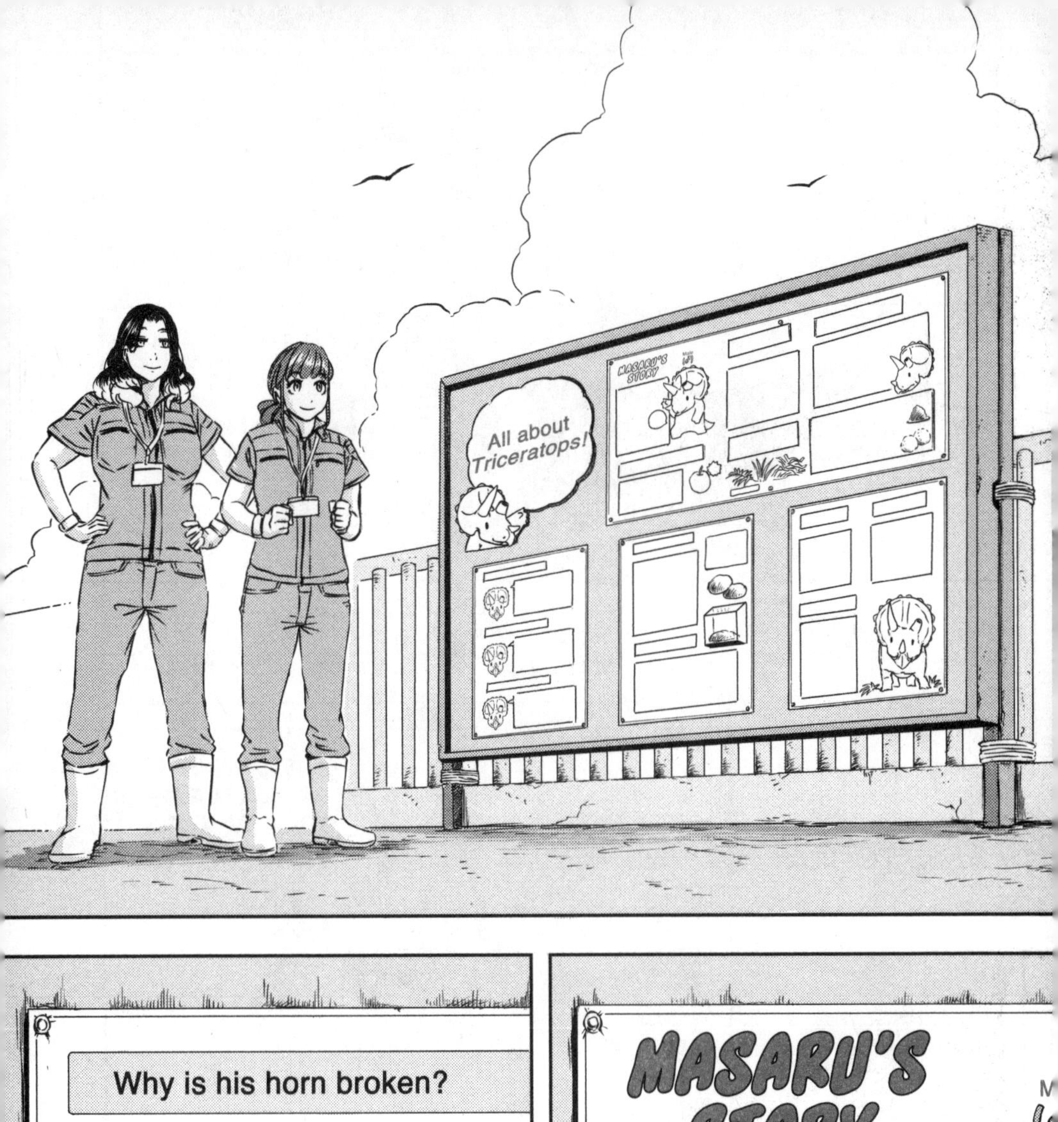
All about Triceratops!

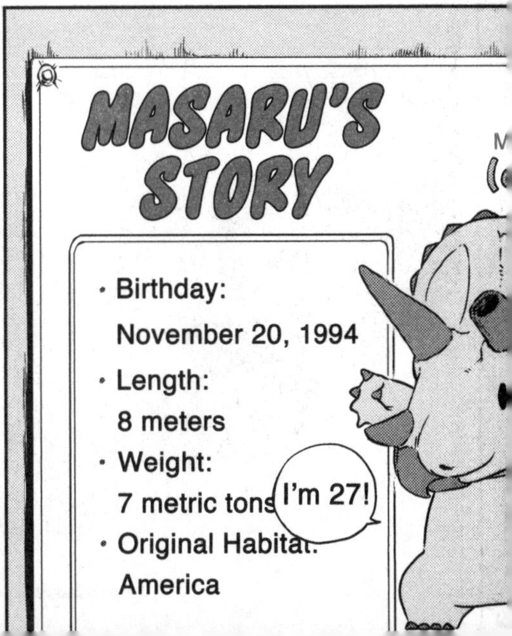
MASARU'S STORY
• Birthday:
November 20, 1994
• Length:
8 meters
• Weight:
7 metric tons
• Original Habitat:
America
I'm 27!

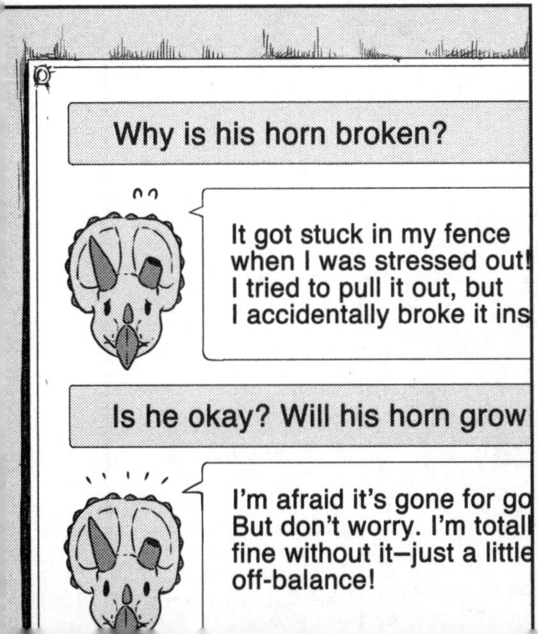
Why is his horn broken?
It got stuck in my fence
when I was stressed out!
I tried to pull it out, but
I accidentally broke it ins
Is he okay? Will his horn grow
I'm afraid it's gone for go
But don't worry. I'm totall
fine without it–just a little
off-balance!

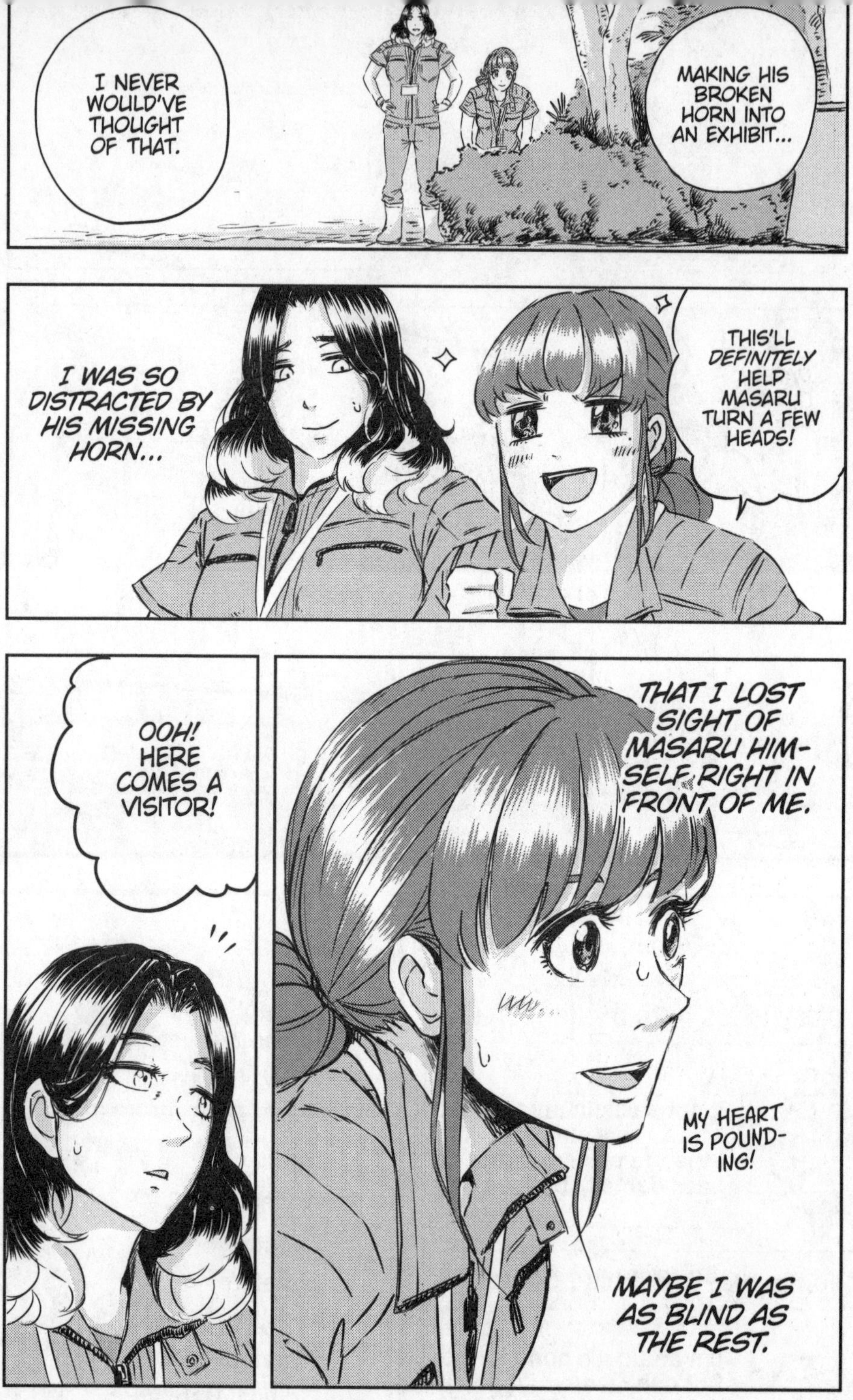
MAKING HIS BROKEN HORN INTO AN EXHIBIT...
I NEVER WOULD'VE THOUGHT OF THAT.
THIS'LL DEFINITELY HELP MASARU TURN A FEW HEADS!
I WAS SO DISTRACTED BY HIS MISSING HORN...
THAT I LOST SIGHT OF MASARU HIMSELF RIGHT IN FRONT OF ME.
MY HEART IS POUNDING!
MAYBE I WAS AS BLIND AS THE REST.
OOH! HERE COMES A VISITOR!

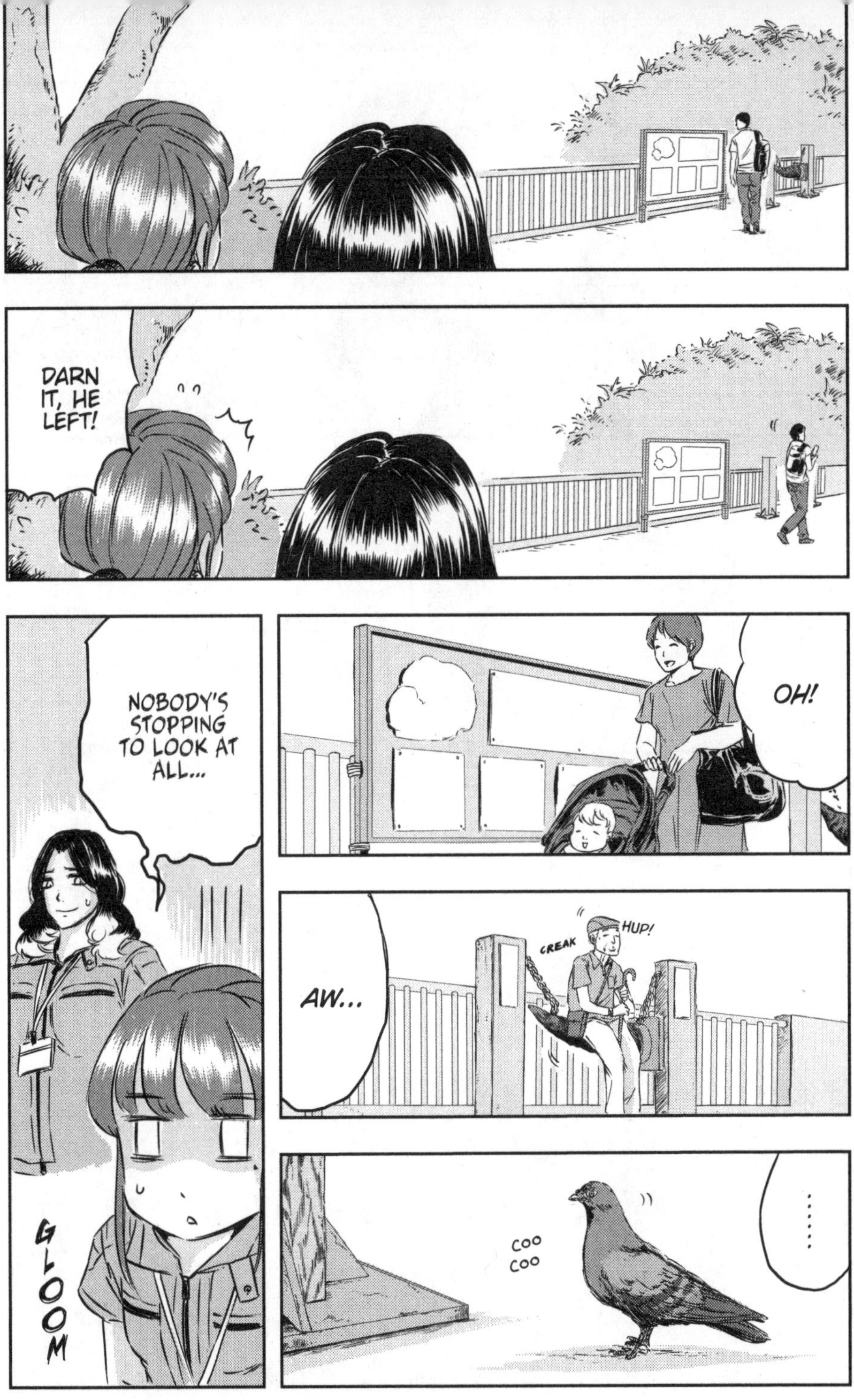
DARN IT, HE LEFT!
OH!
HUP!
CREAK
AW...
......
COO COO
NOBODY'S STOPPING TO LOOK AT ALL...
GLOOM

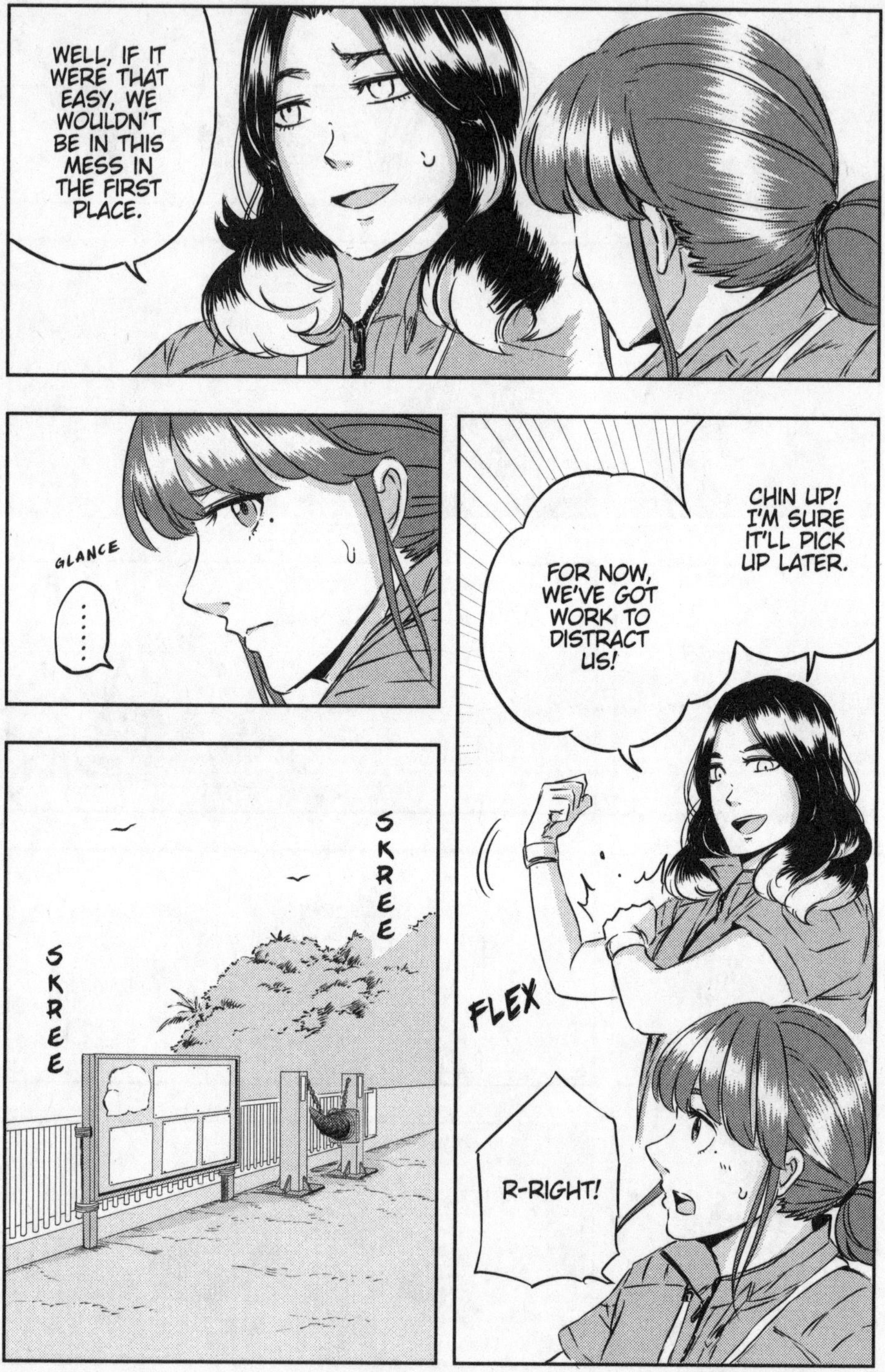
WELL, IF IT WERE THAT EASY, WE WOULDN'T BE IN THIS MESS IN THE FIRST PLACE.
CHIN UP! I'M SURE IT'LL PICK UP LATER.
FOR NOW, WE'VE GOT WORK TO DISTRACT US!
FLEX
R-RIGHT!
GLANCE
......
SKREE
SKREE

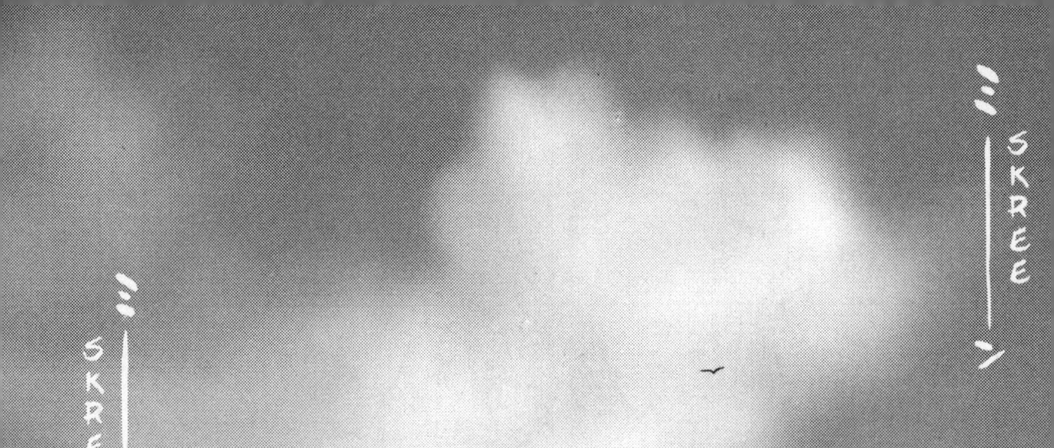
SKREE
SKREE
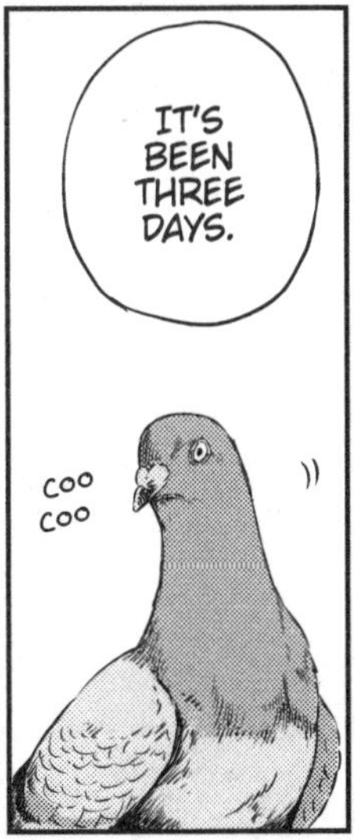
IT'S BEEN THREE DAYS.
COO COO
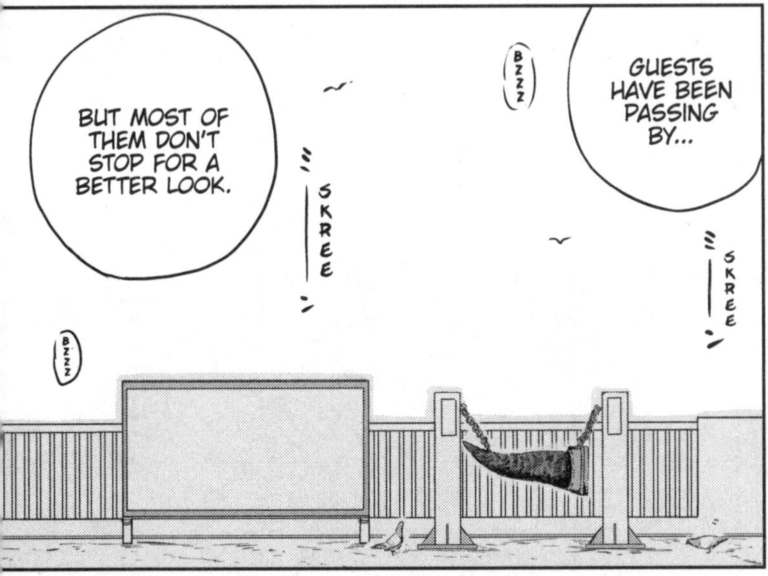
GUESTS HAVE BEEN PASSING BY...
BZZZ
SKREE
SKREE
BUT MOST OF THEM DON'T STOP FOR A BETTER LOOK.
BZZZ

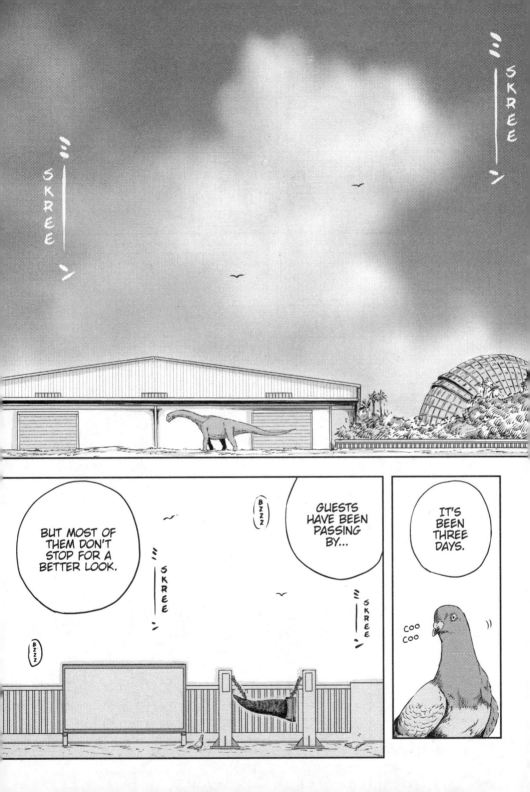

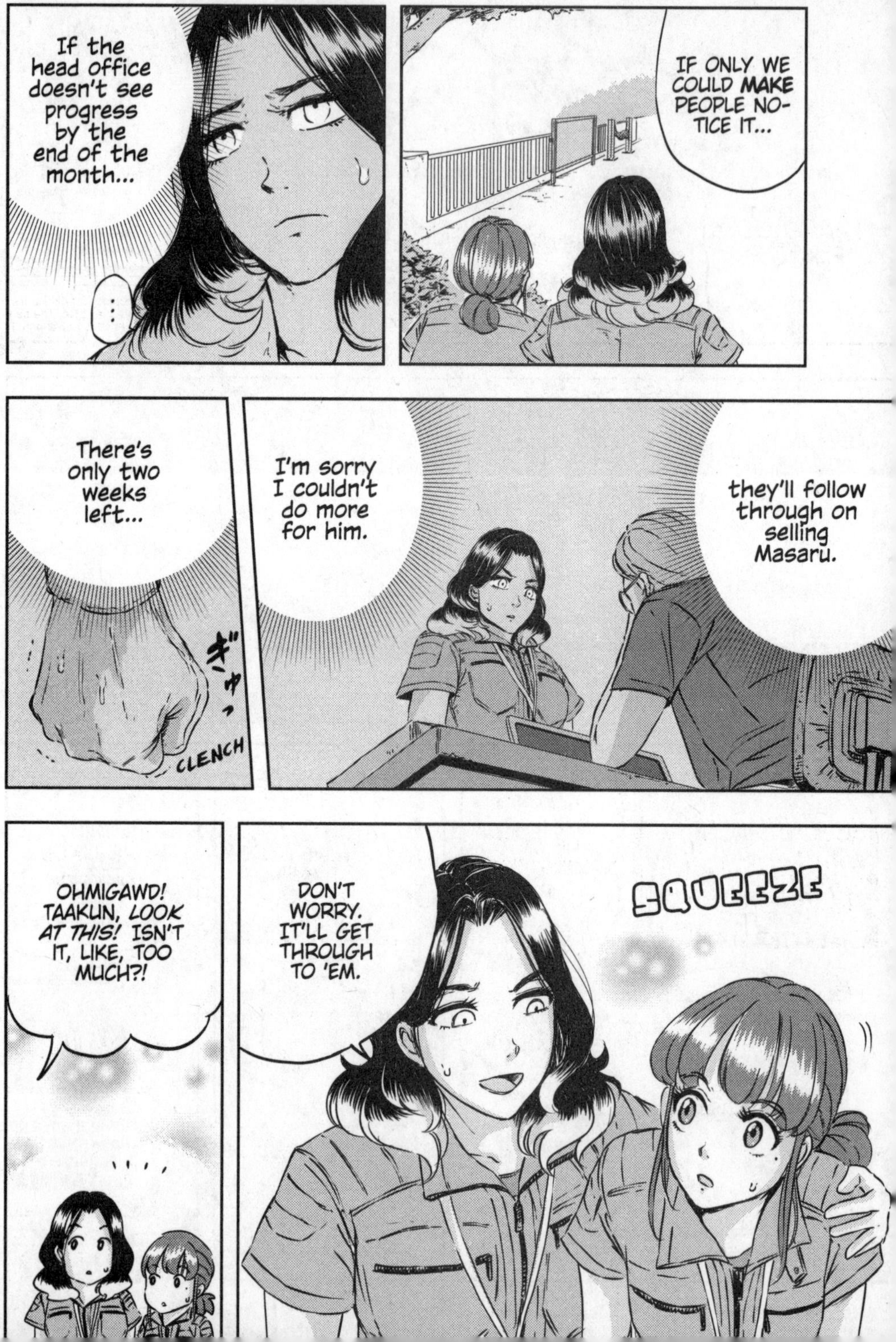
IF ONLY WE COULD MAKE PEOPLE NO-TICE IT...
If the head office doesn't see progress by the end of the month...
...
they'll follow through on selling Masaru.
I'm sorry I couldn't do more for him.
There's only two weeks left...
ギュッ
CLENCH
SQUEEZE
DON'T WORRY. IT'LL GET THROUGH TO 'EM.
OHMIGAWD! TAAKUN, LOOK AT THIS! ISN'T IT, LIKE, TOO MUCH?!

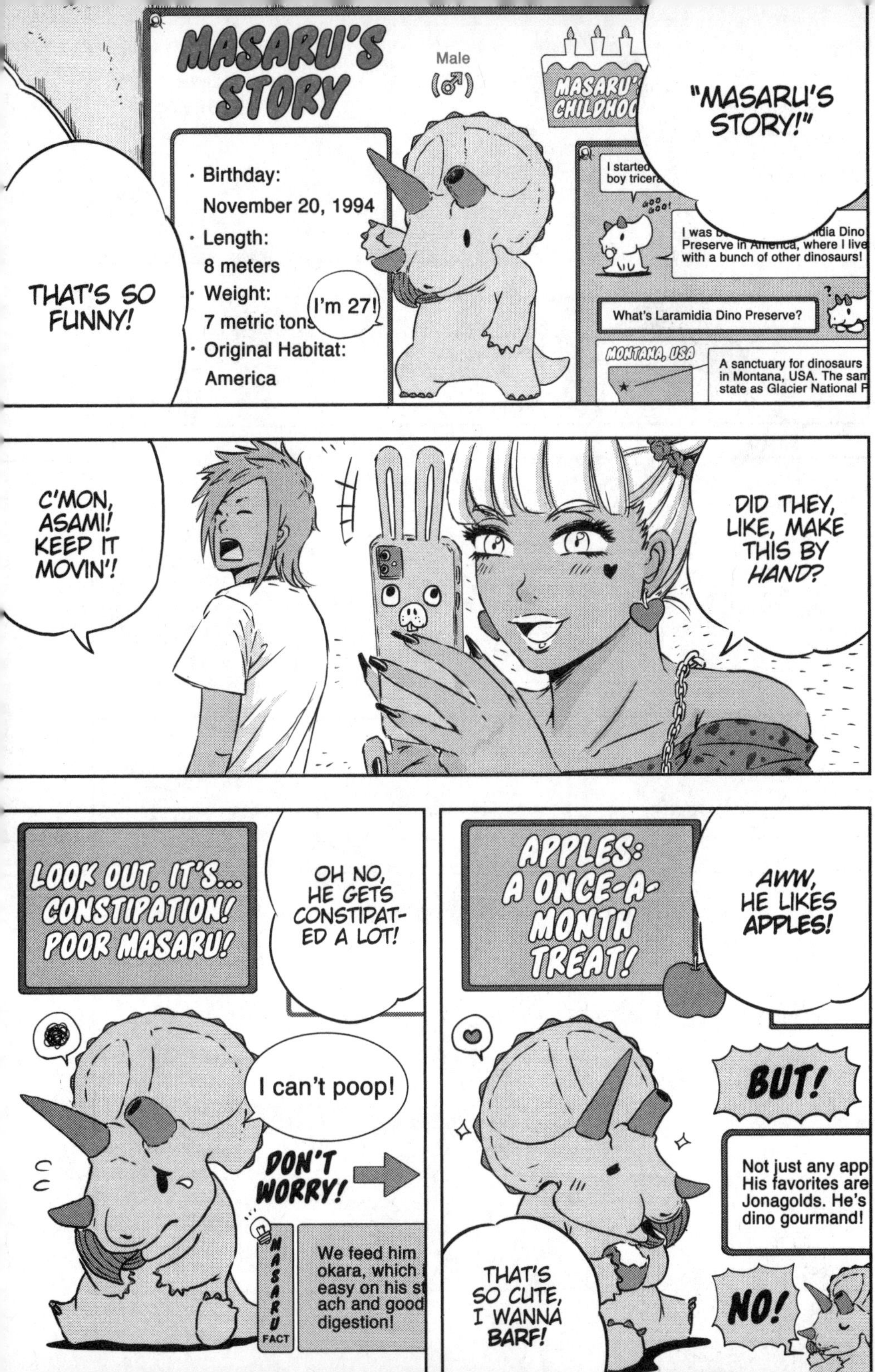
"MASARU'S STORY!"
MASARU'S CHILDHOO
MASARU'S STORY
Male (♂)
· Birthday: November 20, 1994
· Length: 8 meters
· Weight: 7 metric tons
· Original Habitat: America
I'm 27!
I started
boy tricera
GOO GOO!
I was b dia Dino Preserve in America, where I live with a bunch of other dinosaurs!
What's Laramidia Dino Preserve?
MONTANA, USA
A sanctuary for dinosaurs in Montana, USA. The sam state as Glacier National
THAT'S SO FUNNY!
DID THEY, LIKE, MAKE THIS BY HAND?
C'MON, ASAMI! KEEP IT MOVIN'!
APPLES: A ONCE-A-MONTH TREAT!
AWW, HE LIKES APPLES!
BUT!
Not just any app His favorites are Jonagolds. He's dino gourmand!
NO!
THAT'S SO CUTE, I WANNA BARF!
OH NO, HE GETS CONSTIPAT-ED A LOT!
LOOK OUT, IT'S... CONSTIPATION! POOR MASARU!
I can't poop!
DON'T WORRY!
MASARU FACT
We feed him okara, which easy on his st ach and good digestion!

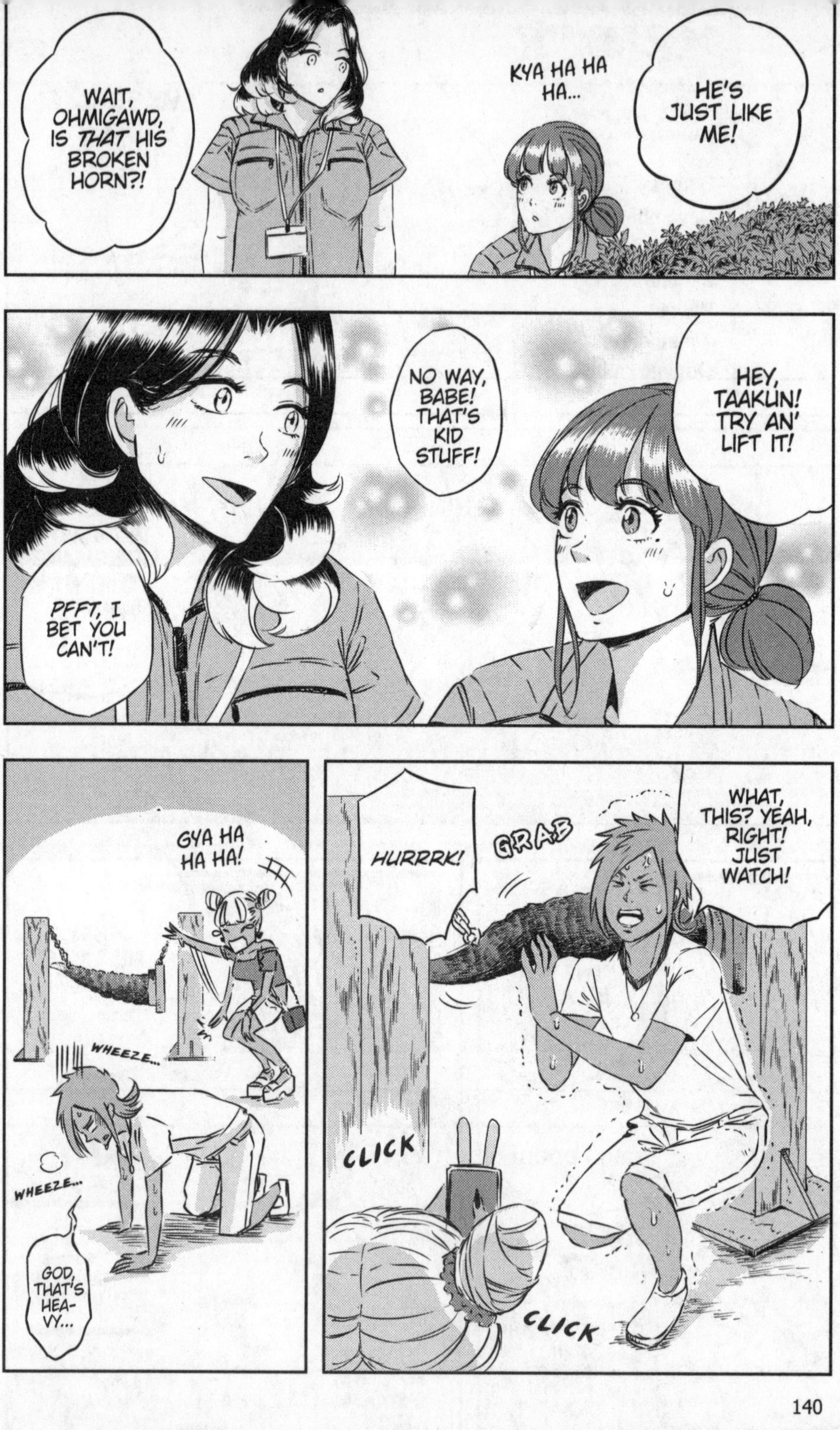
HE'S JUST LIKE ME!
KYA HA HA HA...
WAIT, OHMIGAWD, IS *THAT* HIS BROKEN HORN?!
HEY, TAAKUN! TRY AN' LIFT IT!
NO WAY, BABE! THAT'S KID STUFF!
PFFT, I BET YOU CAN'T!
WHAT, THIS? YEAH, RIGHT! JUST WATCH!
GRAB
HURRRK!
CLICK
CLICK
GYA HA HA HA!
WHEEZE...
WHEEZE...
GOD, THAT'S HEA-VY...

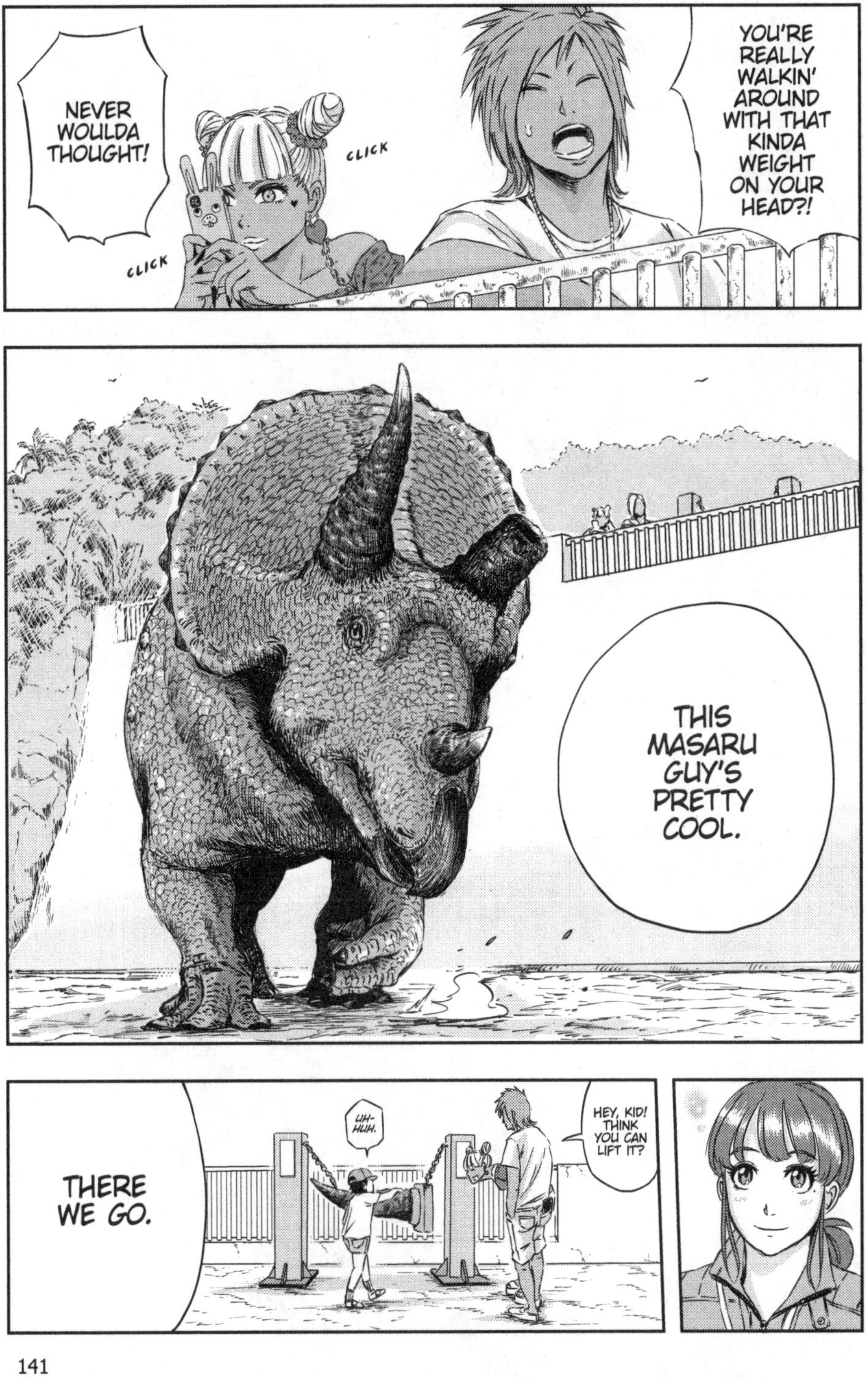

YOU'RE REALLY WALKIN' AROUND WITH THAT KINDA WEIGHT ON YOUR HEAD?!
CLICK
NEVER WOULDA THOUGHT!
CLICK
THIS MASARU GUY'S PRETTY COOL.
HEY, KID! THINK YOU CAN LIFT IT?
UH-HUH.
THERE WE GO.

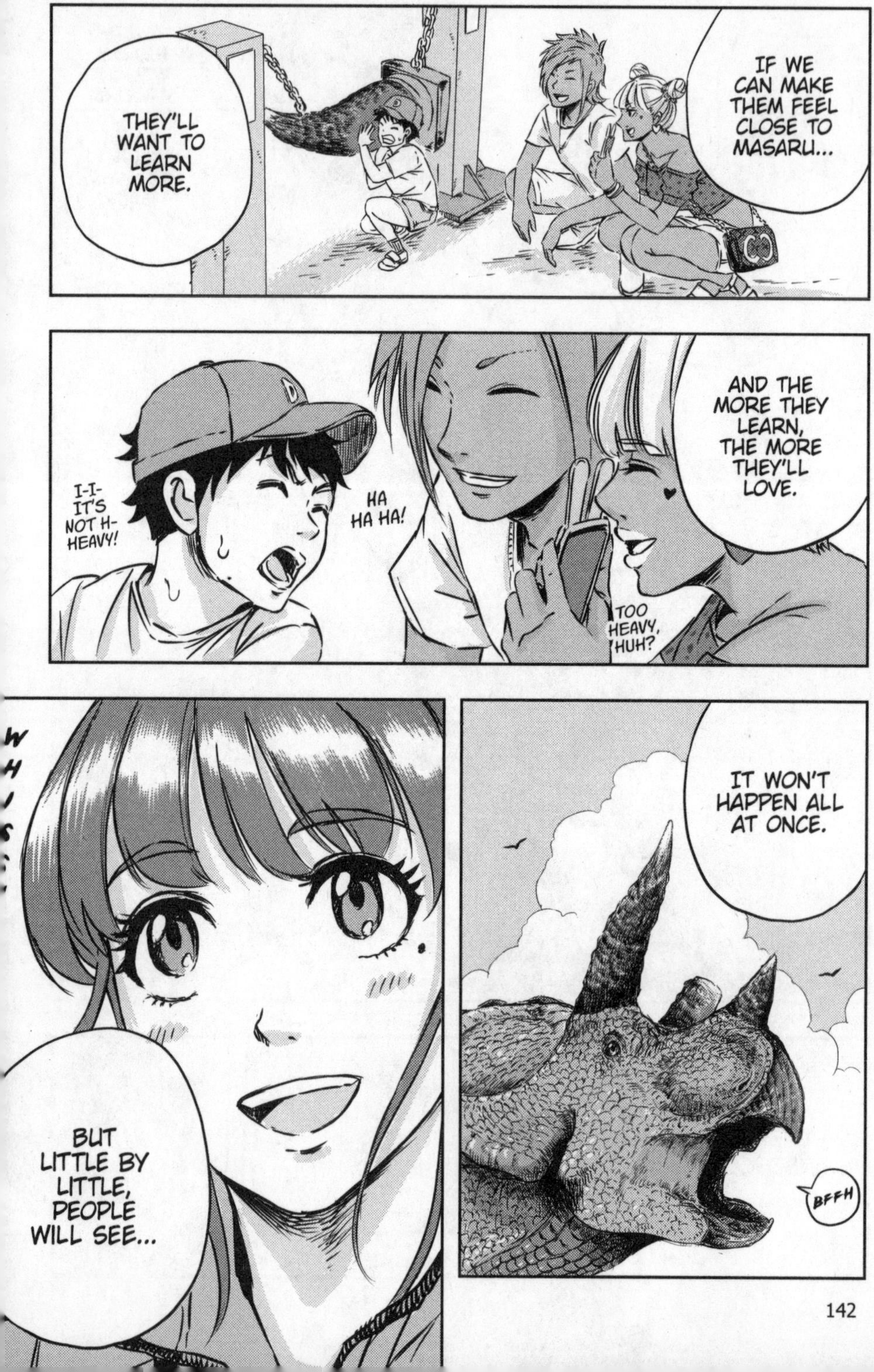
IF WE CAN MAKE THEM FEEL CLOSE TO MASARU...
THEY'LL WANT TO LEARN MORE.
AND THE MORE THEY LEARN, THE MORE THEY'LL LOVE.
TOO HEAVY, HUH?
HA HA HA!
I-I-IT'S NOT H-HEAVY!
IT WON'T HAPPEN ALL AT ONCE.
BFFH
BUT LITTLE BY LITTLE, PEOPLE WILL SEE...

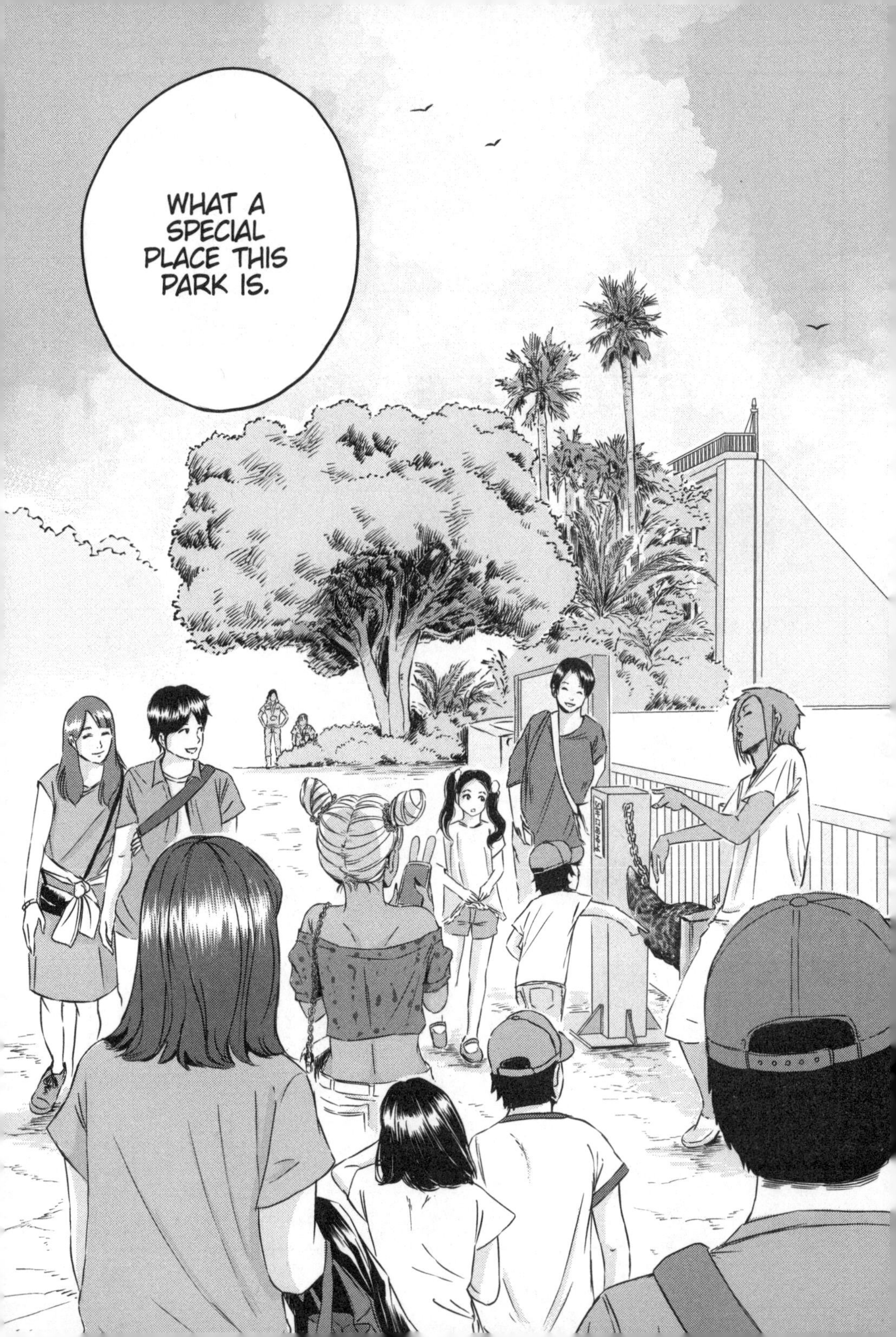
WHAT A SPECIAL PLACE THIS PARK IS.

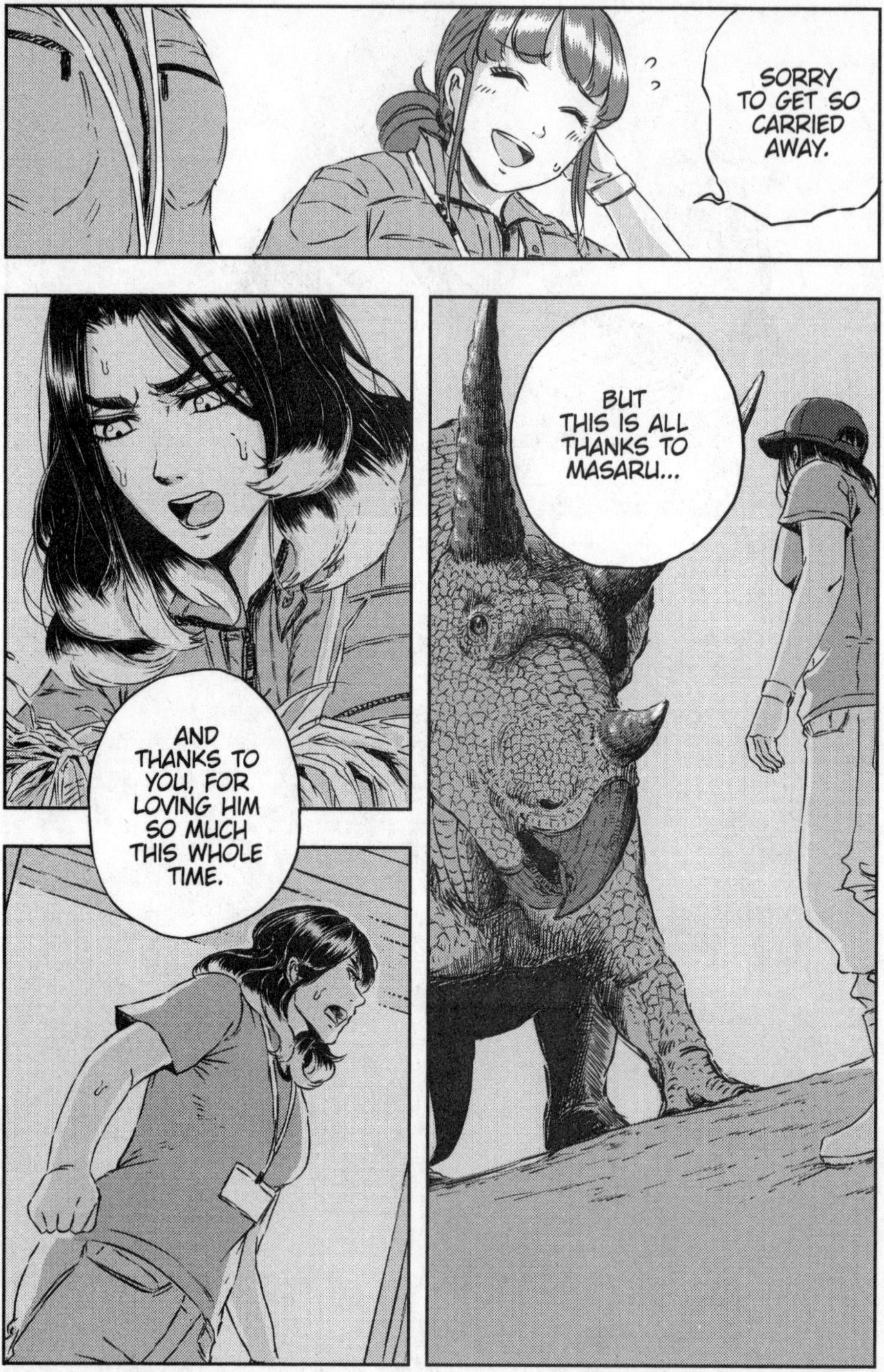
SORRY TO GET SO CARRIED AWAY.
BUT THIS IS ALL THANKS TO MASARU...
AND THANKS TO YOU, FOR LOVING HIM SO MUCH THIS WHOLE TIME.

THIS COULDN'T HAVE HAPPENED WITHOUT YOU, KARIN-SAN.

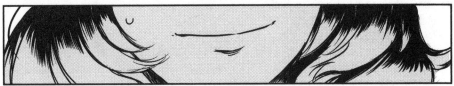

LOOK, TAAKUN! LOOK, LOOK, LOOK!

JEEZ, YOU--!

SQUEEZE

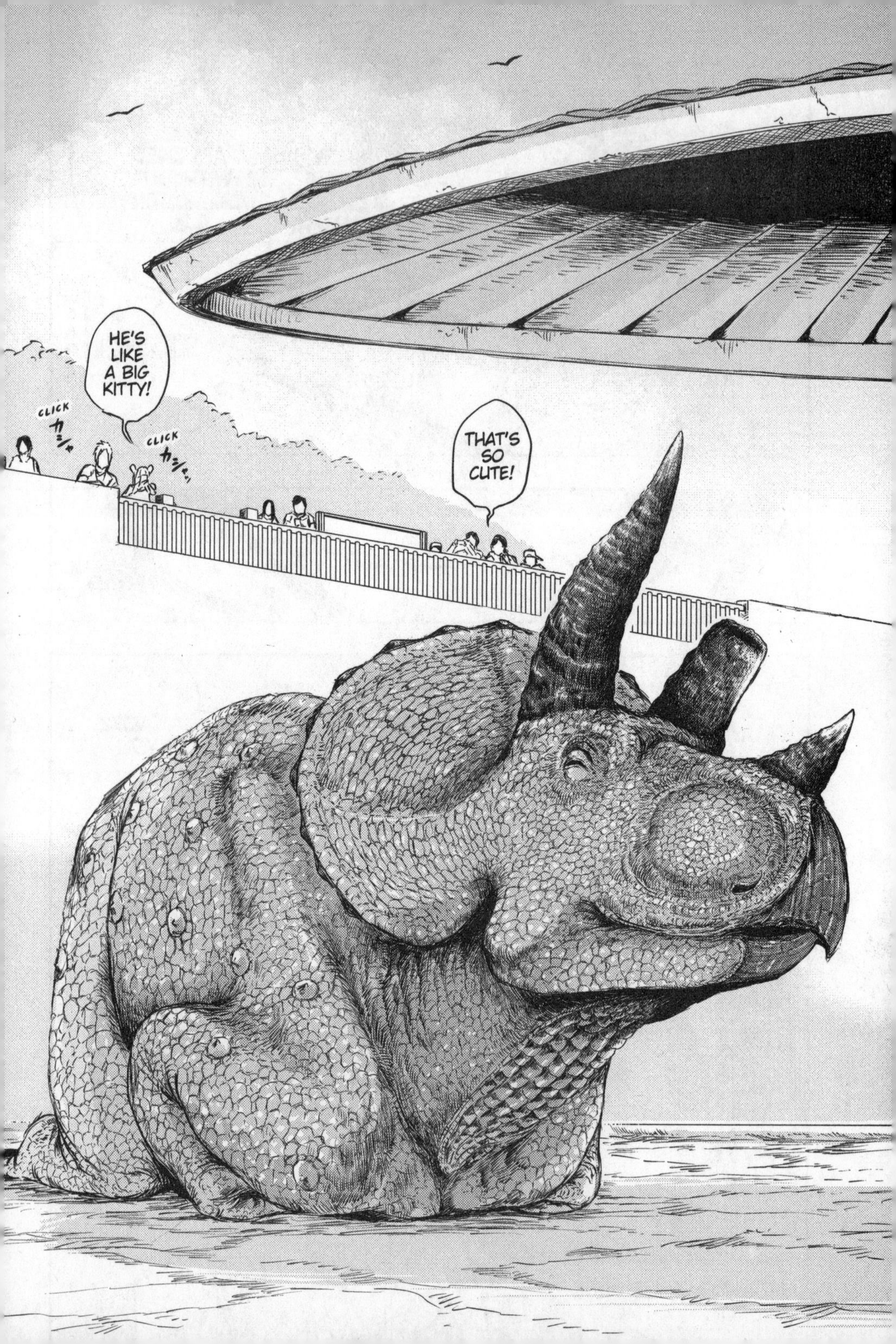
THAT'S SO CUTE!
HE'S LIKE A BIG KITTY!
CLICK
CLICK

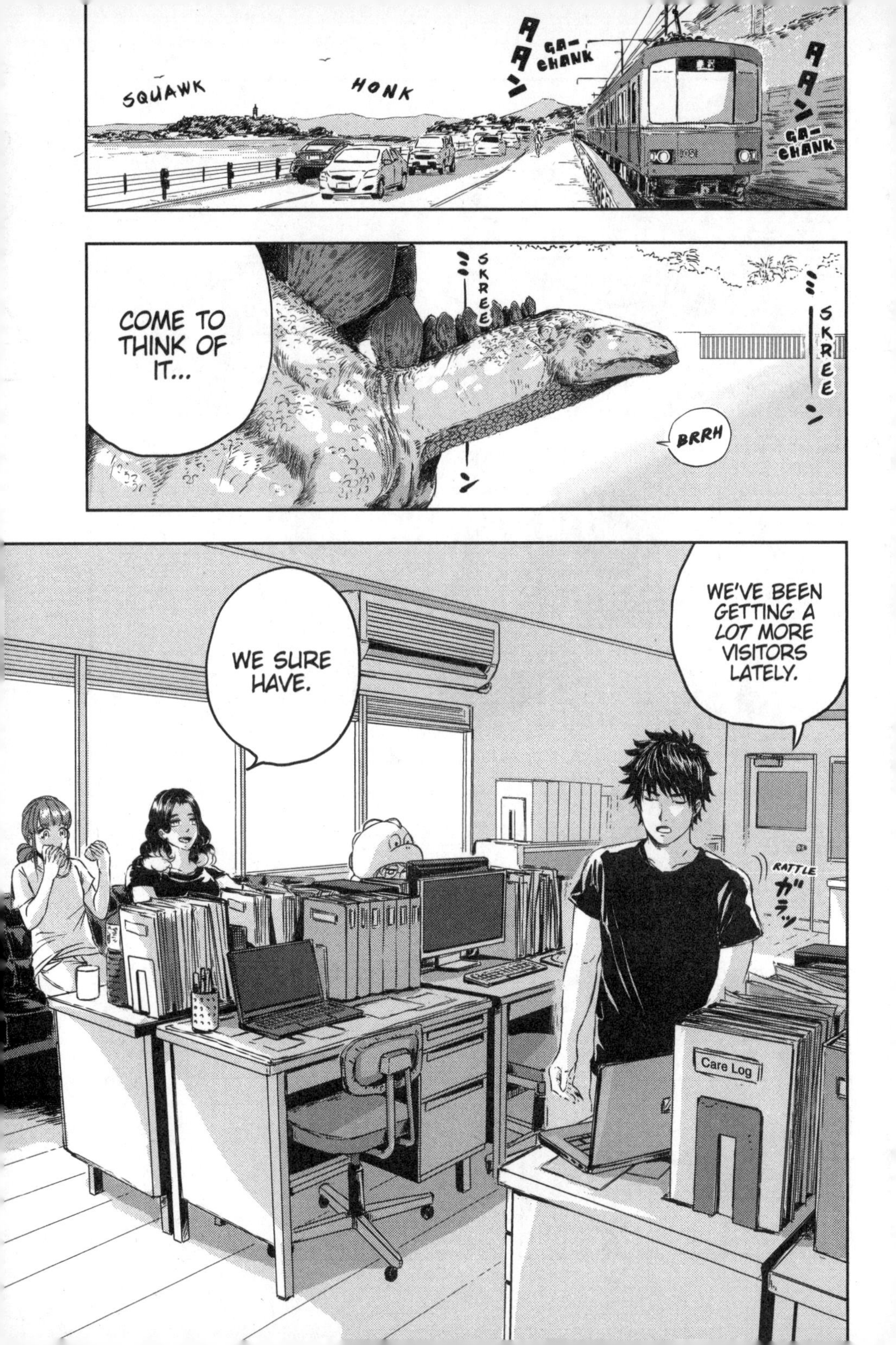

ガタン
GA-CHANK
ガタン
GA-CHANK
HONK
SQUAWK
SKREE
SKREE
BRRH
COME TO THINK OF IT...
WE'VE BEEN GETTING A LOT MORE VISITORS LATELY.
RATTLE
ガラッ
Care Log
WE SURE HAVE.

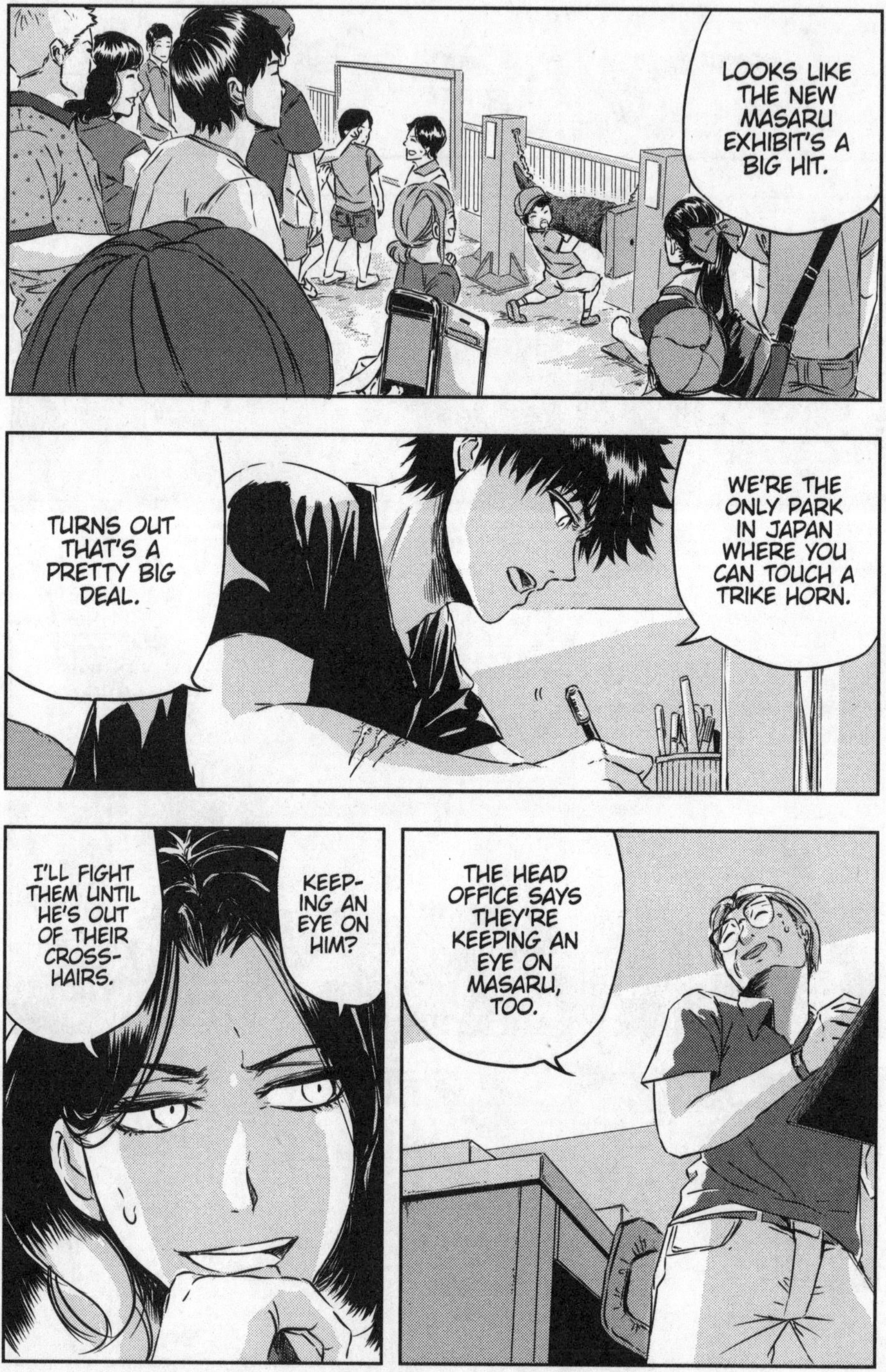
LOOKS LIKE THE NEW MASARU EXHIBIT'S A BIG HIT.
WE'RE THE ONLY PARK IN JAPAN WHERE YOU CAN TOUCH A TRIKE HORN.
TURNS OUT THAT'S A PRETTY BIG DEAL.
THE HEAD OFFICE SAYS THEY'RE KEEPING AN EYE ON MASARU, TOO.
KEEP-ING AN EYE ON HIM?
I'LL FIGHT THEM UNTIL HE'S OUT OF THEIR CROSS-HAIRS.

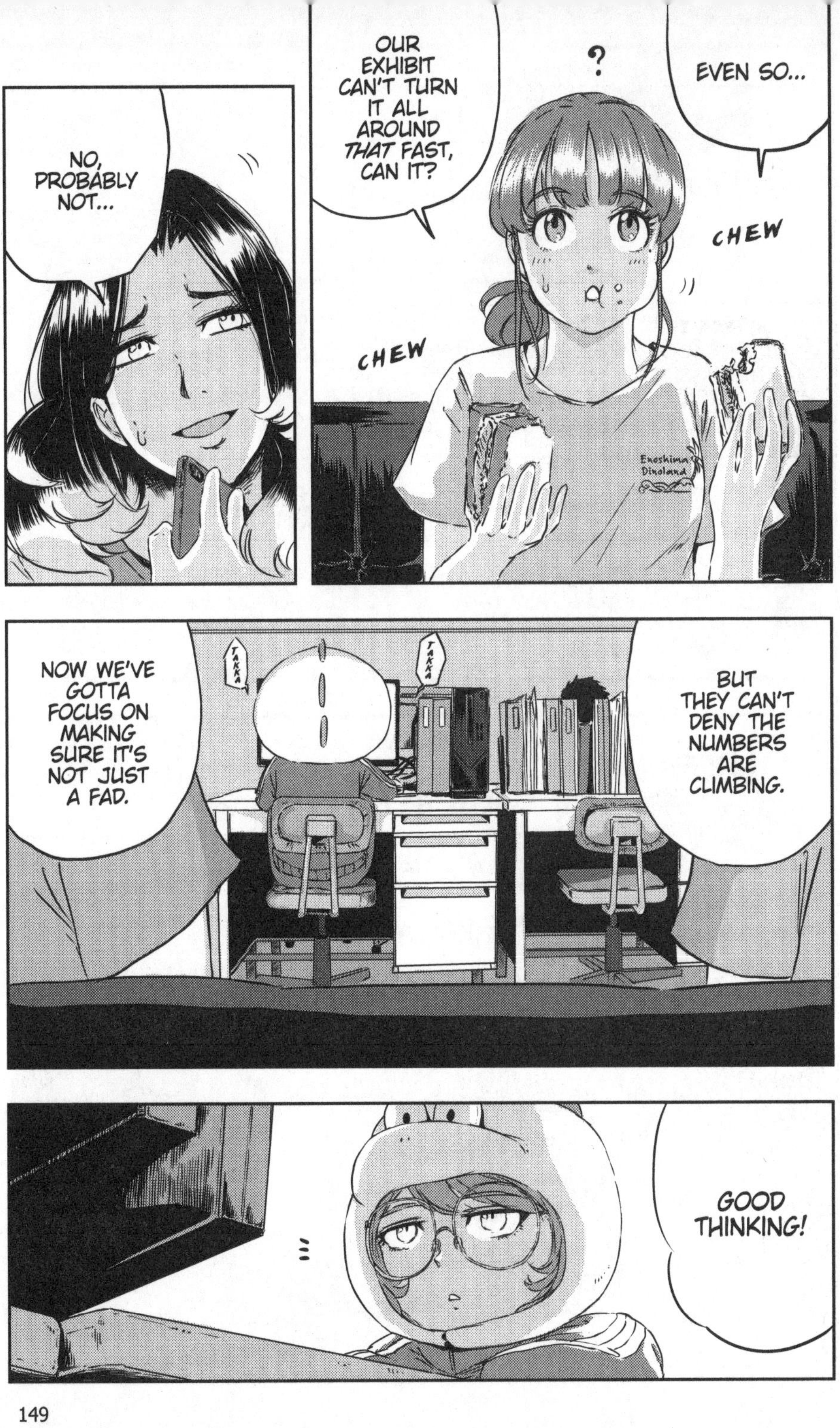
EVEN SO...
?
OUR EXHIBIT CAN'T TURN IT ALL AROUND *THAT* FAST, CAN IT?
CHEW
CHEW
NO, PROBABLY NOT...
BUT THEY CAN'T DENY THE NUMBERS ARE CLIMBING.
TAKA
TAKA
NOW WE'VE GOTTA FOCUS ON MAKING SURE IT'S NOT JUST A FAD.
GOOD THINKING!

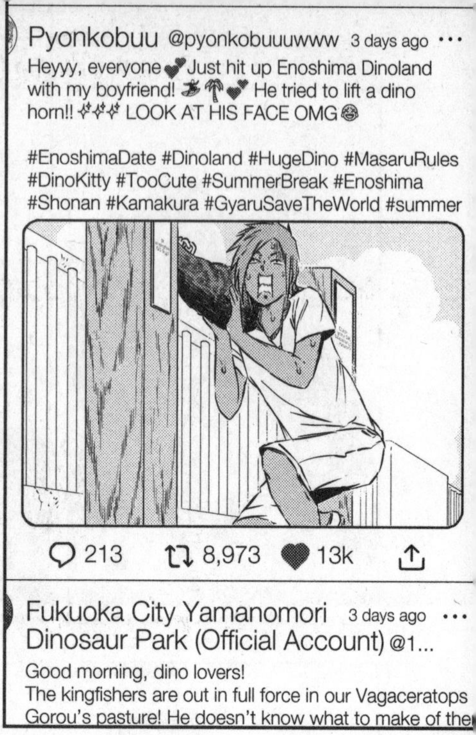
Pyonkobuu @pyonkobuuuwww 3 days ago ···
Heyyy, everyone 💕 Just hit up Enoshima Dinoland with my boyfriend! 🏄🌴💕 He tried to lift a dino horn!! ✨✨✨ LOOK AT HIS FACE OMG 😂
#EnoshimaDate #Dinoland #HugeDino #MasaruRules #DinoKitty #TooCute #SummerBreak #Enoshima #Shonan #Kamakura #GyaruSaveTheWorld #summer
213 8,973 13k
Fukuoka City Yamanomori Dinosaur Park (Official Account) @1... 3 days ago ···
Good morning, dino lovers!
The kingfishers are out in full force in our Vagaceratops Gorou's pasture! He doesn't know what to make of the

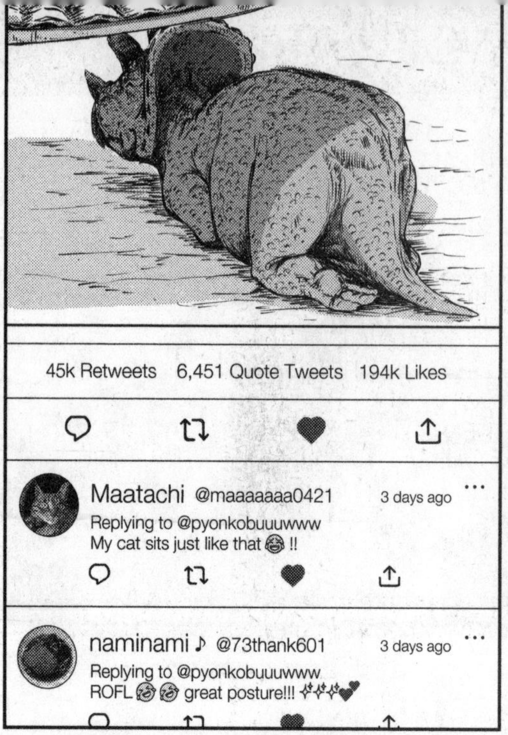
45k Retweets 6,451 Quote Tweets 194k Likes
Maatachi @maaaaaaa0421 3 days ago ···
Replying to @pyonkobuuuwww
My cat sits just like that 😂 !!
naminami ♪ @73thank601 3 days ago ···
Replying to @pyonkobuuuwww
ROFL 😂😂 great posture!!! ✨✨✨💕

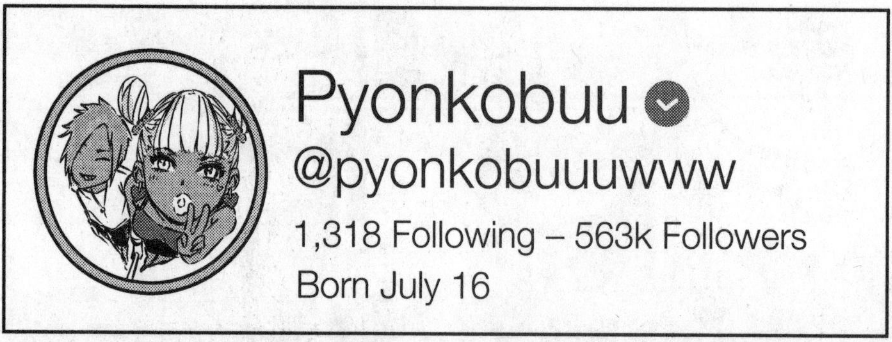
Pyonkobuu
@pyonkobuuuwww
1,318 Following – 563k Followers
Born July 16

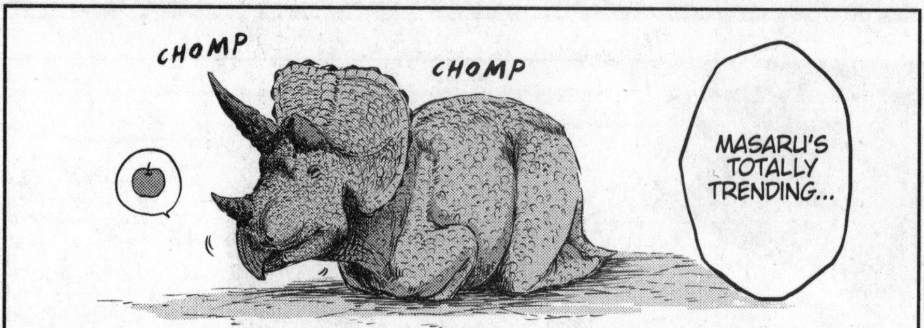
MASARU'S TOTALLY TRENDING...
CHOMP
CHOMP

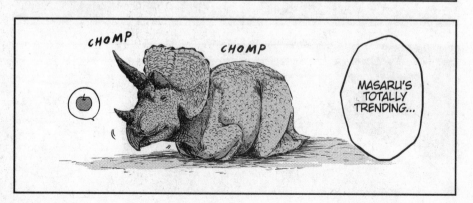

Dr. Dino's Lab Log

FILE. 04 Follow Doubt to Discovery!

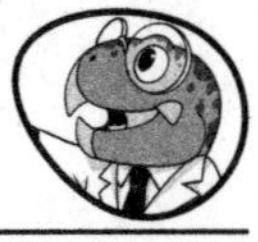

I know this might sound strange, but do me a favor: touch your forearm for me. You know, the part from your elbow to your wrist, with your palm pointed forwards. Feel the bone that connects the outside of your elbow to your thumb? That's called the radius. The other forearm bone, which goes from the back of your elbow to your pinky finger, is called the ulna. This two-bone structure isn't unique to humans. Other mammals have it, frogs have it, lizards have it, and—you guessed it—dinosaurs had it.

Now try standing at attention, with your arms down and against your sides. Keep those two forearm bones parallel to each other. Hold your hands with the backs angled slightly behind you, thumbs towards the front and pinkies to the rear. If you were to get down on all fours from this position, your fingertips would point off to the sides.

So how can you turn your fingertips towards the front instead? In some mammals (including humans), the radius and ulna cross over so that the radius is on the outside at the elbow, but on the inside at the wrist. This puts the thumb on the inside and the pinky outwards, but indeed pointed forwards! This crossover is called pronation, and it comes naturally to you and me. But most animals actually cannot pronate, and dinosaurs were no exception!

Let's look at crocodiles and lizards to see how they manage. They stand with what would be their armpits spread, with elbows pointed out to the sides. By doing this, they keep their radius and ulna parallel, while also pointing their forelimb toes forward.

Now, how about *Triceratops*? Did they handle this like mammals, or like lizards? Actually, there was a great deal of debate about it! But both sides of that discussion based their position on a particular question: "How did *Triceratops* stand with its toes pointed forward?" That was the very premise of the debate.

But hang on a second! Who says *Triceratops* had to point its toes forward in the first place?

That question suddenly came to me while I was studying *Triceratops* as a grad student. Maybe, I thought, it actually kept its armpits closed, with its radius forwards and ulna to the rear; then, the tops of its front feet and its toes would be angled out to the side, just like sea lions walking on land. That idea coincided with fossilized footprints that showed toes pointed outward. Standing like that, *Triceratops'* first, second, and third toes (which likely supported more of its weight) would still be pointed to the front. With careful observation, it became clearer and clearer to me that this sort of movement, with the tops of the feet angled outwards, would have come naturally to dinosaurs.

Fortunately, we've found plenty of articulated skeletons that belonged to *Triceratops'* relatives. They can be seen in museums in Tokyo, Ottawa, and New York. We've also found a *Vagaceratops* specimen in a crouching position—and it's crouched in a position like the one I just described. Its palms cover its chest, with its wrists slightly bent towards the inside. In other words, it has its forelimbs tucked under its body like a resting cat! Its hindlimbs are positioned with the tops of the feet downwards, though, perhaps because it couldn't bend its heels very far. The end result is a pose that resembles the traditional Japanese sitting posture of *seiza*.

…I sure do devote a lot of page space to how dinosaurs sat down, don't I?

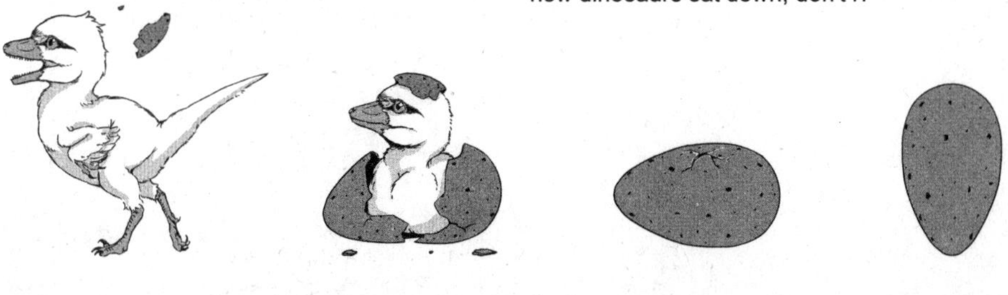

DINOSAUR SANCTUARY

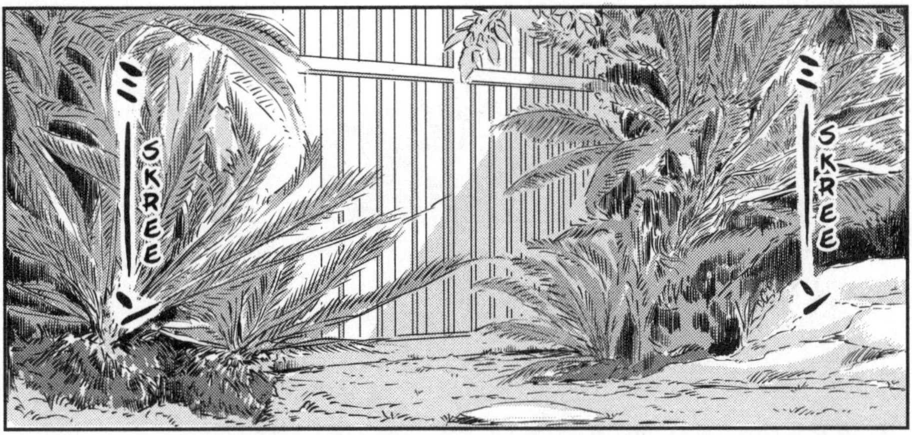
SKREE
SKREE

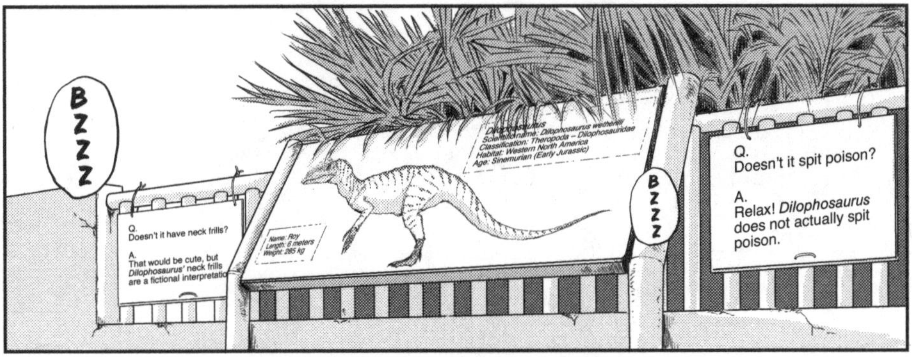
Q.
Doesn't it spit poison?
A.
Relax! *Dilophosaurus* does not actually spit poison.
BZZZ
Classification: Theropoda – Dilophosauridae
Habitat: Western North America
Age: Sinemurian (Early Jurassic)
Name: Roy
Length: 6 meters
Weight: 285 kg
Q.
Doesn't it have neck frills?
A.
That would be cute, but *Dilophosaurus'* neck frills are a fictional interpretatio
BZZZ

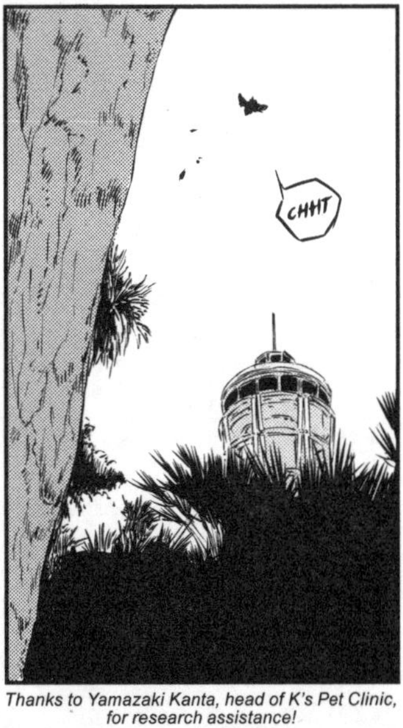
CHHT

Thanks to Yamazaki Kanta, head of K's Pet Clinic, for research assistance!

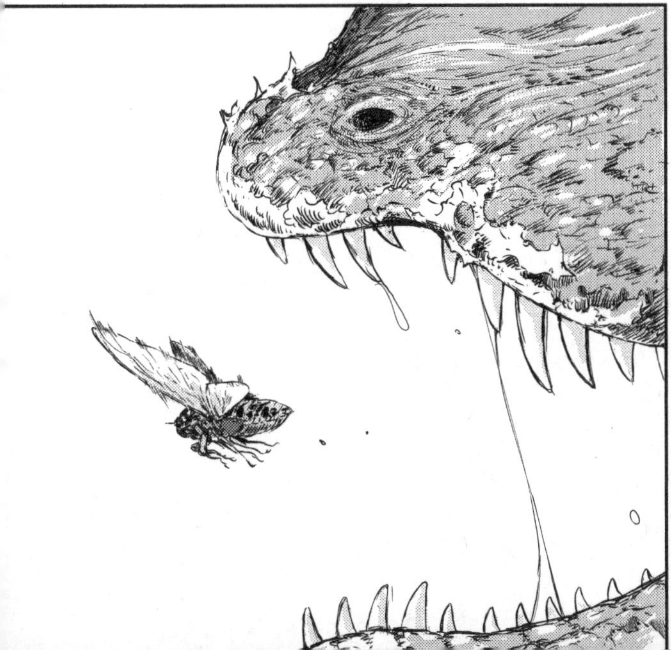

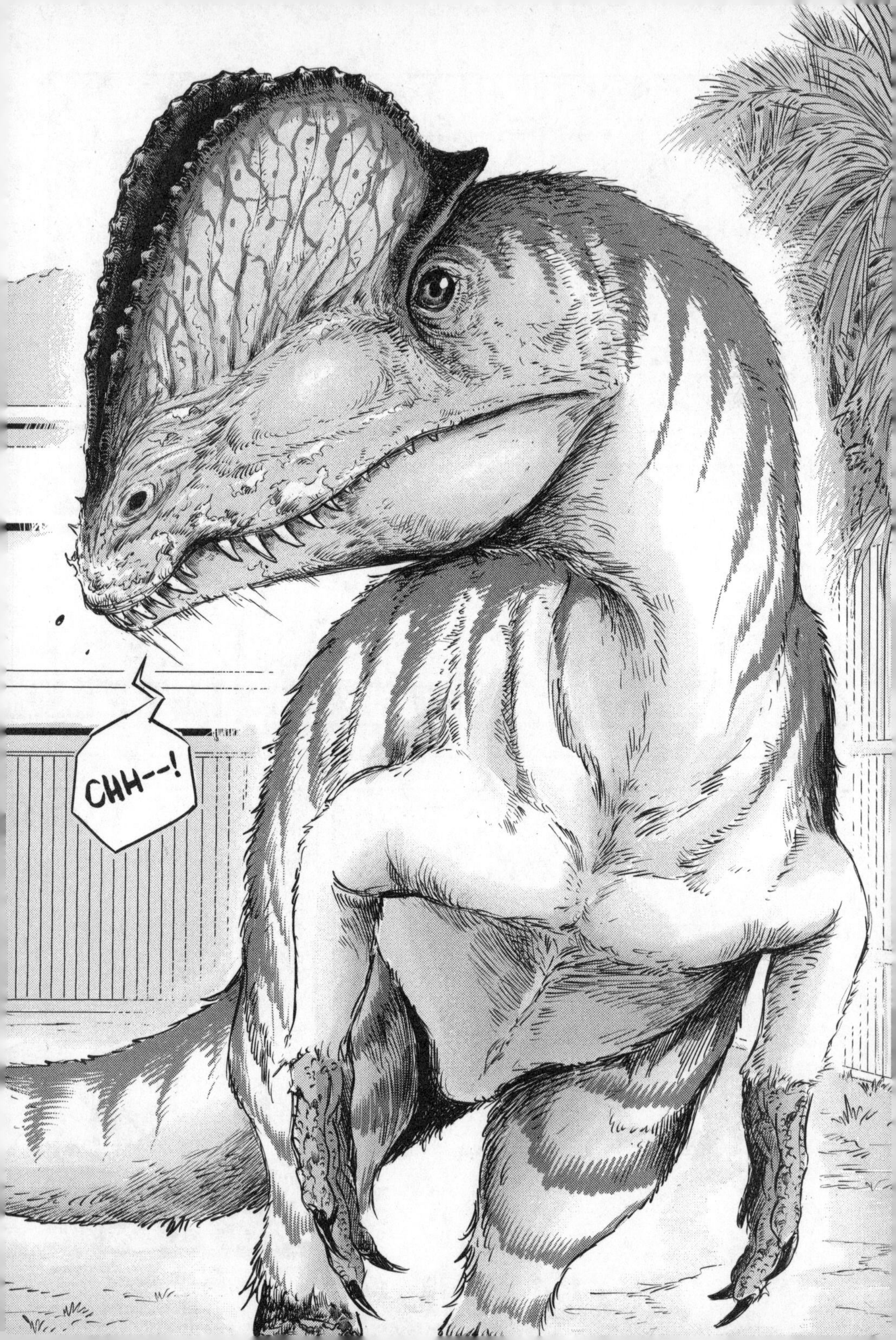
CHH--!

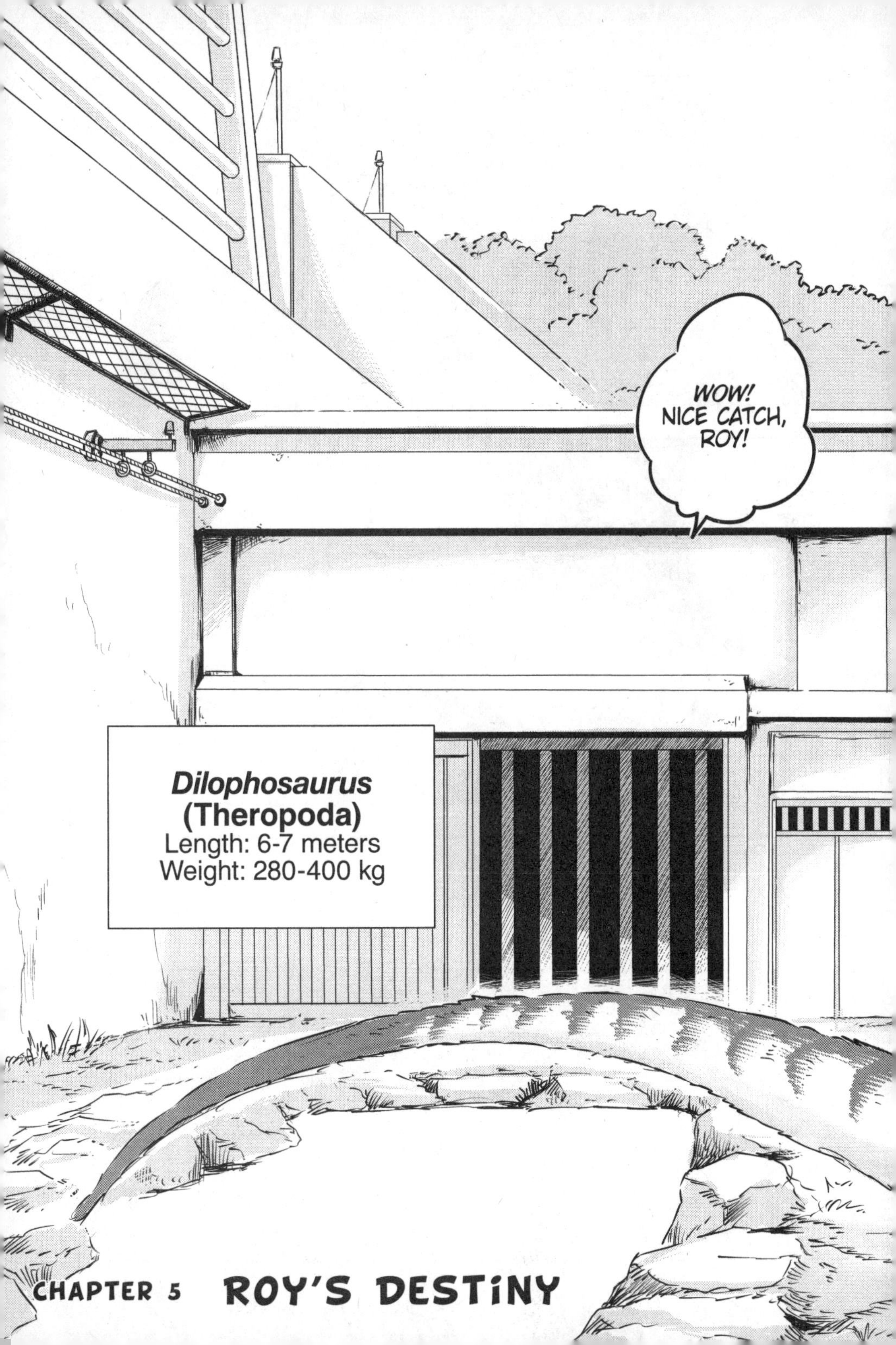
WOW! NICE CATCH, ROY!
Dilophosaurus (Theropoda)
Length: 6-7 meters
Weight: 280-400 kg
CHAPTER 5 ROY'S DESTINY

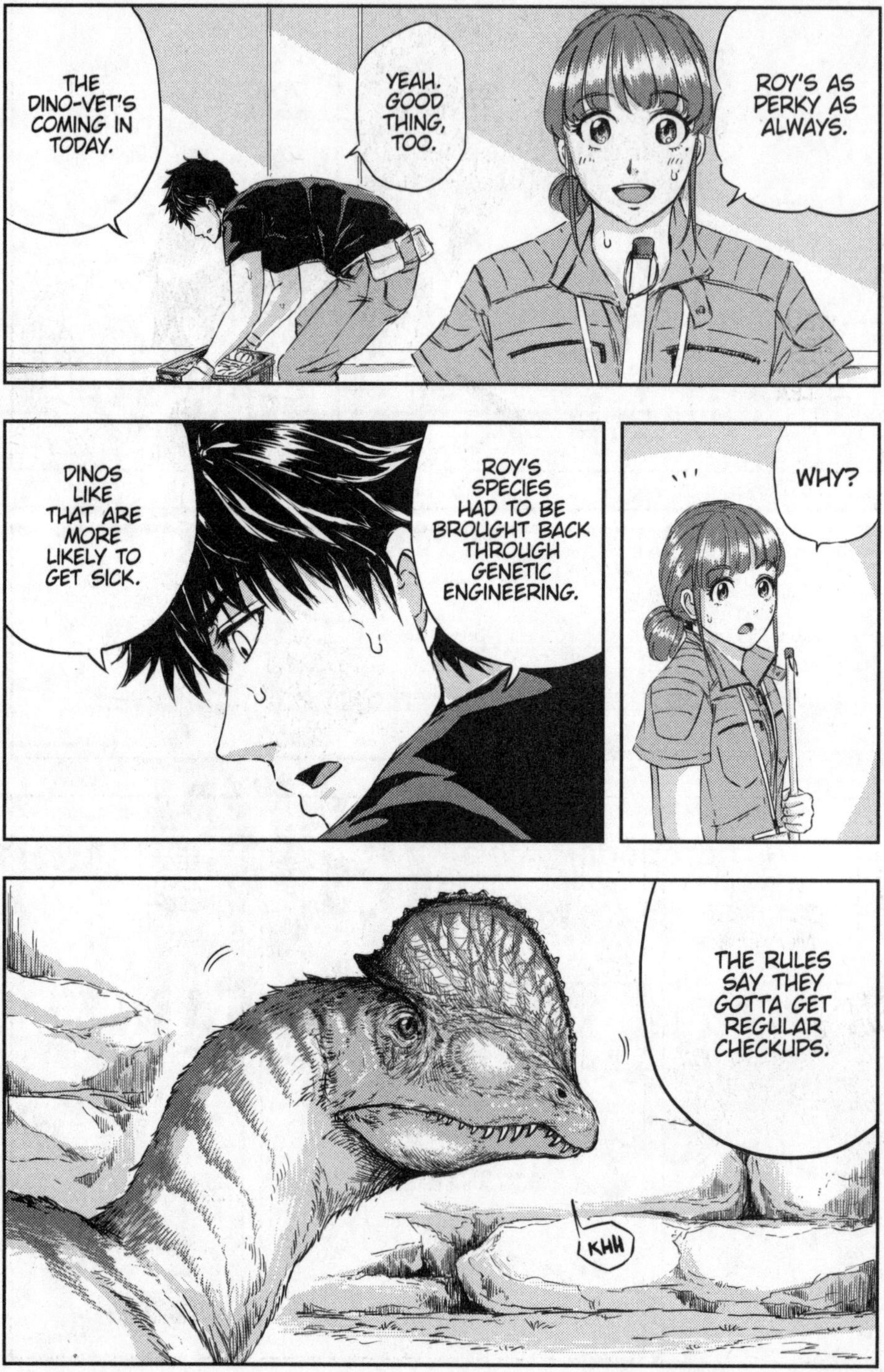
ROY'S AS PERKY AS ALWAYS.
YEAH. GOOD THING, TOO.
THE DINO-VET'S COMING IN TODAY.
WHY?
ROY'S SPECIES HAD TO BE BROUGHT BACK THROUGH GENETIC ENGINEERING.
DINOS LIKE THAT ARE MORE LIKELY TO GET SICK.
THE RULES SAY THEY GOTTA GET REGULAR CHECKUPS.
KHH

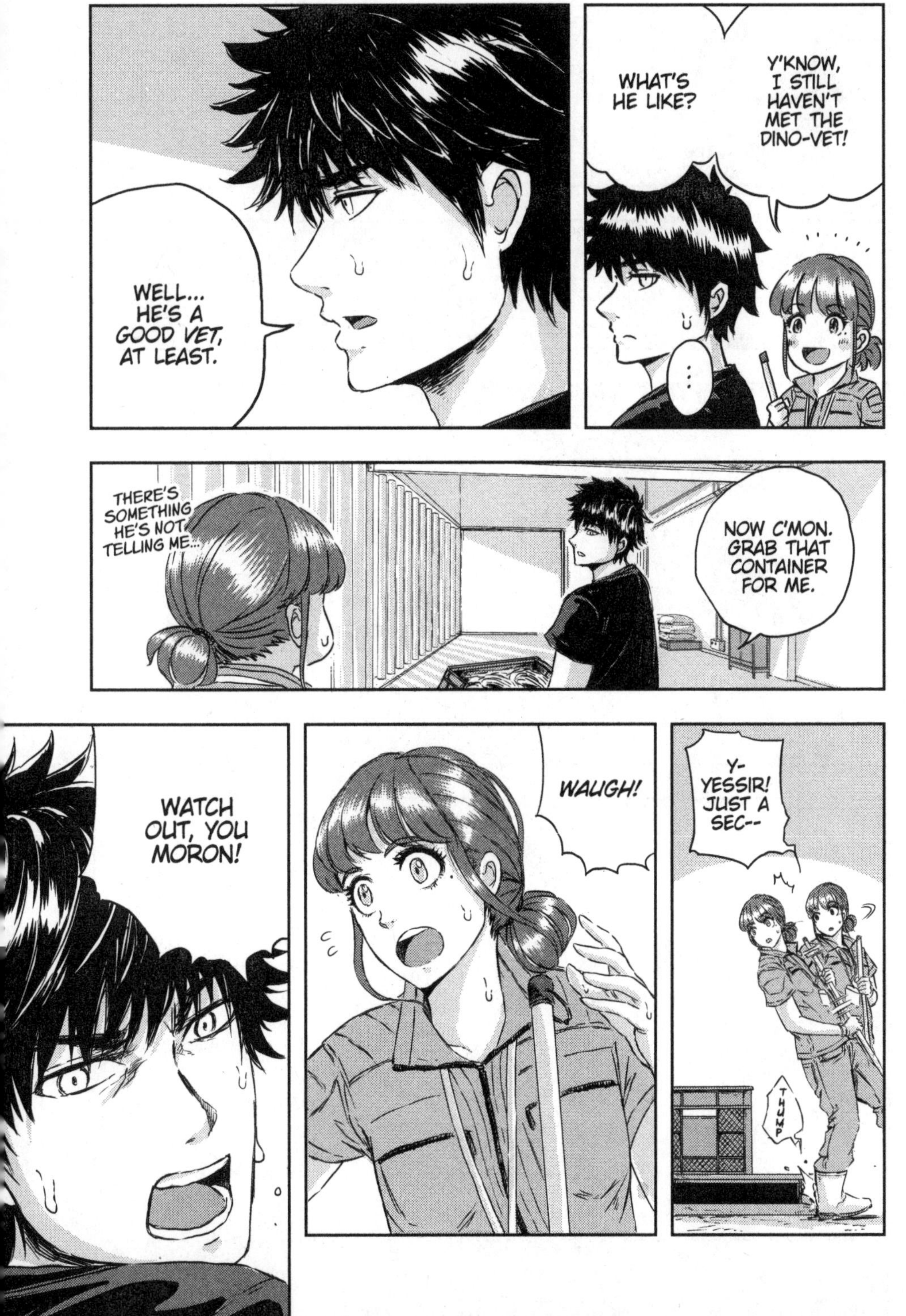
Y'KNOW, I STILL HAVEN'T MET THE DINO-VET!
WHAT'S HE LIKE?
...
WELL... HE'S A GOOD VET, AT LEAST.
NOW C'MON. GRAB THAT CONTAINER FOR ME.
THERE'S SOMETHING HE'S NOT TELLING ME...
Y-YESSIR! JUST A SEC--
THUMP
WAUGH!
WATCH OUT, YOU MORON!

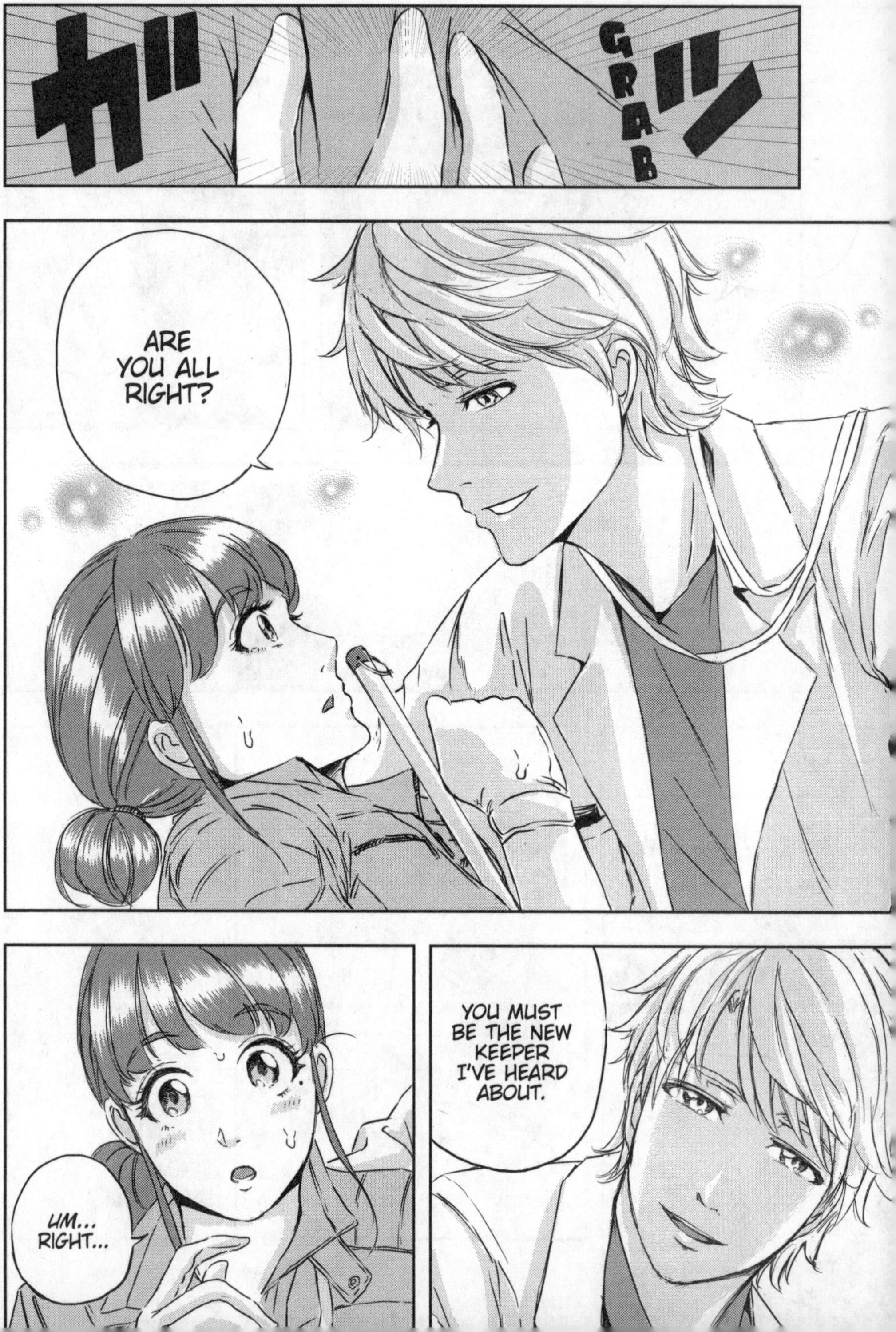
GRAB
ARE YOU ALL RIGHT?
YOU MUST BE THE NEW KEEPER I'VE HEARD ABOUT.
UM... RIGHT...

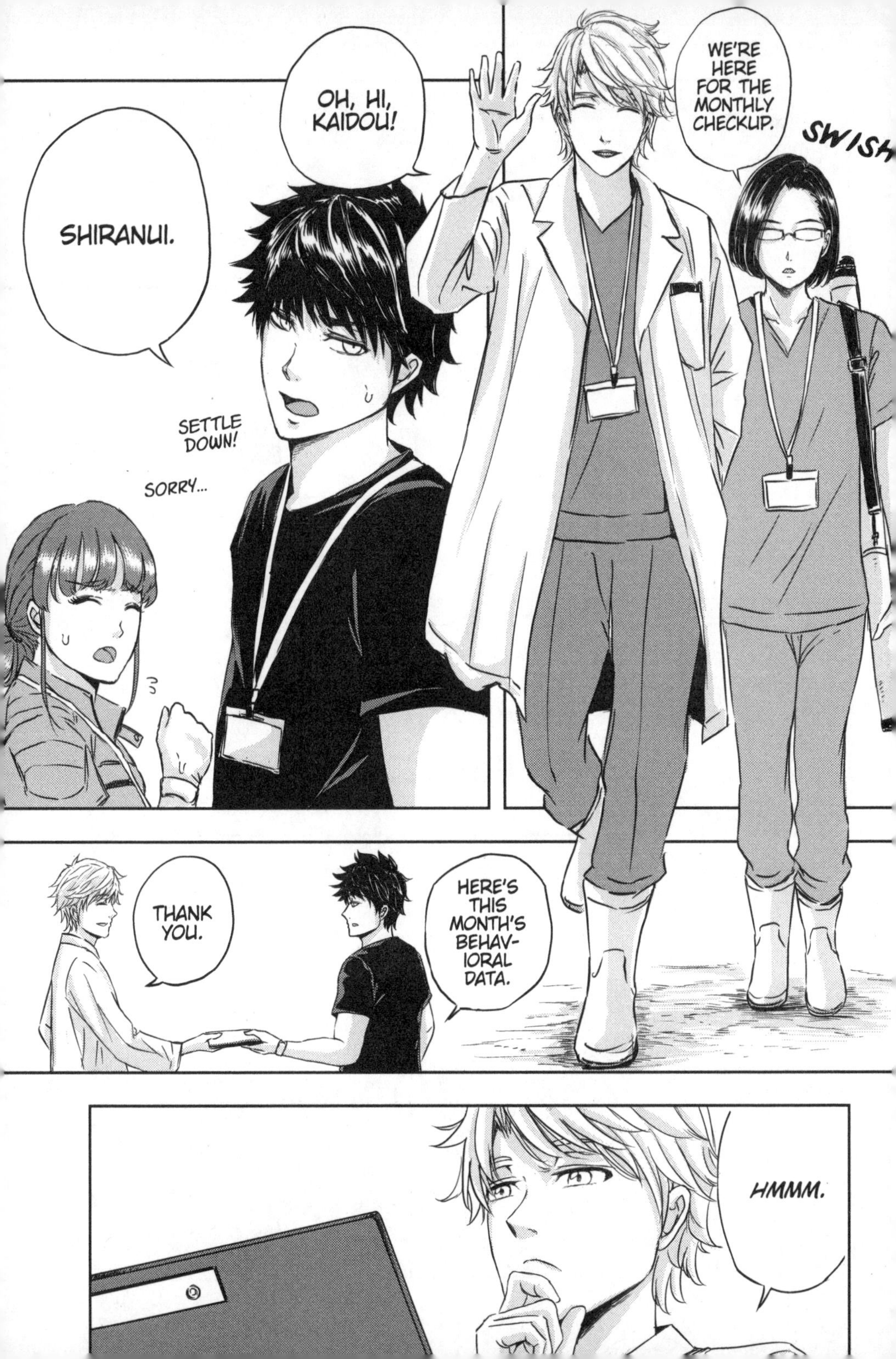
WE'RE HERE FOR THE MONTHLY CHECKUP.
SWISH
OH, HI, KAIDOU!
SHIRANUI.
SETTLE DOWN!
SORRY...
HERE'S THIS MONTH'S BEHAV-IORAL DATA.
THANK YOU.
HMMM.

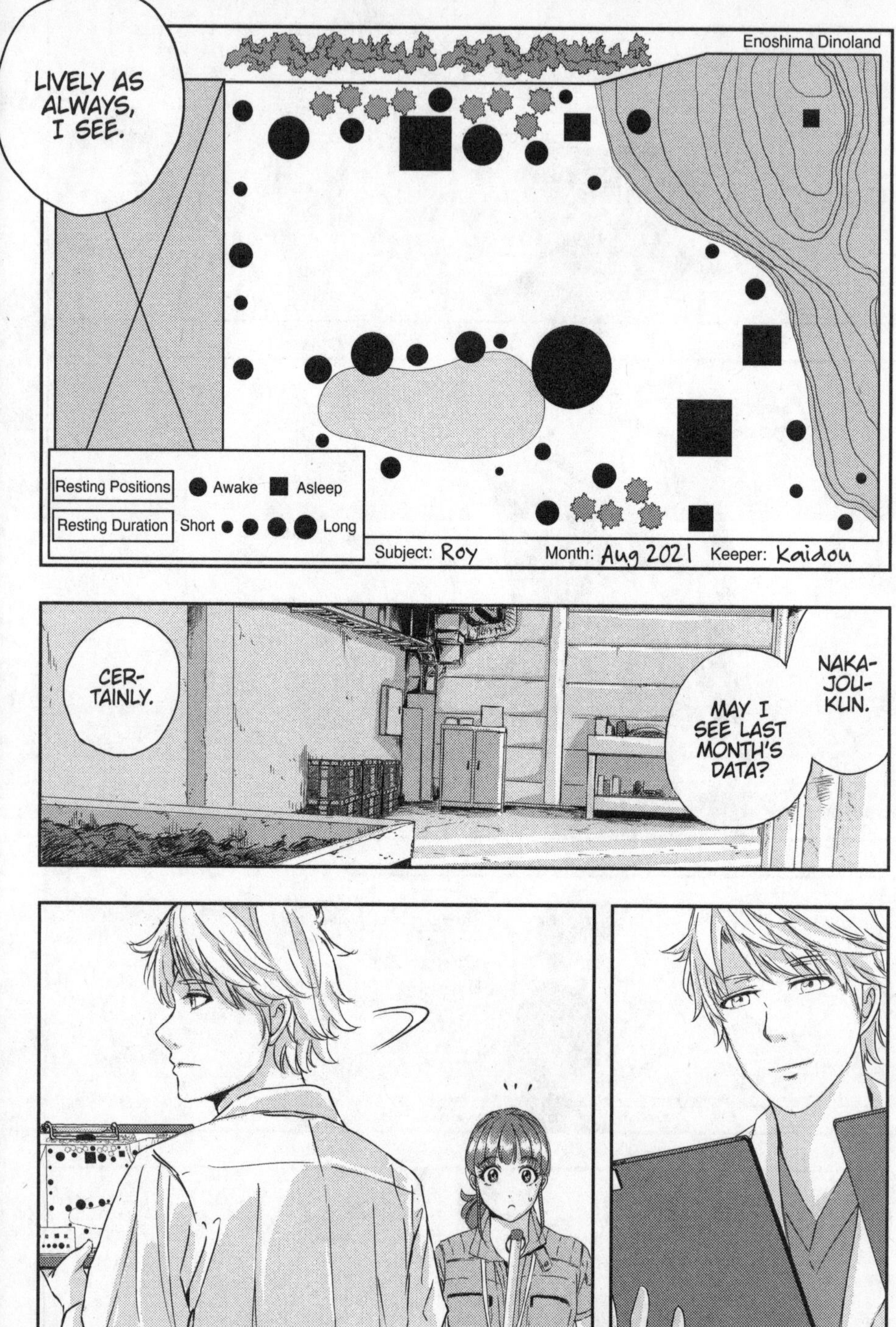
Enoshima Dinoland
LIVELY AS ALWAYS, I SEE.
Resting Positions
Awake
Asleep
Resting Duration
Short
Long
Subject: Roy
Month: Aug 2021
Keeper: Kaidou
NAKA-JOU-KUN.
MAY I SEE LAST MONTH'S DATA?
CER-TAINLY.

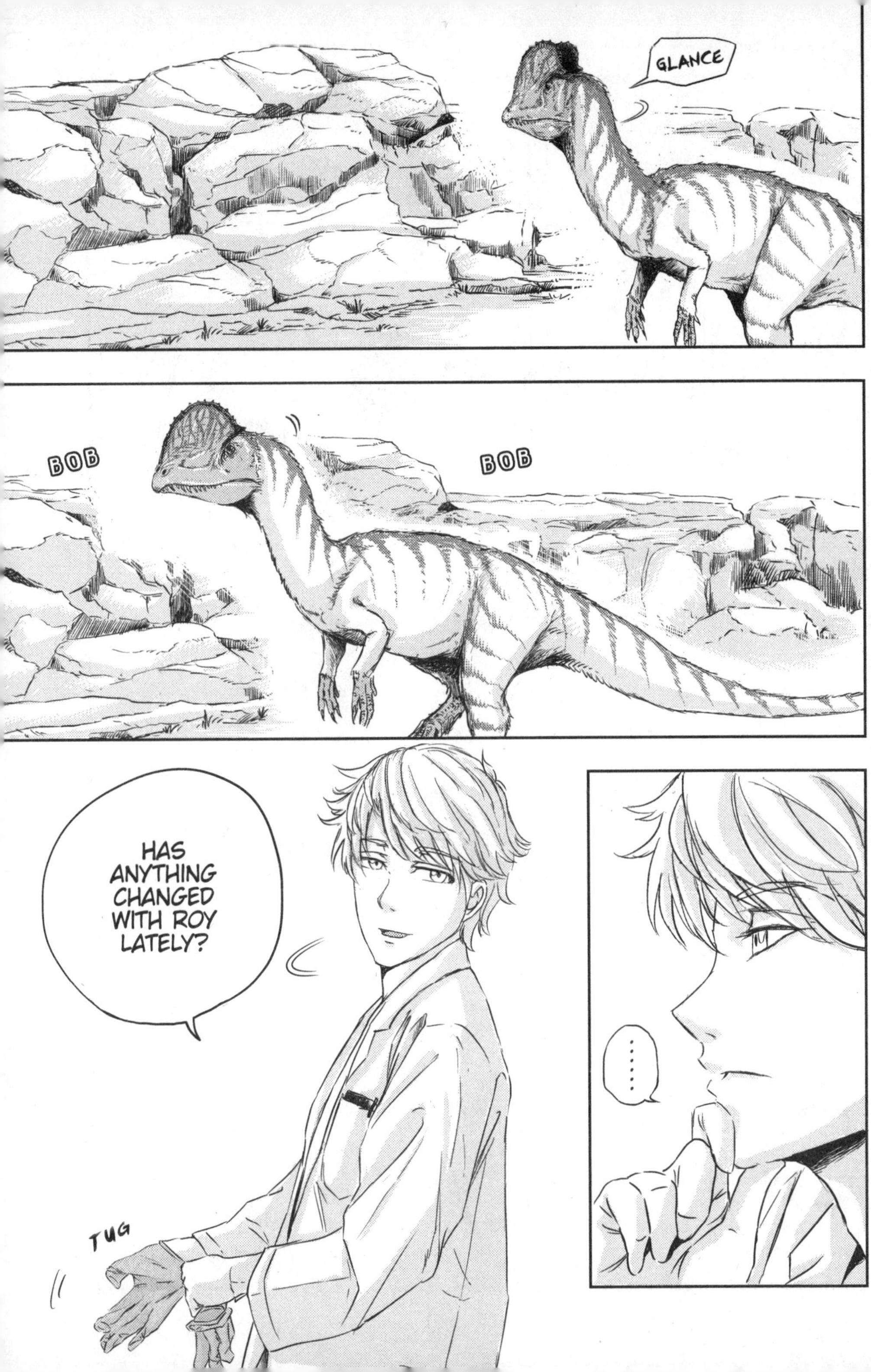
GLANCE
BOB
BOB
......
HAS ANYTHING CHANGED WITH ROY LATELY?
TUG

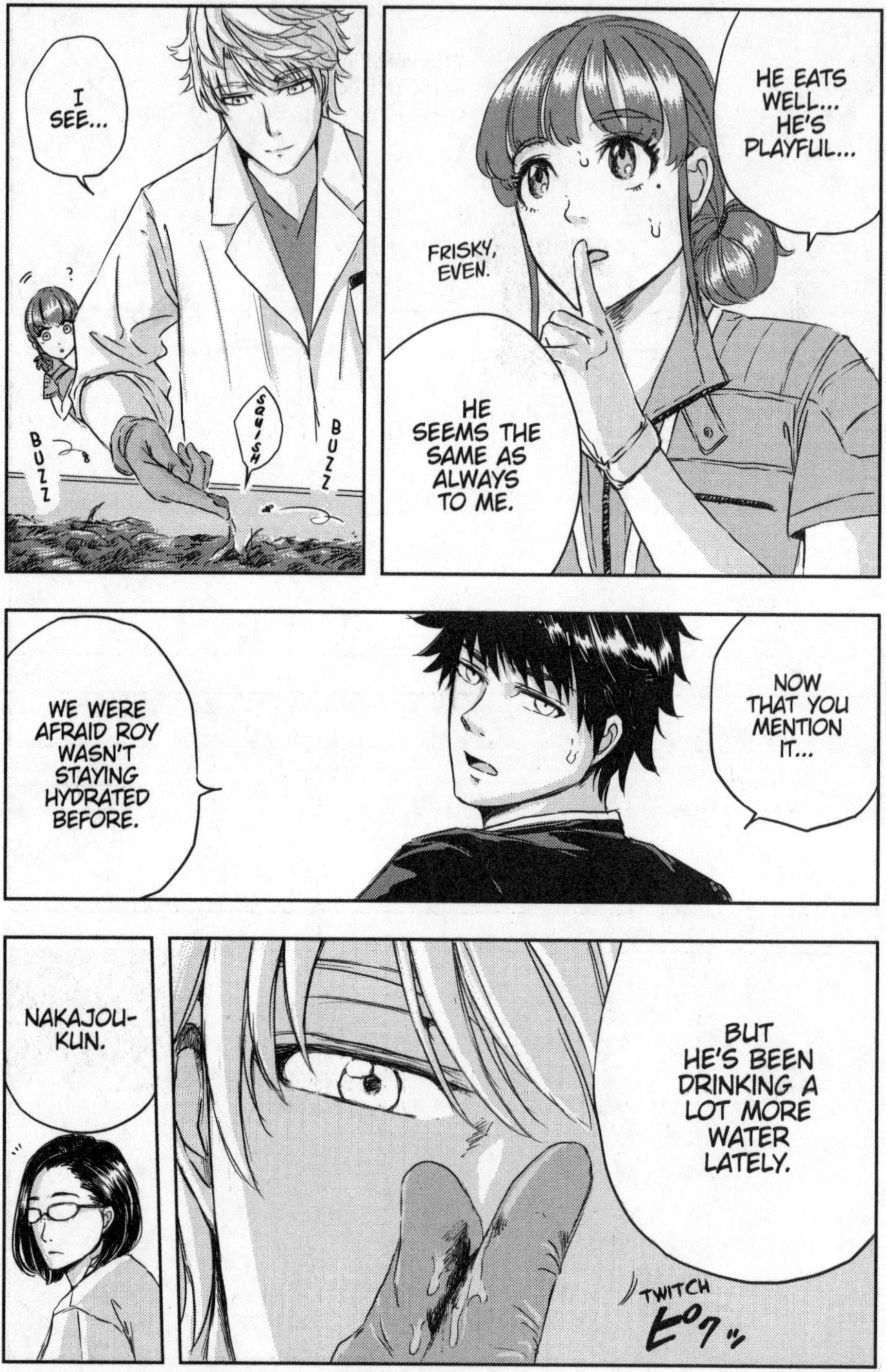
HE EATS WELL... HE'S PLAYFUL...
FRISKY, EVEN.
HE SEEMS THE SAME AS ALWAYS TO ME.
I SEE...
?
BUZZ
SQUISH
BUZZ
NOW THAT YOU MENTION IT...
WE WERE AFRAID ROY WASN'T STAYING HYDRATED BEFORE.
BUT HE'S BEEN DRINKING A LOT MORE WATER LATELY.
TWITCH
ピクッ
NAKAJOU-KUN.

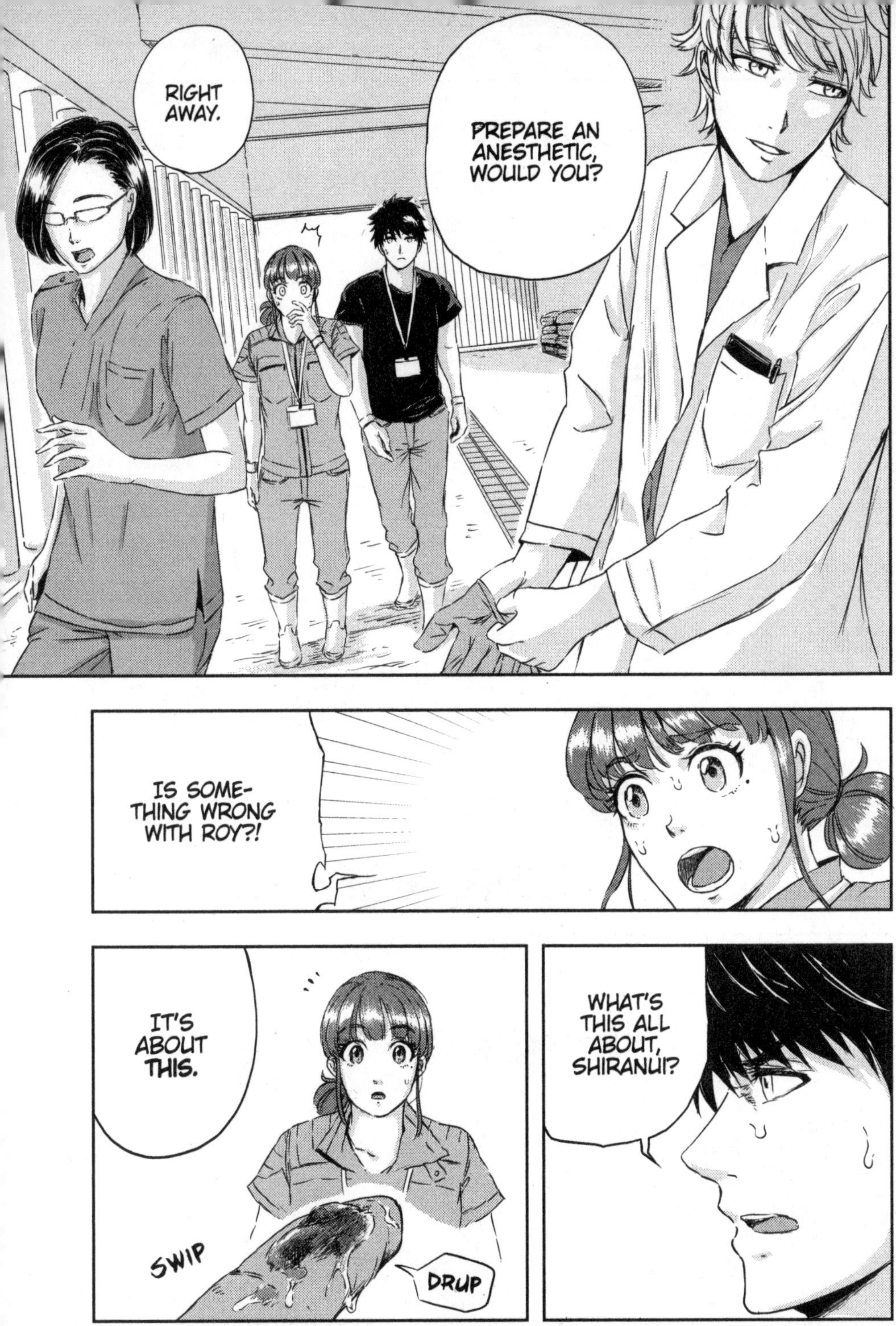
PREPARE AN ANESTHETIC, WOULD YOU?
RIGHT AWAY.
IS SOME-THING WRONG WITH ROY?!
WHAT'S THIS ALL ABOUT, SHIRANUI?
IT'S ABOUT THIS.
SWIP
DRUP

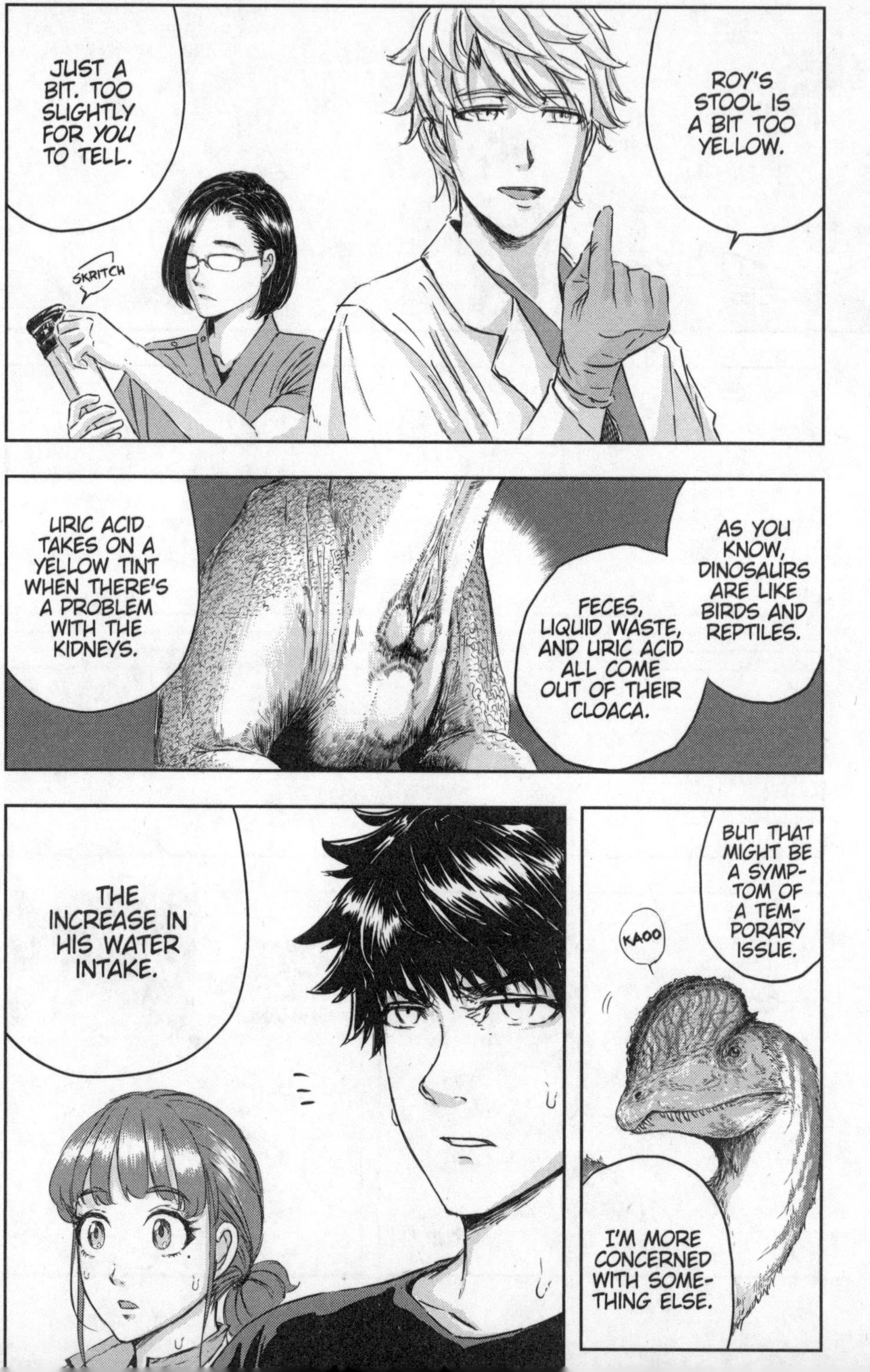
ROY'S STOOL IS A BIT TOO YELLOW.
JUST A BIT. TOO SLIGHTLY FOR *YOU* TO TELL.
SKRITCH
AS YOU KNOW, DINOSAURS ARE LIKE BIRDS AND REPTILES.
FECES, LIQUID WASTE, AND URIC ACID ALL COME OUT OF THEIR CLOACA.
URIC ACID TAKES ON A YELLOW TINT WHEN THERE'S A PROBLEM WITH THE KIDNEYS.
BUT THAT MIGHT BE A SYMP-TOM OF A TEM-PORARY ISSUE.
KAOO
I'M MORE CONCERNED WITH SOME-THING ELSE.
THE INCREASE IN HIS WATER INTAKE.

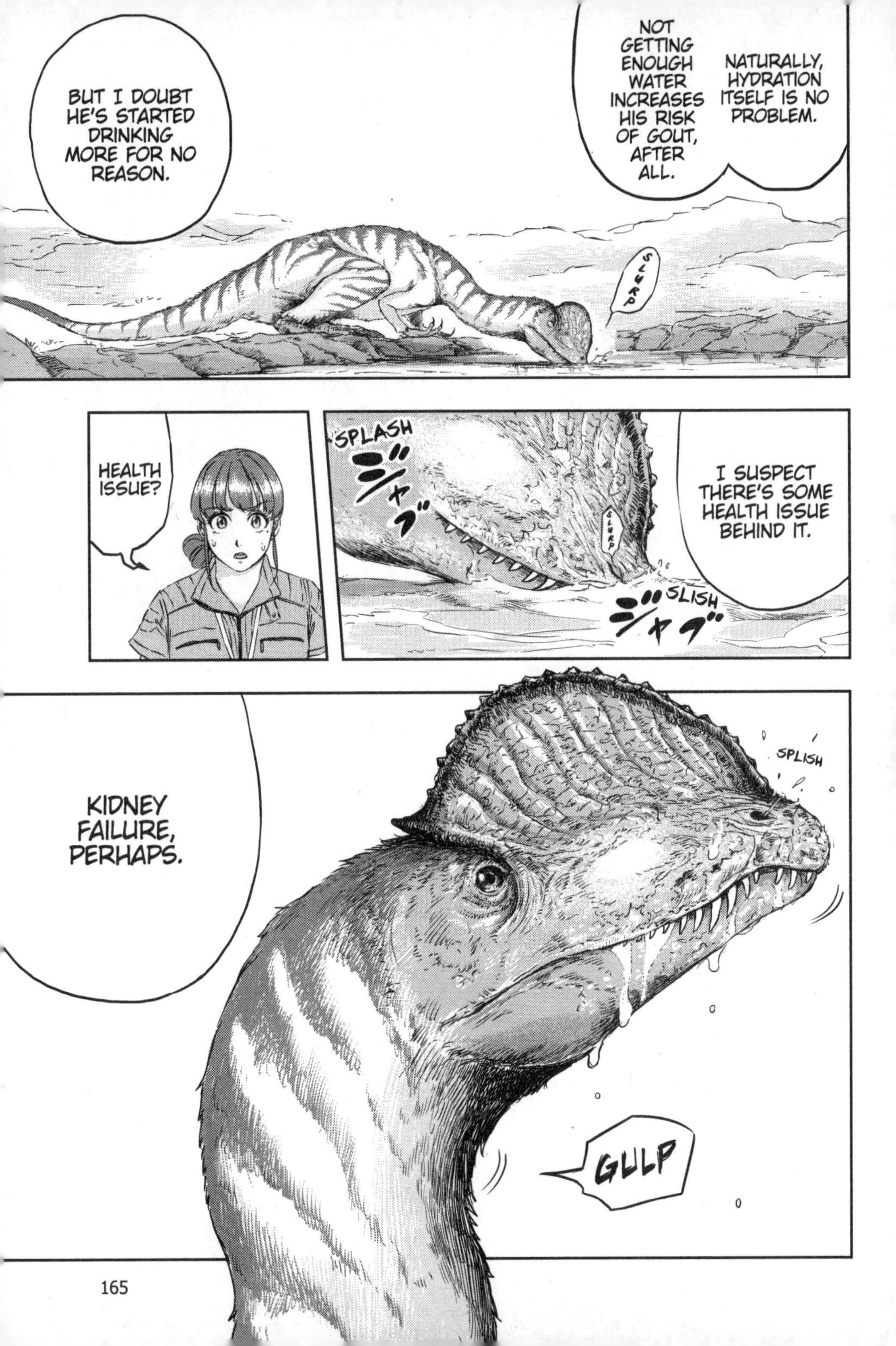
NATURALLY, HYDRATION ITSELF IS NO PROBLEM.
NOT GETTING ENOUGH WATER INCREASES HIS RISK OF GOUT, AFTER ALL.
BUT I DOUBT HE'S STARTED DRINKING MORE FOR NO REASON.
SLURP
I SUSPECT THERE'S SOME HEALTH ISSUE BEHIND IT.
SPLASH
ジャブ
SLURP
SLISH
ジャブ
HEALTH ISSUE?
SPLISH
KIDNEY FAILURE, PERHAPS.
GULP

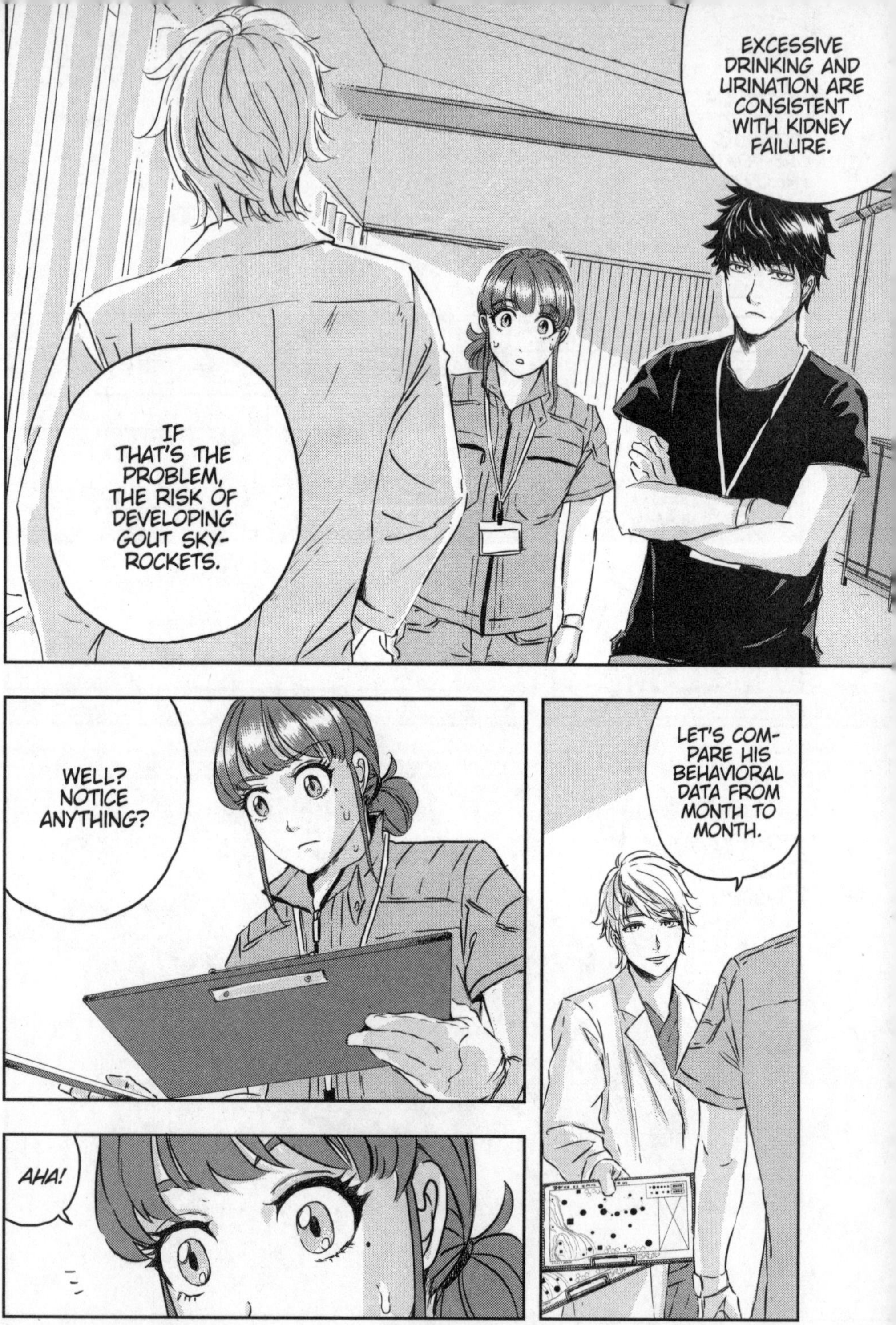
EXCESSIVE DRINKING AND URINATION ARE CONSISTENT WITH KIDNEY FAILURE.
IF THAT'S THE PROBLEM, THE RISK OF DEVELOPING GOUT SKY-ROCKETS.
LET'S COM-PARE HIS BEHAVIORAL DATA FROM MONTH TO MONTH.
WELL? NOTICE ANYTHING?
AHA!

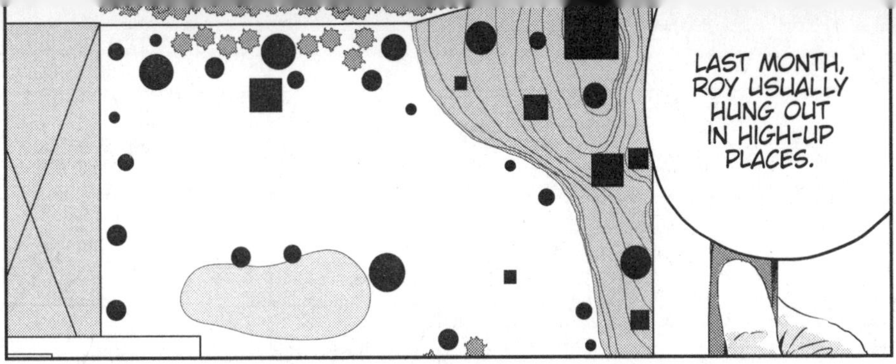
LAST MONTH, ROY USUALLY HUNG OUT IN HIGH-UP PLACES.

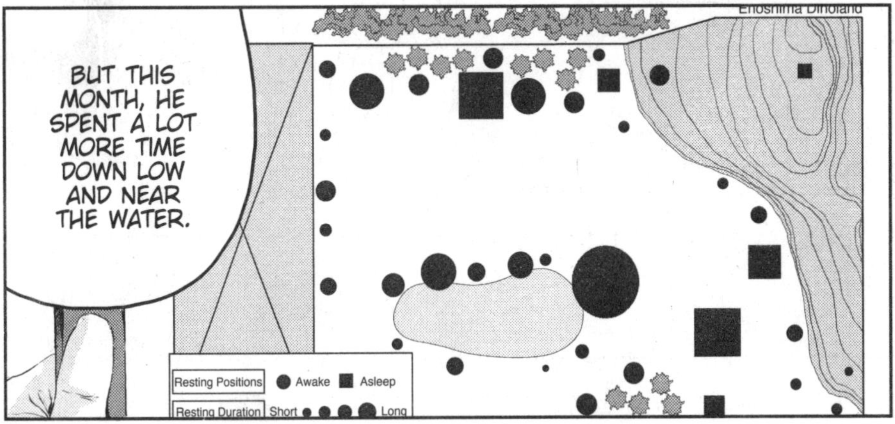
Enoshima Dinoland
BUT THIS MONTH, HE SPENT A LOT MORE TIME DOWN LOW AND NEAR THE WATER.
Resting Positions
Awake
Asleep
Resting Duration
Short
Long

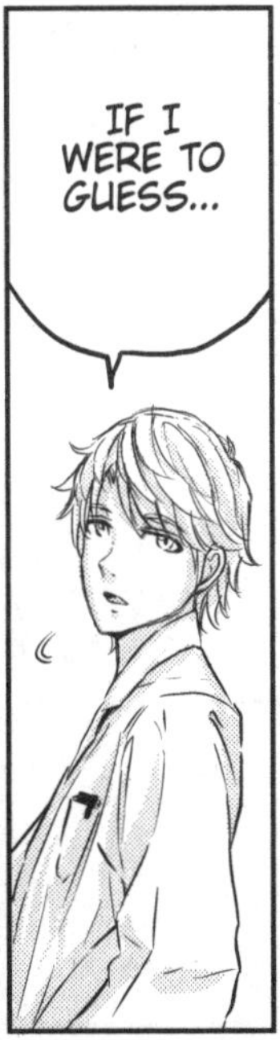
IF I WERE TO GUESS...

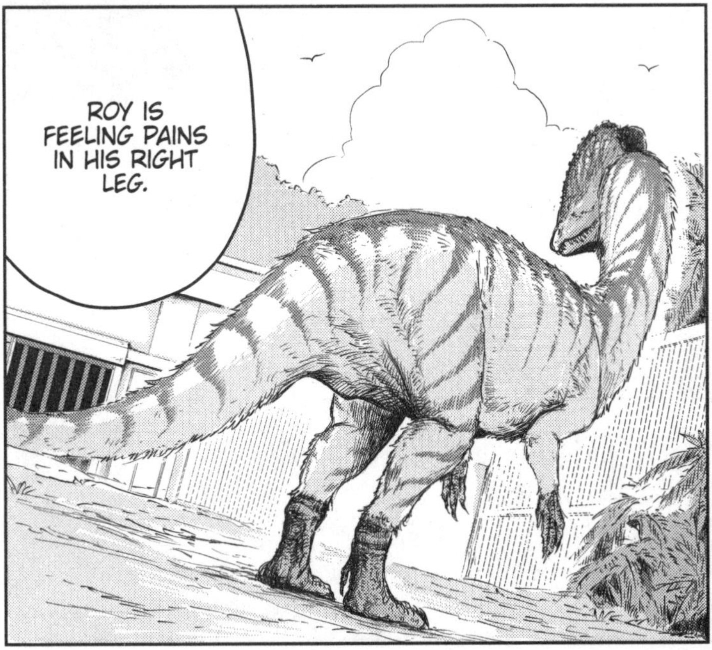
ROY IS FEELING PAINS IN HIS RIGHT LEG.

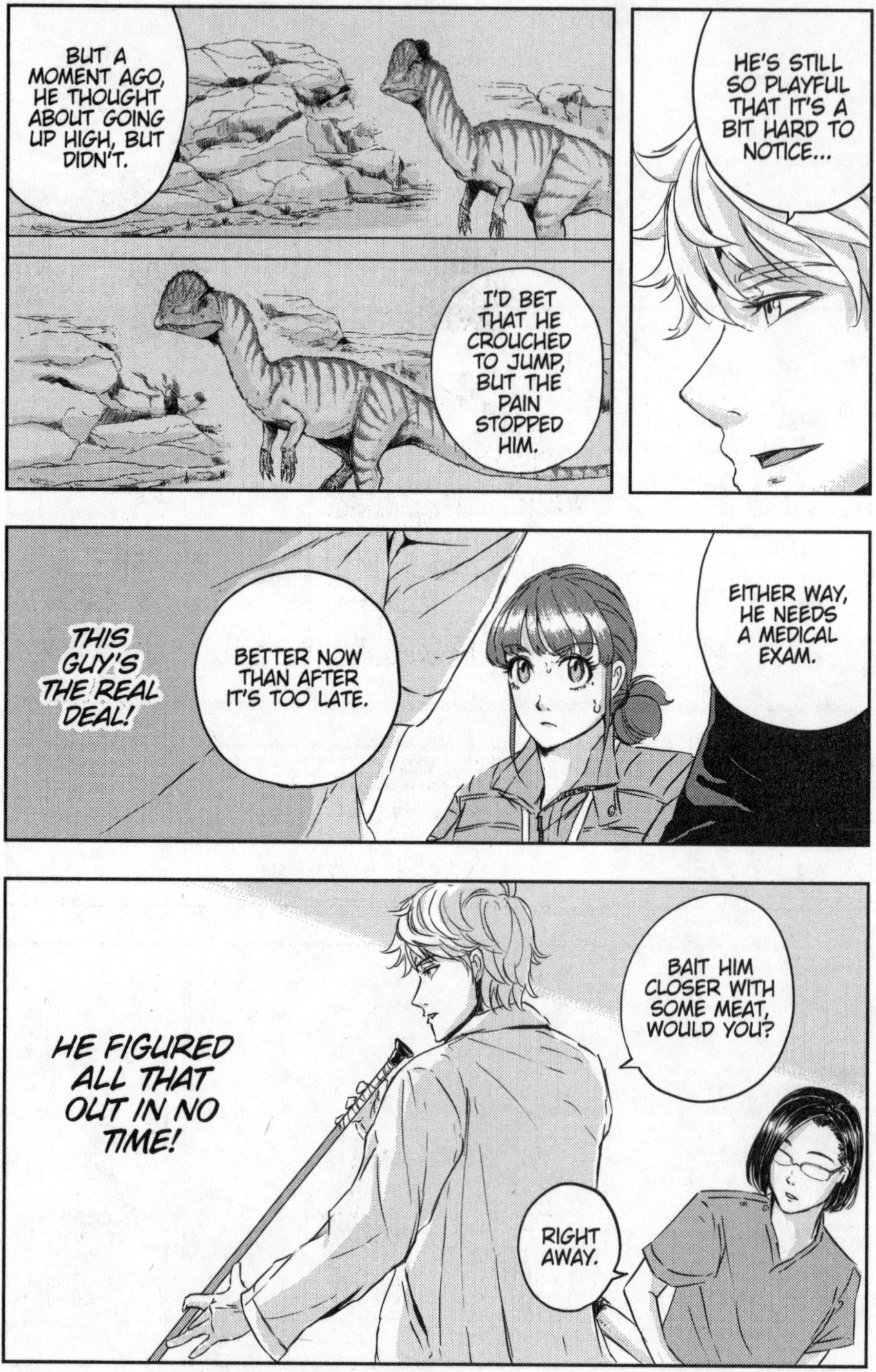
HE'S STILL SO PLAYFUL THAT IT'S A BIT HARD TO NOTICE...
BUT A MOMENT AGO, HE THOUGHT ABOUT GOING UP HIGH, BUT DIDN'T.
I'D BET THAT HE CROUCHED TO JUMP, BUT THE PAIN STOPPED HIM.
EITHER WAY, HE NEEDS A MEDICAL EXAM.
BETTER NOW THAN AFTER IT'S TOO LATE.
THIS GUY'S THE REAL DEAL!
BAIT HIM CLOSER WITH SOME MEAT, WOULD YOU?
RIGHT AWAY.
HE FIGURED ALL THAT OUT IN NO TIME!

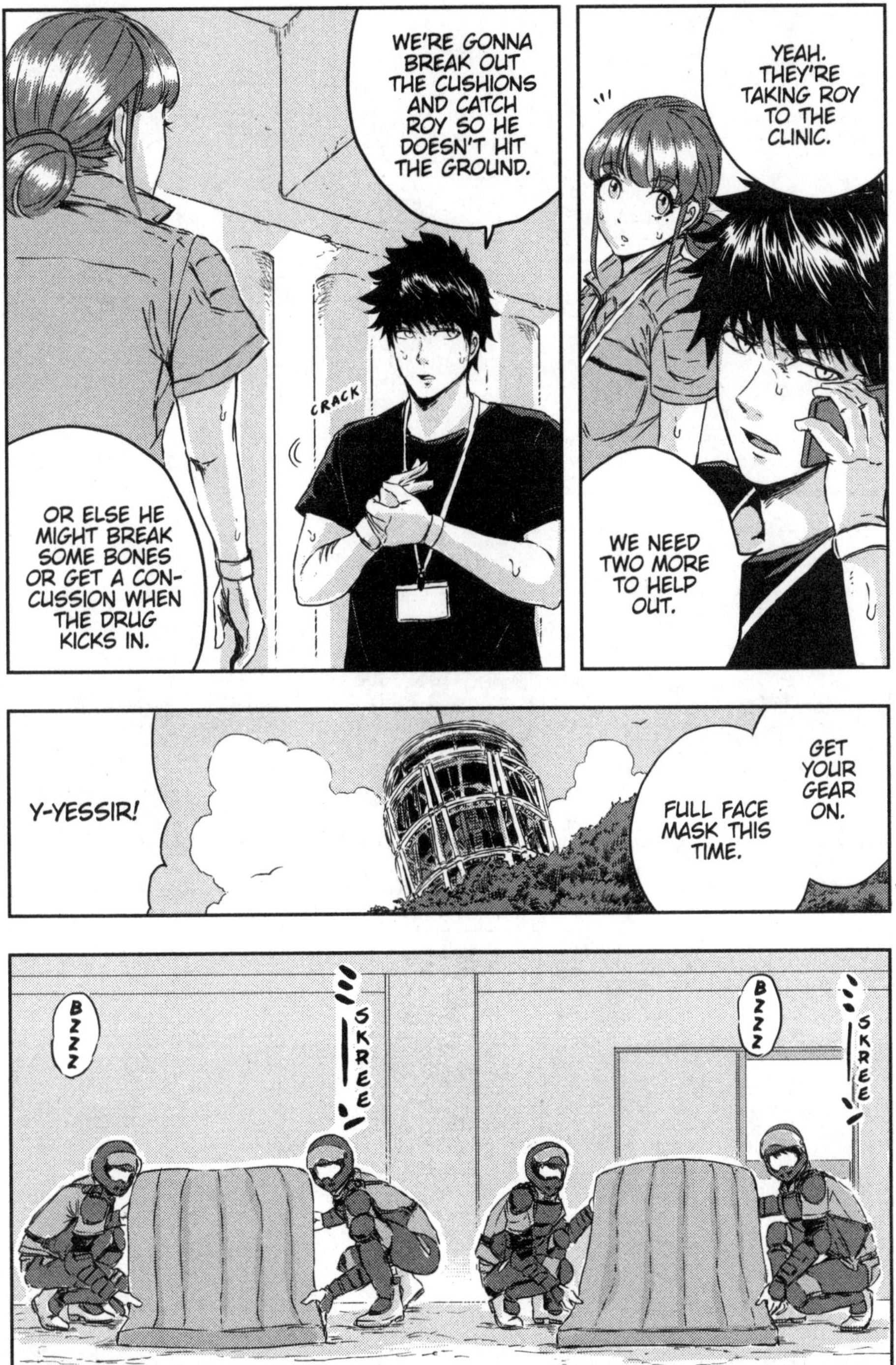
YEAH. THEY'RE TAKING ROY TO THE CLINIC.
WE NEED TWO MORE TO HELP OUT.
WE'RE GONNA BREAK OUT THE CUSHIONS AND CATCH ROY SO HE DOESN'T HIT THE GROUND.
CRACK
OR ELSE HE MIGHT BREAK SOME BONES OR GET A CONCUSSION WHEN THE DRUG KICKS IN.
GET YOUR GEAR ON.
FULL FACE MASK THIS TIME.
Y-YESSIR!
SKREE
BZZZ
SKREE
BZZZ

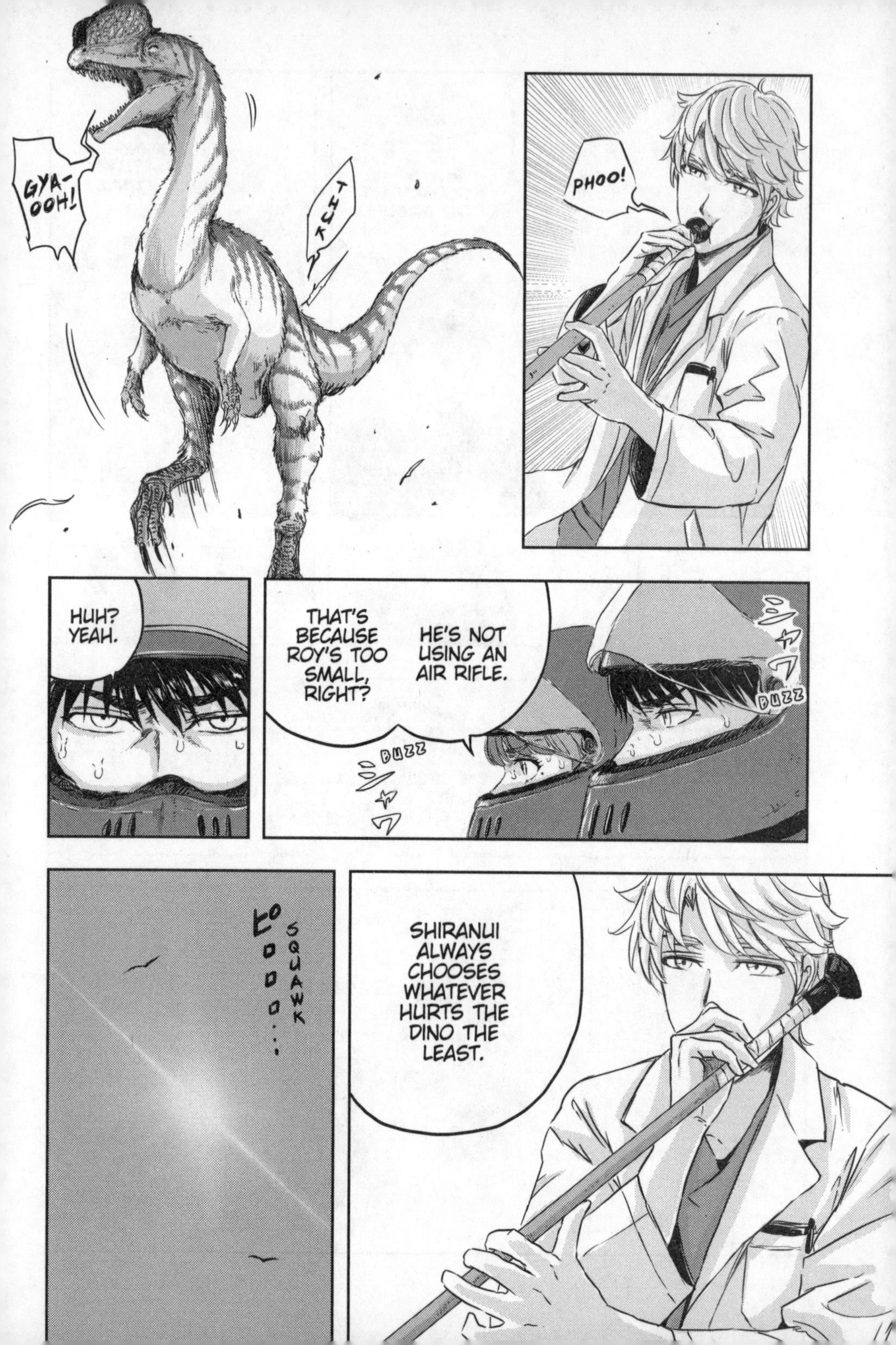
PHOO!
GYA-OOH!
HE'S NOT USING AN AIR RIFLE.
THAT'S BECAUSE ROY'S TOO SMALL, RIGHT?
BUZZ
BUZZ
HUH? YEAH.
SHIRANUI ALWAYS CHOOSES WHATEVER HURTS THE DINO THE LEAST.
SQUAWK

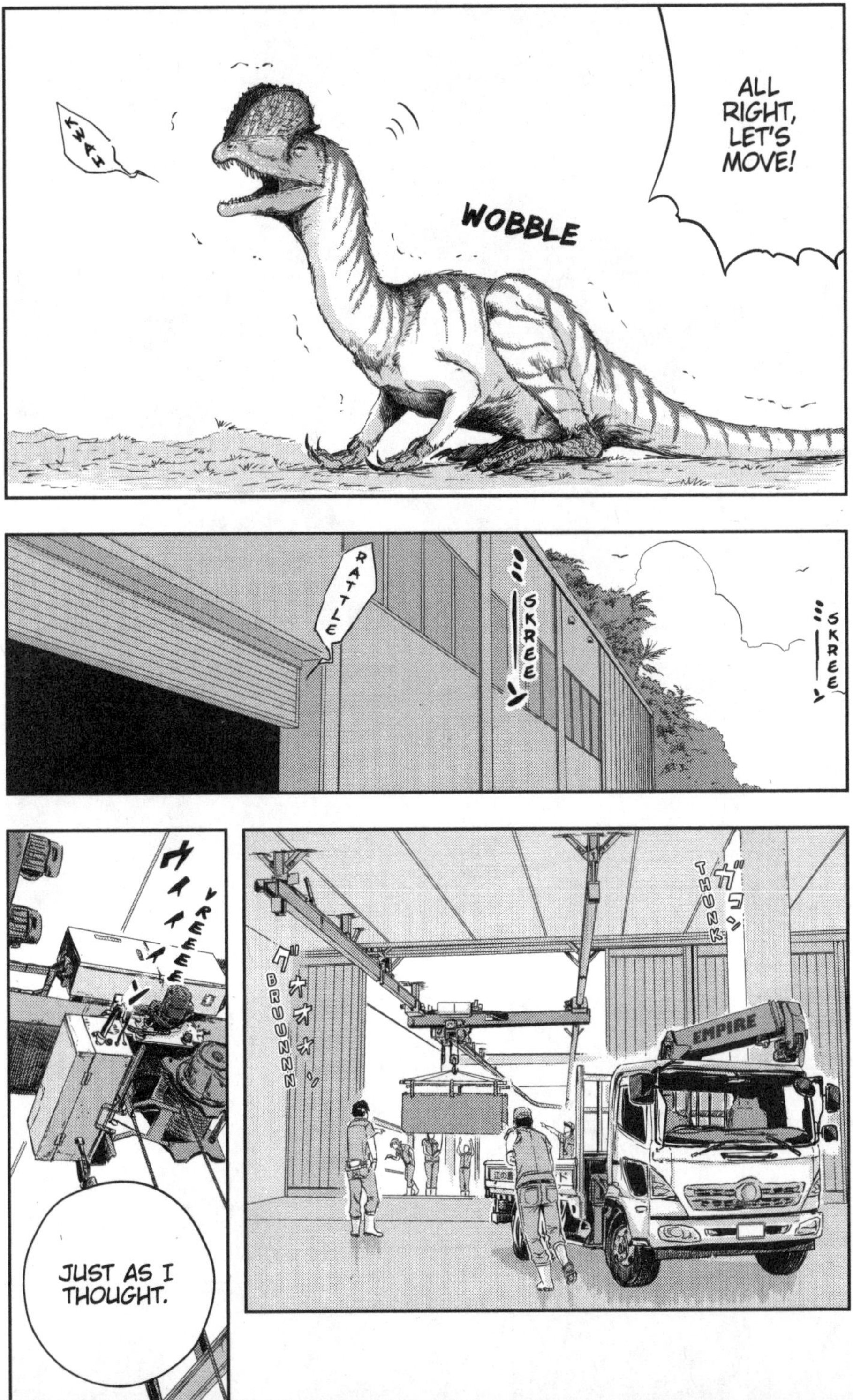
ALL RIGHT, LET'S MOVE!
KWAH
WOBBLE
SKREE
SKREE
RATTLE
THUNK
BRUUNNN
VREEEEE
JUST AS I THOUGHT.

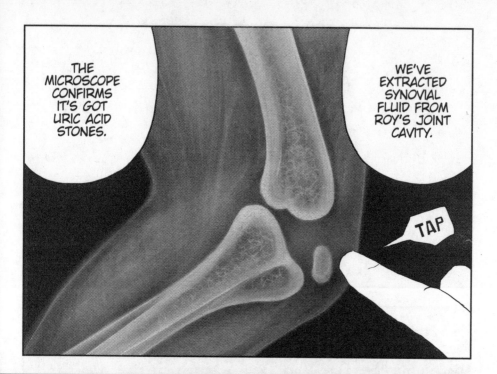

WE'VE EXTRACTED SYNOVIAL FLUID FROM ROY'S JOINT CAVITY.
TAP
THE MICROSCOPE CONFIRMS IT'S GOT URIC ACID STONES.
BEEP
BEEP
HIS RIGHT LEG PAIN IS DUE TO JOINT INFLAMMATION CAUSED BY GOUT.
HSHHH
HSHHH

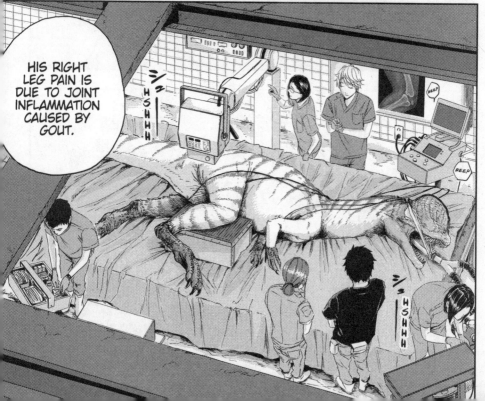

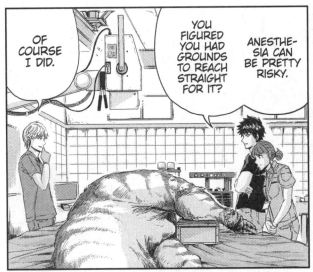

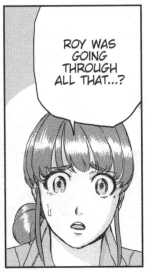

ROY WAS GOING THROUGH ALL THAT...?
ANESTHE-SIA CAN BE PRETTY RISKY.
YOU FIGURED YOU HAD GROUNDS TO REACH STRAIGHT FOR IT?
OF COURSE I DID.
LOOK. DO YOU SEE WHAT'S HAPPENING HERE?
HE'S SHEDDING HIS SKIN. SO?
THE SHEDDING ITSELF ISN'T IMPORTANT.

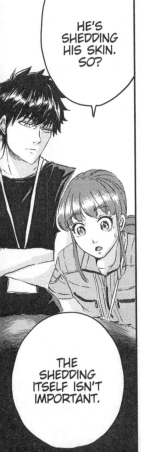

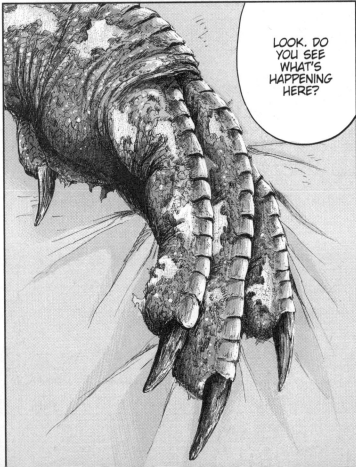

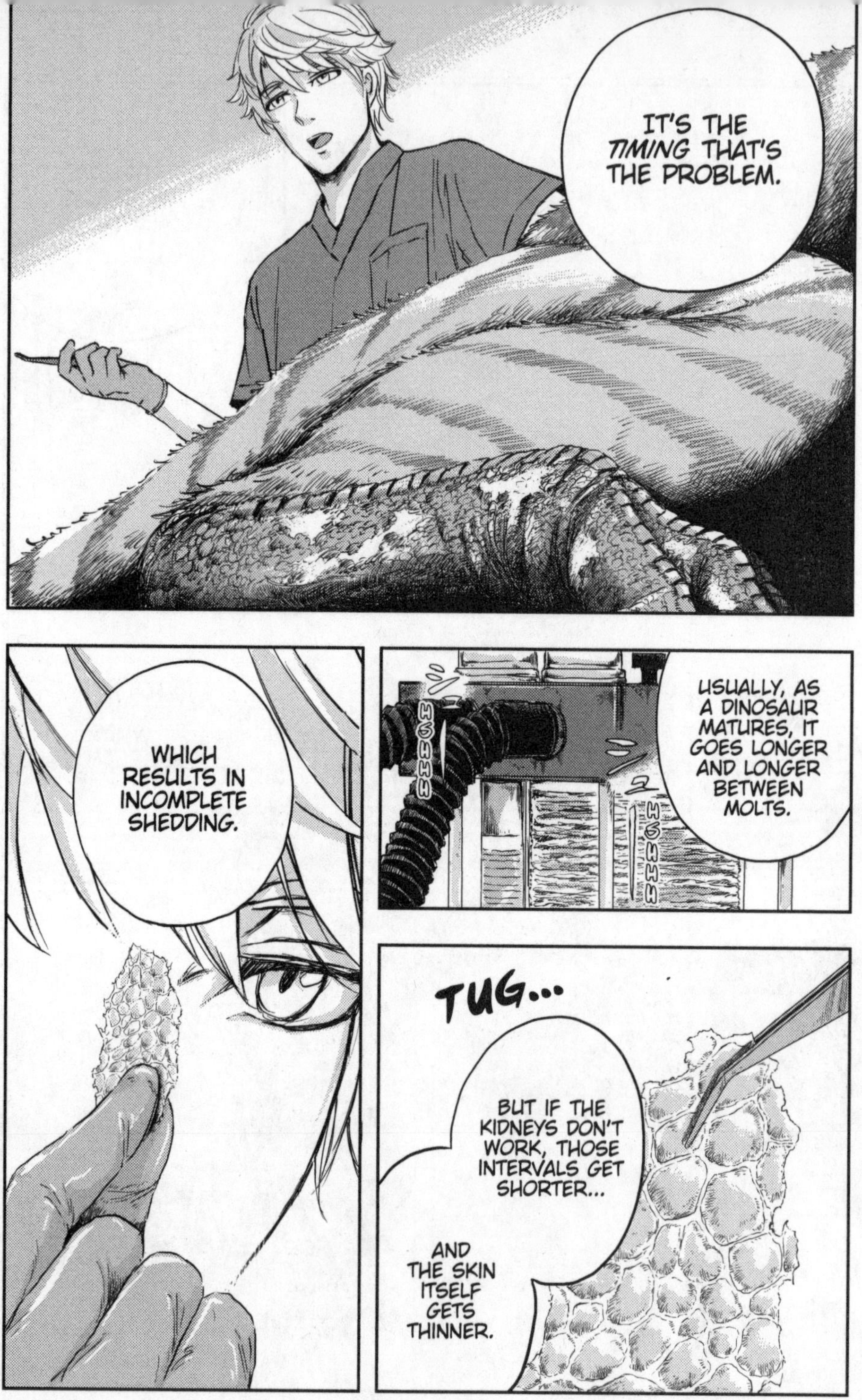
IT'S THE *TIMING* THAT'S THE PROBLEM.
USUALLY, AS A DINOSAUR MATURES, IT GOES LONGER AND LONGER BETWEEN MOLTS.
HSHHH
HSHHH
TUG...
BUT IF THE KIDNEYS DON'T WORK, THOSE INTERVALS GET SHORTER...
AND THE SKIN ITSELF GETS THINNER.
WHICH RESULTS IN INCOMPLETE SHEDDING.

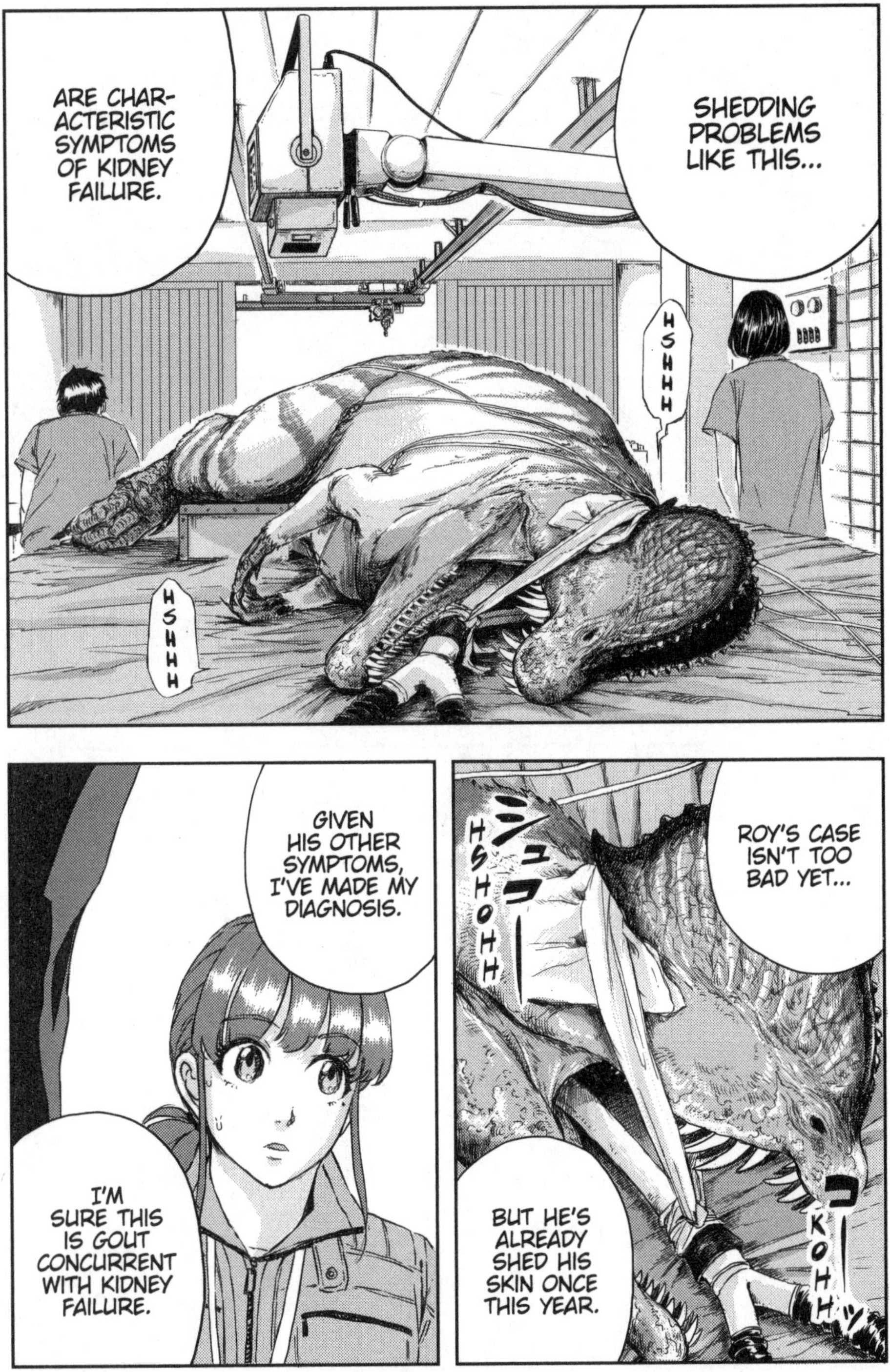
SHEDDING PROBLEMS LIKE THIS...
ARE CHAR-ACTERISTIC SYMPTOMS OF KIDNEY FAILURE.
HSHHH
HSHHH
ROY'S CASE ISN'T TOO BAD YET...
HSHOHH
BUT HE'S ALREADY SHED HIS SKIN ONCE THIS YEAR.
KOHH
GIVEN HIS OTHER SYMPTOMS, I'VE MADE MY DIAGNOSIS.
I'M SURE THIS IS GOUT CONCURRENT WITH KIDNEY FAILURE.

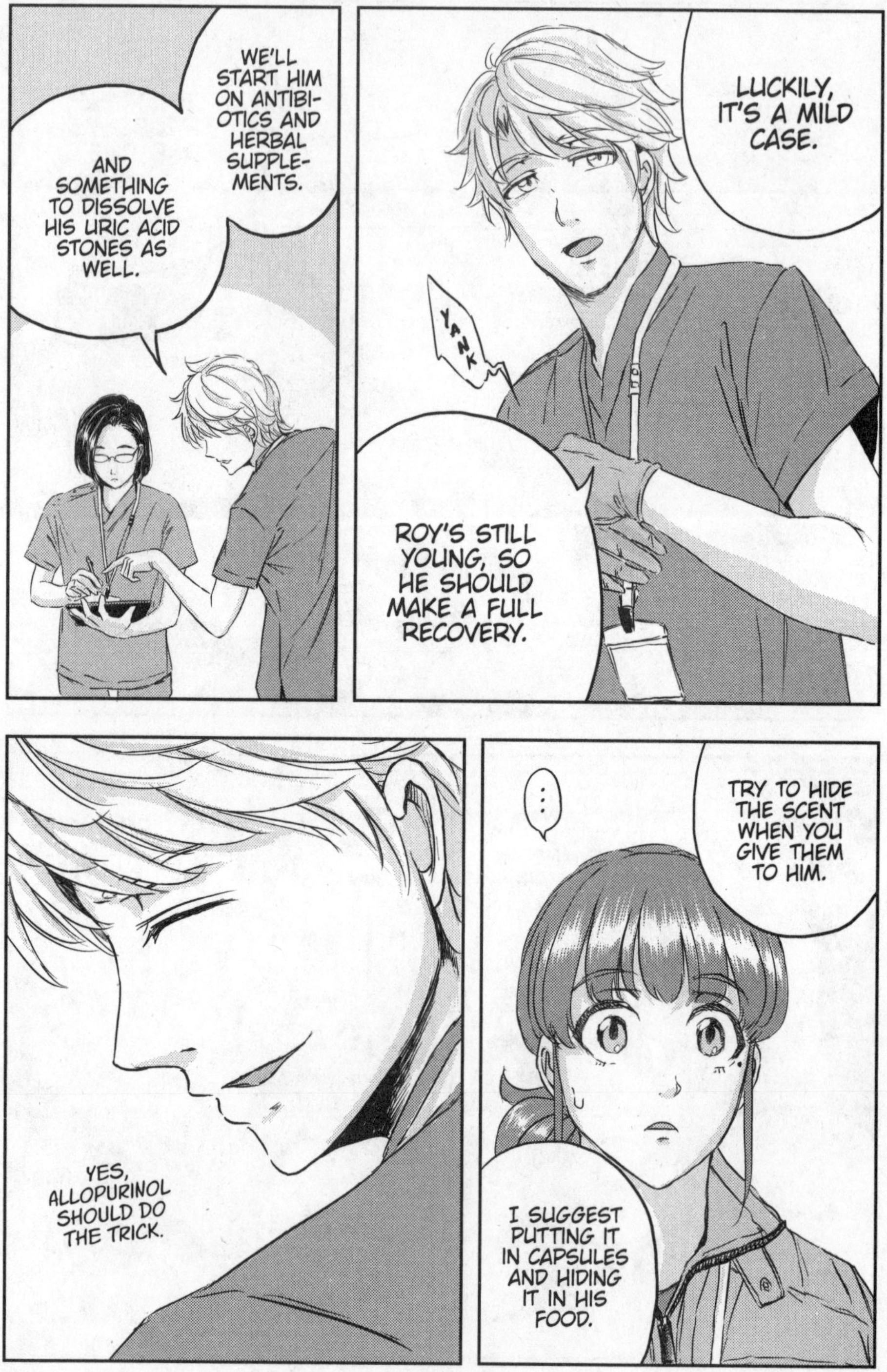
LUCKILY, IT'S A MILD CASE.
YANK
ROY'S STILL YOUNG, SO HE SHOULD MAKE A FULL RECOVERY.
WE'LL START HIM ON ANTIBIOTICS AND HERBAL SUPPLEMENTS.
AND SOMETHING TO DISSOLVE HIS URIC ACID STONES AS WELL.
TRY TO HIDE THE SCENT WHEN YOU GIVE THEM TO HIM.
...
I SUGGEST PUTTING IT IN CAPSULES AND HIDING IT IN HIS FOOD.
YES, ALLOPURINOL SHOULD DO THE TRICK.

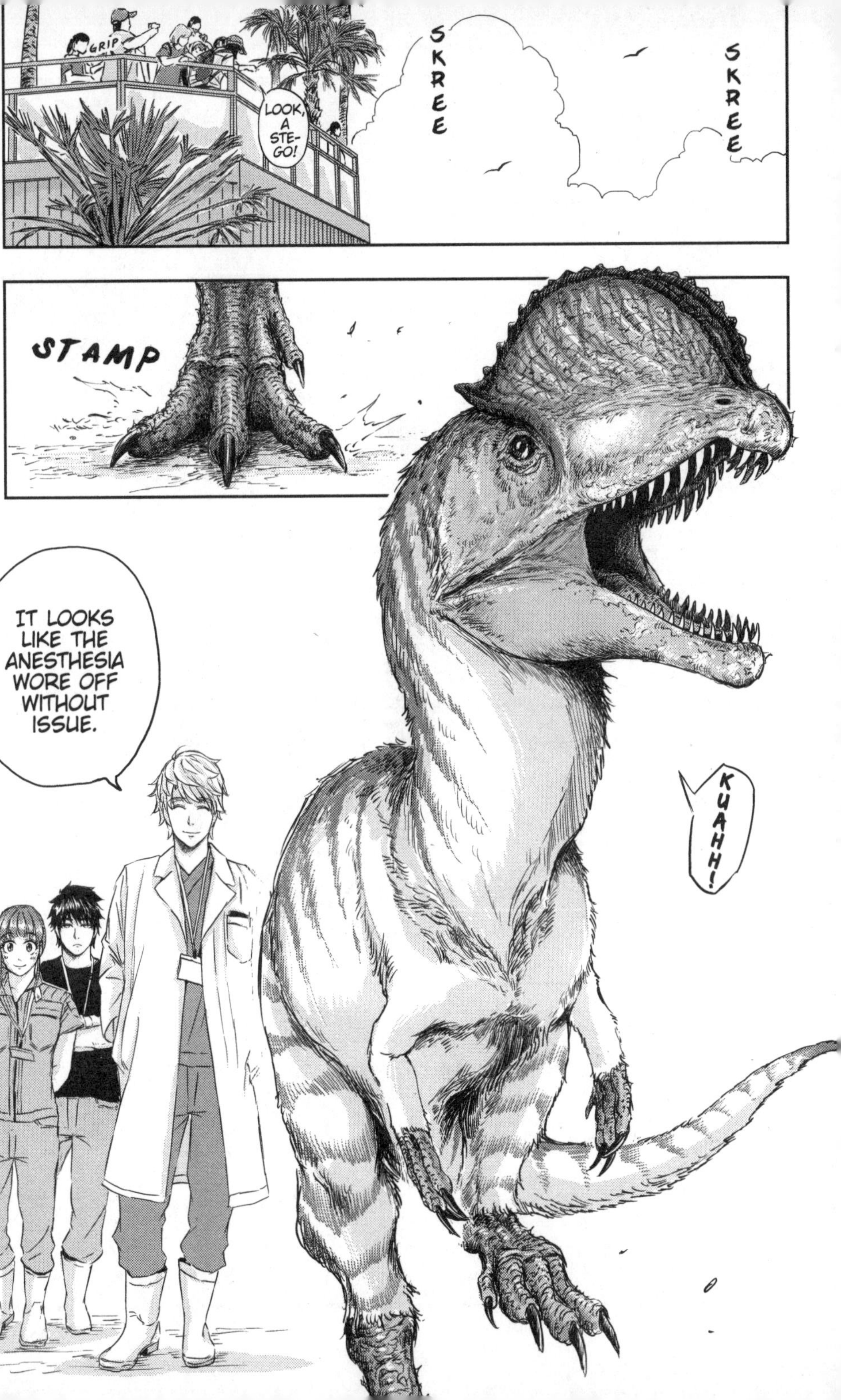
SKREE
SKREE
GRIP
LOOK, A STE-GO!
STAMP
KUAHH!
IT LOOKS LIKE THE ANESTHESIA WORE OFF WITHOUT ISSUE.

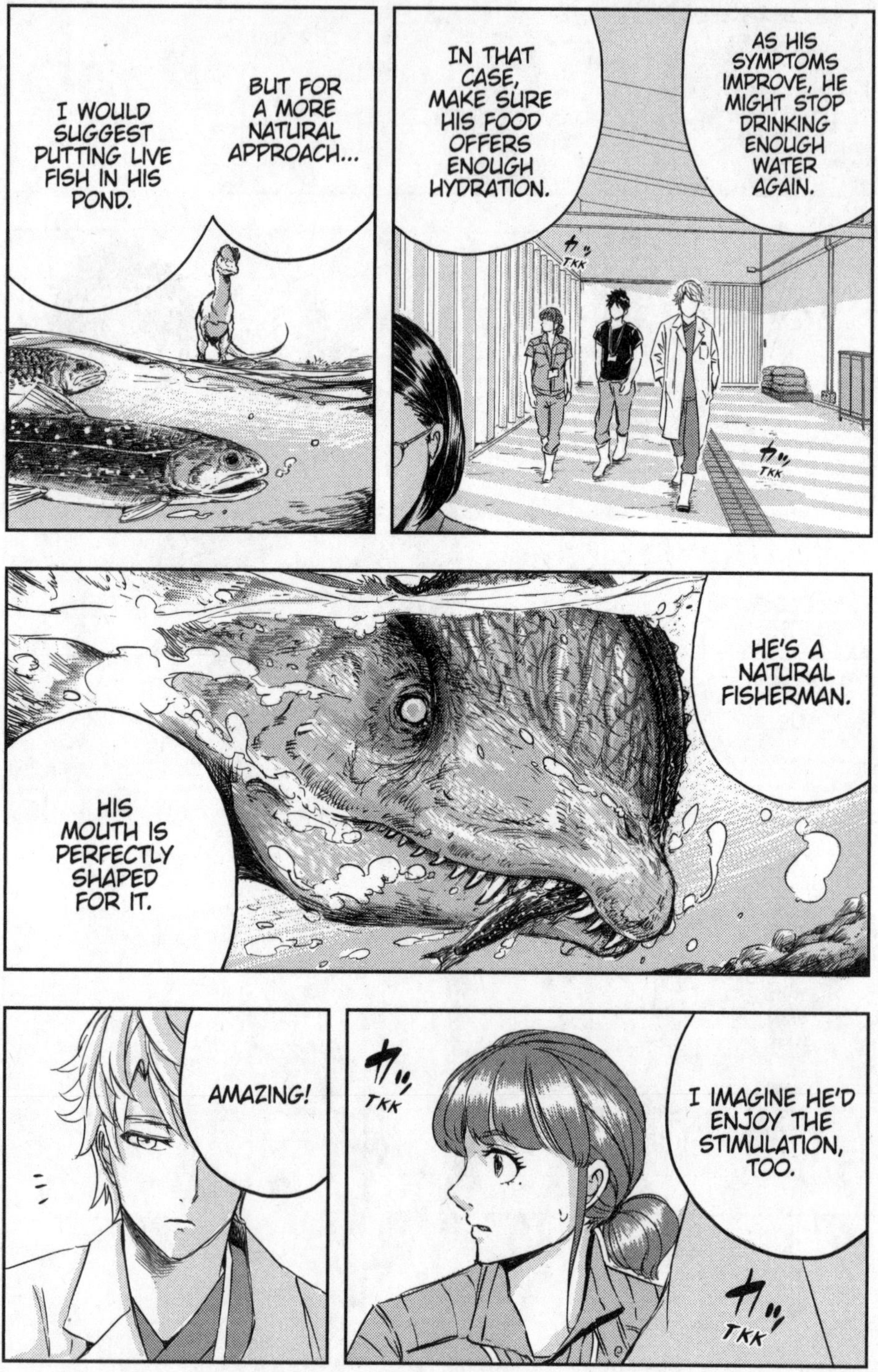
AS HIS SYMPTOMS IMPROVE, HE MIGHT STOP DRINKING ENOUGH WATER AGAIN.
IN THAT CASE, MAKE SURE HIS FOOD OFFERS ENOUGH HYDRATION.
TKK
TKK
BUT FOR A MORE NATURAL APPROACH...
I WOULD SUGGEST PUTTING LIVE FISH IN HIS POND.
HE'S A NATURAL FISHERMAN.
HIS MOUTH IS PERFECTLY SHAPED FOR IT.
I IMAGINE HE'D ENJOY THE STIMULATION, TOO.
TKK
TKK
AMAZING!

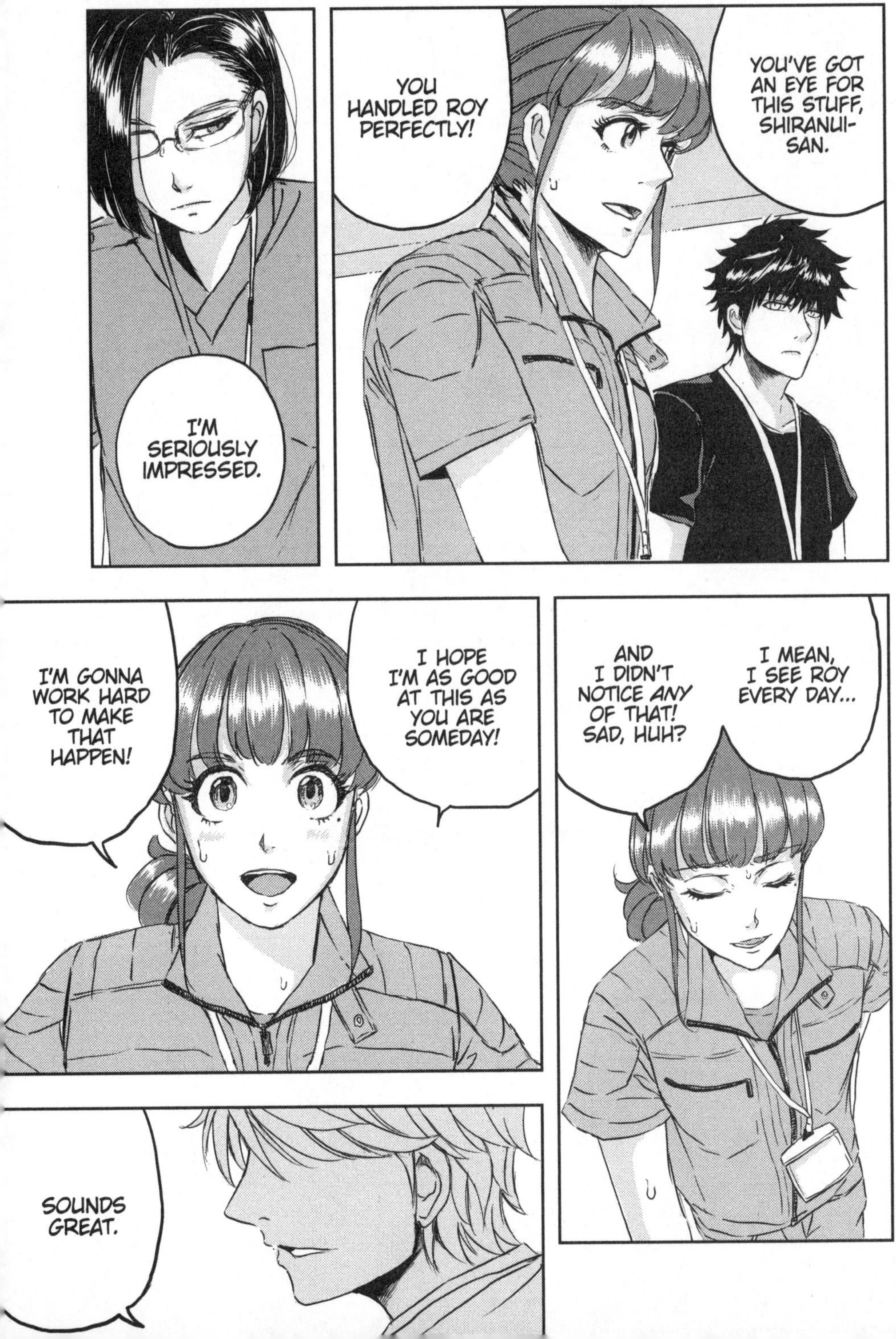
YOU'VE GOT AN EYE FOR THIS STUFF, SHIRANUI-SAN.
YOU HANDLED ROY PERFECTLY!
I'M SERIOUSLY IMPRESSED.
I MEAN, I SEE ROY EVERY DAY...
AND I DIDN'T NOTICE ANY OF THAT! SAD, HUH?
I HOPE I'M AS GOOD AT THIS AS YOU ARE SOMEDAY!
I'M GONNA WORK HARD TO MAKE THAT HAPPEN!
SOUNDS GREAT.

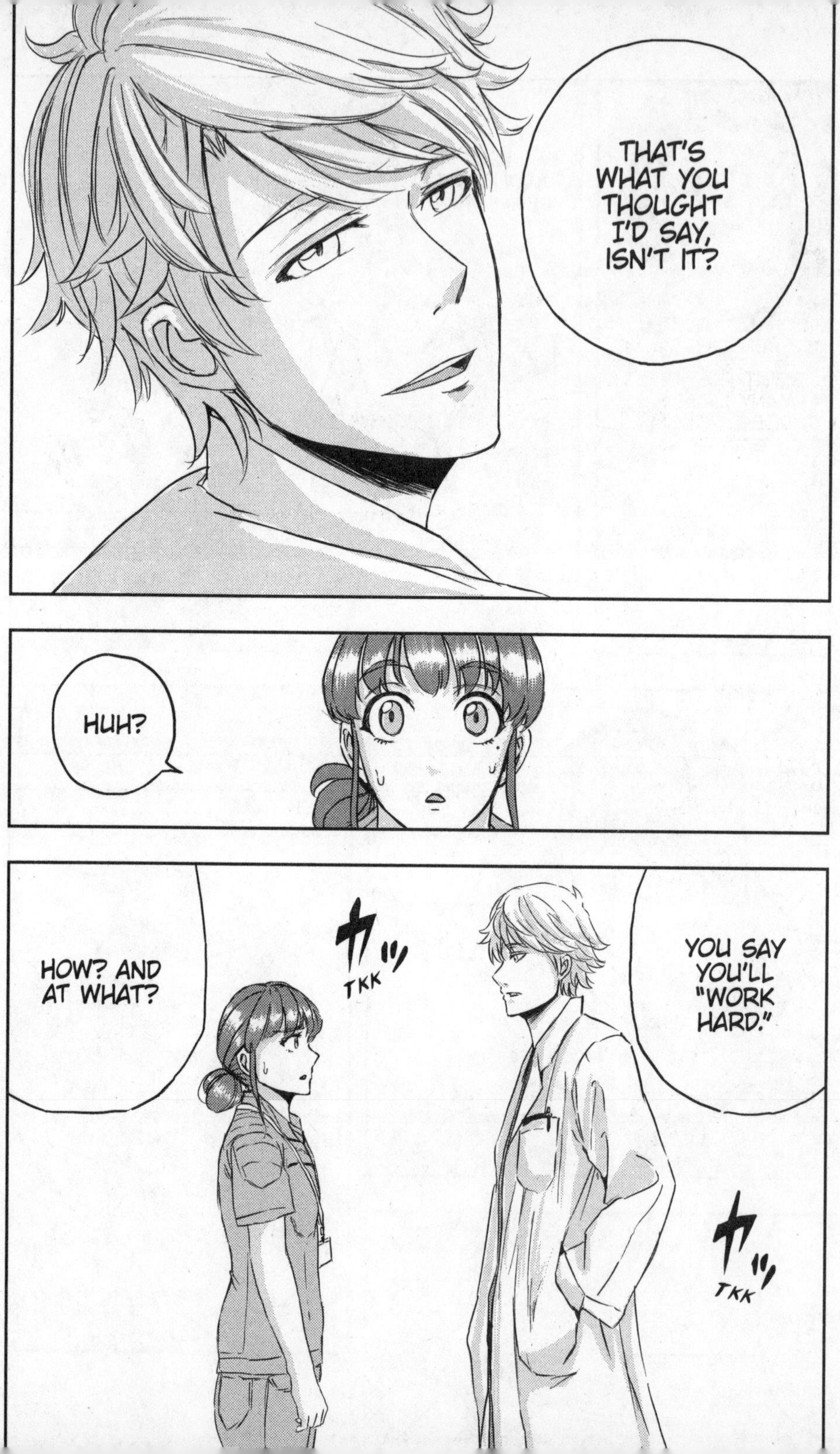
THAT'S WHAT YOU THOUGHT I'D SAY, ISN'T IT?
HUH?
YOU SAY YOU'LL "WORK HARD."
TKK
HOW? AND AT WHAT?
TKK

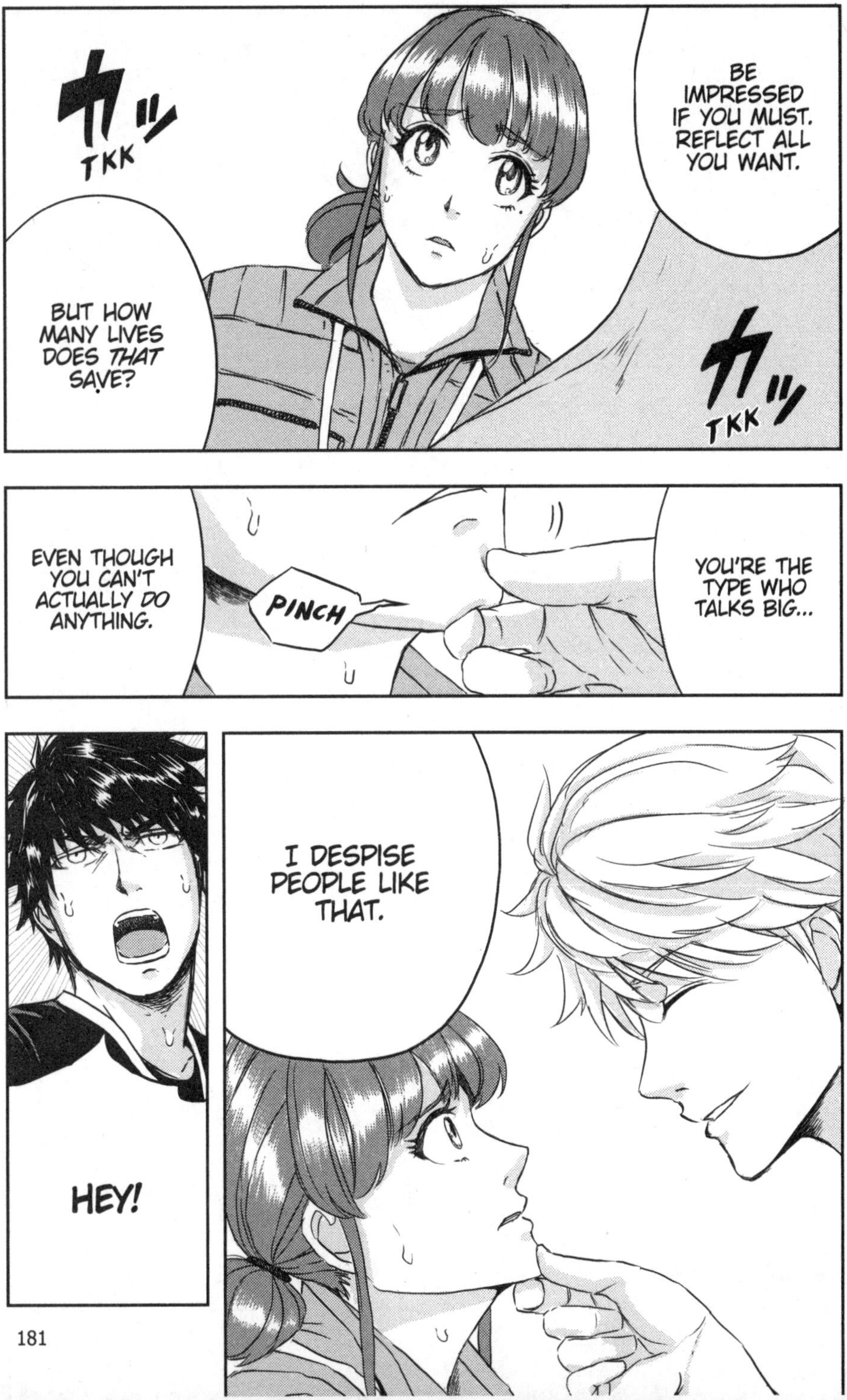
BE IMPRESSED IF YOU MUST. REFLECT ALL YOU WANT.
カッ TKK
カッ TKK
BUT HOW MANY LIVES DOES *THAT* SAVE?
YOU'RE THE TYPE WHO TALKS BIG...
PINCH
EVEN THOUGH YOU CAN'T ACTUALLY *DO* ANYTHING.
I DESPISE PEOPLE LIKE THAT.
HEY!

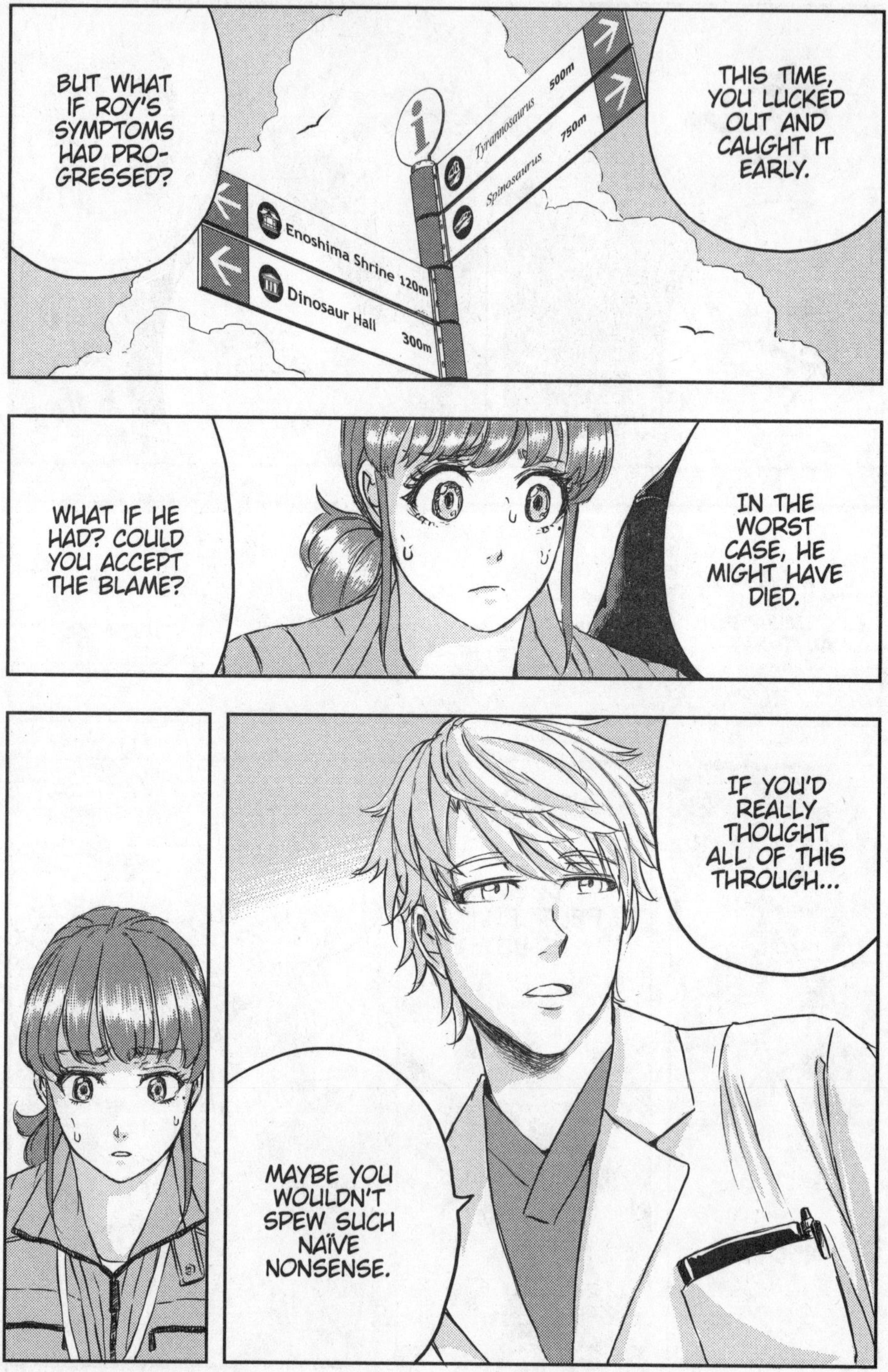
THIS TIME, YOU LUCKED OUT AND CAUGHT IT EARLY.
Tyrannosaurus 500m
Spinosaurus 750m
BUT WHAT IF ROY'S SYMPTOMS HAD PRO-GRESSED?
Enoshima Shrine 120m
Dinosaur Hall 300m
IN THE WORST CASE, HE MIGHT HAVE DIED.
WHAT IF HE HAD? COULD YOU ACCEPT THE BLAME?
IF YOU'D REALLY THOUGHT ALL OF THIS THROUGH...
MAYBE YOU WOULDN'T SPEW SUCH NAÏVE NONSENSE.

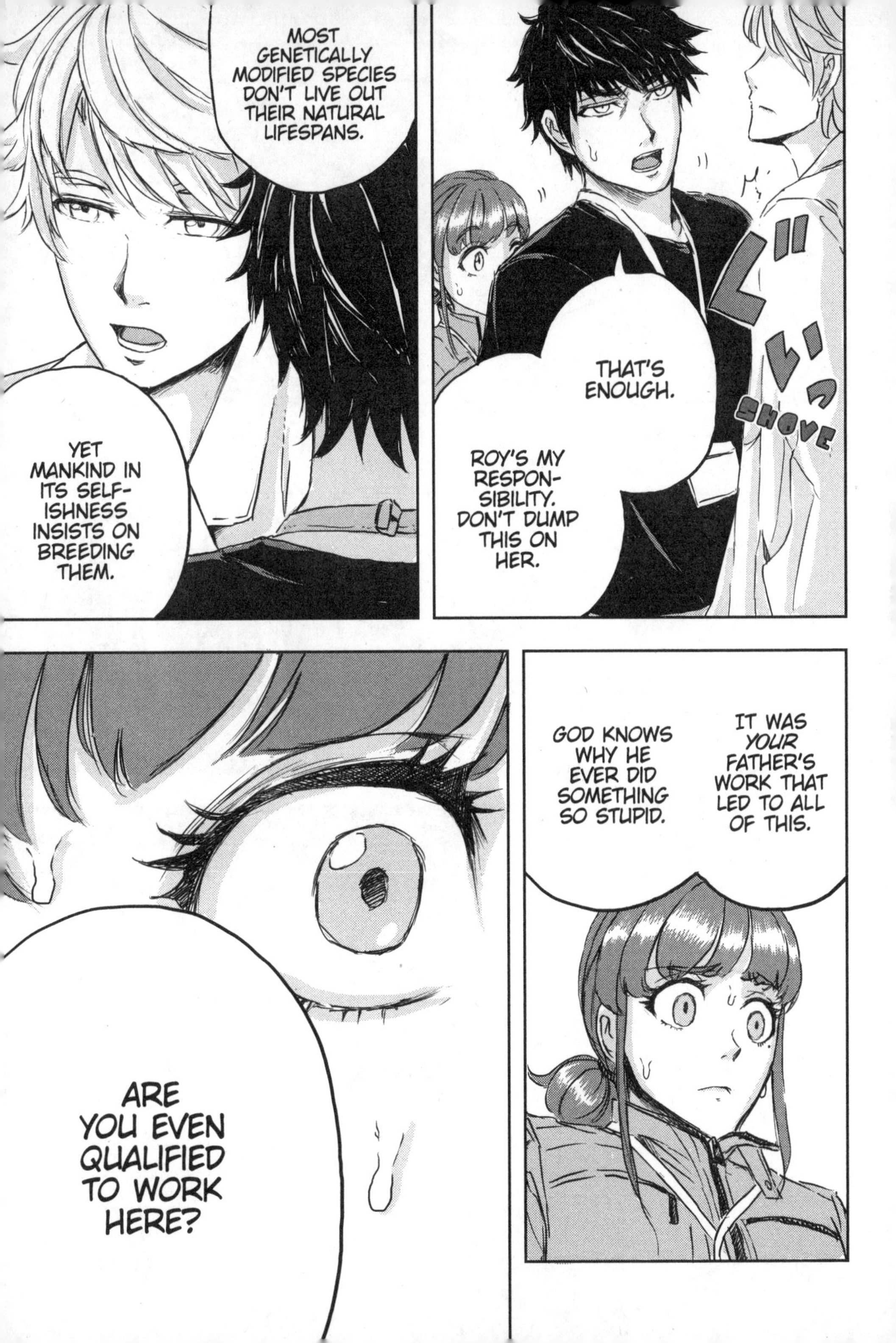

THAT'S ENOUGH.
ROY'S MY RESPON-SIBILITY. DON'T DUMP THIS ON HER.
SHOVE
MOST GENETICALLY MODIFIED SPECIES DON'T LIVE OUT THEIR NATURAL LIFESPANS.
YET MANKIND IN ITS SELF-ISHNESS INSISTS ON BREEDING THEM.
IT WAS *YOUR* FATHER'S WORK THAT LED TO ALL OF THIS.
GOD KNOWS WHY HE EVER DID SOMETHING SO STUPID.
ARE YOU EVEN QUALIFIED TO WORK HERE?

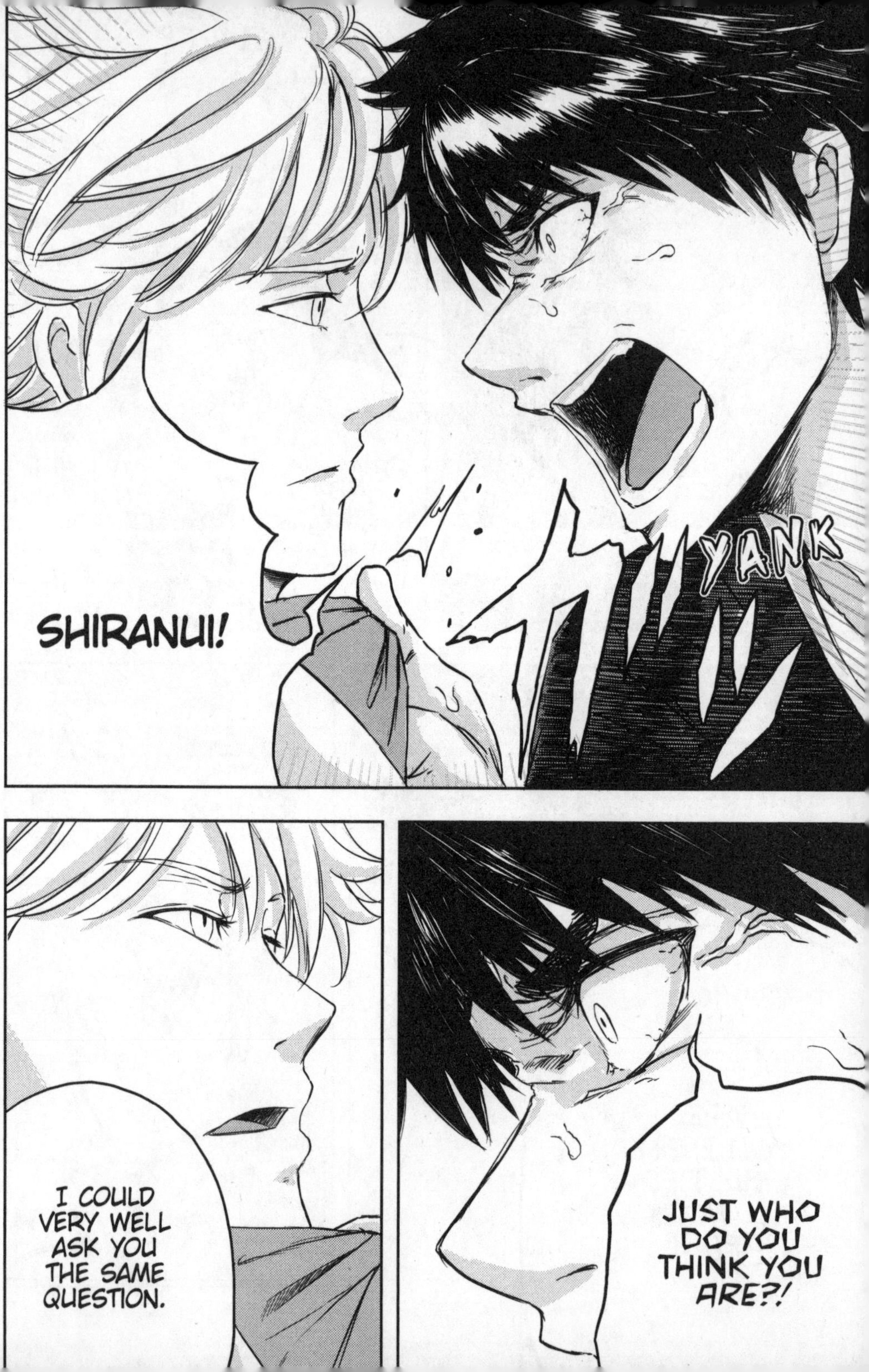
YANK
SHIRANUI!
JUST WHO DO YOU THINK YOU ARE?!
I COULD VERY WELL ASK YOU THE SAME QUESTION.

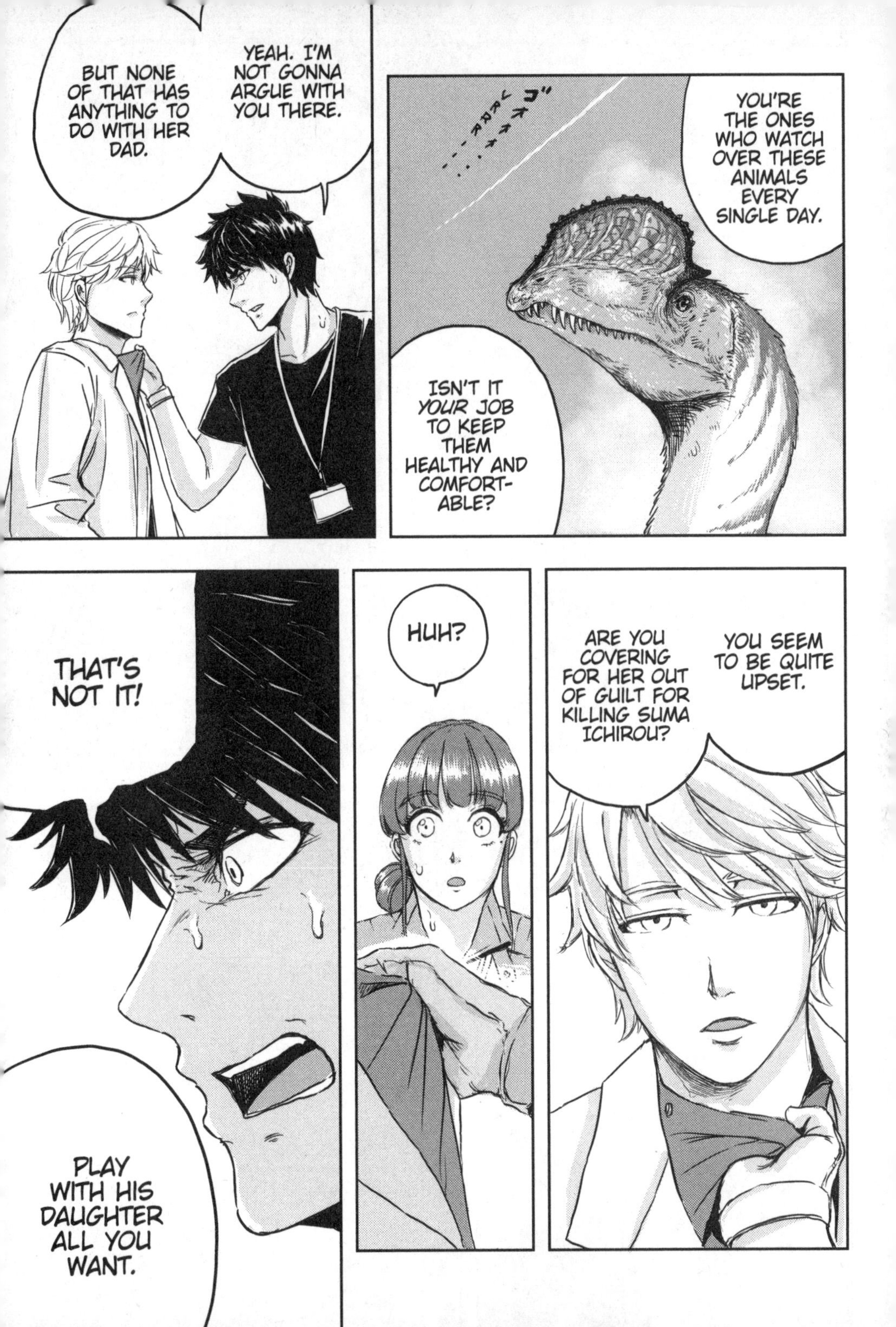
YOU'RE THE ONES WHO WATCH OVER THESE ANIMALS EVERY SINGLE DAY.
ISN'T IT *YOUR* JOB TO KEEP THEM HEALTHY AND COMFORT-ABLE?
YEAH. I'M NOT GONNA ARGUE WITH YOU THERE.
BUT NONE OF THAT HAS ANYTHING TO DO WITH HER DAD.
YOU SEEM TO BE QUITE UPSET.
ARE YOU COVERING FOR HER OUT OF GUILT FOR KILLING SUMA ICHIROU?
HUH?
THAT'S NOT IT!
PLAY WITH HIS DAUGHTER ALL YOU WANT.

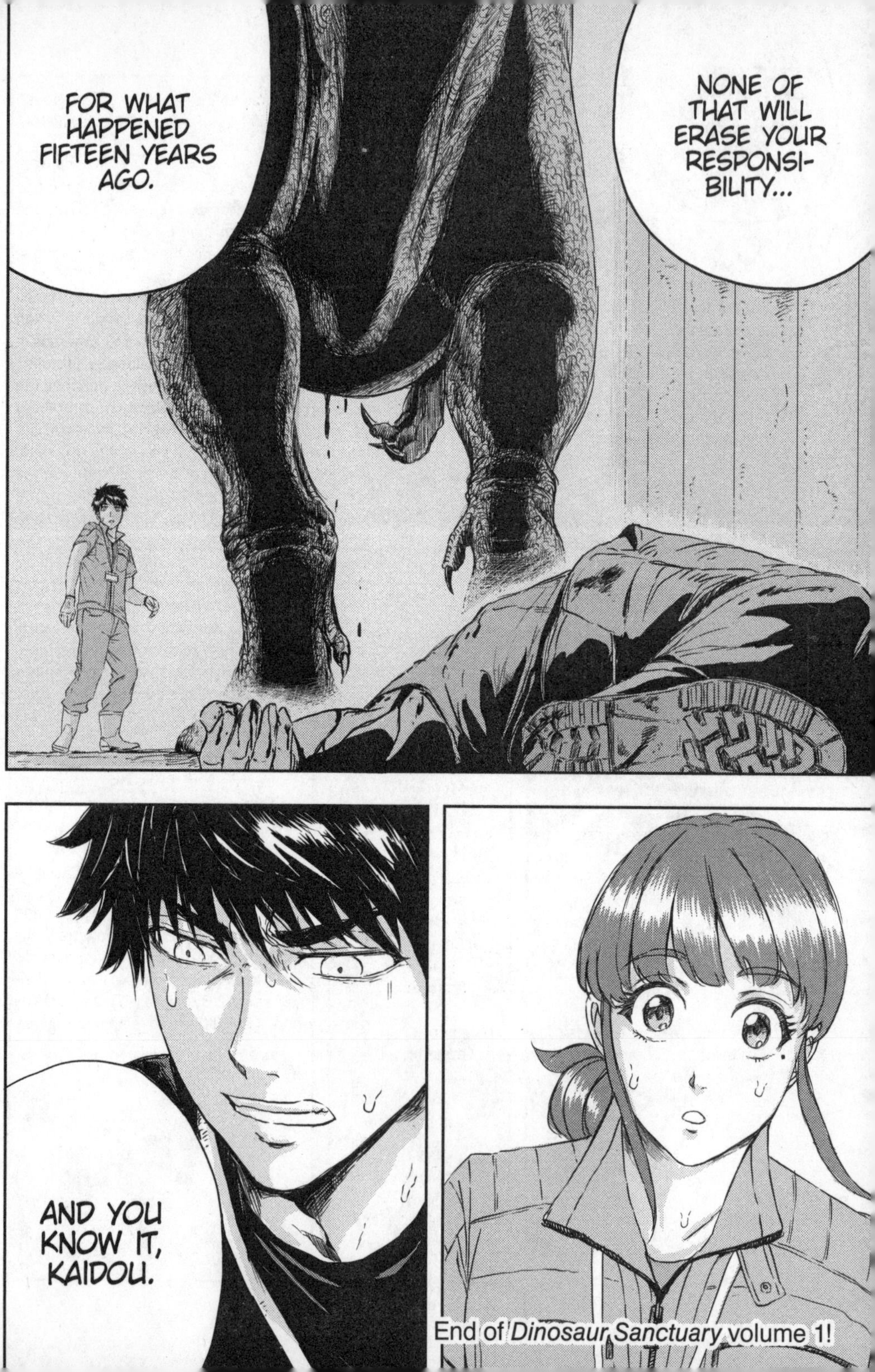
NONE OF THAT WILL ERASE YOUR RESPONSI-BILITY...
FOR WHAT HAPPENED FIFTEEN YEARS AGO.
AND YOU KNOW IT, KAIDOU.
End of *Dinosaur Sanctuary* volume 1!

Dr. Dino's Lab Log

FILE. 05 The More You Look, the More You See

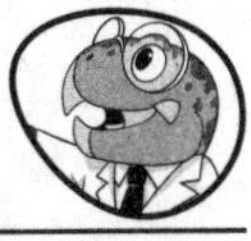

When you study dinosaur biomechanics, you get a lot of chances to check and consult on portrayals of dinosaurs, from drawings and figures to 3D CGI models. Every one of these checks is a chance to take another painstakingly close look at all the available materials on the dinosaur in question's bone structure. While that might sound tedious, it's actually rather fun because it provides new opportunities for fascinating discoveries!

Dilophosaurus brought me a lot of these new little discoveries. For starters, its teeth were much longer than I'd imagined! Also its spine didn't reach very high, and it's not particularly wide. Compared to other theropods, *Dilophosaurus* probably wasn't as good at activating the muscles that kept its torso and tail straight. The little indentation towards the end of its snout is another unique characteristic. It's one we also see on crocodiles and conger eels, and it seems like it would have helped *Dilophosaurus* catch prey that was small enough to hold in its mouth. (Not that I have any certain basis for this; it's just conjecture.)

My biggest *Dilophosaurus* surprise, though, came when I noticed that it had bones that resembled patella—kneecaps. These bones are found among the tendons where its thigh muscles went around its knees to connect to the shins. In most mammals and birds, kneecaps are ossified (formed fully into bone), but in other animals, they've remained soft cartilage. And cartilage doesn't get left behind in fossils. If *Dilophosaurus* really had bony patella, that makes it a remarkably rare dinosaur on the evolutionary pathway to birds.

Incidentally, the first fossil specimen to be given the name *"Dilophosaurus"* appears to have had an injured leg. When I saw that Kinoshita-sensei had given Roy troubles with his knees, I thought it was a very fitting tribute!

Now let's shift gears and take a look at dinosaur hands. Some of the bones at the tips of their fingers are formed into sharp points, and as we know, keratin built up over these bones to make claws. We call these bones unguals, which means "relating to a claw, nail, or hoof."

Some of you may know that the bones that make up your fingers and toes are called phalanges. These claw bones—and fingertips in general—are called distal phalanges (distalis). That's one of three terms we use to describe the finger and toe bones of mammals. The others are medial phalanges (media: the middle of the finger or toe) and proximal phalanges (proxima: at the base of the finger or toe). Finger bones in mammals are generally distributed in a pattern of 2-3-3-3-3. Your thumb has two phalanges, and your other four fingers have three. But dinosaurs' manual phalanges were typically arranged in a 2-3-4-3-2 pattern. We use the words "distal," "medial," and "proximal" to describe their phalanges' shapes, too, but since these words are based on their position in mammal fingers (which only go up to three bones), their meanings may change when used to discuss dinosaur fingers instead. It's important to be extra careful!

This might surprise you, but dinosaurs only had unguals from their first to middle fingers. Their would-be ring and pinky fingers had no claw bones. This is a trait they shared with their close relatives, crocodiles and pterosaurs. So if you see a picture of a dinosaur with claws on fourth or fifth fingers, please note that it's a little fishy!

Lastly, theropod dinosaurs originally had five fingers, but as they evolved, they gradually lost the two that lacked claws. *Dilophosaurus* lost its pinkies to evolution; in time, it would lose its ring finger as well. By the time *Tyrannosaurus* came around, it didn't even have a middle finger.

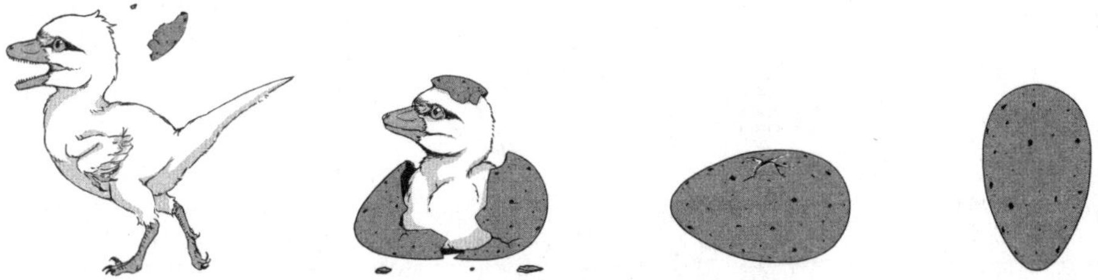

Afterword

One December day in 2020, an offer came to me through my mentor, Dr. Manabe Makoto: "Someone needs scientific oversight on a dinosaur manga. Are you interested?"

Once I'd read the pitch, I was interested indeed. In fact, part of me was giddy about it! The next step was to take a Zoom meeting with Mr. Kinoshita and his editor. I left that meeting feeling confident that they were ready to face down the task of faithfully recreating dinosaur ecology to the greatest extent.

Looking back on my own life, it feels like I've learned quite a lot from manga myself. I was happy to work on *Dinosaur Sanctuary* in hopes that it might help all of you to make some discoveries of your own.

I may have pelted Mr. Kinoshita and the editor with a deluge of comments, but they always stepped up to catch everything I pitched with all their might. I'm extremely grateful to them for putting forth all that effort. And, of course, I'm thankful for all of your encouraging feedback as readers, too!

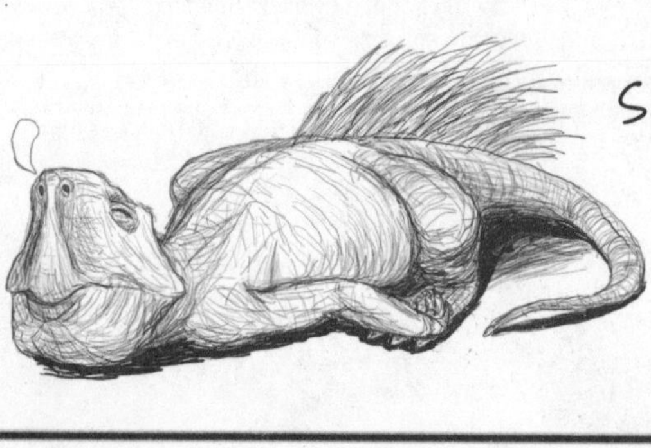

Shin-ichi Fujiwara

藤原慎一

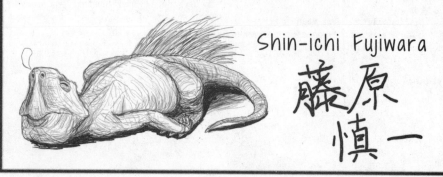

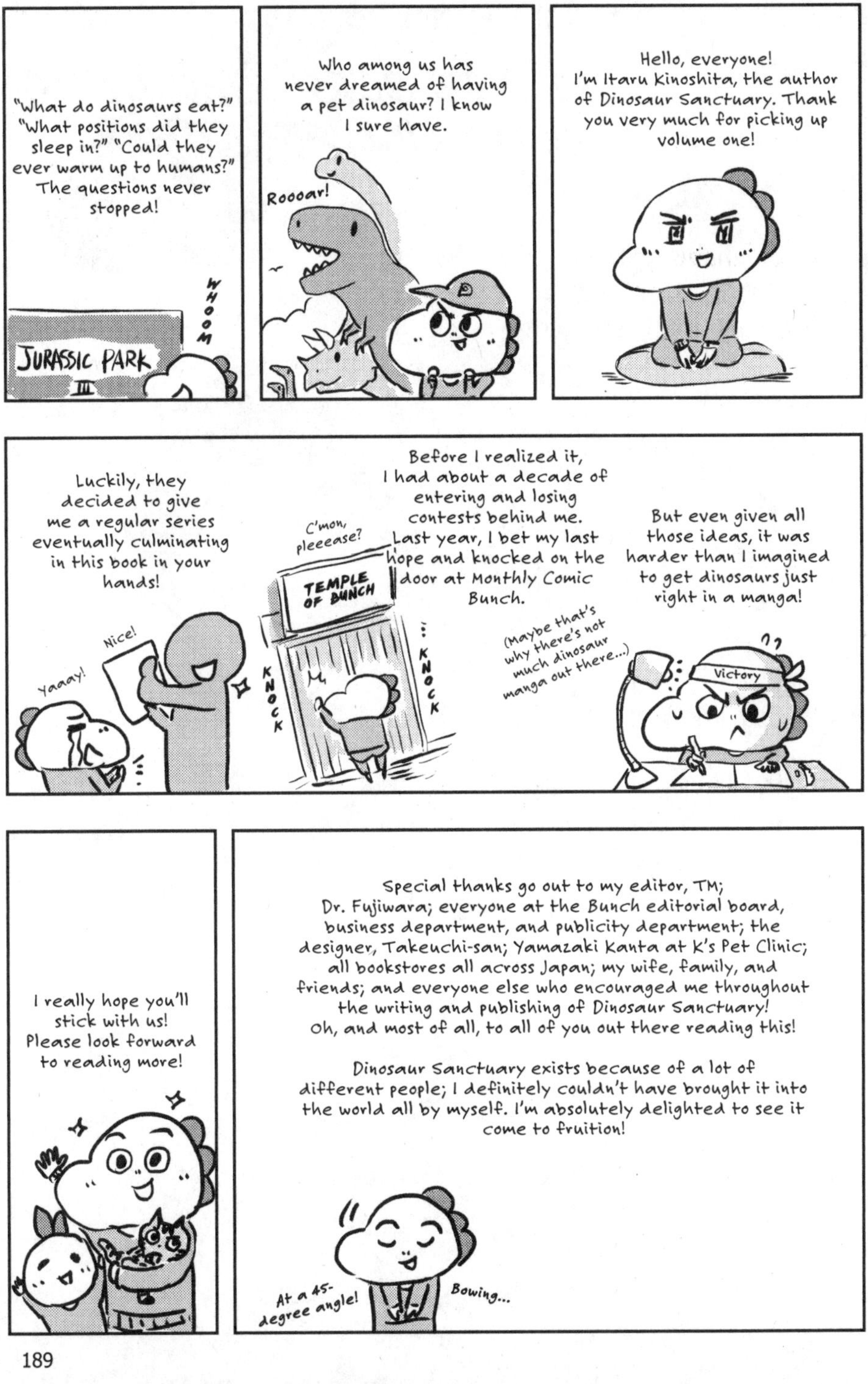
Hello, everyone! I'm Itaru Kinoshita, the author of Dinosaur Sanctuary. Thank you very much for picking up volume one!
Who among us has never dreamed of having a pet dinosaur? I know I sure have.
Rooooar!
"What do dinosaurs eat?" "What positions did they sleep in?" "Could they ever warm up to humans?" The questions never stopped!
WHOOOM
JURASSIC PARK III
But even given all those ideas, it was harder than I imagined to get dinosaurs just right in a manga!
Victory
(Maybe that's why there's not much dinosaur manga out there...)
Before I realized it, I had about a decade of entering and losing contests behind me. Last year, I bet my last hope and knocked on the door at Monthly Comic Bunch.
C'mon, pleeease?
TEMPLE OF BUNCH
KNOCK
KNOCK
Luckily, they decided to give me a regular series eventually culminating in this book in your hands!
Nice!
Yaaay!
Special thanks go out to my editor, TM; Dr. Fujiwara; everyone at the Bunch editorial board, business department, and publicity department; the designer, Takeuchi-san; Yamazaki Kanta at K's Pet Clinic; all bookstores all across Japan; my wife, family, and friends; and everyone else who encouraged me throughout the writing and publishing of Dinosaur Sanctuary! Oh, and most of all, to all of you out there reading this!
Dinosaur Sanctuary exists because of a lot of different people; I definitely couldn't have brought it into the world all by myself. I'm absolutely delighted to see it come to fruition!
Bowing...
At a 45-degree angle!
I really hope you'll stick with us! Please look forward to reading more!

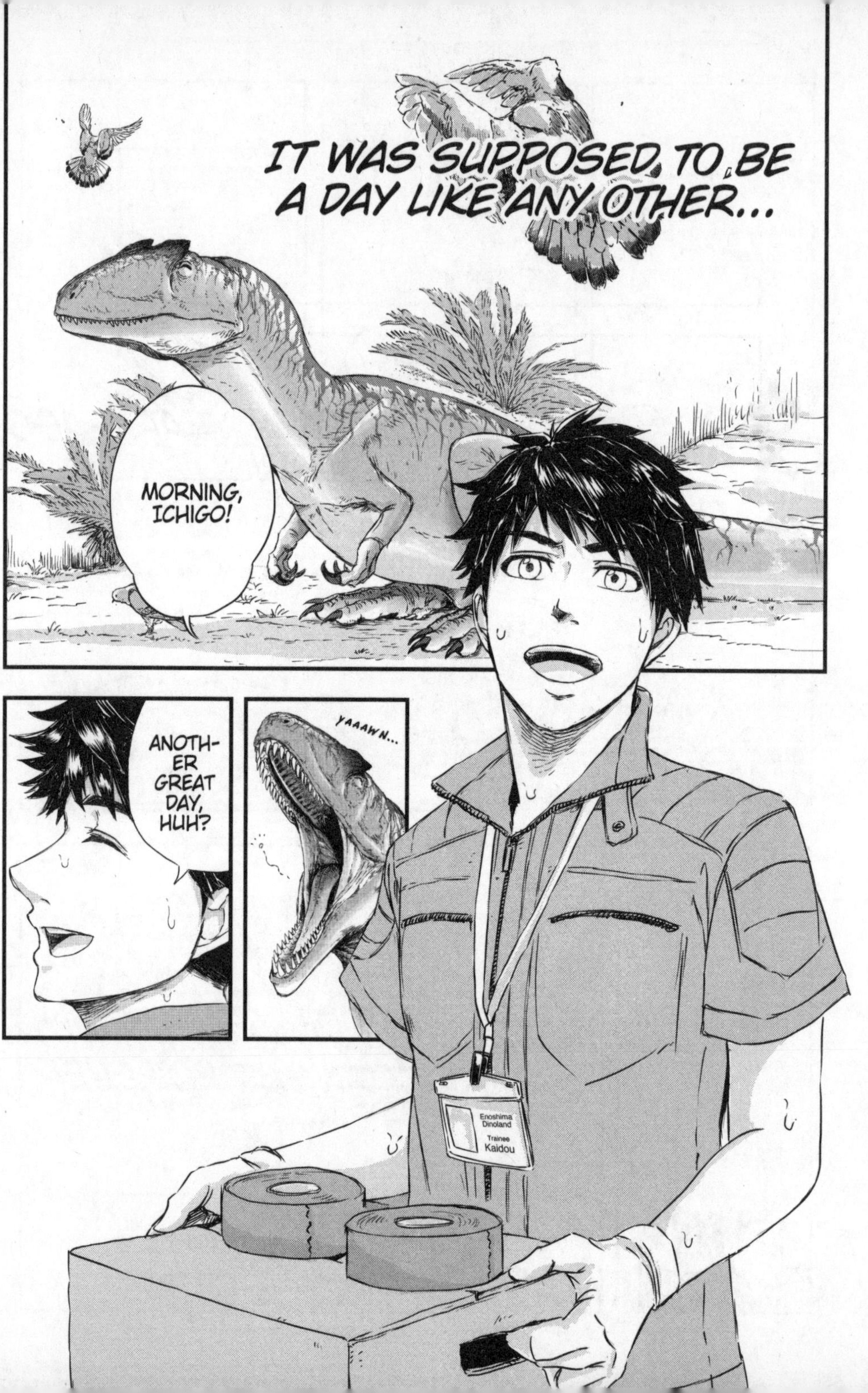
IT WAS SUPPOSED TO BE A DAY LIKE ANY OTHER...
MORNING, ICHIGO!
YAAAWN...
ANOTH-ER GREAT DAY, HUH?
Enoshima Dinoland Trainee Kaidou

ICHIGO'S ESCAPED!
RIGHT NOW...
FIFTEEN YEARS AGO, AT DINOLAND...
ICHIGO'S HEADING FOR THE GENERAL VISITORS' AREA!
HUMANITY'S RELATIONSHIP WITH DINOSAURS CHANGED FOREVER.

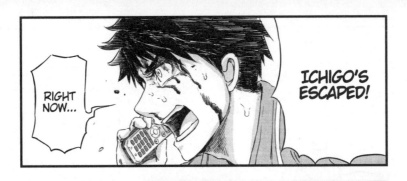

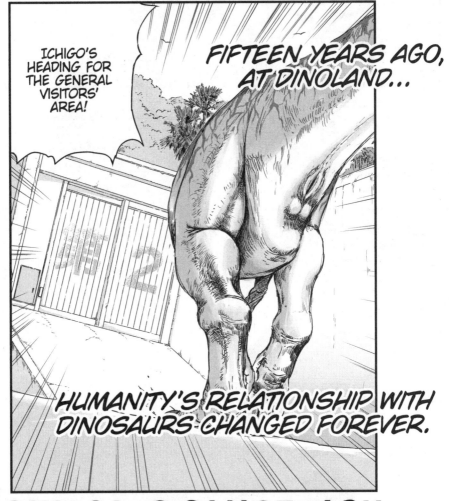

DINOSAUR SANCTUARY
VOLUME 2 COMING SOON!

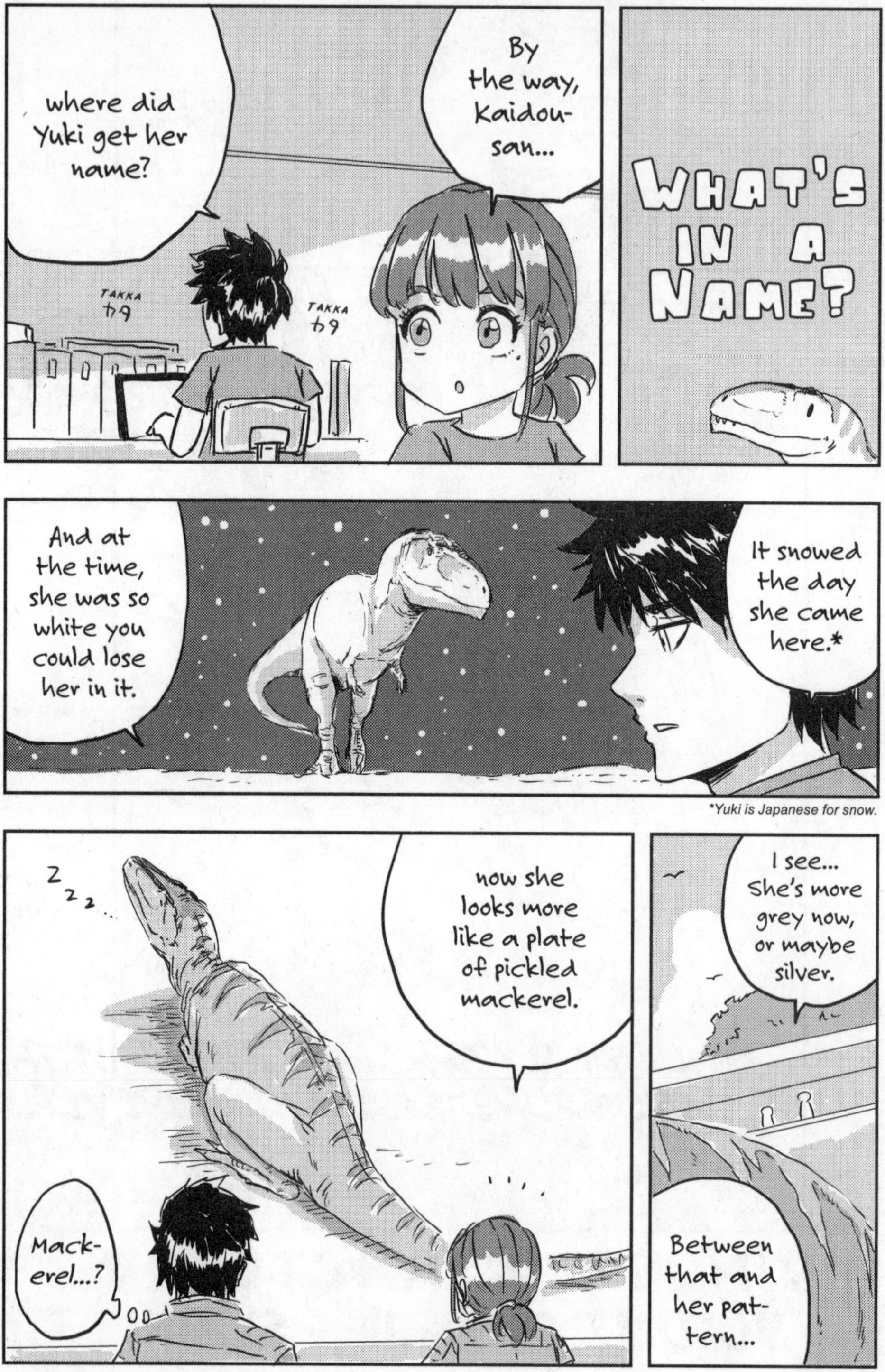
WHAT'S IN A NAME?
By the way, Kaidou-san...
where did Yuki get her name?
TAKKA
TAKKA
It snowed the day she came here.*
And at the time, she was so white you could lose her in it.
I see... She's more grey now, or maybe silver.
Between that and her pattern...
now she looks more like a plate of pickled mackerel.
Z z z...
Mack-erel...?

*Yuki is Japanese for snow.

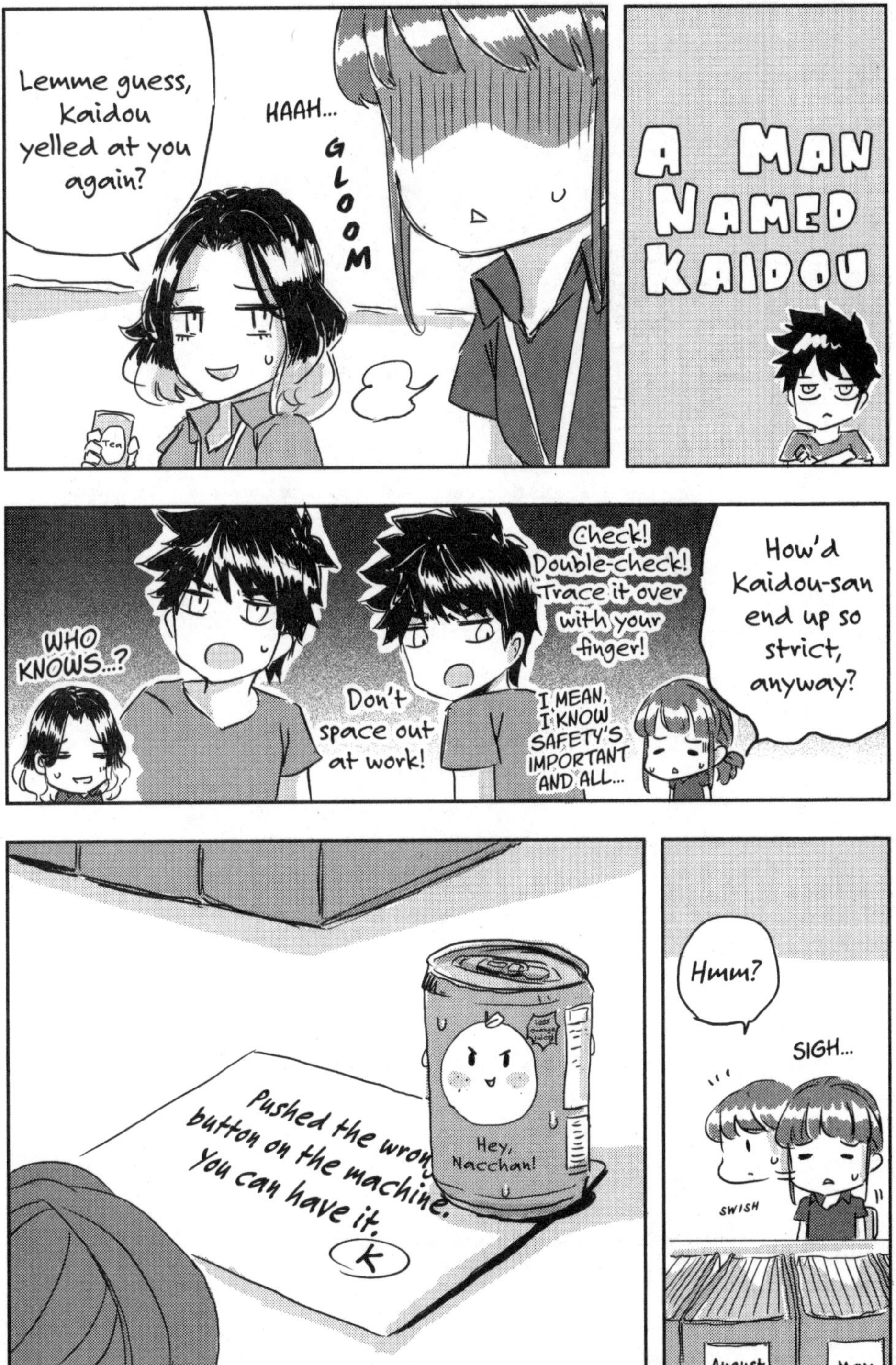
A MAN NAMED KAIDOU
HAAH...
GLOOM
Lemme guess, kaidou yelled at you again?
Tea
How'd Kaidou-san end up so strict, anyway?
Check! Double-check! Trace it over with your finger!
I MEAN, I KNOW SAFETY'S IMPORTANT AND ALL...
Don't space out at work!
WHO KNOWS...?
Hmm?
SIGH...
SWISH
August
May
Hey, Nacchan!
Pushed the wrong button on the machine. You can have it.
K

Itaru Kinoshita

Kinoshita made his manga debut with
Gigant wo Ute for Kodansha.

His favorite dinosaur is *Giganotosaurus*.

Supervisor:
Shin-ichi Fujiwara

Fujiwara is a lecturer at the
Nagoya University Museum.

He has a doctorate from
the University of Tokyo.

His fields of specialization
are functional morphology and
vertebrate paleontology, and his
favorite dinosaur is *Psittacosaurus*.

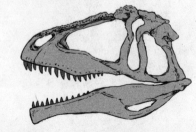

DINOSAUR SANCTUARY

SEVEN SEAS ENTERTAINMENT PRESENTS

DINOSAUR SANCTUARY

story and art: **ITARU KINOSHITA**   research consultant: **SHIN-ICHI FUJIWARA**   **VOLUME 1**

TRANSLATION
John Neal

LETTERING
JM Iitomi Crandall

COVER DESIGN
M. Lyn Hall

PROOFREADER
Leighanna DeRouen

SENIOR COPY EDITOR
Dawn Davis

EDITOR
Linda Lombardi

PRODUCTION DESIGNER
Christina McKenzie

PRODUCTION MANAGER
Lissa Pattillo

PREPRESS TECHNICIAN
Jules Valera

PRINT MANAGER
Rhiannon Rasmussen-Silverstein

EDITOR-IN-CHIEF
Julie Davis

ASSOCIATE PUBLISHER
Adam Arnold

PUBLISHER
Jason DeAngelis

DINOSAN
© Itaru Kinoshita 2021
All Rights Reserved.
English translation rights arranged with SHINCHOSHA PUBLISHING CO.
through Tuttle-Mori Agency, Inc, Tokyo

Seven Seas press and purchase enquiries can be sent to Marketing Manager Lianne Sentar at press@gomanga.com. Information regarding the distribution and purchase of digital editions is available from Digital Manager CK Russell at digital@gomanga.com.

Seven Seas and the Seven Seas logo are trademarks of Seven Seas Entertainment. All rights reserved.

ISBN: 978-1-68579-324-1
Printed in Canada
First Printing: September 2022
10 9 8 7 6 5 4 3 2 1

READING DIRECTIONS

This book reads from *right to left*, Japanese style. If this is your first time reading manga, you start reading from the top right panel on each page and take it from there. If you get lost, just follow the numbered diagram here. It may seem backwards at first, but you'll get the hang of it! Have fun!!

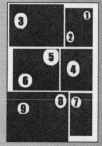

Follow us online: www.SevenSeasEntertainment.com